Global Capitalism, Global War, Global Crisis

Global Capitalism, Global War, Global Crisis. How can these conditions be understood in terms of their internal relationship to capture capital's connection to the states-system of uneven and combined development, social reproduction, and the contradictions facing humanity within world-ecology?

This book assesses the forces of social struggle shaping the past and present of the global political economy from the perspective of historical materialism. Based on the philosophy of internal relations, the character of capital is understood in such a way that the ties between the relations of production, state-civil society and conditions of class struggle can be realised. Conceiving the internal relationship of Global Capitalism, Global War, Global Crisis as a struggle-driven process is a major contribution of this book, providing a novel intervention on debates within theories of 'the international'. Through a set of conceptual reflections, on agency and structure and the role of discourses embedded in the economy, class struggle is established as our point of departure. This involves analysing historical and contemporary themes on the expansion of capitalism through uneven and combined development (Global Capitalism), the role of the state and geopolitics (Global War) and conditions of exploitation and resistance (Global Crisis). The conceptual reflections and thematic considerations raised earlier in this book are then extended in a series of empirical interventions. These include a focus on the 'rising powers' of the BRICS (Global Capitalism), conditions of the 'new imperialism' (Global War) and the financial crisis since the 2007–8 Great Recession (Global Crisis). As a result of honing in on the internal relations of Global Capitalism, Global War, Global Crisis the final major contribution of this book is to deliver a radically open-ended dialectical consideration of ruptures of resistance within the global political economy.

T0381582

Andreas Bieler is Professor of Political Economy and Fellow of the Centre for the Study of Social and Global Justice (CSSGJ) in the School of Politics and International Relations at the University of Nottingham. He is the author of *Globalisation and Enlargement of the European Union* (2000) and *The Struggle for a Social Europe* (2006), as well as co-editor of *Free Trade and Transnational Labour* (2015) and *Chinese Labour in the Global Economy* (2017). He maintains a blog on trade unions and global restructuring at http://andreasbieler.blogspot.co.uk.

Adam David Morton is Professor of Political Economy in the Department of Political Economy at the University of Sydney. He is the author of *Unravelling Gramsci* (2007) and *Revolution and State in Modern Mexico* (2011), which was awarded the 2012 Book Prize of the British International Studies Association (BISA) International Political Economy Group (IPEG). He edits the blog *Progress in Political Economy* (PPE) that was awarded the 2016 International Studies Association (ISA) Online Media Caucus Award for the Best Blog (Group) and the 2017 International Studies Association (ISA) Online Media Caucus Award for Special Achievement in International Studies Online Media: http://ppesydney.net/.

Global Capitalism, Global War, Global Crisis

Andreas Bieler
University of Nottingham

Adam David Morton
University of Sydney

CAMBRIDGE
UNIVERSITY PRESS

CAMBRIDGE
UNIVERSITY PRESS

University Printing House, Cambridge CB2 8BS, United Kingdom

One Liberty Plaza, 20th Floor, New York, NY 10006, USA

477 Williamstown Road, Port Melbourne, VIC 3207, Australia

314-321, 3rd Floor, Plot 3, Splendor Forum, Jasola District Centre, New Delhi - 110025, India

79 Anson Road, #06-04/06, Singapore 079906

Cambridge University Press is part of the University of Cambridge.

It furthers the University's mission by disseminating knowledge in the pursuit of education, learning and research at the highest international levels of excellence.

www.cambridge.org
Information on this title: www.cambridge.org/9781108452632
DOI: 10.1017/9781108596381

First published 2018

A catalogue record for this publication is available from the British Library

Library of Congress Cataloging in Publication data
Names: Bieler, Andreas, 1967– author. | Morton, Adam David, 1971– author.
Title: Global capitalism, global war, global crisis / Andreas Bieler, Adam Morton.
Description: New York : Cambridge University Press, 2018. | Includes bibliographical references and index.
Identifiers: LCCN 2017057575 | ISBN 9781108479103 (hardback) | ISBN 9781108452632 (paperback)
Subjects: LCSH: Economic policy. | Economic development. | Geopolitics. | Global Financial Crisis, 2008–2009.
Classification: LCC HD87 .B54 2018 | DDC 337–dc23
LC record available at https://lccn.loc.gov/2017057575

ISBN 978-1-108-47910-3 Hardback
ISBN 978-1-108-45263-2 Paperback

1. A Necessarily Historical Materialist Moment; 2. The Centrality of Class Struggle; 3. The Material Structure of Ideology; 4. Capitalist Expansion, Uneven and Combined Development and Passive Revolution; 5. The Geopolitics of Global Capitalism; 6. Exploitation and Resistance; 7. Global Capitalism and Rising Powers; 8. Global War and the New Imperialism; 9. Global Crisis and Trouble in the Eurozone; 10. Ruptures in and beyond Global Capitalism, Global War, Global Crisis.

For our families

Contents

Tables

Figures

Acknowledgements

Producing a book on relationality produces its own relationality. For Marx, the threads of the inner connection of the production process under capitalism get more and more lost, so that the relations of production give the appearance of independence from one another and value ossifies into its independent forms. For us, it is important to recover the threads of the inner connection not just of capital but also of our own production process with this book, in order to trace the rich totality of its many determinations and relations. The following are the dialectical ties that stretch across conditions of space as well as changes over time, forming a cluster of our own internal relations.

The origin story of this book stretches back to the British International Studies Association (BISA) annual conference that was held in Durham in December 1996. As we were graduate students at the time, it was the first conference presentation for Andreas and the first conference attendance for Adam during which we began chatting over coffee about shared theoretical and political interests. Since then, more than twenty-one years of friendship have flourished based on academic and activist collaboration. This has developed through joint work on conference papers and their conversion into journal articles, book chapters and edited volumes. It has also entailed combined participation in some of the major fora of protest and resistance over that same time period, whether that be within the European Social Forum, the World Social Forum or in the movement against the Iraq War, as well as through our teamwork within the Centre for the Study of Social and Global Justice (CSSGJ) at the University of Nottingham, setting up events in the form of conferences and seminars, establishing and maintaining the Marxism Reading Group or jointly supervising PhD students.

Despite posing the question of a joint monograph over this time period, it was only really in the Sydney spring of September 2014 that the basis of the present book emerged more clearly following a two-week workshop to bring the formal proposal together. Thereafter, work on this book started in earnest and resulted in a three-year period of intense collaborative labour with the manuscript being finalised, again in Sydney, this time in the 'winter' of July 2017. From Nottingham to Sydney, then, this book owes a massive debt to a rich totality of determinations and relations beyond just us.

To start, we want especially to thank Chris Hesketh and Cemal Burak Tansel for delivering comments on the whole draft manuscript and rising to the provocation of delivering 'what you really think' amidst juggling their own priorities. A special mention and thank you is also in order to Colin Wight, whose mentoring and advice was intrinsic to the successful realisation of this book. From the shores of Ceredigion at the University of Wales, Aberystwyth to the shores of New South Wales at the University of Sydney his counsel has been crucial. We are equally grateful to Jenny Chan, Elaine Hui, Hongyi Lai, Chun-Yi Lee and Stefan Schmalz for their comments on Chapter 7 and to Roland Erne and Jamie Jordan for their feedback on Chapter 9. Furthermore, we are grateful to Matthew Ryan for his outstanding assistance in organising the compilation of the Bibliography as well as Jokubas Salyga and Kayhan Valadbaygi for the preparation of the Index.

We are indebted to John Haslam at Cambridge University Press for maintaining his interest in this book, giving us important support at the right times and especially for judiciously handling the review process. His patient assistance was intrinsic in bringing this book to fruition. Equally, thanks are due to the reviewers of the manuscript who gave overwhelmingly positive and constructively critical feedback when others may well have reached for the hatchet.

In terms of our teaching, the thoughts and conditions expressed in this book have been developed through both joint and individual delivery of a number of modules or units. These have notably included, at the master's level, (M14022) Theories and Concepts in International Relations and, at the undergraduate level, (M12089) IPE and Global Development at the University of Nottingham. Courses delivered within the Department of Political Economy at the University of Sydney have included the second-year unit (ECOP2613) The Political Economy of Global Capitalism and, especially, at the fourth-year honours level, (ECOP4001) Analytic Foundations of Historical Materialism. We want to thank all our students – past, present and future – for their engagement. There is no lip service paid to our conviction that mutual benefits arise from teaching and research, which are experienced reciprocally by teachers and students.

Over the years we have greatly benefited from discussions with a large number of colleagues. These considerations too have had a vital impact on the writing of this volume. Here, we want to thank our joint and individual PhD students, the participants in both the Marxism Reading Group (at the University of Nottingham) and the Past & Present Reading Group (at the University of Sydney), as well as colleagues Pinar Bilgin, Werner Bonefeld, Ian Bruff, Gareth Bryant, Tony Burns, Damien Cahill, Ron Chilcote, Joe Collins, Robert W. Cox, Neil Davidson, Bill Dunn, Randall Germain, Stephen Gill, Barry Gills, Jan Willem Goudriaan, Penny Griffin, Sandra Halperin, Shahar Hameiri, Steve Hobden, Ben Holland, Elizabeth Humphrys, Peter Ives, Bob Jessop, Martijn Konings, Rob Lambert, Ingemar Lindberg, Jim Mittelman, Cerwyn Moore, Alf Nilsen, Robert O'Brien, Bertell Ollman, Gerardo Otero, Karin Pampallis, Roy Pedersen, Hugo Radice, Sébastien Rioux, William Robinson, David Ruccio, Mark Rupert, Ariel Salleh, Graham M. Smith, Susanne Soederberg, Frank Stilwell, Marcus Taylor, Tad Tietze, Simon Tormey, Jacqui True, Asbjørn Wahl and Eddie Webster. For Andreas, colleagues from the Transnational Labour Project in Oslo, including Roland Erne, Darragh Golden, Idar Helle, Knut Kjeldstadli, Tiago Matos and Sabina Stan, are greatly appreciated for their support. For Adam, the ongoing debates with Erik Olin Wright on the philosophy of internal relations, while hosted at the A. E. Havens Center for Social Justice as a visiting scholar in the Department of Sociology at the University of Wisconsin–Madison, were highly valued. Similarly, the freedom to write this book while hosted by Kim Förster as a visiting scholar at the Canadian Centre for Architecture (CCA) in Montreal when undertaking new research in June 2017 was extremely cherished.

Of course, despite all the advice and assistance from all of these colleagues, full and final responsibility for any remaining errors or omissions in this book is ours alone.

Abbreviations

ACFTU	All-China Federation of Trade Unions
AIFM	alternative investment fund manager
BRICS	Brazil, Russia, India, China and South Africa
CCP	Chinese Communist Party
CDM	Clean Development Mechanism
CEE	Central and Eastern Europe
CETA	Comprehensive Economic and Trade Agreement
CTA	Central de Trabajadores de la Argentina (Argentine Workers' Central Union)
ECB	European Central Bank
ECI	European Citizens' Initiative
EFSF	European Financial Stability Facility
EMU	Economic and Monetary Union
EPSU	European Federation of Public Service Unions
ESF	European Social Forum
ETUC	European Trade Union Confederation
EU	European Union
FCO	Foreign and Commonwealth Office
FDI	foreign direct investment
GFC	global financial crisis
GVC	global value chain
IMF	International Monetary Fund
IPE	international political economy
IR	international relations
LAWAS	Latin American Workers' Association
MIC	military-industrial-academic complex
NGO	non-governmental organisation
OPEC	Organization of the Petroleum Exporting Countries
ORHA	Office of Reconstruction and Humanitarian Assistance
PAH	Plataforma de Afectados por la Hipoteca (Platform for People Affected by Mortgages)
PASOK	Panhellenic Socialist Movement

PRD	Pearl River Delta
SEWA	Self-Employed Women's Association
SGP	Stability and Growth Pact
SIGTUR	Southern Initiative on Globalisation and Trade Union Rights
SOE	state-owned enterprise
TC	textile and clothing
TCC	transnational capitalist class
TMSA	Transformational Model of Social Activity
TNC	transnational corporation
TNS	transnational state
TSCG	Treaty on Stability, Coordination and Governance in the EMU
TTIP	Treaty on Trade and Investment Partnership
TVE	township and village enterprises
USAID	United States Agency for International Development
VOC	Varieties of Capitalism
WTO	World Trade Organization

Introduction

1   A Necessarily Historical Materialist Moment

The global political economy is currently undergoing unparalleled change. Emerging economies around Brazil, Russia, India, China and South Africa (the BRICS) challenge the assumed historically dominant and advanced position of Western capitalist states. Especially China, it seems, is potentially on course to 'catch up' developmentally and overtake even the United States. China was the world's leading exporter in 2014, exporting goods valued at a total of $2,342.31 billion USD.[1] In second place, the United States exported only 69 per cent of this amount, followed by Germany in third place with 64 per cent of Chinese exports. Chinese ascendancy is also reflected in impressive economic growth rates. Double-digit GDP growth rates during the mid-1990s and then again in the mid-2000s culminated in an increase of 14.2 per cent in 2007. The figures have declined since, due to the global economic crisis, but are still comparatively high at around 7 per cent today. GDP growth in the United States, by comparison, was between 4.1 per cent (at its highest increase) and −2.8 per cent (at its lowest) across the period of 2000 to 2015. Indian growth rates of around 8 per cent since 2000 come closest to China among the BRICS, while the performances of Brazil, Russia and South Africa are more varied and clearly at a lower level.[2]

Will it be feasible to integrate these states harmoniously into the global political economy, or are we likely to witness further interstate and global conditions of war between hegemonic rivals such as the United States and key contender states such as China? In many respects, we are already in a period of sustained war with the global 'war on terror' engulfing ever more countries stretching from Afghanistan and Iraq, ranging via Libya to encompass and destabilise the whole region around Syria. Of course, the global 'war on terror' does not simply unfold in 'peripheral' spaces but is

---

[1] World Atlas, 'Exports by country – 20 largest exporting countries' (14 June 2016), www.worldatlas.com/articles/exports-by-country-20-largest-exporting-countries.html; accessed 7 September 2016.

[2] World Development Indicators, www.databank.worldbank.org/data/; accessed 6 September 2016.

again and again also waged in the heartland of global capitalism with terror attacks in Paris in November 2015 and Brussels in March 2016 being just two recent horrendous moments. The consequences of the Iraq War, in 2003, have been brought again to the forefront by the *Report of the Iraq Inquiry*, or 'Chilcot Report', published in the United Kingdom on 6 July 2016, which arguably demonstrates the horrors of these ongoing struggles more than any other incident. As early as 2001, as the Chilcot Report indicates, the Middle East Department of the Foreign and Commonwealth Office (FCO) recommended a new approach to reassess the United Kingdom's 'fundamental interests' in Iraq, a key component of which was to ensure a 'level playing field' for UK companies in relation to any containment of Iraq (Iraq Inquiry, 2016: Vol. 9:457). 'Since the U.S.-led, UK-backed invasion of Iraq in 2003, estimates of the lives lost to violence vary from a quarter of a million to 600,000. The number of injured will surely be several times that, and the number of men, women and children displaced from their homes is put at between 3.5 and 5 million, somewhere between one in 10 and one in six of the population.'[3] The United Kingdom's decision to participate in the U.S.-led invasion was made without having exhausted all potential peaceful options, a deliberate exaggeration of the threat posed by Saddam Hussein and no clear understanding of the post-war challenges and the necessary plans to meet them.[4]

The upheavals of developmental 'catch up' and interstate rivalry shaped by global capitalism as well as the causes and consequences of global war, finally, are of a piece with the global economic crisis since 2007–8, regarded as the Great Recession akin in its severity to the Great Depression of the 1930s, which in particular has pushed several states in the Eurozone to the brink of bankruptcy. Greece alone had to be bailed out three times, with the latest 'rescue package' implemented – some would argue imposed – on 13 July 2015, just over a week after a majority of 61 per cent of voters had rejected further austerity in exchange for another bailout agreement on 5 July 2015. It included the transfer of €50bn (£35bn) worth of Greek assets to an independent fund for privatisation, further pension cuts, increases in VAT and other taxes and a liberalisation of the economy, including

---

[3] *The Guardian*, 'The Guardian view on the Chilcot report: a country ruined, trust shattered, a reputation trashed' (6 July 2016), www.theguardian.com/commentisfree/2016/jul/06/the-guardian-view-on-the-chilcot-report-a-country-ruined-trust-shattered-a-reputation-trashed; accessed 7 September 2016.

[4] BBC News, 'Chilcot report: findings at-a-glance' (6 July 2016), www.bbc.co.uk/news/uk-politics-36721645; accessed 7 September 2016; *The Guardian*, 'Chilcot report: key points from the Iraq inquiry' (6 July 2016); www.theguardian.com/uk-news/2016/jul/06/iraq-inquiry-key-points-from-the-chilcot-report; accessed 7 September 2016.

labour markets.[5] Ireland, Portugal and Cyprus too had to accept conditionality programmes in exchange for bailout packages. The social and economic consequences are dramatic. Youth unemployment, unemployed people between the ages of fifteen and twenty-four as a percentage of the total labour force in this age group, reached 52.4 per cent in Greece, 34.8 per cent in Portugal and 26.9 per cent in Ireland in 2014. Other countries struggling in the Eurozone include Italy and Spain, registering youth unemployment of 42.7 per cent and 53.2 per cent respectively in 2014 (OECD Employment Outlook, 2016: 221). Greece's situation is probably the most dramatic. National debt has reached 180 per cent of GDP, general unemployment is high – at around 25 per cent, the highest in Europe – and 'consumption and exports had also fallen, by 6.4% and 7.2%, in the second quarter' of 2016.[6] Against the background of the continuing recession, a humanitarian crisis is unfolding especially in healthcare.[7] Unsurprisingly, these dynamics of Global Capitalism (the rise of the BRICS), Global War (the war in Iraq), Global Crisis (the Eurozone crisis) are interlinked. In Brazil, against the background of economic recession, the centre-left President Dilma Rousseff has been removed from power without a popular vote. The insistence is that her successor revives the economy through further austerity measures.[8] Equally, the developmental 'catch up', or equalisation of growth in China has resulted in highly uneven development or differentiation elsewhere. Drastic increases in Chinese output of steel have strongly contributed to the collapse of the steel sector in the United Kingdom.[9] Finally, the rise of China as such may have hastened the decision-making of key geopoliticians within U.S. statecraft in relation to the invasion of Iraq, with a view to securing control over the global oil supply to maintain a dominant geopolitical position.

[5] *The Guardian*, 'Greece bailout agreement: key points' (13 July 2015), www.theguardian.com /business/2015/jul/13/greece-bailout-agreement-key-points-grexit; accessed 7 September 2016.

[6] *The Guardian*, 'A year after the crisis was declared over, Greece is still spiralling down' (13 August 2016), www.theguardian.com/business/2016/aug/13/greek-economy-still -spiralling-down-year-after-crisis-declared-over; accessed 7 September 2016.

[7] *The Guardian*, 'Greek debt crisis: "Of all the damage, healthcare has been hit the worst"' (9 July 2015), www.theguardian.com/world/2015/jul/09/greek-debt-crisis-damage -healthcare-hospital-austerity; accessed 7 September 2016.

[8] *The Guardian*, 'Brazil's Dilma Rousseff impeached by senate in crushing defeat' (1 September 2016), www.theguardian.com/world/2016/aug/31/dilma-rousseff -impeached-president-brazilian-senate-michel-temer; accessed 7 September 2016.

[9] *The Guardian*, 'China steel giant to raise output by 20% in grim outlook for UK industry' (31 March 2016), www.theguardian.com/business/2016/mar/31/china-steel-giant-to -raise-output-by-20-in-grim-outlook-for-tata; accessed 7 September 2016.

Global Capitalism, Global War, Global Crisis – this book offers a fresh analysis of these themes by arguing that the conditions of Global Capitalism, Global War, Global Crisis have to be understood in terms of their internality. In order to do so, our argument is that the inner connections between Global Capitalism, Global War, Global Crisis are best realised through a relational method that captures capital's internalisation through the states system of uneven and combined development, geopolitics and the global crisis conditions facing humanity that are themselves embedded within world ecology. We argue therefore that the conditions of Global Capitalism, Global War, Global Crisis can be uniquely analysed from a historical materialist perspective in a way that transcends the shortcomings of competing studies on 'the international'. Our argument is that the extant literature on global politics and global political economy across international relations (IR) and international political economy (IPE) continuously separates out, in different ways, both the material *content* and/or the ideational *form* of 'the international' as well as agency and/or the structure of 'the international'. Thus, material content and ideational form, agency and structure within international studies are treated ontologically as dualisms, often as discrete or at best as interacting separate elements. A dialectical understanding of material conditions and ideational form, of agency and structure, in contrast, can begin to grasp the internality of Global Capitalism, Global War, Global Crisis. This book is a contribution to the critique of ontological dualisms shaping understandings of 'the international' and an assertion of the necessity of historical materialism in furthering a dialectical analysis of the inner connections of Global Capitalism, Global War, Global Crisis.

The dominant dualist framing of history across international studies involves positing distinct spheres (such as the realms of 'agents' and 'structures', the 'ideal' and the 'material', 'politics' and 'economics' or 'states' and 'markets') as separate spheres or variables that, at best, are held in an externally *inter*acting relationship that fails to grasp their *inner* actions. The presupposition of always-already treating social ontologies as separate and then interacting realms is therefore reliant on a relationship of *ontological exteriority* (Morton, 2013). With Eric Wolf (1982/1997: 3):

[T]he world of humankind constitutes a manifold, a totality of interconnected processes, and inquiries that disassemble this totality into bits and then fail to reassemble it falsify reality. Concepts like 'nation', 'society', and 'culture' name bits and threaten to turn names into things. Only by understanding these names as bundles of relationships, and by placing them back into the field from which they were abstracted, can we hope to avoid misleading inferences and increase our share of understanding.

By positing a world that is made up of logically independent things – an atomistic approach to ontology – the elements may only, again at best, then come to relate as interdependent. But, most significantly, the inner connections that are constitutive of social relations are rent asunder by this commitment to ontological exteriority. Four brief examples will suffice for the purposes of our argument in this introduction.

Witness, first, a canonical statement in *The Political Economy of International Relations* by Robert Gilpin on how states and markets presumably interact in wealth creation.

The historical relationship of state and market is a matter of intense scholarly controversy. Whether each developed autonomously, the market gave rise to the state, or the state to the market, are important historical issues whose resolution is not really relevant to the argument of this book. State and market, whatever their respective origins, have independent existences, have logics on their own, and interact with each other. (Gilpin, 1987: 10)

By clearly separating state and market from the very beginning of his enquiry, Gilpin does not even attempt to investigate their internal relations. This dualist framing or view of states and markets, however, pervades wider reflections on 'the international', not least the theory of history posited by neorealists. The second prominent example of the dualisms at the core of mainstream accounts of 'the international' is, of course, Kenneth Waltz's 'systemic' explanation of international politics that claimed to avoid the 'distraction' of detail and the vagaries associated with domestic politics. Instead, the focus became the structure of the international system that was based on self-help or anarchic principles within which functionally undifferentiated units (states) operated, albeit with a varying distribution of capabilities (Waltz, 1979: 111–14). Based on an adherence to principles of parsimony – to be very sparse and logically tight, to omit certain things, to develop elegant definitions – the purpose of theory here is to identify regularities and repetitions by isolating one domain from the wider social context. As a consequence, a neorealist approach to 'the international' establishes the autonomy of international politics consisting of fully formed states-as-actors in the effort to develop 'a necessarily slender explanatory construct' (Waltz, 1990: 31–2). Hence 'definitions of structure must leave aside, or abstract from, the characteristics of units, their behaviour, and their interactions' (Waltz, 1979: 79). Yet the international states system is here abstracted from history, leading to a failure to account for the social bases of state power or the historically specific ideologies and material practices that have constituted and sustained state identities across different orders. Having assumed the nature of state identities and the states system, 'history becomes for neo-realists a quarry providing raw materials with which to illustrate variations on always recurrent themes' (Cox, 1981: 133). 'One person's elegance', in terms of an adherence to principles of parsimony, 'is another's oversimplification' (Cox, 1985/1996: 53).

Within political economy, Susan Strange, our third example, challenges state-centric analysis. Nevertheless, by establishing four separate *distinguishable* structures of power (security, production, finance, knowledge) that are then externally related to each other as *interacting* sources in the world economy, she equally ends up fetishising such concepts by abstracting them from the social relations of capitalism (Strange, 1988: 26; see Germain, 2016 for a contemporary reinterpretation). Finally, the dualist framing or external separation of material content and ideational form equally bedevils more recent sophisticated accounts of world politics. Observe, as our fourth indicative illustration, John Hobson's attempt to reveal the making of modern world politics through 'Eastern agency' and how he abstracts out ideas, institutions and technologies as different elements of 'resource portfolios'. The constituent parts of these resource portfolios are regarded as separate, connected only in exterior relation to each other, to account for the making of modern world politics. Emblematic is his statement that 'materialist causes must be factored in alongside the role of identity if we are to craft a satisfactory explanation of the rise of the West' (Hobson, 2004: 25–6). But note that the relation of the 'material' and the 'ideational' is held through their a priori ontological exteriority. Our purpose in this book, though, is not to rehash a critique of mainstream accounts of 'the international'. Instead, our argument is that the necessarily historical materialist moment of dialectics still awaits thinking about 'the international' in order to grasp the internal relations of Global Capitalism, Global War, Global Crisis in shaping contemporary world order.[10]

Our assertion of the necessarily historical materialist moment of dialectics in rethinking 'the international' is attached to a *philosophy of internal relations* that has been deeply overlooked to date.[11] The philosophy of

---

[10] Some noteworthy exceptions that attempt to grasp the import of dialectics for rethinking political economy and world order would include Alker (1996), Alker and Biersteker (1984), Brincat (2010) and Heine and Teschke (1996).

[11] Bertell Ollman comments that relational categories permeate the considerations of Marx as much as inter alia G. W. F. Hegel, Baruch Spinoza, Gottfried Wilhelm Leibniz, Georg Lukács, Herbert Marcuse, Jean-Paul Sartre or Henri Lefebvre (Ollman, 1976: 276, 2015: 13). Debates on the uneven and combined development of 'the international' have noted that the use of internal relations as a theoretical presupposition is 'hardly common' and that the internal relations perspective has an 'insignificant presence' in

internal relations implies that the character of capital is considered as a social relation in such a way that the internal ties between the relations of production, state-civil society and conditions of class struggle can be realised. As the hallmark of historical materialism this philosophy of internal relations makes explicit a conception of capital through which connections are maintained and contained as aspects of a self-forming whole. As Karl Marx (1858/1973: 408) put it in the *Grundrisse*, 'the tendency to create the *world market* is directly given in the concept of capital itself.' Through this philosophy of internal relations, the dialectical method of historical materialism therefore focuses on internally related causes and conditions, rather than positing logically independent factors existing side by side. As Bertell Ollman (1976: 48), a key exponent of the philosophy of internal relations, establishes:

With the philosophy of internal relations, the problem is never how to relate separate entities but how to disentangle a relation or group of relations from the total and necessary configuration in which they exist.

The first section of this introductory chapter to this book will thus assert the radical social ontology of the philosophy of internal relations (see also Rupert, 1995) in order to analyse Global Capitalism, Global War, Global Crisis. Our aim is to stress, in accord with Derek Sayer (1987: 25, emphasis added), that 'the connection between people's productive relations with nature, or labour process, and their productive relations between themselves, or social relations of production, is *internal* and *necessary*, not *external* and *contingent*.'[12] This foray into the philosophy of internal relations is an essential backstop to the rest of this book. Hence the first section of this introductory chapter is crucial to establish our radical social ontology, or a conception of categories as internally related to one another, which is regarded as an indispensable and defining part of a materialist philosophy of history shaping our argument. These are the

reconsiderations of 'the international' (Cooper, 2013: 586–7). This intervention is remiss, though, in its neglectful engagement with anterior developments of precisely the internal relations perspective on such questions (Bieler and Morton, 2008; Rupert, 1995). Elsewhere, critical Realism – particularly in the work of Roy Bhaskar – can equally lay claim to formulating similar concerns in the vocabulary of dialectics, albeit with established shortcomings (see Bhaskar, 1993 and Ollman, 2003 and, on the wider contribution of critical Realism to international studies, see Joseph, 2007; Joseph and Wight, 2002; Kurki, 2008; Wight, 2006, 2007). There is also the reinvigoration of dialectics in the special issue of *Globalizations* entitled 'Dialectics and World Politics' edited by Brincat (2014) with significant contributions by Ollman (2014) and Teschke and Cemgil (2014).

[12] The world ecology perspective on the double internality of capitalism-in-nature and nature-in-capitalism is a recent extension of the philosophy of internal relations approach to capitalism; see Moore (2015).

analytic foundations of historical materialism that will become the analytic foundations of this book. The philosophy of internal relations is a revolt against the *violence of abstraction* through which concepts all too commonly become fetishised, or treated as things, so that such material features come to replace specific social relations (Sayer, 1987). Yet, despite the richness of this literature, the common charge against historical materialism is still a caricatured accusation of economic determinism. The task in this first section of this chapter is therefore also to address how the philosophy of internal relations as the hallmark of historical materialism vitiates the taboo term of 'economism'. The taboo of 'economism' is often levelled against a straw Marxism as a disciplinary discourse or boundary in order to prevent engagement with the separation of the political and the economic (Ashley, 1983). Our argument is that a historical materialist philosophy of internal relations offers a novel series of vantage points from which to consider the constitution of productive activity in relation to the institutional and social forms of capitalism, allowing a comprehension of the historical specificity of capitalism. Charges of the taboo term of 'economism' against historical materialism will therefore be revealed as nothing more than a furtherance of criticism in the form of parody (Fine and Saad-Filho, 2004: 171).

Once capital is established as a social relation in our reasoning we are then directed to its *buried history* in treating the political economy of state formation, class struggle and relations of production within a substantive historical sociology (Sayer, 1987: 135). The second section therefore delves into some of the rich debates within historical materialism on the internality of the modern capitalist state to conditions of class struggle shaped by relations of production. Our interest at this juncture of this chapter is grabbed by Henri Lefebvre's (1975/2009: 114) comment that we need to focus on 'the revolt of the "lived" against abstractions, of the everyday against economism, of the social and civil society against the "high rate of growth", whose demands are upheld by the State'. The revolt against the violence of abstraction is therefore mobilised in the second section of this chapter through a focus on the internal ties between the relations of production, state-civil society and conditions of class struggle, which will provide a series of threads that will be woven into the remainder of the chapters that constitute this book. Historical materialism does not relegate the 'economic' and the 'political' to *spatially separate spheres* but conceives of the social constitution of the economy so that relations of production are embodied in juridical-political and ideological forms (Wood, 1995). In making this argument the central focus of the second section of this chapter, and by realising the inner tie of relations of production, state-civil society and class struggle, we therefore aim to establish the panoramic historical sociology of this book (Sayer, 1985: 221). This entails returning full circle to the philosophy of internal relations and its method of studying history backward to ask: *what had to have happened in the past for capitalism as a mode of production to emerge and consolidate?* (Ollman, 2003: 119, 2015: 18).

It should then become clear that the first section of the present chapter on the radical social ontology and philosophy of internal relations relates subsequently to Part I of this book on Conceptual Reflections linking the relationality of agency–structure (Chapter 2) and the material structure of ideology (Chapter 3). Meanwhile, the second section of this introductory chapter – focusing on the buried history of the internal ties between the relations of production, state-civil society and conditions of class struggle – links to Part II of this book on Thematic Considerations containing a relational conception of capitalist expansion and uneven and combined development (Chapter 4), the geopolitics of capitalist accumulation (Chapter 5) and conditions of exploitation and resistance through class struggle (Chapter 6). This is the scaffolding around which this book is constructed that then establishes a series of vantage points in Part III on Empirical Interventions from which a relational conception of the inner tie of Global Capitalism (Chapter 7), Global War (Chapter 8), Global Crisis (Chapter 9) can be advanced and is finally realised.

A Radical Social Ontology and the Taboo of 'Economism'

Asserting the importance of the philosophy of internal relations and its relevance to rethinking Global Capitalism, Global War, Global Crisis puts us on guard against posing such processes as a series of external relations of opposition. Our caution here is cast against the violence of abstractions and recourse to raw facts as key principles. It was E. P. Thompson (1968: 224–5) who stated, in *The Making of the English Working Class*, that:

When we encounter some sonorous phrase such as 'the strong ebb and flow of the trade cycle' we must be put on our guard. For behind this trade cycle there is a structure of social relations, fostering some sorts of expropriation (rent, interest, and profit) and outlawing others (theft, feudal dues), legitimising some types of conflict (competition, armed warfare) and inhibiting others (trade unionism, bread riots, popular political organisation) – a structure which may appear, in the eyes of the future, to be both barbarous and ephemeral.[13]

---

[13] This extract also shapes the renewal of historical materialism in the work of Ellen Wood (1995: 89).

We, therefore, have to be on guard against the use of fetishised concepts, categories or raw facts, which are often abstracted from their alienated forms of appearance under the social relations of capitalism. Yet, as Ollman (1976: 17) indicates, the average social scientist starts with a conception of factors or relations that are treated as logically independent of one another where each *relatum* is taken as a self-subsistent entity existing apart from the other. This philosophy of external relations treats the world as constituted of things external to each other, remaining independent, relatively isolated and static, meriting analysis only when 'bumping' into each other (Ollman, 2015: 10). As discussed earlier, the exogenous interaction of states, akin to the analogy of billiard balls, independently operating within a system of international anarchy would be the example par excellence from neorealist international theory. Central to a dialectical method, in contrast, is the philosophy of internal relations in which entities take their meaning in and through their relationality with each other. The full complexity of the inneraction of entities, then, can be assessed only after their prior identity has been accepted as linked within a relational viewpoint. As Ollman (1976: 270) highlights, both issues of identity and difference can then be established:

The identity of mode of production and relations of production, private property and the division of labour, production and consumption, base and superstructure, class and state ... constitutes the ontological basis for the investigation of their actual differences.

Connections are therefore maintained and contained as aspects of each part, as both 'process' and 'relation', forming together the whole in which they exist. Various philosophical sources for treating internally related aspects as part of the same whole may be established. Yet it is Karl Marx's conception of capital that establishes factors conventionally thought of as external as, instead, treated as co-elements in a single structure or relational whole within a materialist theory of history (Ollman, 1976: 14). For example, witness Marx's emphasis on the metabolic inneraction between humanity and nature in order to realise 'the everlasting nature-imposed condition of human existence' (Marx, 1867/1990: 290). What historical materialism manages to capture, then, is the 'spiral form of development' of concepts, categories and their conditions to establish the manifold ways in which entities are internally related as part of a dialectical method of inquiry (Engels, 1883/1987: 313). A relational ontology therefore avoids positing entities in external interaction, or succumbing to the pitfall of ontological exteriority, by asserting instead a focus on the internal ties that bind exploitation through value, labour, private property, class, capital, interest, commodities, the state, nature, religion or ideology, to name just a few possible points of departure. This is why Ollman asserts so adroitly a powerful rereading of Vilfredo Pareto's comment that 'Marx's words are like bats. You can see in them both birds and mice' (Ollman, 1976: 3; Pareto, 1902: 332). In short, the relational method of conceiving a world contained in each of its parts is a hallmark of historical materialism. The enterprise of historical materialism puts us on guard against the reified domains of trade cycles, states or market relations and shifts the focus from purely 'technological' factors as the typical refuge of economics and capitalist ideology to the internal relations of political economy (Wood, 1995: 90). Within this enterprise, a radical social ontology exists wherein 'the state is internally related to the class-based organisation of production in civil society' (Rupert, 1995: 23). Our aim therefore is to have the philosophy of internal relations taken seriously as a contribution to the critique of political economy (Ollman, 1976: 262).

Within critical political economy circles, Karl Polanyi is often understood as a significant contributor to analysing the shifting place occupied by a 'substantive' notion of economy as an instituted process within embedded and enmeshed institutions and as a result he is often presented as a radical alternative to mainstream approaches (e.g. Block and Somers, 2014; Blyth, 2002; Burawoy, 2003). In defining the militant creed of liberalism and the doctrine of *laissez-faire* it was in *The Great Transformation* that Polanyi famously highlighted how the road to the free market was opened by an enormous increase in centrally organised and controlled interventionism enforced by the state. 'There was nothing natural about *laissez-faire*', Polanyi (1944/1957: 139) states, 'free markets could never have come into being merely by allowing things to take their course'. Although Polanyi displays a greater sensitivity to the rise of 'market society' and a substantive focus on economy as an instituted process (Polanyi, 1953/1959: 166–8), his view is still one of the state intervening in capitalist political economy without treating the capitalist market as a specific social form (Wood, 2002a: 21–6). The consequence, again, is that of a theoretical dualism that still opposes 'economy' and 'society': between an 'economy' embedded in social relations or social relations embedded in the 'economy'. In concurrence with Kurtuluş Gemici, viewing embeddedness as a gradational concept still means delineating 'spheres' of economy and society, as the market economy becomes the dominant economic system in history, which presupposes economy as an autonomous sphere without social content and reifies the market economy in the way that mainstream economics conceptualises it. 'Strictly speaking, economy and society as bounded ontic entities do not exist. As a result, one cannot be embedded in the other, nor can the embeddedness level change over time' (Gemici, 2007: 26). Hence there is a resurrection of the conceptualisation of the 'economic' and the 'social' as belonging to different social spheres (see Krippner, 2001). The implication is that there is still an assumption of separateness existing between the spaces of economic *and* social relations expressed in market society. Hence a view that posits intervening in capitalist political economy through countermoves to ameliorate market society within the logic of capitalism (Wood, 1997: 556–8). Polanyi, in the most critical terms, was 'condemned in advance to being unable to do more than describe the shifting place of the economy in various societies, without ever really being able to pose the theoretical problem of its effect upon the functioning and evolution of societies, and therefore of its role in history' (Godelier, 1986: 200–1).

By contrast, we want to draw attention to Antonio Gramsci's more acute critique of 'historical economism' as emblematic of a philosophy of internal relations, which he situated within the nexus between free trade ideology, trade unionism and 'statolatry' as part of his ongoing theorisation of an enlarged conception of the state. In his prison writings from 1930 to 1932, there is a generative understanding of 'civil society' not as a separate sphere in opposition to the 'state' but as an element in dialectical unity with 'political society'. Gramsci quite clearly spells this out by formulating the issue around, in his words, the 'identity-distinction between civil society and political society' (Gramsci, 2007: 317, Q8§142) within the state.[14] The tendency to view the state as both a perpetual entity and to concentrate solely on direct governmental responsibility within political society was dismissed as 'statolatry'. His transcendence of 'statolatry' thus came to be famously rendered as 'State = political society + civil society, in other words hegemony protected by the armour of coercion' (Gramsci, 2007: 75, Q6§88). Added to this was also a critique of 'economism' within his wider reflections on state–civil society relations, which has profound importance for an understanding of the separation of the 'economic' and the 'political' in capitalism. Written across 1932–4, in a singular note entitled 'Some theoretical and practical aspects of "economism"', there was a further detailing of the merely methodological distinction between political society and civil society because:

---

[14] A specific convention associated with citing the *Prison Notebooks* is adopted throughout this book. In addition to giving the reference to the selected anthologies, the notebook number (Q) and section (§) accompanies all citations, to enable the reader to trace their specific collocation. The concordance table used is that compiled by Marcus Green and is available at the website of the International Gramsci Society: www.internationalgramsci society.org/.

[I]t is asserted that economic activity belongs to civil society, and that the State must not intervene to regulate it. But since in actual reality civil society and State are one and the same, it must be made clear that *laissez-faire* too is a form of State 'regulation', introduced and maintained by legislative and coercive means. It is a deliberate policy, conscious of its own ends, and not the spontaneous, automatic expression of economic facts. (Gramsci, 1971: 160, Q13§18)

For Gramsci, the struggle over hegemony is therefore exercised within 'the decisive nucleus of economic activity', which should not be misunderstood as recourse to 'economism'. 'Even from the point of view of the classical economists', Gramsci recognised, 'the state intervenes at every moment of economic life, which is a continuous web of transfers of property' (Gramsci, 2007: 10, Q6§10). Or, to coin a pertinent phrase, capitalism exists within the web of life (Moore, 2015). According to Gramsci, then, the traits of economism appeared in many guises but could be linked to:

1) the search for historical connections that *assume* the motives of self-interest rather than taking processes of class formation into account, 'with all their inherent relations';
2) the doctrine whereby economic development is reduced to the course of technical change in the instruments of work; and
3) the dogma according to which both economic and historical development are made to depend directly on the changes in some important element of production e.g. the discovery of a new raw material.

'The discovery of new fuels and new forms of energy, just as of new raw materials to be transformed', he continues, 'is certainly of great importance, since it can alter the position of individual states; but it does not determine historical movement, etc.' (Gramsci, 1971: 163, Q13§18). Hence, confronted with certain events, Gramsci argued that the simplification of economism asks '"who profits directly from the initiative under consideration?"', but it would only be a fallacious reply if one simply assumed that 'the ones who profit directly are a certain fraction of the ruling class' (Gramsci, 1971: 166, Q13§18). Instead, the struggle against economism should be conducted, he argues, through analysis that focuses on the social content and the balance of forces that 'can and must be carried on by developing the concept of hegemony' (Gramsci, 1971: 165, Q13§18).

Here, then, we find explicitly displayed the internal relation or dialectical unity of state and civil society, rather than their separation as externally related factors. In accord with Peter Thomas (2009: 69 n.89, emphasis added), 'Gramsci's argument that the distinction between the state and civil society is, properly understood, methodological rather than organic, is crucial for grasping the *dialectical dimensions* of his concept of the state.' But 'it was also precisely against the notion of an "ontological" identity of the two terrains of the modern social formation that Gramsci polemicised' (Thomas, 2009: 69). Thus, with the integral state – combining as a dialectical unity the moments of civil society and political society in constructing hegemony – there was contained, in their internal relation, the elements of a theorising of the modern state. As Gramsci (1992: 128, Q1§43) sums up, basic concepts have to be adapted to diverse peculiarities by presenting and re-presenting them in their positive aspects and traditional negations, to 'always order each partial aspect in the totality'. The novelty of this theorisation, viewing state–civil society relations as a dialectical unity of the integral state, is therefore in its contribution to the perspective of a historical materialist philosophy of internal relations of the capitalist state form. This is what was meant in striving to establish 'the ethical content of the state', drawing together political society and civil society within a theory of the integral state and, 'all the forms of life which are implicit in its internal relations' (Gramsci, 2007: 20, Q6§24, 1971: 177, Q13§17). As Gramsci (1992: 128–9, Q1§43) concludes: 'Finding the real identity underneath the apparent differentiation and contradiction and finding the substantial diversity underneath the apparent identity is the most essential quality of the critic of ideas and the historian of social development.'

The spatial separation of spheres such as 'state' and 'civil society', positing such relations as external to one another, is therefore rejected from the standpoint of a historical materialist philosophy of internal relations. Allied with this, historical materialism also does not relegate the 'economic' and the 'political' in capitalism to spatially separate spheres. As becomes clearer throughout the chapters constituting Part I of this book on Conceptual Reflections, our focus on the social constitution of the economy means that relations of production do not stand apart from or precede juridical-political forms, whereby a 'material' productive base is held in exteriority to ideological 'superstructural' conditions (Wood, 1995: 61). For Marx (1847/2010: 166), in *The Poverty of Philosophy*, 'ideas, these categories', are 'as little eternal as the relations they express. They are historical and transitory products' that are the abstract ideal expressions of social relations. Hence, in Chapter 2, we conceptualise the internal relations between agency and structure by arguing that the social relations of production generate the structuring conditions of capitalism as well as collective social class agency. Drawing on the work of E. P. Thompson, this shift to asserting class in internal relationship to underlying relations of production recognises the antagonisms that generate conflicts and struggles through which class identity emerges (Thompson, 1978: 149). This is relayed by an emergent process of class formation whereby particular communities experience new structures of exploitation and identify new points of antagonistic interest centred around issues of class struggle, even though forms of class consciousness – involving a conscious identity of common interests – may not have immediately formed (Morton, 2011/2013: 204–9). Subsequently in Chapter 3, the philosophy of internal relations is applied to the role of ideas in international theory. Rather than understanding ideas as a separate, explanatory category, we argue that we can comprehend the way ideas are internally related to material structures through the 'material structure of ideology' expressed in four steps: 1) there is a focus on issues such as architecture alongside street layouts (as well as street names), and the social function performed by libraries, schools, publishing houses, newspapers and journals; 2) these condensations of hegemony are diffused through indirect forms of capillary power, mediated through society to exercise class relations; 3) as a consequence, ideologies are viewed as historically produced through ceaseless struggle, taking on substance through practical activity bound up with systems of meaning embedded in the economy; and (4) such activity is linked to the role of organic intellectuals in the struggle over hegemony, exercising an ideological social function in a broad sense across state–civil society relations. Thus, both chapters indicate how our historical materialist viewpoint conceptualises the social forms that relations of production take, above all through the form of state itself as well as the mediations in civil society exerted by a mode of production (Sayer, 1985: 251; Wood, 1995: 96). This means there is a *differentiation* of the 'economic' sphere from the 'political' to be made in capitalism but not a *separation*.

Despite Gramsci's own critical engagement with 'economism', this is still the predominant criticism of historical materialism from across the social sciences. Indicative here would be three examples drawn from interdisciplinary literatures on political economy, historical sociology and geographical studies. First, there is the claim that there is 'a pervasive inclination' towards economism within political economy and therefore that economism is the 'hallmark' of explicitly Marxist approaches to state debates (Phillips, 2005: 83, 100). But witness in this accusation the stark separation of the 'political' and the 'economic' that is enforced by the critic. Running with the logic, historical materialist analyses of state transformation are dismissed as having 'a tendency towards economic determinism and a heavily structuralist account of politics, in which states, state strategies and, indeed, the class relations they represent derive from the processes and imperatives of global capitalist accumulation' (Phillips, 2005: 100). Furthermore, the follow-on claim is that such a Marxist stance identifies that 'a "logic" of economic (capitalist) globalisation exists, and a determinist argument that states are essentially subordinated to it and intrinsically defined by it' (Phillips, 2005: 100). Although there is no recourse to clarifying who such perpetrators are, notice how it is the detractor that presents the economic sphere as a distinct, independently existing sphere (linked to capitalism) whose elements are separated from the political aspects of life (linked to the state). Second, some scholarship has similarly accused historical materialist approaches of taking 'the economic and financial domains as unproblematic or material starting points to their enquiries', thus failing 'to enquire how financial knowledge, including statistics and indices, has been historically developed' (de Goede, 2003: 80). These historical materialist perspectives are then accused of economism in that class identity is deemed to be presented as preceding the political and, thus, driving explanation in a determinist way. 'The point to be emphasised here', de Goede (2003: 90) argues, 'is that ... culture, discourse and ideology remain largely in the domain of the superstructure, and of secondary importance to the study of the economic base which ultimately determines the objective economic interests of agents'. In other words, there is supposedly an undue distinction 'between the material sphere of the economic and the ideational sphere of the political' (de Goede, 2003: 90). But here again the categories of separation are enforced and adopted by the detractor while overlooking the diversity of historical materialism in order to reject it on the basis of a blanket objection of economism (Laffey, 2004: 467–8). Third, in debates on the geographical and spatial practices of modernity there is the thinly substantiated contention that political economy reduces modernity to capitalism so that 'accounts of modernity become accounts of the all-powerful machinations of a hegemonic and abstract capitalist force' (Radcliffe, 2007: 25). But despite a worthwhile move to reveal how conceptions of modernity contain distinctively geographical and spatial power relations, there is a failure here to acknowledge a clear historical materialist focus on the historical specificity of capitalism, which avoids any conflation with modernity. After all, the project of modernity and the Enlightenment had little to do with capitalism. It belonged to distinctively *non*-capitalist practices so that any conflation of modernity with capitalism should be avoided because 'the identification of capitalism may disguise the specificity of modernity too' (Wood, 1997: 544).

Across these instances, economism is commonly cast as a *taboo term* that, following Richard Ashley's salutary acknowledgement, 'has no other purpose than to secure the boundaries of disciplinary discourse when argument threatens to stray into alien terrain or by warning when alien argument threatens to penetrate or subordinate the discipline's time-honoured rules of discourse' (Ashley, 1983: 463). The charge of 'economism' and the use of it as a taboo term are therefore embedded within a wider set of disciplinary articulations that attempt to exclude questions and arguments from political discourse. Through the use of a taboo term such as 'economism', critics charge that all references to capitalism or class relations by historical materialists are economistic and 'having so reduced them, they can find the arguments guilty of reductionism and reject them out of hand. They can regard the arguments as economistic theories that fail to respect disciplinary boundaries, neglect political causes of political outcomes, and bring their explanations to rest in "economic causes"' (Ashley, 1983: 467). However, the languid turn to the taboo blanket term of 'economism' is problematic on at least two counts. First, the interdisciplinary practice of using such a term fails to register the radical aspect of the critique of political economy that historical materialism claims, which is to relate internally the capitalist state's material problematic to the emergent class-based organisation of property relations in civil society. By so doing, indulging in the use of the taboo term of 'economism' immunises issues of class exploitation from political contestation and places such appraisers uncritically within the capitalist state's own violent abstractions to naturalise the given order. Second, these indicative critics present historical materialism as relying on an account of the material economic realm (base) as a distinct sphere separate from the ideational (superstructure) of the political to deny any notion of causality within social relations. The result is what Perry Anderson has recognised as the complete *randomisation of history* due to the stress on absolute contingency (Anderson, 1983: 48). As Gramsci forewarned, 'it is not true that the philosophy of praxis "detaches" the structure from the superstructures when, instead, it conceives their development as intimately bound together and necessarily interrelated and reciprocal' (Gramsci, 1995: 414, Q10II§41i). Hence, the significance of recognising the internality of the ways in which private property is legally ensured by the state, so that forms of power such as 'the law' may be seen as *both* an instrument through which definitions of property are imposed or maintained *and* an ideology in active relationship to social norms through which class relations are mediated (Gramsci, 2007: 69, Q6§84; 83–4, Q6§98; Heino, 2018; Thompson, 1975: 261; Wood, 1995: 22). Productive relations are therefore in part meaningful in terms of their very definition in law in civil society, although 'the anatomy of this civil society ... has to be sought in political economy' (Marx, 1859/1987: 262). The task, as mentioned earlier, is then one of investigating history backwards to ask: *what had to have happened in the past for capitalism as a mode of production to emerge and consolidate?* This is now the purpose of the next section, to outline how posing this question will assist in delivering the plan of the main parts of this book beyond our meta-theoretical concerns, in terms of the historical sociological analysis in Part II on Thematic Considerations on capitalist expansion and uneven and combined development (Chapter 4), the geopolitics of capital accumulation (Chapter 5), and conditions of exploitation and resistance through class struggle (Chapter 6). This will then enable us to provide a series of vantage points on the political economy of world order through the internal ties of Global Capitalism (Chapter 7), Global War (Chapter 8), Global Crisis (Chapter 9) in order to reveal intrinsic features of capitalism from the explanatory approach of historical materialism in Part III of this book on Empirical Interventions.

The Buried History of Political Economy

Lost in the haste and haze of indictments against historical materialism as 'economistic' is an understanding of the specific conceptualisation it can offer of the *social constitution of the economy* linking state power within capitalism to prevailing social property relations or relations of production (Corrigan, Ramsey and Sayer, 1980; Wood, 1995: 25). In Part II of this book, we move towards uncovering the historical specificity of capitalism. This entails engaging with the panoramic historical sociology that Marx and wider classic historical materialists offer to establish the inner tie of relations of production, state-civil society and conditions of class struggle in such a way that moves beyond the economic forms of phenomena, which is the basis of this book in rethinking Global Capitalism, Global War, Global Crisis. We begin to address here the central question as to what had to have happened in the past for capitalism as a mode of production to emerge and consolidate. Chapter 4, especially, highlights how, under feudalism, agrarian property was largely privately controlled by a class of feudal lords who extracted a surplus from the peasants by politico-legal relations of direct compulsion (Anderson, 1974a: 150–1, 1974b: 404–7). Under capitalist social property relations, however, 'free' wage labour and the private ownership of the means of production are, by contrast, constituted differently as the direct producers are no longer in possession of their own means of subsistence but are compelled to sell their labour power for a wage in order to gain access to the means of production (Wood, 1995: 35–6). The market, in this focus on social property relations, does not therefore represent an opportunity but a compulsion mediated by the state to which both appropriators and expropriators (capital and labour) are subjected, through the imperatives of competition, profit maximisation and survival (Wood, 2002a: 96–8,

102). Although mindful of the point that relations of production are not simply or completely reducible to forms of exploitation (see Banaji, 2010), the historical process of primitive accumulation reconstituting peasants (and the social position of women) in possession of the means of subsistence into propertyless individuals compelled to sell their labour is crucial for the emergence of capitalism. As Marx points out:

[T]he transformation of the individualised and scattered means of production into socially concentrated ones, of the pigmy property of the many into the huge property of the few, the expropriation of the great mass of the people from the soil, from the means of subsistence, and from the means of labour, this fearful and painful expropriation of the mass of the people forms the prelude to the history of capital. (Marx, 1867/1990: 928)

An important facet of Part II is therefore how varied forms of surplus extraction can be differentiated by focusing on the defining features of pre-capitalist and capitalist property relations and how the latter have become interiorised within the states system. In terms of the connection between the emergence of capitalism and the rise of the modern state, we hold the common argument in Chapter 4 that in the historically peculiar and specific case of England the processes developed in tandem. State formation and capitalist development there went hand in hand as the social transformations that brought about capitalism were the same that characterised the apparent differentiation of state and civil society leading to the constitution of the capitalist state (Wood, 1991: 27). Therefore, the 'specificity of state sovereignty lies in its "abstraction" from civil society – an abstraction which is constitutive of the private sphere of the market, and hence inseparable from capitalist relations of production' (Rosenberg, 1994: 123–4). In contrast, the state emerging out of feudal and absolutist property relations elsewhere meant that there was still a largely direct coercive function to the extraction of surplus through 'extra-economic' means. Hence Chapter 4, on uneven and combined development, also establishes how forms of class agency through passive revolutions are differently related to the institution and/or outward expansion of capitalism on a world scale.

The challenge for Chapter 5 is to conceptualise the state as a condensation of class forces in a way that emphasises its internal relations with social property relations, with the wider interstate system and with global capitalism. As alluded earlier, mainstream IR and IPE theories commit to a philosophy of external relations which *either* ascertain the continuing dominance of states in the global political economy *or* analyse how markets and new actors have taken over traditional state authority. In contrast to such attempts to analyse the external relations between the political (or the state) and the economic (or the market) we focus again on the internal relations between global capitalism and geopolitical rivalry. In particular, we argue that in order to conceptualise global restructuring, we need to analyse the way and the extent to which the interests of transnational capital have become internalised within specific forms of state. Chapter 6 then focuses on conditions of exploitation, resistance and class struggle, indicating that the analysis of class struggle against exploitation needs to be cast widely beyond the direct confrontation between workers and employers at the workplace. Only if we understand the internal relations between the wider dynamics of capitalist exploitation extending into the sphere of social reproduction can we conceptualise how the social relations of ethnicity, gender and sexuality are internally constitutive of class, rather than separate, external factors of analysis. From a philosophy of internal relations perspective, the social relations of race, gender and sexuality are thus internally constitutive of class, rather than external to it (McNally, 2015).

The dialectics of the philosophy of internal relations sets up the possibility to establish a vantage point from which to view, consider, link and rethink a set of relations as parts of a self-forming whole. As explained by Ollman, the abstraction of vantage point offers a sense of the different ordering parts shaping the whole, providing insight into what is important and, in reconstructing intricate relations, enables a grasp of what historical and contemporary features coexist in shaping capitalism across space and time (Ollman, 2003: 75). This methodological commitment means that the meta-theoretical considerations on class struggle (Chapter 2) and the materiality of ideas (Chapter 3), in Part I of this book on Conceptual Reflections, and the conditions of capitalist expansion through uneven and combined development (Chapter 4), geopolitics (Chapter 5) and exploitation and resistance (Chapter 6), in Part II of this book on Thematic Considerations, can be understood in the contemporary era through a set of Empirical Interventions in Part III of this book, internally relating global capitalism to the so-called rising powers of the BRICS, but, especially, to the insertion of China within the uneven and combined development of Global Capitalism (Chapter 7); Global War and conditions of the new imperialism linked to the political economy of the invasion of Iraq in 2003 as an expression of the geopolitical dynamics of capital accumulation (Chapter 8); and Global Crisis based on the uneven and combined developmental outcome of the Great Recession since the global financial crisis of 2007–8, notably across the Eurozone, situated within the web of conditions of ecological crisis and austerity (Chapter 9). These vantage points will provide a varied perspectival approach to the political economy of world order in order to reveal intrinsic features of capitalism within our explanatory approach of historical materialism. As Ollman (2003: 105) delineates this approach:

Sticking with one vantage point will restrict understanding any relation to its identical or different aspects ... Abstracting the vantage points that bring out the difference between two or more aspects of an interactive system also highlights the asymmetry in their reciprocal effect.

The assumption of internal relations in ontology and epistemology is assisted across the last three chapters of this book by the historical method of 'postholing' in order to unravel the dynamics of Global Capitalism, Global War, Global Crisis. The historical method of postholing invites theory about why historical change occurs and demands a theoretical perspective of history beyond explanations of immediate contingencies or sheer chance (Sennett 1977/2002: 42).[15] The chapters constituting Part III of this book will therefore depict the sweep of historical forces and at the same time some of the richness of detail which comes from delving into specific moments of Global Capitalism, Global War, Global Crisis.

'It is felt that the dialectic', stated Gramsci (1971: 435, Q11§22), 'is somewhat arduous and difficult, in so far as thinking dialectically goes against vulgar common sense'. This book nevertheless asserts the intrinsic importance of the dialectical approach of the philosophy of internal relations, as the hallmark of historical materialism, in order to understand better Global Capitalism, Global War, Global Crisis. The final chapter outlines radical ruptures of social transformation in and beyond Global Capitalism, Global War, Global Crisis as a basis for shaping the future.

---

[15] Elsewhere, in his account of the intellectual origins of the Russian Revolution, Edmund Wilson (1940/1972: 140–1) captures a similar sentiment in detailing the 'spotlighting method' to stress moments of intellectual production as representative of processes of social situations.

Part I

Conceptual Reflections

2   The Centrality of Class Struggle

Every approach within the social sciences implicitly or explicitly adopts a conceptualisation of the relation between structure and agency. Importantly, as Colin Wight reminds us, 'the agent-structure problem cannot be solved in the sense of a puzzle with an answer, but rather represents competing visions of what the social world is and what it might become' (Wight, 2006: 4). The purpose of this chapter is to lay out our vision of the agent–structure problem, informed by historical materialism and the philosophy of internal relations as introduced in Chapter 1.

Because any theory has to engage with the agency–structure problem, this issue has been of considerable importance in the broader social science literature. While making no claims to presenting a comprehensive overview, the first section in this chapter looks at some of the more recent key interventions on agency and structure across wider social science debate. Since Alexander Wendt's (1987) seminal article, considerable effort has been spent on developing discussions of the agency–structure problem in international relations (IR). The second section of this chapter assesses more closely key developments in this respect with a particular emphasis on constructivist and poststructuralist scholarship. The third section of this chapter then explores our own, historical materialist conceptualisation of the relation between agency and structure, which will underpin the discussions in the remainder of this book. As Wight emphasises, the agent–structure problem is an ontological question of the nature of the object we are investigating, its constituent elements and the way they are related to each other (Wight, 2006: 63). Hence, this section also includes a discussion of the key structuring conditions of capitalism as well as social class forces as the main collective agents. The objective from a historical materialist perspective, as introduced in Chapter 1, is to emphasise how the philosophy of internal relations enables an appreciation of agent–structure issues within a critical theory of world order. Thus, a further contribution is made to establishing our historical materialist approach in relation to other IR theories, which is one of the key purposes of Part I in this book.

Diverse Interventions in the Social Sciences

Structuralism and intentionalism are two social science approaches that adopt a monocausal view on the agency–structure debate. While the former denies human beings any autonomy in their actions, the latter completely ignores the structures in which agents' activities are located. Both are unsatisfactory. As Walter Carlsnaes points out (1992: 250), 'as long as actions are explained with reference to structure, or vice versa, the independent variable in each case remains unavailable for problematisation in its own right.' Therefore, we need to consider how the dialectical relationship between structure and agency can be encapsulated. Anthony Giddens' theory of structuration offers one such attempt. Giddens 'prefers the idea of a duality, in which structure and agency are seen as two sides of the same coin, to that of a dualism in which structure and agency are externally related – two separate coins which periodically knock against one another' (Hay, 1995: 197). The notion of duality implies that social structures are constituted by human agency and are, at the same time, the medium of this constitution. Both are internally related through social practices. In Giddens' own words (1984: 25):

The constitution of agents and structures are not two independently given sets of phenomena, a dualism, but represent a duality. According to the notion of the duality of structure, the structural properties of social systems are both medium and outcome of the practices they recursively organise.

As positive as this approach may look at first sight, it is not without problems. First, Giddens' definition of structure and the closely related notion of duality are problematic. 'In structuration theory "structure" is regarded as rules and resources recursively implicated in social reproduction' (Giddens, 1984: xxxi). Being the medium and the outcome of social practices, structure enjoys no existence on its own, i.e. 'no existence independent of the knowledge that agents have about what they do in their day-to-day activity' (Giddens, 1984: 26). It has a 'virtual existence' only when instantiated by actors. Nevertheless, according to Margaret Archer, an elaborated structure has properties which cannot be reduced to social practices made up of rules and resources instantiated via human interaction in the present. Similarly, Giddens' definition lacks a differentiation between various types of structural properties. He does not comprehend that 'at any given time some properties are more resilient or engender more resistance to change than others' (Archer, 1990: 78).

This lack of differentiation makes Giddens exaggerate voluntarism and minimise constraint. His 'voluntaristic bias means that institutions are what people produce, not what they confront and have to grapple with in ways which are themselves conditioned by the structural features involved' (Archer, 1990: 79). Overall, as Colin Hay shows, Giddens' redefinition of 'structure' as rules and resources implemented in interaction opens up a new dualism, this time between agency and systems. Of course, Giddens' approach offers a rich insight into social interaction, 'but this is achieved by detaching the micro-practices of everyday life from their broader social and political context' (Hay, 1995: 198; see also Wight, 2006: 141–4). Hence, the problem of structure and agency has not been solved by relating the two to each other in a new way but by redefining them.

Additionally, due to the notion of duality, an analysis of the potential for change in a particular historical situation is diminished. 'Conceptual insistence on the simultaneity of freedom for action and the stringency of constraints inhibits any theoretical formulation of the conditions under which either will predominate' (Archer, 1990: 82). Consequently, structuration theory cannot adequately promote questions about how actors may transform their social situations or when they merely replicate existing structures. Following the same line of argument, the notion of duality within structuration theory does not provide the scope to acknowledge that structure and agency work at different time intervals. 'It can, therefore, never incorporate theoretically the two most important dualistic assumptions: 1) that structural features logically pre-date the actions that transform them; and 2) that structural elaboration logically post dates those actions' (Archer, 1990: 83). Overall, despite its path-breaking achievement in highlighting that the dualism of agency and structure needs to be reviewed in order to overcome the traditional determinist bias of both structuralism and intentionalism, structuration theory does not offer a satisfactory solution.

In order to overcome the limits of duality, Archer suggests the morphogenesis approach. She incorporates the analysis of time into the agency–structure problem by noting the time gap between the original formation of structure, interactions then taking place within it and the resulting elaborated structure to argue that 'this invites analytical dualism when dealing with structure and action' (Archer, 1982: 458, 1995: 89–92). Time is crucial as a factor, since it helps us to realise that while there are no social structures without people, it does not follow that there are particular social structures only because of the people present at a particular point in time. Some structures are the consequences of actions by people in the past. A dualistic separation of structure and agency explains, then, why actors encounter social structures as objects, although they are made by human beings. 'In structural conditioning, systemic properties are viewed as the emergent or aggregate consequences of past actions. Once they have been elaborated over time they are held to exert a causal influence upon subsequent interaction' (Archer, 1995: 90). Morphogenesis, in short, argues that:

> Action is ceaseless and essential both to the continuation and further elaboration of the system, but subsequent interaction will be different from earlier action because conditioned by the structural consequences of that prior action. Hence the morphogenetic perspective is not only dualistic but sequential, dealing in endless cycles of structural conditioning/social interaction/ structural elaboration, thus unravelling the dialectical interplay between structure and action. (Archer, 1990: 76)

In short, morphogenesis permits a focus on both agency and structure and promotes the analysis of their dialectical interplay over time. Its central assumption of analytical dualism, furthermore, makes it possible to investigate when different degrees of determinism or voluntarism might prevail. 'Morphogenesis tackles the respective weightings of the two aspects by analysing the stringency of constraints and degrees of freedom in different structural and cultural contexts and for different social groups' (Archer, 1990: 82, 1995: 294–344). Nevertheless, the break-up of the interaction between action and structure over time into intervals gives the impression that every action leads to an elaboration of the structure as a whole within which it took place. Thereby, Archer does not specify that there are different types of structural properties overlapping each other at a particular point in time. The most important structures are, of course, the most deeply embedded ones, i.e. the ones which provide the overall framework of action during a particular historical period, such as feudalism or capitalism as specific modes of production. These structures are, furthermore, the most unlikely ones to change immediately. Even if every action changed the structure, we would have to distinguish between changes of deep structural properties, which are important for the conditioning of action, and changes of microstructural properties, which have no, or a less, significant impact on the framework of action.

   A further approach in the social sciences to the issue of agency structure is Roy Bhaskar's Transformational Model of Social Activity (TMSA), drawing on scientific Realism as a meta-theoretical approach (Bhaskar, 1975). As Wight (2006: 29) outlines:

> A commitment to depth realism presupposes that there are things, entities, structures and/or mechanisms that operate and exist independently of our ability

to know or manipulate them. It also presupposes that appearances do not exhaust reality, that there are things going on, as it were, beyond and behind the appearances that are not immediately accessible to our senses. The laws of nature, the entities, structures or mechanisms which are often not empirically 'observable', are what Bhaskar terms the 'intransitive objects of knowledge' and exist independently of (wo)man and independently of his/her ability to know them.

Within IR, Roy Bhaskar's approach has been received in different ways. There are those who argue that from a TMSA perspective the generative mechanisms that make up structures are unobservable objects, which are completely independent from human beings as agents (Doty, 1997: 370). Although these entities, including social structures, are unobservable, they 'must nevertheless be regarded as really existent because they have effects' (Suganami, 1999: 377). It is, then, the task of scientific inquiries to analyse the empirically visible effects by referring them back to the unobservable structures and their causal mechanisms. As a result, however, structure is understood as given and beyond change, there is little room for agency and science becomes a modified positivist enterprise. Alternatively, in Wight's (1999: 119) reading, 'Bhaskar makes clear that social structures are ... concept dependent; activity dependent; and time–space dependent,' leaving room for transformative human agency (also see Joseph and Wight, 2002). This reading is closely related to Colin Hay's position that, in contrast to structuration theory, the TMSA employs analytical dualism in its investigation. Structures do not determine outcomes, but define the potential range of alternative strategies. Agents have the opportunity of choosing from several strategies within the structure. Hence, 'strategic action is the dialectical interplay of intentional and knowledgeable, yet structurally-embedded actors and the preconstituted (structured) contexts they inhabit' (Hay, 1995: 200–1). Structures, being both constraining and enabling, do not determine action, but they define the framework within which agents can choose several alternative strategies. Enabling features may favour some agents over others in a particular structural setting. Eventually, structure may also be transformed by agency over time (Hay, 1995: 201). In short, agency is located in structure, but not determined by it.

For the morphogenesis approach as well as the TMSA, agency and structure play independent roles often at different times in line with analytical dualism. In our own, historical materialist approach we go beyond analytical dualism by stressing the philosophy of internal relations introduced in Chapter 1 and the internality of structure and agency rather than their exterior relation. As a next step, however, we first evaluate the way in which general developments in the social sciences on the agent–structure problematic have played out within the IR discipline.

International Relations and the Agent–Structure Problematic

Structuralist and intentionalist approaches can also be found in IR. The world systems approach associated with Immanuel Wallerstein is discussed in more detail in Chapter 4. Here, it serves as a clear example of an approach in which developments are explained by referring exclusively to the structural level. According to Wallerstein, 'the major social institutions of the capitalist world-economy – the states, the classes, the peoples, and the households – are all shaped (even created) by the ongoing workings of the world-economy' (Wallerstein, 1990: 508). Kenneth Waltz's (1979) neorealism, also called structural Realism, is equally an example of a structuralist approach in our view. Some argue that it would be an example of an agency-centred account (e.g. Dessler, 1989: 448; Wendt, 1987: 339), as states as the main ontological units are perceived to be prior to the interstate system. In other words, the latter is the result of the prior positioning of the former. Nevertheless, Waltz's emphasis on the distribution of capabilities between different states as a system-level property being the main explanatory variable in the analysis of international outcomes clearly puts him into the structuralist camp as a 'methodological structuralist' (Wight, 2006: 75). Waltz 'attempts to arrive at explanations without recourse to the motives of individuals and views structure as a domain that is autonomous of individual powers and propensities' (Wight, 2006: 131). By contrast, Hans Morgenthau's realist perspective is an example of an intentionalist approach (Wight, 2006: 76). Regarding the search for dominance rooted in human nature, international politics is understood as a struggle for power. The explanation of international developments rests, therefore, on the analysis of agency, not the wider structure (Morgenthau, 1946, 1966). Against the background of further developments within the social sciences more generally, efforts have been undertaken in IR to reach a more satisfactory conceptualisation of the agency–structure problem. In the following, we investigate more closely constructivist as well as poststructuralist developments.

The Constructivist Challenge: Anarchy Is What States Make of It

Wendt, who explicitly initiated the debate on agency and structure in IR, claims to have developed structuration theory as the basis for a new research agenda with the aim of overcoming the limitations of structuralist approaches. 'The core of this agenda is the use of structural analysis to theorise the conditions of existence of state agents, and the use of historical analysis to explain the genesis and reproduction of social structures' (Wendt, 1987: 365). Both methodologies within a structurationist investigation are combined through dialectical analysis, conceptualising agents and structures as mutually constituted or co-determined (Wendt, 1987: 350). Structural research starts with concrete historical events and then abstracts to the social and internal organisational structures that have provided the conditions for the events to occur. Hence, it is questioned how the underlying social conditions, which provided particular structural limits and opportunities, came about. Then historical research follows, which involves questioning why certain events unfolded in the way they did. A combination of 'structural-historical' analysis thus provides explanation by structurally theorising causal powers, practices and interests and historically tracing the significant choices and interactions that led to specific events and the reproduction (or transformation) of social structures (Wendt, 1987: 364).

Along these lines, Wendt criticises state-centric IR theories for taking the interests and identity of states as given, i.e. exogenous to the process of state interaction. Instead, he suggests 'a cognitive, intersubjective conception of [a] process in which identities and interests are endogenous to interaction' (Wendt, 1992: 394). As a result, 'each identity is an inherently social definition of the actor grounded in the theories which actors collectively hold about themselves and one another and which constitute the structure of the social world. Identities are the basis of interests' (Wendt, 1992: 398). Hence, structure does not only consist of material capabilities, but also intersubjectively constituted identities and interests within the system. 'It is through reciprocal interaction ... that we create and instantiate the relatively enduring social structures in terms of which we define our identities and interests' (Wendt, 1992: 406). This implies that structure is endogenous to process and changing practices of interaction will change intersubjective meanings and thereby the overall structure. In other words, states can change and influence the structure through collective action. Equally, identities and interests may also change, as they are no longer deduced from an unchanging, international, anarchic system. Consequently, rather than comprehending the interstate system characterised by anarchy and state interests as maximising security as fixed, they are understood as changeable depending on collective agency by states as the constituent units. 'If we treat identities and interests as always in process during interaction, then we can see how an evolution of cooperation might lead to an evolution of community' (Wendt, 1994: 390). Hence, anarchy is what states make of it. Wendt identifies three different macro-level structures. There could be the

Hobbesian structure characterised by constant war between states, in line with a neorealist understanding. Equally, however, the structure could be Lockean based on rivalry between states (not excluding the use of violence but also implying the possibility of cooperation) or, finally, Kantian characterised by collective security. The dominant state role in these three structures would be enemy, rival and friend, respectively (Wendt, 1999: 246–312).

Several criticisms can be made concerning Wendt's structurationist approach. First, his definition of structure is oscillating between two different social ontologies. As Wight (1999: 118, 126) outlines, Wendt defines structure according to Giddens and argues that 'the deep structure of the state system . . . exists only in virtue of the recognition of certain rules and the performance of certain practices by states; if states ceased such recognition or performances, the state system as presently constituted would automatically disappear' (Wendt, 1987: 359). However, Wendt also appears to draw predominantly on Bhaskar's work regarding structure as a set of real but unobservable internal and external relations. Thus, he argues that 'because social structures have observable effects, we can potentially claim that they are real entities despite being possibly unobservable' (Wendt, 1987: 357). Such a combination of Giddens' structuration theory with Bhaskar's understanding of structure is, however, deeply problematic, if not meta-theoretically incommensurable despite the appeal of cross-paradigmatic theories (Archer, 1995: 137–49; Doty, 1997: 370; Wight 1996: 313–17, 1999: 117). In any case, it does not help to formulate a clear position on the agency–structure debate.

Second, Wendt's 'structural-historical' analysis, in line with an analytical dualist approach, engages with both structure and agency at different time intervals. The way the two are, however, related to each other is perceived in purely external terms. For example, Wendt analyses the structure consisting of material capabilities as well as intersubjectively constituted identities and interests while focusing on the agency of states, which are still considered the main actors in IR. Wendt does not depart from rationalist assumptions about state agents but, instead, attempts to ground such assumptions within an intersubjectivist epistemology. This generally results in an attempt to understand how prevailing social and power relationships and institutions, regardless of their social construction, develop. Little attention is thus paid to identifying the contradictions that might lead to transforming the structures of the existing world. Overall, Wendt is still committed to being a statist and a realist (Wendt, 1992: 424, 1999: 43). The constitution of the international structure and the existence of states as main agents is simply assumed, adopted from neorealist analysis. There is no attempt made at understanding their internal relation. Put differently, agents and structure are held as ontologically exterior, or always-already separate spheres that are then combined as interacting realms. The problem of ontological exteriority is that the inner connection, or internal relationship, of entities is overlooked if they are held as separate and then combined (see Morton 2013: 139–43). In our own conceptualisation of structure and agency we therefore draw on the philosophy of internal relations, essential to historical materialism, as discussed in Chapter 1.

Poststructuralist Practices and Agency–Structure

The agency–structure debate in IR has also been under scrutiny from a poststructural 'gaze'. As Doty (1997: 371–2) argues:

[T]he difficulty ... is the oppositional logic within which the agent–structure problem has been articulated, i.e. the agent–structure problem has been formulated within a system of thought that defines structures and agents as two distinct, fully constituted and opposed entities each with essential properties, while the central feature of structures, as defined in the agent–structure problematique, makes problematic this very distinction.

Hence, rather than overcoming the dualism of agency and structure, the approaches would have to prioritise at one point either agency or structure in their explanations. That is, they revert either to 'a structural determinism or alternatively to an understanding of agency which presumes pregiven, autonomous individuals' (Doty, 1997: 366). As an alternative to the discussion of agency and structure as such, Doty recommends a concentration on practice. Provided practice is decentred and its indeterminacy acknowledged, she claims, the dichotomy of agency and structure can be overcome. 'Practices, because of their inextricable link with meaning, have an autonomy which cannot be reduced to either the intentions, will, motivations, or interpretations of choice-making subjects or to the constraining and enabling mechanisms of objective but socially constructed structures' (Doty, 1997: 377). In short, both agency and structure are the effect of indeterminate, decentred practices. Another tendency to develop poststructuralist positions is evident in Hidemi Suganami's work. Similar to Doty's approach, agents and structures are not considered to have a pregiven, independent existence. Rather, they are partly the result of a narrative, of stories told about them. Overall, agency, structure and narrative form a complex relationship shaping each other:

[A] society is what it partly is and agents are what they partly are partly because of the stories told about them. But stories, in turn, are told by agents acting as story-tellers as enabled by their social structures (which here include conventions of story-telling). (Suganami, 1999: 379)

Doty's and Suganami's alternatives may look convincing at first sight. Nevertheless, Wight points to a core problem associated with poststructuralist approaches. 'What in Doty's account enables practices? What are the conditions of possibility for practices? What are the causal powers and processes that produce practices? These questions are never fully addressed' (Wight, 2006: 82–3). In other words, it is not clear what practices mean for Doty, what enables them. By asserting the total indeterminacy and decentred nature of practices – an 'indeterminate determinism' (Wight, 1999: 121) – she 'cannot explain practices, except of course by recourse to more practices. In effect a viciously circular argument' (Wight, 1999: 123). Just as Nicos Poulantzas (1978: 151) levied against Michel Foucault, discursive practices of power become hypostatised, leading to power understood not as a social relation but as a phagocyte, meaning that discourse comes to recursively consume discourse, a point developed further in Chapter 3 on ideology. For the present discussion, Suganami's and Doty's accusation that agency–structure theorists have to decide on either structure or agency as fundamental in a particular explanation is brittle. As we argue from a historical materialist conceptualisation of agency–structure, it is possible to relate actors to their surrounding structures, as being even engendered by structures, and realise at the same time that they always have several possible strategies from which to choose a particular course of action. 'There is simply no conflict between structure as a necessary condition for agency and the fact that agents can act otherwise' (Wight, 1999: 120).

In the next section, we outline our historical materialist position on the agent–structure problematic, going beyond analytical dualism with a focus on the philosophy of internal relations. Equally, by drawing on a historicist method of enquiry, we incorporate the intersubjective realm as important for the identity and interests of agents.

A Historical Materialist Position on Agency–Structure

According to Martin Hollis and Steve Smith, accounts of the social world can be divided into two traditions – one that develops an 'external' story modelled on the natural sciences by focusing on detecting cause-and-effect relationships (explanation) and another that develops an 'inside' story by conveying the meanings attached to actions and events by the actors themselves that is more interpretative (understanding). Although it might be appealing to combine a natural science approach with an interpretative one, it is argued that there are always two stories to tell – either explaining or understanding (Hollis and Smith, 1990: 6–7). In terms of agency–structure, the two stories entail 'one based on the intersubjective and subjective choices made by individuals; the other based on structural forces external to those individuals and which may be unknown to those agents' (Wight, 2006: 88). Whether it is two different epistemologies – explaining and understanding – or whether the ontologies of structure and agency require different modes of investigation, a reconciliation between structure and agency is not possible for Hollis and Smith. To overcome this impasse, Wight argues that 'all adequate resolutions of the agent–structure problem will require a metatheoretical perspective that can elaborate the properties of agents and structures and their interrelationships at the level of social ontology, as well as situating a philosophical account of the social sciences that can allow for the possibility of either a rapprochement between interpretative understanding and structural explanation or perhaps a transcendence of the dichotomy' (Wight, 2006: 89).

In line with Wight's privileging of ontological issues and criticism of our previous work on agency–structure for emphasising methodological questions (Wight, 2006: 85), we take here a clear ontological starting point to our engagement with the agency–structure problem. This is also based on Robert Cox's (1992/1996: 144) understanding that 'ontology lies at the beginning of any enquiry. We cannot define a problem in global politics without presupposing a certain basic structure consisting of the significant entities involved and the form of significant relationships among them ... There is always an ontological starting point.' As introduced in Chapter 1, the social relations of production are the ontological starting point of our historical materialist analysis. In order to avoid economic determinism:

Production ... is to be understood in the broadest sense. It is not confined to the production of physical goods used or consumed. It covers also the production and reproduction of knowledge and of the social relations, morals, and institutions that are prerequisites to the production of physical goods. (Cox, 1989: 39)

The social relations of production therefore refer to everyday patterns of behaviour involved in the production and consumption of physical goods as well as the discursive institutional and cultural tactics established to ensure the hegemony of existing social relations.

Within capitalism, production is organised around the private ownership of the means of production and 'free' wage labour. It is this understanding which generates the key ontological properties of structure and agency. First, there are the structuring conditions of capitalism, the way production and accumulation of surplus value is set up. At the same time, these social relations of production also engender social class forces as the key collective agents. As a result of private property and wage labour, two main classes oppose each other in capitalism, on one hand capital, the owners of the means of production, and on the other labour, those who are indirectly forced to sell their labour power in order to survive. However, importantly this does not suggest a homogeneous understanding of identities in their class relevance. Depending on the forms of capital within the overall process of surplus accumulation, we can distinguish between different circuits of financial and industrial capital and labour as well as, depending on which level production is organised, between national and transnational fractions of capital and labour (Bieler, 2000: 10–11, 2006: 32–5; Cox, 1981: 147; van Apeldoorn, 2002: 26–34; van der Pijl, 1984: 4–20). In short, different class fractions are regarded as emerging through the way production is organised in capitalism. It is this focus on the social relations of production as the generator of both structure and agency that facilitates a focus on the internal relations, which allows us to assess the structuring conditions of capitalism with a focus on the role of class agency. The next subsection explores in more detail the wider structuring conditions of global capitalism, followed by a subsection on conceptualising the role of class agency.

The Structuring Conditions of Global Capitalism

The particular set-up of capitalist social relations of production around the private ownership of the means of production and wage labour implies two crucial structuring conditions. First, because labour and capital both reproduce themselves through the market, there is a constant emphasis on competitiveness and a related pressure for further technological innovation in a relentless struggle for ever higher profit levels. As Marx (1867/ 1990: 381) noted, 'under free competition, the immanent laws of capitalist production confront the individual capitalist as a coercive force external to him.' In order to remain competitive every capitalist is forced to innovate production in order to produce more goods at lower costs, generally through the introduction of new technology in the production process. 'If accumulation is not carried on, if the apparatus of production is not constantly modernised, then one's own enterprise is faced with the threat of being steamrolled by competitors who produce more cheaply or who manufacture better products' (Heinrich, 2012: 16). Nevertheless, the technological advantage gained is never permanent, because as soon as one capitalist has moved ahead, others are forced to catch up in order to remain competitive themselves. Once this step has occurred, there is then renewed pressure to move ahead technologically yet again, and so forth (Harvey, 1982/2006: 120). In other words, this constant pressure towards technological innovation is a key structuring condition of capitalist social relations of production. 'Competition subordinates every individual capitalist to the immanent laws of capitalist production, as external and coercive laws' (Marx, 1867/1990: 739).

Nevertheless, what is logical for the individual capitalist is problematic for capital as a whole. When every capitalist attempts to produce more goods with fewer workers through the application of new technology, there will be fewer and fewer people who can actually buy those goods. In other words, there are tensions between growth and technological progress which are 'just too powerful to be contained within the confines of the circulation of capital' (Harvey, 1985: 132). Hence, there will be a crisis of overproduction/underconsumption linked to a declining rate of profit. 'We see here', Harvey argues, 'the necessary contradiction that arises when each capitalist strives to reduce the share of variable capital in value added within the enterprise while speculating on selling his output to workers employed by other capitalists' (Harvey, 1982/2006: 134). With Michael Lebowitz (1992/2003: 12, original emphasis), capital, 'tends to expand the production of surplus value *beyond* its ability to realise that surplus value'. Expressed differently, there is a situation of a surplus of both capital and labour, which can no longer be brought together in a productive way within capitalist social relations of production, leading to a crisis of overaccumulation (Harvey, 1985: 132). Thus, Marx identified the following economic cycle: 'feverish production, a consequent glut on the market, then a contraction of the market, which causes production to be crippled. The life of industry becomes a series of periods of moderate activity, prosperity, overproduction, crisis and stagnation' (Marx, 1867/1990: 580). This crisis tendency of capitalism can be identified as the second structuring condition of capitalism.

Rosa Luxemburg had already pointed to 'the inherent contradiction between the unlimited expansive capacity of the productive forces and the limited expansive capacity of social consumption under conditions of capitalist distribution' (Luxemburg, 1913/2003: 323; also see Bieler et al., 2016). These crises, she argued, cannot be solved within capitalism itself. Instead, new markets have to be opened up elsewhere. 'The decisive fact is that the surplus value cannot be realised by sale either to workers or to capitalists, but only if it is sold to such social organisations or strata whose own mode of production is not capitalistic' (Luxemburg, 1913/2003: 332). Ray Kiely engages critically with Luxemburg's analysis of the outward dynamic of the capitalist mode of production. Historically, capitalist accumulation did not functionally depend on absorbing ever more non-capitalist space. Before World War I, for example, most capital was invested in, and trade took place between, industrialised countries (Kiely, 2010: 79–81). And yet, at the same time, it is a fact that capitalism did expand outwardly in encompassing the whole globe. As early as 1848 Marx and Engels wrote about how capital overcomes periodic crises 'on the one hand through the enforced destruction of a mass of productive forces; on the other through the capture of new markets and a more thoroughgoing exploitation of old ones' (Marx and Engels, 1848/1998: 18). The enforced destruction of productive forces and a more intensive exploitation of existing capitalist social relations of production links to Kiely's emphasis on developments internal to industrialised countries. The capture of new markets, however, refers to Luxemburg's focus on outward expansion. The notion of uneven and combined development becomes relevant especially in relation to the geographical outward expansion of capitalist accumulation.

The notion of uneven and combined development goes back to the work of Leon Trotsky. In 1906, he analysed the location of Russia within the world economy. While Russia was economically backward based on a large sector of inefficient agriculture indicating the unevenness of development in relation to advanced Western countries, a number of small pockets of highly developed industries, especially in military-related production, were established as a result of foreign pressure by more developed neighbours in the West. 'The Russian State, erected on the basis of Russian economic conditions, was being pushed forward by the friendly, and even more by the hostile, pressure of the neighbouring State organisations, which had grown up on a higher economic basis' (Trotsky, 1906/ 2007: 27). Hence, capitalist expansion also leads to 'combined development' as a result of 'the sociological outcome of international capitalist pressures on the internal development of non-capitalist societies' (Rosenberg, 2006: 319). In short, in response to the crisis tendencies of capitalist social relations of production, there is an inherent dynamic of outward expansion along uneven and combined developmental lines. 'In the process of its development, and consequently in the struggle with its internal contradictions, every national capitalism turns in an ever-increasing degree to the reserves of the "external market", that is, the reserves of world economy' (Trotsky, 1929/2007: 137).

The focus on competitiveness and the tendency towards crisis are structuring conditions of capitalist social relations of production. Equally, it can be argued that the pressure towards outward expansion is to some extent a structuring condition resulting from the need to overcome crisis albeit on a temporary basis. Nevertheless, it is at this point that one has to be careful not to slide into a purely structuralist argument. First, restructuring within industrialised countries and the intensified exploitation of the existing workforce are always contested and never conflict free. It is in this contestation that the agency of resistance plays a crucial role. As Harry Cleaver (1979/2000: 89) argues, capital's focus on increasing productivity is not only the result of competition with other employers; it is also a response to workers' struggles, establishing a new way of controlling labour; see also Chapter 6 for an expansion. Equally, Beverly Silver (2003) demonstrates that whenever capital relocated production into new areas to avoid labour unrest in existing facilities, soon novel moments of resistance erupted in these new locations. Clearly, in relation to capitalism's outward spatial expansion, the way and the extent to which non-capitalist space is incorporated also depends on the level of resistance against this expansion. 'The production of economic landscapes is the result of political conflict, between labour and capital and between different segments of labour and of capital who might have quite different visions for how the landscape should be structured' (Herod, 2006: 158). Or, with Cox's (1983: 171, 1987: 150) spatial sensitivity, 'hegemony is more intense and consistent at the core and more laden with contradictions at the periphery', where it may wear thin.[1] In other words, while the pressure for outward expansion results from capitalism's crisis tendencies, the way this unfolds and the extent to which this spatiality unfolds is very much also a result of class struggles, reflecting the internal relation between the structure of the social relations of production and class agency. The next section now looks at the conceptualisation of class agency.

Conceptualising Class Agency

In general under capitalism, a common assumption is that nobody is forced to work for a particular employer. However, without owning one's own means of production, people are indirectly forced to look for paid employment. They are forced to sell their labour power in order to reproduce themselves. Thus, to understand the inequalities and exploitation characteristic of capitalism, we need to investigate the 'hidden abode of production, on whose threshold there hangs the notice "No admittance except on business." Here we shall see, not only how capital produces,

---

[1] This emphasis is in lockstep with Gramsci's own spatial acknowledgement that 'in periods of crisis, it is the weakest, most peripheral segment that reacts first' as a rupture within state formation processes (see Gramsci, 1992: 130, Q1§43).

but how capital is itself produced. The secret of profit-making must at last be laid bare' (Marx, 1867/1990: 279–80). It is 'the netherworld of production, outside and beneath the market, where economic necessity compels workers owning only their labour power to seek employment' (Barker, 2013: 44). This is specific about the capitalist historical period and this is why the state and market appear to be separate, while they are ultimately only two different forms of the same underlying configuration of the social relations of production. Class is here a relational concept with workers having to sell their labour power to those who own the means of production, i.e. capital.

From within historical materialism, there is often an uneasiness voiced about structural varieties of Marxism, which overlook the importance of (class) agency. In a survey of classical Marxist political economy, Harry Cleaver outlines how many of these authors separate the economic from the political:

> They analysed capitalist growth and accumulation independently of working-class initiative. Because of this it is of secondary importance that some of these authors endorsed social democracy and/or collaborated with capitalist governments (e.g. Bernstein, Kautsky, Hilferding, Bauer, Sternberg) while others endorsed a 'revolutionary' perspective (e.g. Luxemburg, Lenin, Pannekoek, Mattick). In all cases, by reading *Capital* as political economy they limited themselves to a critique of capitalist anarchical instability or exploitative nature. (Cleaver, 1979/2000: 34)

As a result, agency is written out of history. Marx's work, while used to analyse the 'objective' structures of the current political economy, cannot seemingly provide any direction for alternative class strategy.

In response to such an ahistorical, political economy approach, Cleaver suggests a political reading of Marx which puts class agency at the heart of analysis. Rather than identifying laws related to the structure of the capitalist social relations of production, he emphasises that all law-like structures are ultimately the result of class struggle between capital and labour. 'The "laws of motion" of capitalist society are the direct product of the class struggle and denote only what capital has had the strength to impose, given the rising power of the working class' (Cleaver, 1979/2000: 88). Along similar lines, Alf Nilsen puts forward a social movement approach with a heavy emphasis on agency. The main stress is on class struggle between social movements from below and social movements from above, the outcome of which determines the structural, institutional setting. 'Such structures – and the social formations in which they inhere – are not static,' Nilsen argues. 'Rather they are internally contradictory totalities that undergo constant processes of change as a result of contention between dominant and subaltern social groups over the structuration of needs and capacities' (Nilsen, 2009: 114; also see Nilsen 2010: 14–16).

Praxis and its social organisation is posited as both the subject and object of social movements. Praxis is the subject of social movements in that movement activity is nothing more and nothing less than the conscious deployment of capacities to satisfy needs. Praxis is also the object of social movements in that movement activity seeks to effect changes in or maintain those structures through which human activity is socially organised, and/or the direction in which those structures are to develop (Nilsen, 2009: 114–15).

In other words, as Nilsen and Cox write elsewhere, 'we see social structures and social formations as the sediment of movement struggles, and as a kind of truce line continually probed for weaknesses and repudiated as soon as this seems worthwhile – by social movements from above and social movements from below' (Nilsen and Cox, 2013: 66; see also Cox and Nilsen 2014: 99–158). But the danger inherent in this social movement from above/social movement from below approach is that structure and agency come to mirror one another. The prioritisation of agency leaves it difficult to discern how the agency of social movements (above or below) is structurally conditioned and contingently articulated in *different* ways.

E. P. Thompson also warns against a static, structural definition of class in developing what has been termed an *emergentist* theory of class composition and struggle (Morton 2011/2013: 208, 268). Rather than upholding a static model of capitalist productive relations from which classes and consciousness derive and correspond to, Thompson places emphasis on emergent processes of class formation. This means analysing contexts within which particular communities experience new structures of exploitation and points of antagonistic interest, even though forms of class consciousness – involving a conscious identity of common interests – may not have immediately formed (Thompson, 1978). Therefore Thompson does not 'see class as a "structure", nor even as a "category", but as something which in fact happens (and can be shown to have happened) in human relationships' (Thompson, 1968: 8). Hence, 'class is defined by men as they live their own history, and, in the end, this is its only definition' (Thompson, 1968: 10). Class is, therefore, a historical category, observed behaviour over time. However, unlike Cleaver as well as Cox and Nilsen, Thompson's theory of class does not dismiss the social relations of production in structurally conditioning class emergence as a form of *structured agency* that is then contingently articulated in specific historical circumstances. As Thompson makes clear:

[T]he class experience is largely determined by the productive relations into which men [*sic*] are born – or enter involuntarily. Class-consciousness is the way in which these experiences are handled in cultural terms: embodied in traditions, value-systems, ideas, and institutional forms. If the experience appears as determined, class-consciousness does not. (Thompson, 1968: 8–9)

In short, what has to be avoided is the deduction of specific ideas, interests and strategies of workers from their location in the social relations of production. But this does not imply that the structural setting of class agency should be dismissed. As Marx (1852/1984: 10) famously said himself:

Men [*sic*] make their own history, but they do not make it as they please; they do not make it under circumstances chosen by themselves, but under circumstances directly encountered, given and transmitted from the past. The tradition of all the dead generations weighs like a nightmare on the brains of the living.

Stuart Hall (1986: 42) further conceptualises how we can understand the impact of the structuring conditions of capitalism on class agency:

The economic aspect of capitalist production processes has real limiting and constraining effects (i.e. determinancy), for the categories in which the circuits of production are thought, ideologically, and vice versa. The economic provides the repertoire of categories which will be used, in thought. What the economic cannot do is (a) to provide the contents of the particular thoughts of particular social classes or groups at any specific time; or (b) to fix or guarantee for all time which ideas will be made use of by which classes. The determinancy of the economic for the ideological can, therefore, be only in terms of the former setting the limits for defining the terrain of operations, establishing the 'raw materials', of thought. Material circumstances are the net of constraints, the 'conditions of existence' for practical thought and calculation about society.

In other words, within each given structural setting, agents are not completely free in their actions, but they nonetheless have a range of strategies at their disposal from which they can choose. Hence, our argument is that analysis commences with a focus on the structuring conditions of capitalist social relations of production, which by default implies that structure matters. Of course, (class) agency remains crucial, but strategies cannot be analysed in isolation of structure. As mentioned earlier, it is accepted that structures are always instantiated by human beings, but this may be the result of actions in the past, with structures opposing social class forces as objective constraints in the present. These structures do not determine agency in the present. They may prevent, constrain or enable agency and they may be changed by collective agency. Thus, within any particular structural setting, social class forces can choose from a limited variety of different strategies. It is this process, the decision on which strategy to adopt within a particular structural setting, which is played out in processes of class struggle. Thus, 'this approach replaces the notion of fixed ideological meanings and class-ascribed ideologies with the concepts of ideological terrains of struggle and the task of ideological transformation' (Hall, 1996: 41). The material is, thus, determining only in the first instance.

Colin Barker (2013: 43) further elaborates that, 'conceptually and historically, "class struggle" precedes any "formation" of classes as potential actors, or any necessary "consciousness" of class.' The focus, thereby, has to be on struggles around exploitation and resistance. As Ste. Croix makes clear, 'bring back exploitation as the hallmark of class, and at once class struggle is in the forefront, as it should be' (Ste. Croix, 1981: 57). Importantly, this focus on class struggle around exploitation and resistance ensures that social forces are not simply reduced to material aspects, but also include other forms of identity involved in struggle such as ethnic, nationalist, religious, gender or sexual forms. In short, '"non-class" issues – peace, ecology, and feminism – are not to be set aside but given a firm and conscious basis in the social realities shaped through the production process' (Cox, 1987: 353). In Chapter 6, we discuss in more detail how through a focus on class struggle within the whole 'social factory' – including the sphere of social reproduction – gender, race and ecological concerns become tightly integrated into the analysis. When analysing class struggle, moreover, the distinction between class-in-itself and class-for-itself is relevant. A class-in-itself can be identified due to the way production is organised, but it may not yet have developed a class consciousness in struggle and, thus, become a class-for-itself. William Robinson, for example, argues that transnational labour so far has only developed into a class-in-itself resulting from the organisation of production at the transnational level. 'But this emerging global proletariat is not yet a class-for-itself; that is, it has not necessarily developed a consciousness of itself as a class, or organised itself as such' (Robinson, 2004: 43; see also Robinson, 2014: 51). The transition from a class-in-itself to a class-for-itself is made through the emergence of class struggle. People 'experience exploitation (or the need to maintain power over those whom they exploit), they identify points of antagonistic interest, they commence to struggle around these issues and in the process of struggling they discover themselves as classes, they come to know this discovery as class-consciousness' (Thompson, 1978: 149). Hence, although classes-in-themselves can be identified through a focus on the social relations of production, the analytical emphasis then has to turn towards the analysis of class struggle and the potential of forming class consciousness. In sum, social class forces are shaped by their location within the social relations of production, but neither their particular strategy nor their interests and identities are determined. Analysing Global Capitalism, Global War, Global Crisis therefore requires a careful appreciation of the structuring conditions of capitalist social relations of production, as well as the strategies of various social class forces.

In order to ensure an analytical focus on the internal relations of the agent–structure problem in particular and empirical research more generally, we employ a historicist epistemology in the section that follows.

A Historicist Epistemology

When exploring the internal relations between the structuring conditions of capitalist social relations of production and social class forces, we draw on the work of Antonio Gramsci, who in accounting for movement and historical change appreciated the traces left in historical phases by preceding phases. Stress is therefore placed on the relationship between past history and the social conditions of the present because residues from the past shape all social forms in the present. As Gramsci stated (1971: 353, Q10II§54), 'each individual is the synthesis not only of existing relations, but of the history of these relations. He [or she] is a précis of the past.' This dialectical conception of past and present, then, provides a basis for appreciating 'the sum of effort and sacrifice which the present has cost the past and which the future is costing the present ... which conceives the contemporary world as a synthesis of the past and of all past generations, which projects itself into the future' (Gramsci, 1971: 34–5, Q12§2). Between past and present, the 'real dialectics of history' (Gramsci, 1978: 15–16) involve the realm of necessity, those social residues or traces of the past determining the present, and the realm of freedom within which possibilities of change can conceivably be obtained. What emerges within this historicist conception of philosophy and history, therefore, is a concern with the structural conditions of existence, the realm of necessity, initially inherited from past forms of thought and action, as well as concern for the realisation of agency, the realm of freedom, that is both determined and determining. 'History is at once freedom and necessity' (Gramsci, 1977: 75). The terrain of politics was thus conceived in a way that avoided voluntarism, assuming that people move in 'the turbid void' of their own desires and dreams, while not excluding the possibility of organising the conditions under which freedom might be achieved (Gramsci, 1971: 171–2, Q13§16, 1977: 325).

The passage from 'necessity to freedom' was also conceived as a passage from 'objective to subjective' (Gramsci, 1971: 367, Q10II§6i):

Structure ceases to be an external force which crushes man [*sic*], assimilates him to itself and makes him passive; and is transformed into a means of freedom, an instrument to create a new ethico-political form and a source of new initiatives.

Just as an emphasis on how the past shapes the present was important for this theory of history then so too was the combination of objective–subjective elements. The 'objective' social world of 'abstract natural forces' or 'intractable natural laws' that confronts people, which is instantiated in forms of thought and practice inherited from the past, 'does not exist on its own, in and for itself, but only in an historical relationship with the men [*sic*] who modify it' (Gramsci, 1971: 34, Q12§2; 346, Q11§59; 467, Q11§30). Additionally, people were themselves conceived as a combination of individual subjective elements and mass objective or material elements in constant and active relationship with each other (Gramsci, 1971: 360, Q10II§48ii). These are important points about knowledge of the social world as a human construction, i.e. the internal relation between structure and agency. They can be illustrated as follows. In a classic passage from the *Prison Notebooks* Gramsci questions the notion of the 'reality' of the 'external world' by taking up the example of geographical terms like 'North' and 'South' or 'East' and 'West'. This is done in order to reject the rather straightforward approach developed by Bertrand Russell, who argued that geographical positions such as North–South or East–West would exist regardless of whether humans knew of such distinctions. As Gramsci states (1971: 447, Q11§20):

It could be objected [against Russell] that without the existence of man [*sic*] one cannot think of 'thinking', one cannot think at all of any fact or relationship which exists only in so far as man exists. What would North–South or East–West mean without man? They are real relationships and yet they would not exist without man and without the development of civilisation.

Such geographical distinctions are therefore arbitrary and dependent upon particular human conventions. Yet it is also noted that they arise from a specific form of European civilisation that was universalised through imperialist expansion and world hegemony. This resulted in references to Japan as the 'Far East', Egypt as the 'Near East' or Muslim and Arab civilisations as 'Eastern' (Gramsci, 1971: 447, Q11§20). Such geographical notions, though, are not merely subjective mental images. As Gramsci makes clear, references of North–South were to become objectified or treated as real tangible entities because they are 'real facts, they allow one to travel by land and by sea, to arrive where one has decided to arrive, to ... objectivise reality, to understand the objectivity of the external world' (Gramsci, 1971: 447–8, Q11§20). An historical fact is therefore real insomuch as it corresponds to the 'historical subjectivity of a social group' (Gramsci, 1995: 347–8, Q10I§8). Yet, although 'reality' is mediated by thought, this does not mean that it is *only* constituted by thought (Femia, 1998: 89). The *ensemble* of social relations that makes up the social world is therefore mediated by a combination of 'objective' and 'subjective' elements. As Gramsci asserts (Gramsci, 1971: 445–6, Q11§17, emphasis added):

> It might seem that there can exist an extra-historical and extra-human objectivity. But who is the judge of such objectivity? Who is able to put himself [*sic*] in this kind of 'standpoint of the cosmos in itself' and what could such a standpoint mean? ... *Objective always means 'humanly objective' which can be held to correspond exactly to 'historically subjective': in other words, objective would mean 'universal subjective'* ... We know reality only in relation to man, and since man is historical becoming, knowledge and reality are also a becoming and so is objectivity.

The geographical positions of North–South, as 'historically subjective' human constructions, would thus become accepted as 'universal' subjective definitions, or intersubjective understandings, of the social world while retaining a 'humanly objective' sense because of the direct physical impact they would have on people's lives (see also Gramsci, 1995: 290–2, Q11§37; 402–3, Q10II§6iii; 406–15, Q10II§41i). Hence, there is an identity between subject and object. The historicist method does not entail collapsing agency into ideational practices. Ideas of the social world arise from, as well as construct, the material conditions in which social groups exist. The world is to some extent given, in the *first instance*, by the material conditions of the past which then set certain limits upon social practices and the conditions of existence for thought and action in the present and future. It is in this move from 'historical subjective' to 'universal' subjective and, thus, 'humanly objective' definitions that the internal relations between class agency and the structuring conditions of capitalism, which precisely include intersubjective understandings of institutions and norms, are revealed.

In short, our argument is that this historicist epistemology focuses on the unity of the subjective and the objective by understanding how structures of the social world are made and also by explaining how such structures confront people as part of 'objective' social reality. As such it avoids a positivist emphasis on positing causal laws to human nature and interaction outside or prior to history. 'Structures are formed by collective human activity over time. Structures, in turn, mould the thoughts and actions of individuals. Historical change is to be thought of as the reciprocal relationship of structures and actors' (Cox, 1995: 33). At the same time, our historicist conception does not collapse unspecified structures and power relations into an equally unspecified account of agency that fails to account for what power is and who the social forces are in shaping modern capitalism (as Knafo, 2010, 2014). On the basis of a historical materialist social ontology and historicist epistemology it is then possible to analyse both the structural setting of capitalism, within which different strategies can be pursued, as well as class agency (Bieler, 2014: 115–16).

Conclusion: Agency in Structure

As discussed in this chapter, in relation to the agent–structure problematic, we go beyond a strategy of analytical dualism. Unlike constructivism, however, we focus on the internal relations of structure and agency, not their external relations. The particular historical materialist social ontology combined with a historicist method of analysis reveals these internal relations. Capitalist social relations of production shape the various structuring conditions as well as engender social class forces as key collective agents. Moreover, we maintain that there are always several different layers of structures overlapping each other, which may appear to social class forces in a given historical situation, to different degrees, as objective and unchangeable. Although originally brought about through human interaction, the state and market within capitalist social relations, for example, appear as separate, objective entities and therefore shape and constrain, but also enable class agency. Nonetheless, the fact that it is so difficult to change deeply embedded structures does not imply that change is impossible. A first step to engendering such change is questioning the objective status of structures. Only if it is realised that a particular structure is the result of class agency in the past and not an objective 'given' is it possible to think about how to change it through class struggle in the present. It is in this sense that our historical materialist approach and its focus on open-ended class struggle contributes to change by attempting to unmask the apparent objective status of structures. This is precisely their inherent critical quality. The exact form and content of class agency and the way it relates to structure is open-ended and determined within the crucible of class struggle.

In sum, class struggle is the moment when agency meets structure, when labour and capital, the two main collective forces opposing each other in capitalism, meet the structuring conditions of capitalist social relations of production. Class struggle is the process in which class identities are formed and transformed. It is the moment when structuring conditions are confirmed or changed. It is through the prism of class struggle that we unravel the internal relations between the structuring conditions of capitalism and class agency and can, therefore, analyse best Global Capitalism, Global War, Global Crisis. In the next chapter, we assess in detail how we can conceptualise the role of ideas in their internal relation to materiality, thereby further establishing the importance of pursuing a historical materialist line of enquiry.

3   The Material Structure of Ideology

The argument of this chapter is that an approach drawing from sources within historical materialism is most adept in appreciating the internal relations, expressed within the notion of the material structure of ideology, between the ideational and material realms as mediators of configurations of class forces. This approach is intrinsic to the argument of this book in its attempts to assess the conditions of Global Capitalism, Global War, Global Crisis thematically in Part II and empirically focused in Part III.

Similar to the relation between structure and agency discussed in Chapter 2, the conceptualisation of the role of ideas within international relations (IR) and international political economy (IPE) has become increasingly important over recent years. Neorealism and liberal institutionalism generally treat ideas as exogenous to states' interest formation and interaction. It has been pointed out, however, that such approaches cannot answer important 'questions of which economic theories and beliefs are most likely to shape the definition of interests in international relations and why and how it is that particular sets of ideas prevail in the international arena' (Woods, 1995: 161; see also Jacobsen, 2003: 41). A first set of attempts to deal with this problem resulted in an amendment to these approaches by simply adding an additional focus on ideas (e.g. Adler and Haas, 1992; Goldstein and Keohane, 1993; Haas, 1992). For example, some scholars have tried to identify institutional and/or actor-centred causal mechanisms. Ideas acquire causal relevance, it is argued, when they become embedded as organisational rules and procedures in institutions (Goldstein and Keohane, 1993: 20–4; Yee, 1996: 88–92). These approaches are based on a positivist understanding of social science, which involves a separation of subject and object and the search for clear cause–effect relationships.

A problem befalling this literature, however, is that while ideas are still treated as causes, as possible additional explanatory variables, this leaves no space for understanding ideas as partly constituting the wider social totality. Ideas are merely seen as commodities, as objects which influence

51

other objects. This 'reinforces the notion that "ideas" are distinct from interests and that their role, in practice, is limited to manipulation; and it obscures the constitutive function of "ideas"' (Laffey and Weldes, 1997: 207). In short, the emphasis on empirical analysis of observable behaviour prevents mainstream IR approaches from capturing the structural quality of ideas in the form of 'intersubjective meanings' (Yee, 1996: 102).

Since these early debates, three sets of theoretical perspectives have more recently emerged which challenge neorealist and liberal institutionalist approaches more fundamentally in the way they conceptualise the role of ideas: social constructivist, poststructuralist and historical materialist contributions. As post-positivist theories, they all commonly question the notion that it is possible to establish causal relationships within a given objective reality. Hence, they share a rather different concentration on the analysis of structural change. They all agree that ideas can be part of overall structural conditions in the form of intersubjective meanings, i.e. collectively held beliefs. They differ, however, in their underlying normative rationale and how precisely intersubjectivity can be conceptualised due to their different ontological/epistemological approaches (Smith, 1995: 24–6, 1996: 35, 38). This chapter critically discusses these approaches, aiming to establish the pivotal contributions of an historical materialist conceptualisation of the role of ideas, embedded in material social practices, to IR theory.

In the first main section we focus on social constructivism, which has argued that ideas, in the form of intersubjective meanings, are as much part of the structure confronting agents as are material processes. Hence ideas may constrain or enable agency. Additionally, ideas may change as the result of individual and collective agency and the establishment of new intersubjective meanings. In short, extending our focus from Chapter 2, there is a very close relationship between ideas, practice and the overall structure, within which agency operates. Importantly, however, agency often remains under-conceptualised across social constructivist approaches. Moreover, while the latter can establish *how* specific ideas might become part of the overall structure, social constructivists are unable to explain *why* a particular set of ideas became part of the structure and not another, rival set of ideas at a particular moment in time.

The subsequent section then analyses poststructuralist contributions to the analysis of discourse in and beyond IR theory. Poststructuralism has generally criticised social constructivism for not questioning more directly the way structure and subjects are constituted. Simply adding an ideational dimension to structural conditions does not overcome the problem of separating structure and agency, as argued in the previous chapter. Rather, the focus has to be on how the constitution of the social subject is directly linked to the discursive founding of the social order. One implicates the other and cannot be analytically separated. As a result, poststructuralists concentrate on power/knowledge relations articulated through discourse around the moments when a new founding myth is created and a new social order (along with social subjects) is constituted. Similar to constructivist approaches, however, while it is outlined *how* a particular discourse can gain dominance at a specific point in time, the question is not addressed as to *why* a certain discourse and not another is successful. The underlying power structures promoting individual discourses are overlooked.

It is by stressing the importance of such underlying power structures that the turning point towards historical materialism is made. Drawing on the philosophy of internal relations, as introduced in Chapter 1, we argue that it is the dialectical way ideas prevail in interrelationship with material properties that can be subsumed within an historical materialist theory of history. This allows us to show that for historical materialism the philosophy of praxis does not detach structure from superstructure but conceives their development as intimately bound together and related internally (Gramsci, 1995: 414, Q10II§41i). Hence this chapter shows how ideas can be conceived as material social processes through which signs become part of the socially created world within global capitalism in a way that surpasses the deficits of social constructivist and poststructuralist approaches alike. This is crucial in identifying *who* the key (class) agents are, *how* certain ideas have emerged as dominant and *why* this is so within the specificity of global capitalism.

Social Constructivism: The Ideal/Material as Always-Already Separate and Combined

Social constructivists consider ideas to be 'intersubjective meanings', defined as 'the product of the collective self-interpretations and self-definitions of human communities' (Neufeld, 1995: 77). Together, these intersubjective meanings make up a 'web of meaning', which is as much a part of the social totality, the structures human beings are confronted with, as material social practices. It is argued, consequently, that 'the practices in which human beings are engaged cannot be studied in isolation from the "web of meaning", which is, in a fundamental sense, constitutive of those practices, even as it is embedded in and instantiated through those same practices' (Neufeld, 1995: 76). Social constructivists widely accept this definition. For example, Emanuel Adler (1997: 322) argues that 'constructivism is the view that the manner in which the material world shapes and is shaped by human action and interaction depends on dynamic normative and epistemic interpretations of the material world.' The close link between ideas and practice is further highlighted, albeit from a different stance, by Mark Laffey and Jutta Weldes (1997: 209) who define ideas as 'symbolic technologies', which 'are, most simply, intersubjective systems of representations and representation-producing practices.' In other words, ideas are not objects to be fetishised but intersubjectively constituted forms of social action that shape social reality.

As outlined in Chapter 2, Alexander Wendt (1992, 1994, 1999) develops this social constructivist line and criticises state-centric approaches such as neorealism for taking the interests and identity of states as given. By contrast, he argues that identities and interests are part of the overall structure in the form of 'intersubjective meanings' and that, therefore, structure is endogenous to process and changing practices of interaction will change 'intersubjective meanings' that partly constitute social totality. Hence, when discussing neorealist scholarship on the nature of the international system, he concludes that 'anarchy is what states make of it.' Depending on the dominant 'intersubjective meanings' collectively held by states, the international system may also be characterised by state rivalry or collective security. While clearly an advance over neorealist IR theory, there are, however, several problems with Wendt's understanding. First, as demonstrated in Chapter 2, his constructivism does not allow him to conceptualise which actors are important for his analysis. Instead, he simply falls back on the neorealist understanding that states are the most important international actors (Wendt, 1992: 424, 1999: 39, 43). Thus, Wendt's variant of social constructivism suffers from state-centricity and an empiricist methodology (Campbell, 1996: 12; Wight, 2004: 273–9). Second, Wendt also continues to take 'the view that material conditions are in fact independent of ideas' (Palan, 2000: 590). This makes it difficult to analyse why certain ideas and not others gain efficacy in terms of structural importance. For example, Wendt cannot explain why it is *anarchy* that is characteristic of the international system, at a particular moment in time, rather than *rivalry*.

Friedrich Kratochwil and John Ruggie, in turn, have highlighted that the intersubjective quality of convergent expectations, as the basis for international regimes, is not accessible to mainstream approaches, which treat ideas simply as independent variables. Instead, the incorporation of social constructivist insights and methods is necessary for explanation to proceed (Kratochwil and Ruggie, 1986: 771). Kratochwil argues that international relationships resemble the intersubjective dimension of games. Positivists can only observe the 'facts' of overt behaviour. 'Beyond that lies the realm of intersubjective rules which are constitutive of social practice, and which an interpretive epistemology has to uncover' (Kratochwil, 1988: 277; see also Kratochwil, 1989). This focus on constitutive rules may provide a non-causal, explanatory account in certain situations plus a narrative explanatory form, which 'is established through a process of successive interrogative reasoning between explanans and explanandum' (Ruggie, 1998: 34). Without a conception of constitutive rules, it is 'impossible to provide endogenously the non-causal explanations that constitutive rules embody and which are logically prior to the domain in which causal explanations take effect' (Ruggie, 1998: 24).

This research agenda has set out to problematise the identities and interests of states, to open up the historical constitution of the states system and to reflect on issues of systemic change. Intersubjective frameworks of meaning are attached to social norms that are not taken as simple descriptive categories but as components of generative structures that shape, condition and constrain action (Ruggie, 1982, 1983, 1993). For example, rather than assuming an undifferentiated states system inceptive from the 1648 Peace of Westphalia, Ruggie attempts to account for the historical specificity of medieval and modern geopolitical orders to reveal the social construction of transformations in the international states system. The shift from the medieval to the modern international system is surmised as an instance of change in the basic structure of property rights, alongside transformations in strategic behaviour among major actors, and alterations in epistemic conditions consisting of political doctrines and metaphysical assumptions (Ruggie, 1983: 281–3, 1993: 168–9). Elsewhere, in his analysis of 'embedded liberalism' in the post–World War II economic order, Ruggie also asks why it was that the social purpose of the post-war order continued to be maintained to some extent after the collapse of Bretton Woods in the 1970s, despite the fact that the United States had ceased to maintain this system as a hegemon. In response, he argues that international regimes are not only a reflection of the underlying power structure but are also 'a fusion of power and legitimate social purpose' (Ruggie, 1982: 404). Hence, while the underlying power structure changed with the purported decline of us hegemony, the regime of embedded liberalism was maintained due to the continuation of its legitimised social purpose.

However, while Ruggie's analyses of either the shift from the medieval to the modern international states system, or the evolving monetary and trade regimes since the early 1970s, can demonstrate various features constitutive of geopolitical orders, he cannot explain *why* this has happened and *why* other political authority structures did not come to dominate. As one compelling critique attests, no clear, definitive argument is permitted to emerge within these accounts of system transformation, as all factors of explanation are held to be equally irreducible to one another (Teschke, 2003: 27–32). In this variant, social constructivism offers a causally indeterminate sketch of the modern states system and 'fails to identify those social agents that sustained, lived out, and changed property titles – not merely as formal institutions, but as politically maintained and actively negotiated social relations' (Teschke, 2003: 29, 1998: 330). A pluralist framework is thus evident within social constructivist arguments that grants the same indistinguishable weight to different factors in explaining changes in the international states system. Yet, in terms of tracing the causes and consequences of the capitalist states system, social constructivists can be subjected to C. Wright Mills' (1959: 154) criticism that 'what are often taken as historical explanations would better be taken as part of the statement of that which is to be explained'. This means that within social constructivism there is confusion over the relation between explanandum (or principle of historical explanation) and explanans (or point of reference that itself explains the changing character of the modern world) (Anderson, 1992: 121; Rosenberg, 2000: 3). While no clearcut distinction is implied by this contrast, to treat social facts specifically in terms of the latter would endow them with a sense of absolute autonomy, eliding how particular material institutional forms condition and circumscribe discursive power relations in a determinate historical conjuncture. The problem identified within this version of social constructivism is the assumption that a straight switch took place from the medieval to the modern states system. Citing Ruggie (1998: 25–6, 1993: 150–1), 'the personalised and parcellised structure of political authority relations in feudal society collapsed and was replaced by the completely different institutional system of modern states.' Following Teschke (2003: 31), the fault here is that by identifying one major shift – or sovereignty switch – from the medieval to the modern periods, pre-capitalist absolutist and modern forms of sovereignty are conflated. As a result, the different trajectories of European state formation and the uneven development of transitions from feudalism to capitalism during the age of absolutism are obliterated (Morton 2005: 498–502). This is traced in Chapter 4 on capitalist expansion and uneven and combined development.

Social constructivism has elsewhere increasingly been applied in comparative IPE. Mark Blyth analyses the embedding as well as disembedding of the US and Swedish political economies in the twentieth century and the role ideas have played within these processes of structural change. In times of crisis, he argues, 'ideas allow agents to reduce uncertainty, propose a particular solution to a moment of crisis, and empower agents to resolve that crisis by constructing new institutions in line with these new ideas' (Blyth, 2002: 11). Unlike many other social constructivists, he

links the emergence of new ideas to material relations. His narrative of
disembedding liberalism in Sweden, for example, mentions several times
the importance of business in the promotion and dissemination of neoliberal ideas from the mid-1970s onwards and he highlights specifically
the vast financial resources capital employed to this effect (Blyth, 2002:
209–19, 228, 262, 269). Nevertheless, there is an ad hoc nature to the
linkage of ideas to material relations stemming from an underdeveloped
conceptualisation of the social relations of production, which leads to the
neglect of two interrelated and crucial factors. First, at a methodological
level, Blyth identifies capital, labour and the state as core collective
homogenous actors, a move developed through his critical engagement
with methodological individualism (Blyth, 2002: 13–14). Thereby, Blyth
implicitly draws on a corporatist understanding of agency, without, however, adequately conceptualising or substantiating this choice of actors.[1]
Similar to Wendt, core actors are simply identified on an external basis
and are not internally related within the constructivist approach itself.
This, second, has serious ramifications for the empirical study of the case
of Sweden. Capital was not only important for the direct dissemination
and financing of neoliberal ideas in Sweden but it also held a position of
structural power more broadly due to its ability to transfer production
units abroad. Hence Blyth overlooks the point that it was not capital in
general but Swedish transnational capital in particular that was intrinsic
to the promotion of neoliberal policies, supported on several significant
occasions by forces of transnational labour, such as *inter alia* in the
separate collective wage agreement between employers and trade unions
in the transnational metalworking sector in 1983, the pro–European
Union (EU) membership campaign in 1994 (Bieler, 2000: 46, 102–10)
and the pro–Economic and Monetary Union (EMU) membership campaign in 2003 (Bieler, 2006: 96–7, 143–5). A conceptualisation of the
changing Swedish social relations of production in processes of transnational restructuring would have indicated the growing significance of the
structural power of transnational capital (Bieler, 2006: 59–66).

   Mark Blyth's (2013) discussion of austerity as a dangerous idea similarly demonstrates the shortcomings of social constructivism. In an overview of the intellectual history of 'austerity', he demonstrates well *how* its
key theoretical concepts have been developed over time. Equally he can
trace well the actual implementation of austerity policies covering cases
from the early twentieth century until today, demonstrating that austerity

---

[1] See also Blyth's (2007) agent-centred constructivist investigation of the National
Recovery Administration during the Roosevelt era, in which analysis is again based on
a tripartite separation of state-labour-business.

has been unsuccessful at reducing debt and generating growth. Finally, he discusses potential policy alternatives in the global economic crisis, giving Iceland as a positive example. Suggested measures include letting some banks fail, introducing capital controls and pursuing an expansionary fiscal policy as well as progressive taxation. What he cannot explain, however, is *why* austerity still reigns supreme. Moreover, his reasoning for *why* austerity will eventually be replaced reflects a rather naïve idealism. 'Not because austerity is unfair, which it is, not because there are more debtors than creditors, which there are, and not because democracy has an inflationary bias, which it doesn't, but because austerity simply doesn't work' (Blyth, 2013: 44). As we demonstrate in Chapter 9, austerity has been a class project of European transnational capital, which uses such policies to promote labour market flexibility and restrict trade union rights. For transnational capital, austerity has worked rather well indeed. Only if we analyse the internal relations between the ideology of austerity and its wider material setting can we explain these dynamics. In short, as positive as Blyth's advance is over other constructivist approaches, he does not fully comprehend the importance of material structural conditions in their internal relation to ideas. He adopts a view of material structure and ideas that are always-already separated as variables that are then combined in their external relationship to one another (e.g. Blyth, 2002: 251).

Moreover, as a further example, there is not just a separation but a stark juxtaposition of materialist views of wars and crises as exogenous shocks, on one hand, and the agent-centred constructivist stress on wars and crises as endogenous in terms of their social sources, on the other (Widmaier, Blyth and Seabrooke, 2007: 750). When attempting to understand how elite agents' constructions of wars and crises act as turning points for policy change, social constructivists grant a clear one-sided emphasis to the role of intersubjective consensus formation, persuasion-making engagements and legitimacy-building. As it is argued, an 'agent-centred constructivist approach to war and crisis inverts materialist frameworks [and instead] casts political struggles as arguments over the meaning of events, over how they should be framed and interpreted within various institutional contexts' (Widmaier et al., 2007: 756). In contrast, as Chapter 8 develops, a historical materialist viewpoint draws attention to the internal relationship between the geographical expansion of capitalist accumulation and the geopolitical dynamics of global war.

It could be supposed that cognate arguments on the origins of international norm dynamics and the role of norm entrepreneurs (as generators of norms with platforms within states, international organisations and networks) might resolve questions linked to ideational causation. After all,

Martha Finnemore and Kathryn Sikkink, in asking 'where do norms come from', attempt to trace the origins of ideational causation through norm emergence (based on the persuasion of norm entrepreneurs); norm cascading (linked to the socialising-, legitimatising- and conformity-inducing actions of norm entrepreneurs); and norm internalisation (leading to a taken-for-granted universalisation of norms) (Finnemore and Sikkink, 1998). As alluring as this entrée might be into the social construction of norms, this approach merely repeats the problems already raised. On norm emergence they argue that, for example, the World Bank 'though not tailored to norm promotion, may have the advantage of resources and leverage over weak or developing states they seek to convert to their normative convictions'. On norm cascading they argue that while there may be norms that are congruent between capitalism and liberalism, such 'a formulation is too vague to be useful'. Finally, on norm internalisation there is the position that there is supposedly 'no good way of treating it theoretically' although 'persuasion is central to politics of all kinds and we need a good theoretical apparatus for understanding it' (Finnemore and Sikkink, 1998: 900, 907, 914). This approach to the social construction of norms is precisely what Damien Cahill would critique as an ideas-centred conception of political and economic change (Cahill, 2014). Is it convincing to argue that the World Bank is really not tailored to norms promotion following decades of structural adjustment after the debt crisis in developing countries? How can a focus on the social construction of norms in the contemporary world elide any connection to modern capitalism on the basis of a charge of vagueness? In the variant Finnemore and Sikkink offer, constructivism becomes an ideas-centred approach divorced from the development of capitalism and the institutional and class-embedded nature of neoliberalism. In contrast to social constructivists, Cahill persuasively highlights the always-embedded character of neoliberalism in society through class relations; through the form of the state; and through discourse and ideology that prevents a slide into a constructivist ideas-centred conception of norms. Neoliberalism is, thus, identified as a moment within the history of capitalist social relations, a historically specific moment within the development of capitalism, which has distinct features setting it apart from previous capitalist eras. Hence, to cite Cahill (2014: 76) directly:

Ideas can therefore be thought of as having a materiality in a double sense. On one hand they emerge out of concrete social relations and historical conditions, while on the other they are a material force that structures people's conduct.

We return to this appreciation of the material structure of ideology in our historical materialist conceptualisation of ideas.

In summary, the problem of social constructivism, as a theory of history, is that it is grounded in an idealist understanding of transformations in social relations due to the disembedding of intersubjective ideas, norms and values from the social relations of capitalism in which they cohere. In other words, the interrelatedness and influence of the ideal/material is posed as always-already separate and combined entities, and constructivism fails to live up to its own claims of resolving all manner of contrasting philosophical problems within international theory (see Katzenstein, Keohane and Krasner, 1998; Price and Reus-Smit, 1998). To echo our earlier emphasis, the recurring questions are therefore: *Which* agents shape the core intersubjective beliefs of underlying social and world orders? *How* have their values and beliefs become embodied in state identities and interests and the relevant constitutional structure of the international society of states? *Why* does a particular set of ideas become part of the structure and not another? As it stands, an under-theorised notion of power exists across social constructivist perspectives that fails to ascertain whose interpretations come to constitute the social world, which agents are relevant and why they do so.

The Discourse of Poststructuralism

Poststructuralist accounts are highly critical of social constructivism for not breaking completely with mainstream, positivist IR theory. As Nalini Persram (1999: 171) argues, 'the pseudo-progressive vocabulary of intersubjectivity and all the rest cannot hide the uncritical categories through which constructivism expresses itself.' More problematically, rather than providing a challenge to mainstream approaches, by adopting core assumptions – such as a conception of the state as an anthropomorphic actor (e.g. Wendt, 1999: 10) – social constructivism actually cements the predominance of the mainstream within the discipline, simultaneously closing down alternative critical ways of thinking. In short, simply adding an ideational dimension to the overall structure without questioning how the social and/or world order and the subjects within it are constituted does not go far enough.

The main focus of poststructuralism is the way in which social subjects are constituted in the first place. Instead of seeing structure and agency as two different entities, as argued in the previous chapter, they are taken as directly implicated in each other through discursive practices (Doty, 1997). 'Subjectivity and the social order are constituted together, the social order being the frame within which subjectivities are placed. The social order only comes into existence by our positing it in advance, assuming that it already exists, and in doing this we are ourselves constituted as subjects' (Edkins and Pin-Fat, 1999: 5). As a result, the moment when a new social order is established becomes crucial. Jenny Edkins' distinction between 'politics' and 'the political' is important in this respect. Politics refers to the technical arrangements within an established social order and identified subjects. For example, neorealist IR theory assumes that international politics, as the social or world order, is dominated by states, as the subjects. What neorealists analyse, then, is the politics of state interaction. What they cannot question, however, is the assumed social or world order and the subjects themselves. Subject and state formation is taken for granted. Poststructuralists, by contrast, concentrate on the political, the founding moment, when the myth of a new social or world order is established. According to Edkins (1999: 13), 'the founding moment is the moment of decisioning, the moment that both produces and reproduces the law.' An example of such a founding moment would be the significance of 1989 within processes of European integration, when a new order could be enacted through the inclusion and legitimacy of Central and Eastern Europe within the regional social order.

As a critical strategy, then, poststructuralists turn their attention to these founding moments, when a new master signifier is established. They concentrate on questioning what is generally taken as given. 'In a sense, the duty of the critical intellectual is exactly this not forgetting, this drawing of attention to the produced, artificial, contingent character of any reigning master signifier' (Edkins, 1999: 140). In other words, the IR scholar is set the task of challenging 'the hegemony of the power relations or symbolic order in whose name security is produced, to render visible its contingent, provisional nature' (Edkins, 1999: 142). Accepting, however, the contingent character of a master signifier implies that there can never be a moment of ontological fullness, a moment of establishing clearly the material and ideational basis of a particular social or world order as well as the subjects within it. Hence, the subject is fragmented and decentred: 'in this picture, the subject is always in the process of being constituted; there is no point at which, however briefly, the performance is finished. In some sense the subject does not exist' (Edkins and Pin-Fat, 1999: 1). Accepting any structure as foundational is therefore impossible from a poststructuralist account. It is in this respect that poststructuralism then criticises critical IPE theories. The latter, although claiming to challenge key mainstream assumptions, nonetheless are charged with simply replacing one foundation with another, upholding a view of 'a heroic subject in estrangement' that is presented as 'the necessary, central figure of any labour that would have critical, emancipatory, transformative potentials' (Ashley, 1996: 243, 248). In other words, by taking as foundational the structures of historical processes, which are understood to determine the realms of the possible, analysis within critical IPE remains caught within modernist assumptions (Ashley, 1989: 275).

Poststructuralist reflections on the international engagements of critical activity are thus presented rather differently. Ashley (1996: 242) has pushed himself to consider an 'interpretation of circumstances' in which such critical activity emerges to focus on the undecidability of claims to sovereignty. He casts out the lonely figure of the 'itinerate *condottiere*' that he posits as equivalent to his posture towards understanding the constitutive field of international studies (Ashley, 1996: 250–3). In medieval Italy, *condottieres* led armies for different cities and rulers depending on who paid them most, without attaching themselves too closely to a particular city or ruler on a principled basis. Thus, the itinerate *condottiere* exists in a condition of 'estranged unsituatedness' and 'lives the life of a vagabond' as 'a stranger to every place and faith', who is 'never at home among the people who dwell there' and as a nomad is constantly facing forceful eviction. Similarly, the poststructuralist, Ashley continues, holds an 'ideal of inhabiting a securely bounded territory of truth and transparent meaning beyond doubt, a place given as if by some author beyond time, a place where it is possible to appeal to the word in order to decide what things mean' (Ashley, 1996: 252). Nevertheless, at the same time, because the poststructuralist asserts the artificial nature of any such bounded territory of truth and order, this short-lived order is not mistaken as the concrete realisation of the ideal. Rather, the poststructuralist accepts that the ideal of such a territory of truth can never be fully achieved. This in itself is considered more desirable than the mistaken assumption that there could be something such as an ontologically true social order and its subjects within it.

When this understanding is related to moves in IR theory to consider how ideas defined in a broad way can be conceptualised, it is clear that from a poststructuralist perspective they cannot be regarded as a part of the ontological structure. Instead, there is a conception of ideas *as* discourse (which is more than language) surrounding the political, or the moment a new myth is deployed to establish a particular social/world order. What poststructuralists propose 'is a recognition of the contingency of present political forms and the discourses that we use to produce and describe them' (Edkins and Zehfuss, 2005: 470). Hence, discourses establish the truth for a temporarily limited moment. As a result, poststructuralists claim to reject the very distinction between the material and the ideational expressed within constructivism. 'Discourses provide criteria of intelligibility that establish the conditions of possibility for social being and, as such, cannot be considered as separate from, or secondary

to, the material realm' (de Goede, 2001: 152). For instance, in attempting to criticise the current international financial order, de Goede does
not concentrate on a material structure. Instead 'in order to criticise the
legitimacy deficit in finance and to broaden financial debates, it is imperative to understand how financial science became a historical possibility
and how financial decision making became depoliticised in the first place'
(de Goede, 2001: 151). This is traced through the historical constitution
of financial speculation as a technical issue, which depoliticises the circumstances surrounding notions of risk. Once discourses of financial
speculation as well as the discursive constitution of modern finance
more broadly are deconstructed, the process of thinking about possible
alternatives can then begin (de Goede, 2005: xxvi, 2004).

However, it is doubtful whether these approaches to the role, or social
function, of the theorist in revealing such acts of deconstruction is adequate. Ashley's self-image of the itinerate *condottiere* – a noble who
chooses the life of organising mercenary activity in order to increase
revenue – merely compounds similarly problematic reflections on the
conditions of emergence of poststructuralism in international studies.
For example, it most notably evokes the status of dissident theorists
questioning narratives of sovereignty from the position of disciplinary
exiles (Ashley and Walker, 1990). It also retains resonance within the
assumption that intellectual activity involves constantly shifting ethico-
political responsibility between 'coalitions of support and political
advocacy ... seen as constituted, temporary and issue-based' (Edkins
and Zehfuss, 2005: 468). The itinerate nature of ethical commitments,
furthermore, links with David Campbell's reflections on the duty, obliga-
tion and responsibility of poststructuralist theorising that involves
a struggle for and on behalf of the Other and thus the necessity of
a *deterritorialisation* of responsibility (Campbell, 1999: 50–1). His focus
is cast towards the delineation of ethico-political criteria within international engagements that involve 'a philosophical anthropology of everyday life on a global scale', which is emergent from 'specific, local inquiries
of political questions, inquiries that focus on how problems in international politics are problematised'. These ethico-political criteria are
marked in international studies through 'inside/outside distinctions'
that 'are the geographical-spatial exemplars of self/other demarcations'
(Campbell, 2001: 445–6). Yet within these divergent considerations of
scholarly international engagements (the unrooted, shifting, globe-
travelling *condottiere* and the specific localist of everyday life committed
to deterritorialised responsibility) scant attention is cast to situating poststructuralism within its own historical conditions of emergence. Akin to
developments elsewhere in the social sciences, the point can be sustained

that there is obfuscation within poststructuralism that mystifies its own relationship to social conditions linked to global capitalism which, however fragmented in appearance and circumstance, serve as a structuring principle of social relations (Dirlik, 1994: 331). Teasing out a point from Chapter 1, Ashley (1983: 488–9) has himself raised valid caution about the use of the taboo term of 'economism' (now, in our case, by poststructuralists), indicating a failure to engage with 'the capitalist state's material problematic' and the effects of state legitimations.

Moreover, despite denying ontological foundations, poststructuralists in IPE fall short in a similar manner to social constructivists when attempting to establish the role of discourses within social power relations. Witness the spotlighting that de Goede (2006: 5) brings in order to emphasise 'the importance of discourse and representation for political and economic practice' and the accent on 'the deeply discursive nature of the realms of politics and economics', with these realms posited in terms of their separateness. Louise Amoore outlines well *how* the discourse of linking risk/uncertainty to globalisation 'has become central to programmes of work flexibilisation, casualisation, and fragmentation' (Amoore, 2004: 175), thereby exerting pressure on workers and individualising uncertainty and risk. What she does not explain, however, is *why* this particular discourse became dominant. There is a failure here to uncover the agency and structural power behind discourses of risk. Similarly, in his analysis of the shift away from final salary pension schemes in Anglo-American capitalism, Paul Langley (2004a: 541) asserts that 'there is a need to ask how the current financialisation of capitalism is taking place at the expense of other possible restructurings.' What is missing is the analysis of *why* this shift occurs and *who* has deployed it as a strategy of social power. Elsewhere, in an examination of IPE literature on the New International Financial Architecture, he also claims that analysis should not be restricted to a critical assessment of international financial institutions, 'but should also explicitly recognise the discursive features of authority relations and situate governance networks in the power relations, contestation, contradictions and reproduction of the global financial order' (Langley, 2004b: 84). In practice, however, there is a sole concentration on discourse without examining the internal relation of dominant discourses as material social processes. Debates within poststructuralism have detected this, highlighting a dissatisfaction with the maintenance of a distinction between materiality on one hand and the role of discourse as language and representation on the other. The result is that by adhering to a framework of the politics of representation, 'the place of materiality is still secondary to the politics of representation through which it acquires political significance'

(Lundborg and Vaughan-Williams, 2015: 11). Specifically, statements such as 'the institutional focus of much existing IPE research should be combined with a concern with the discursive dynamics of authority relations' located in global financial governance (Langley, 2004b: 73) echo the always-already separate *and* combined approach to ideal/material relations evident within social constructivism. This separation is most starkly apparent in the clear binary line Louise Amoore (2004: 186, emphasis added) draws between the material and ideational in her account of discourses of risk:

[T]he transformation of working practices must be understood as more than simply a response to the material reality of an uncertain global economy; instead *it relies upon* the ideational production and reproduction of ways of thinking about risk and uncertainty.

What is evident here is precisely an act of inscribing ontological centrality to ideas, a moment that not only clearly establishes and separates the material and ideational dimensions but also grants causal priority to the latter in political economy.[2]

Furthermore, poststructuralists in IPE assert that at any juncture, any political moment, different outcomes are possible within the contingent and conjuncturally specific power relations of global capitalism (Langley, 2004b: 71, 75). The different problem here, though, is that despite uncovering and sequencing how a particular discourse might become established in a specific period of time, total contingency is prioritised. Unambiguously, Charlotte Epstein (2015) focuses on contingency and indeterminacy as the defining features of theorising the social. 'There are as many constructed worlds', she argues, 'as there are cultures and even individualities. Constitutive theorising, then, requires ways of theorising with the unfixity that the focus on contingency sets into play' (Epstein, 2013: 501). The result is what Perry Anderson has recognised as the complete *randomisation of history*. 'Language as a system furnishes the formal *conditions of possibility* of speech, but has no purchase on its actual *causes*' (Anderson, 1983: 48). Thus, while a poststructuralist gaze can be effectively cast over what Foucault (1980: 92, 2003: 24) termed the "'how of power'", in terms of the effects of hegemonic discourses, there is nevertheless abnegation in refraining from asking the *who* of power

---

[2] Such attempts to prioritise ideational production are actually contrary to Michel Foucault's own stance on the exercise of power. 'Power relations, relationships of communication, objective capacities should not,' he argues, 'be confused. This is not to say that there is a question of three separate domains. Nor that there is, on the one hand, the field of things, of perfected technique, work, and the transformation of the real, and on the other, that of signs, communication, reciprocity, and the production of meaning' (Foucault, 2000: 337–8).

(see also Marsden, 1999: 26, 192).[3] This is revealed in Foucault's deliberation on the functioning of society when stating that 'the best conditions for this functioning may be defined internally, without one being able to say "for whom" it is best that things may be like that', thus effacing questions of *cui bono?* intrinsic to political economy (Foucault, 1999: 100).[4] While power may very well be regarded as relational, or produced through social interaction, there is thus little indication of the direct social agents of relational power (Edkins, Pin-Fat and Shapiro, 2004: 2; Edkins and Pin-Fat, 2005: 406). *Who* practices hegemony? *Why* might one discourse have been successful in a specific historical context and underpin the distribution of material entitlements and not other, rival discourses in power struggles? Returning to Foucault, the question of the who of power is an apparently settled one:

> The question of power remains a total enigma. Who exercises power? And in what sphere? We now know with reasonable certainty who exploits others, who receives the profits, which people are involved, and we know how these funds are reinvested. But as for power ... (Foucault, 1977: 213)

Power is purported to be an enigma but the conditions of exploitation under capitalism and questions about who conducts the production, appropriation and distribution of surpluses from labour are apparently all resolved. But what is lost in the game of discursivity and the play of contingency is any point of condensation within social power relations, or, put differently, how the discipline of capital structures concrete individuals and the interpellation of identities. Poststructuralists, to paraphrase Stuart Hall (1996: 136), might therefore save for themselves 'the political', but they deny themselves a politics due to their neglect of historical relations of force. The result is a rendering of capitalist exploitation and domination into a shapeless and contingent world of fetishised self/other differences. This is reflected in a focus on the 'arbitrary play of actions upon actions – actions that are not attributable to any ultimate

---

[3] We are aware here of Foucault's statement that, 'If for the time being, I grant a certain privileged position to the question of "how", it is not because I would wish to eliminate the questions of "what" and "why."' However, his preference for a focus on *power relations* rather than power itself – with power relations regarded as linked but distinct from objective capacities – is still troubling. Power relations become embedded within a complex and indistinct 'ensemble of actions' (Foucault, 2000: 336). With the limits of space preventing a full development of this point, the problem here is locating power within a vague ensemble of social relations, which may throw up a theory of individuality but obscures the history of social formations linked to the conditions of production and reproduction constitutive of material relations of existence in the labour process (Althusser, 2003: 254, 290).

[4] This quotation is referred to in Perry Anderson's (1983: 57) critique of the capsizing of both structure and subject within poststructuralism.

source' (Ashley, 1996: 244; see also Doty, 1997: 377). To draw from Fernando Coronil (1992: 99–100), there is a repudiation of metanarratives here that produces disjointed mini-narratives, which in reacting against the taboo of 'economism', presents a series of free-floating contingent events. The hegemony of discourse therefore becomes a phagocytic essence, absorbing and engulfing everything within the discursive (Poulantzas, 1978: 151), as mentioned in Chapter 2.

By drawing especially on the work of Antonio Gramsci, we turn now to a historical materialist analysis of these issues in an attempt to explain precisely this problem through an emphasis on the internal relation between ideas and material social processes.

The Material Structure of Ideology

Eric Hobsbawm has noted that, following the revolutions of 1830 and despite the regional variations in social and economic organisation across Europe, the decisive importance of capital cities as a locus for revolt gained widespread acceptance. However, by the time further revolution spread across the continent after 1848, 'governments began to replan them in order to facilitate the operation of troops against [the] revolutionaries' (Hobsbawm, 1962: 129). 'For the city planners', he continues, 'the poor were a public danger, their potentially riotous concentrations to be broken up by avenues and boulevards which would drive the inhabitants of the crowded popular quarters they replaced into some unspecified, but presumably more sanitary and certainly less perilous locations' (Hobsbawm 1975: 211). The archetypal example is the hiring of Georges-Eugène Haussmann (1809–92) by Napoleon III to 'modernise' Paris in the 1860s with the building of *grande boulevards* to accommodate new street cafés and single-function urban development (Harvey, 2003a: 107–16). Richard Sennett (1977/2002: 134–5) has summarised this as the transference of an ecology of *quartiers* into an ecology of classes. Antonio Gramsci (1971: 365, Q10II§12) also drew attention to such state-impelled practices and designations where the wider class 'realisation of a hegemonic apparatus' was emphasised in four main ways in contributing to what has been heralded as a spatial political economy perspective (see Bieler and Morton, 2008: 118–22; Morton 2017b, 2017c).

First, he referred to the overarching importance of the 'material structure of ideology', which included issues such as architecture alongside street layouts (as well as street names), and the social function performed by libraries, schools, publishing houses, newspapers and journals, down to the local parish newsletter and the church. Overall awareness of these aspects of social power would 'inculcate the habit of assessing the forces of agency in society with greater caution and precision' (Gramsci, 1995: 155–6, 1996: 53, Q3§49). This is a point that may strike one whether standing on Avenue de la Grande Armée, one of Haussmann's twelve grand avenues radiating from the Arc de Triomphe; or facing El Monumento a la Revolución in México City located on the Plaza de la República; or situated opposite the Republic Monument in Taksim Square in İstanbul and its sculpture to the founder of the Turkish Republic, Mustafa Kemal Atatürk; or located on the more humble but still symbolic Viale Gramsci in Rome (see Therborn, 2017, on spatial patterning, the political naming of streets and state formation within capital cities of power). It is such a focus on the internal relation of the material structure of ideas that has been explored in the work of David Harvey, notably tracing transformations in the built environment of modernist architecture in the early twentieth century – embodied in the work of Le Corbusier, Mies van der Rohe or Frank Lloyd Wright – that unfolded 'less as a controlling force of ideas over production than as a theoretical framework and justification for what practically minded engineers, politicians, builders, and developers were in many cases engaged upon out of sheer social, economic and political necessity' (Harvey, 1989: 69). Likewise, within the postmodernism of the late twentieth-century city, Harvey internally associates speculative land, property development and redevelopment in the built environment, to processes of capital accumulation, market and land-rent allocation and money capital. Linking with our discussion in Chapter 1 on reification, 'the fetishism (direct concern with surface appearances that conceal underlying meanings) is obvious', according to Harvey (1989: 77–8), 'but it is here deployed deliberately to conceal, through the realms of culture and taste, the real base of economic distinctions', which are entailed in establishing enclosed and protected housing and leisure spaces as an expression of class power. Architecture, then, amidst a diverse array of other social condensations (such as cadastral mapping defining property rights over land, the drawing of territorial boundaries for administration, social control and communication routes or literary geographies representing borders and landscapes across space and time) provides an opportunity to question the role played by discursive productive meanings embedded within the economy through analysis of the internal relations within the 'material structure of ideology' (see Morton, 2015). As Harvey (1996: 269) summarises, 'any recourse to a philosophy of dialectics or internal relations leads, either explicitly or implicitly, to a relational view on space and time.'

Second, these social condensations of hegemony are the means by which a '"diffused" and capillary form of indirect pressure' becomes mediated through various organisations – or 'capillary intellectual meatuses' – to exercise hegemonic class relations (Gramsci, 1971: 110, Q15§11, 1985: 194; Q27§2). The significance of this understanding of hegemony through capillary networks is therefore in the dialectical unity of state-civil society referring to 'the system of explicit and implicit "private and public" associations that are woven together in the "state" and in the world political system' (Gramsci, 2007: 187, Q7§35). Gramsci is thus a paramount theorist of capillary power due to his attentiveness to the social class meatuses of 'capillary sources of capitalist profit' (Gramsci, 1977: 82, 1992: 230–1, Q1§151).[5] Hegemony within the realm of civil society is grasped when the citizenry come to believe that authority over their lives emanates from the self. Hegemony is therefore articulated through capillary power – akin to 'an incorporeal government' – when it is transmitted organically through various 'social infusoria' such as schools, street layouts and names, architecture, family, workplace or church (Gramsci, 1977: 143–4). Hence 'within the enwrapping [*involucro*] of political society a complex and well-articulated civil society' is evident, '*in which the individual governs himself*, provided that his self-government does not enter into conflict with political society but becomes, rather, its normal continuation, its organic complement' (Gramsci, 2007: 310, Q8§130, emphasis added).[6] It was this separation, detailed in Chapter 1, that Marx saw as characteristic of the structuring of societies leading to the naturalisation of the distinctive forms of modernity. That is why, in his view:

Security is the highest social concept of civil society ... expressing the fact that the whole of society exists only in order to guarantee to each of its members the preservation of his [*sic*] person, his rights, and his property ... The concept of security does not raise civil society above its egoism. On the contrary, security is the *insurance* of its egoism. (Marx, 1843/1975: 162–3, original emphases)

Hence, for Gramsci, the philosophy of internal relations comes to bear ultimately on his notion of the integral state as a dialectical unity of the moments of civil society and political society. The distinction of the integral state was itself developed out of his reflections on the internal transformation of its constitutive dimensions leading to the emergence of

---

[5] While space restrictions limit full elaboration, this conception differs in marked ways from the focus on discursive formations and architecture in *The Archaeology of Knowledge* (Foucault, 1972); essentially because of the indeterminate determinism within Foucault's notion of capillary power (see Wight, 1999: 121).

[6] See Thomas (2009: 189) for his important sharpening of the understanding of *involucro* as enwrapping in order to grasp a more sophisticated internal articulation and condensation of social relations within a given state form.

the modern state. Therefore, conceptions of 'state' and 'civil society' are actually expressions of a mode of thinking based on 'exterior' observations that overlook their relational internalisation within a conception of the integral state (Thomas, 2009: 137, 140, 401).

Third, according to Gramsci, 'ideology' was neither artificial nor something mechanically superimposed. Rather, ideologies were viewed as historically produced through ceaseless struggle, taking on substance through practical activity bound up with systems of meaning embedded in the economy (Gramsci, 1996: 56, Q3§56). 'Ideas are realised when they find their justification – and the means to assert themselves – in economic reality' (Gramsci, 1994a: 56). Importantly, not all ideas are relevant. 'Ideas only become effective if they do, in the end, connect with a particular constellation of social forces. In that sense, ideological struggle is a part of the general social struggle for mastery and leadership – in short for hegemony' (Hall, 1986: 42). Consequently, ideas represent an independent force when maintained in dialectical connectivity, or internally related, with the social relations of production. For historical materialism 'ideologies are anything but arbitrary; they are real historical facts which must be combated and their nature as instruments of domination exposed ... precisely for reasons of political struggle' (Gramsci, 1995: 395, Q10II§41xii). Importantly, only those ideas can be regarded as 'organic' that 'organise human masses, and create the terrain on which men [sic] move, acquire consciousness of their position, struggle, etc.' (Gramsci, 2007: 171, Q7§19). Related to this is the twofold distinction drawn between 'historically organic ideologies' and those based on extemporary polemics that are 'arbitrary, rationalistic, or "willed"'. Hence highlighting 'real action on the one hand ... and on the other hand the gladiatorial futility which is self-declared action but modifies only the word, not things, the external gesture' (Gramsci, 1971: 307, Q22§5, 2007: 170–1, Q7§19). For Gramsci, 'it is on the level of ideologies that men [sic] become conscious of conflicts in the world of the economy' (Gramsci, 1971: 162, Q13§18). These conflicts can be heuristically analysed in the form of class struggle (Cox, 1985/1996: 57–8).

Fourth, it is here, in the struggle over hegemony between different class fractions, that Gramsci attributed an important role to intellectuals. Thus, 'Gramsci's investigation of the role of intellectuals in modern society is part of his attempt to understand what actually links the world of production and civil or private society with the political realm' (Vacca, 1982: 37). Gramsci understood intellectuals as exercising an ideological social function in a broad sense across the social, political, economic and cultural fields in ways related to the class-structuring of societies. On one hand, traditional intellectuals are those who consider themselves autonomous (the itinerate *condottiere*?) but, more accurately, can be related to socio-economic structures belonging to a specific period of historical time. Examples would include 'ivory tower' intellectuals, who 'can be defined as the expression of that social utopia by which the intellectuals think of themselves as "independent", autonomous, endowed with a character of their own etc.' (Gramsci, 1971: 8, Q12§1). Traditional intellectuals therefore represent 'the culture of a restricted intellectual aristocracy' that is 'given by the man of letters, the philosopher, the artist' (Gramsci, 1971: 9, Q12§1; 393, Q16§9). On the other hand, the category of organic intellectual was predominantly reserved for those intellectuals who stood as the mediators of hegemony articulated by social classes (see Sassoon, 1987: 144, 214). Hence, according to Gramsci:

[E]very social group, coming into existence on the original terrain of an essential function in the world of economic production, creates together with itself, organically, one or more strata of intellectuals which give it homogeneity and an awareness of its own function not only in the economic but also in the social and political fields. (Gramsci, 1971: 5, Q12§1)

Such intellectuals have the function of organising the hegemony of social class forces, and thus capillary power, beyond the coercive apparatus of the state whether in terms of their organic intellectuality as direct members of an intelligentsia; as industrial technicians; as intellectuals of statecraft or as classical Realist geopoliticians; as specialists in political economy, as organisers of 'the "confidence" of investors'; as journalists; or as architects (Gramsci, 1971: 5, Q12§1; 12, Q12§1, 1995: 61–70, Q16§11ii, 1996: 200–1, Q4§49).[7] For Gramsci, organic intellectuals engage in active participation in everyday life, acting as agents or constructors, organisers and 'permanent persuaders' in forming social class hegemony, or by performing a valuable supporting role to subaltern groups engaged in promoting social change, that is then '"mediated" by the whole fabric of society' (Gramsci, 1971: 12, Q12§1; 52–4, Q25§5). Thus, organic intellectuals do not simply produce ideas as norm entrepreneurs; they also concretise and articulate strategies in complex and often contradictory ways, which is possible because of their proximity to the structurally most powerful forces in society. It is their task to develop the 'gastric juices' to digest competing conceptions of social order in

[7] Organic intellectuality is highlighted as intrinsic to understanding the sphere of classical Realist geopoliticians, with Gramsci's studies on hegemony held as 'path-breaking' (Ashley, 1984: 275, 275 n.6). Intellectuals of statecraft refers to 'a whole community of state bureaucrats, leaders, foreign policy experts and advisors throughout the world who comment upon, influence and conduct the activities of statecraft' (Ó Tuathail and Agnew, 1992: 193).

conformity with a hegemonic project (Gramsci, 1994b: 182). Put differently, it is their social function to transcend the particular interests of their own social group which brings 'the interests of the leading class into harmony with those of subordinate classes and incorporates these other interests into an ideology expressed in universal terms' (Cox, 1983: 168). When ideas are thus accepted as common sense – or 'diffuse, uncoordinated features of a generic mode of thought' (Gramsci, 1971: 330, Q11§12) – they become naturalised in the form of intersubjective meanings. Accordingly, it is in this manner that ideas establish the wider frameworks of thought, 'which condition the way individuals and groups are able to understand their social situation and the possibilities of social change' (Gill and Law, 1988: 74). It is through this process that the material structure of ideology plays a decisive role in shaping the terrain of class (-relevant) struggle.

What a realisation of the material structure of ideology amounts to is a dialectical conception of the 'necessary reciprocity' between ideas and material social conditions, in sustaining and possibly transforming state–civil society relations within the conditions of the integral state (Gramsci, 1971: 12, Q12§1, 2007: 340, Q8§182). It is a focus that links the social function of intellectuals to the world of production within capitalist society, without succumbing to the taboo of economism, while still offering the basis for a materialist and social class analysis of intellectuals. Cultural aspects, from literature to architecture, clearly play a significant role within this conception of organic intellectuals where each activity is understood as a material social product having a social function endowed with political significance. The task therefore becomes one of revealing the social functions of organic intellectuals as representative of class fractions within the complex web of relations between rulers and ruled (Morton, 2011/2013: 139–43).

In sum, this mode of enquiry allows us to understand *why* certain ideas attain the presence of 'common sense' in the form of intersubjective meanings and not others. Unlike poststructuralism, collective agency is not abstracted from the prevailing social order (Wood, 1986: 176). The conditions of inequality and exploitation that confront social forces are included in the analysis. It is understood that peoples' identities are constituted within the context of existing social relations, which are to some extent inherited from and shaped by historical and material relations of force. Questions attempting to ascertain what aspects of social experience *make possible* the articulation of certain discourses, within the struggle over hegemony are, thus, at the forefront of analysis. Discourse does not simply act upon people; rather, people act through discourse, so the world cannot be reduced to discourse alone. As Stuart Hall (1997: 31) puts it, 'everything is within the discursive, but nothing is only discourse or only discursive.' Moving beyond idealism and materialism, therefore, means appreciating how Gramsci developed what Peter Ives heralds as a 'double-pronged critique':

[F]or Gramsci, starting from materiality does not posit two realms – material versus non-material, material versus ideal, extra-linguistic versus linguistic – between which there could be 'correspondence'. This does not rule out making pragmatic distinctions between ideas and objects or between words and thoughts. It does mean, however, that the philosophy of praxis cannot rest on divisions between subjectivity and objectivity, reality and thought, nor can it exacerbate them, nor can it equate them with the linguistic and non-linguistic. (Ives 2004a: 7, 9; see also Ives 2004b: 84–9)

This is what a consistently historical materialist approach to the material structure of ideology offers to understanding language as discourse and ideas within situations of class conflict and struggles over hegemony.

An alternative way of grasping the material structure of discourse has emerged in the form of a 'cultural political economy' approach (Sum and Jessop, 2013). Similarly, it is through our specific conception of hegemony that culture is not conceived as separate and then bolted on to the socio-economic realm in an additive way. Our stress is on political economy *as* cultural. As Gramsci (1971: 360, Q10II§48ii), rather soberly, reminds us, 'that the objective possibilities exist for people not to die of hunger and that people do die of hunger, has its importance, or so one would have thought' whilst indicating at the same time that 'the existence of objective conditions ... is not yet enough: it is necessary to "know" them, and know how to use them.' As we have argued, this is far removed from the taboo of economism articulated in Chapter 1. But it *is* a view that reappraises different modes of cultural struggle as a 'critique of capitalist civilisation' (Gramsci, 1977: 10–13).

Conclusion: The Effects of Hegemony

Antonio Gramsci elaborated a distinct theory of history within which ideology was understood in 'its highest sense of a conception of the world that is implicitly manifest in art, in law, in economic activity and in all manifestations of individual and collective life' (Gramsci, 1971: 328, Q11§12). For Gramsci, idealist intellectuals developed a subjective account of history based on the progression of philosophical thought rather than historically specific conditions of class struggle. This resulted in a hypostatising of hegemony, removing social conflict from a quite specific context and treating it as an independent property divorced from any social basis so that 'history becomes a formal history, a history of concepts' (Gramsci, 1995: 338, Q10I§4; 343–4, Q10I§7; 370, Q10II§1). Along this line, social constructivist and poststructuralist engagements with the taboo of economism are strangely silent in acknowledging the forms of class identity, or organic intellectuality, so intrinsic to capital accumulation on a global scale. The result is that both suppress agency linked to class power and political economy so that the overriding economic significance of the promotion of certain discourses, in favour of particular interests and purposes, is missed. Drawing in spirit from Ashley (1984: 281), albeit with a different target in mind, it can be said that social constructivists and poststructuralists end up scoffing at historical materialism's 'warnings and sense limits, misstates its interests, deadens its ironies, empties its concepts, caricatures its rich insights, reduces practice to an endless serial performance of constrained economic choices on the part of one-dimensional characters, and casts the whole of it up before a flat historical backdrop devoid of perspective, contradiction and life'. As Dirlik makes clear, poststructuralism might well then be 'appealing because it disguises the power relations that shape a seemingly shapeless world and contributes to a conceptualisation of that world that both consolidates and subverts possibilities of resistance' (Dirlik, 1994: 355–6; as indicative see Amoore, 2006).

By contrast, the position that ideas are material, a process of articulation within which signs themselves become part of a socially created world, can be subsumed differently within an historical materialist theory of history. What is denied here is not that objects are constituted through discourse; instead the rather different assertion is made that this is itself a material social practice: a practical activity developed through means of social production and reproduction as a material relation. Emphasising this rather different position thus entails realising the production of meaning and ideas as part of material social processes, so that consciousness and thought are necessarily social material activities. An historical materialist theory of history thus throws into relief certain features necessary to understanding the dual process of knowing and being known embedded within the production of ideas. But it does so by expressing textuality in terms of class struggle or specific conflictual social relationships. For 'the philosophy of praxis conceives the reality of human relationships of knowledge as an element of political "hegemony"', linked to the agency of social classes (Gramsci, 1995: 306, Q10II§6iv). In sum, a historical materialist conceptualisation of the role of ideas through its philosophy of internal relations overcomes the shortcomings of constructivist and poststructuralist approaches. Rather than treating ideas and material properties as separate analytical factors, the philosophy of internal relations allows us to comprehend their internal relations as encapsulated in the notion of 'the material structure of ideology'. Social class forces can be identified as core collective actors through a focus on the social relations of production to address the *who* of power (see also Chapter 2). By acknowledging the location of these actors within the social relations of production, i.e. the underlying power structure, it is then possible to address the question as to *why* a certain set of ideas, rooted within these material relations, dominates at a particular point in time.

Having asserted the importance of a historical materialist approach through critical engagements with constructivist and poststructuralist theories, the ground is now prepared for a historical materialist thematic consideration of capitalist expansion, the geopolitics of global capitalism as well as resistance and class struggle in Part II of this book, before turning to empirical analyses of Global Capitalism, Global War, Global Crisis in Part III.

Part II

Thematic Considerations

4   Capitalist Expansion, Uneven and Combined Development and Passive Revolution

Having established the argument for a necessarily historical materialist moment in understanding 'the international' (Chapter 1) and discussed the related implications for the issue of agency and structure (Chapter 2) and the material structure of ideology (Chapter 3), we are now in a position to develop the thematic basis for understanding Global Capitalism, Global War, Global Crisis from a historical materialist perspective. In this chapter, our focus is on debates about the historical emergence of the international states system and the rise of capitalism. The first section contains an excursus on what we regard as several false starts on the origins of capitalist development through the approaches of Barrington Moore on the making of the modern world, Immanuel Wallerstein on the modern world system and Giovanni Arrighi on the origins of our times linked to the analysis of capitalist and territorialist logics. In the subsequent section, we develop our own understanding of the emergence of capitalism. Following Robert Brenner's social property relations approach, we emphasise how capitalism became initially organised around wage labour and the private ownership of the means of production in England and the Netherlands. In turn, capitalism was propelled outward within an already existing interstate system (see Lacher, 2006; Teschke, 2003) along lines of uneven and combined development as a structuring principle of 'the international' (see Anievas and Nişancıoğlu, 2015). In the third section, a more detailed focus on and appreciation of the theory of uneven and combined development is presented, going beyond the assumption that it is a 'rather fragmentary and undeveloped conception' in the work of Leon Trotsky (Romagnolo, 1975: 8 n.2). Specific emphasis is placed on addressing the charge of Eurocentrism against the social property relations approach.

The fourth section of this chapter seeks to address three lines of criticism in the literature around uneven and combined development. First, there is no fully reconstructed theory within the original approach to uneven and combined development and, by extension, contemporary approaches to uneven and combined development have not been adequate in 'accounting for *both* the spatio-temporal dynamics of capitalist development *and* the causal effects of socio-political multiplicity' (Rioux, 2015: 494, original emphasis). The danger here, in Sébastien Rioux's (2015: 494) useful framing, is that the theory of uneven and combined development is 'nothing more than a friendly reminder about the importance of "the international"'. Second, for some time, David Harvey (1982/2006: xix) has prominently opined that historical materialism cannot exist without a solid appreciation of the dialectics of spatio-temporality, hence the agenda-setting advancement of historical-geographical materialism. Yet it is perplexing that much of the recent literature within historical sociology is aspatial (Hesketh and Morton, 2014: 150). There is a failure to develop an internal dialectical perspective on the relationship between the 'political' state and the 'economic' modalities of exploitation. Third, this opens up the need to recognise and then focus on what Ernest Mandel called the 'historical detour', in order to consider how the unfolding of capitalism occurred within societies of socio-economically uneven and combined developmental conditions (Mandel, 1976/1990: 85). Put differently, without the concrete analysis of the spatio-temporal dynamics of uneven and combined development, recent debates have been coy in delivering place-based accounts of the historical detour that capitalism has taken in time and space (see Matin, 2013, for an exception). The result is that 'we are left with the important *identification* of a lateral field of causality, without the latter being incorporated within social theory' (Rioux, 2015: 485, original emphasis). The originality of this chapter within the overall purpose of this book is, therefore, that it asserts the notion of *passive revolution* as precisely a lateral field of causality capable of grasping spatio-temporal dynamics linked to state and class practices of transformation in social property relations within the overriding conditioning situation of uneven and combined development. While in Chapter 2 we demonstrated how the agency of social class forces is internally related to the structuring conditions of capitalism in general terms, this relationship between structure and agency is concretised in Chapter 4 by revealing passive revolution as an affinal concept to uneven and combined development, which delivers a field of causality that captures expressions of state and class agency internally related to the structuring condition of uneven and combined development (Morton, 2011/2013: 35–9, 237–51, 2017a; also see Hesketh, 2017b).

False Starts on the Origins of Capitalism?

In leading attempts to rehistoricise enquiry into the analysis of the social origins of modern states and the emergence of capitalism, Barrington Moore notably decried the predominance of a formalist deductive tradition in the social sciences that resulted in a detrimental mix of static analysis, universal law-like generalisations and the exaltation of parsimonious virtuosity at the expense of a critical spirit (Moore, 1958: 131). Equally, relying on a 'multi-factor' liberal approach that invokes a multiplicity of causes, setting out one after the other within a vague form of eclecticism, encourages a form of 'intellectual chaos' (Moore, 1958: 112, 1967/1993: 135). The consideration of state identities in terms of unchanging substances within mainstream neorealist approaches in international relations (IR) can be clearly linked to the former tendency (e.g. Gilpin, 1987; Waltz, 1979), while the latter strongly reminds us of neo-Weberian and constructivist multicausal accounts of the role of state identity and interest formation (e.g. Hobson, 1997, 2004; Mann, 1986). The contribution of the latter work is that it collapses into an 'undertheorised eclecticism' (Teschke, 2003: 51). Instead, Moore advances in his celebrated *Social Origins of Dictatorship and Democracy* a clear, causally related account of institutional practices and far-reaching structural changes in agricultural production that promoted capitalism and the transition to modernity in Western Europe.

To start with, there is a realisation by Moore of the 'very significant part that the classes in the countryside played in the transformation to industrialism' in order to understand the role of the peasantry and landed classes in 'bourgeois revolutions' that led to capitalist forms of state in England and France and their different origins of political development (Moore, 1967/1993: 3). In England, transformations in land formerly subject to customary rules prescribing methods of cultivation became viewed as an income-yielding investment. Hence, from the fourteenth century onward, the increasing importance of commerce was felt in the countryside, which spread a 'commercial impulse' through 'commercially minded landowners' to overcome the fetters of feudalism and dissolve the land and tenurial relations that had previously bound together lord and peasant. According to his view, this resulted in 'the growth of a commercial and even capitalist outlook in the countryside' at this time (Moore, 1967/1993: 4–6). Yet the impulse for such change in sixteenth- and seventeenth-century England is deemed to come from the towns, which created expanded markets for agricultural products. Therefore 'under the impact of commerce and some industry, English society was breaking apart from the top downward', promoted by the yeomanry and the landed upper classes at the expense of the peasants, creating the pressures that would lead to the Civil War.

Through the breaking of the power of the king, the Civil War swept away the main barrier to the enclosing landlord and simultaneously prepared England for rule by a 'committee of landlords', a reasonably accurate ... designation of Parliament in the eighteenth-century. (Moore, 1967/1993: 16, 19)

By contrast, Moore finds structural differences in the rise of commercial agriculture and thus alternative origins in the processes leading to state formation and modernisation in France. Here, in the era of the Bourbon monarchy, nobles used the prevailing social and political framework of feudalism to squeeze the labour of the peasantry by subjecting them to continued political authority conducted through the demesne. Keeping the peasants on the land as a labour force – as 'wage labourers' – was therefore buttressed by the political institutions of feudalism to produce an income for the noblemen. Thus 'land was useful to the nobleman only insofar as the peasants on it produced an income for him' (Moore, 1967/1993: 53–4, 55). This mix of feudal arrangements with royal absolutism enabled an economic surplus to be extracted by the landed aristocracy from the peasantry to the extent that there proceeded the 'penetration of commercial and capitalist practices into agriculture by feudal methods' (Moore, 1967/1993: 63).

Nevertheless, the confidence in the logic of commercialisation embedded within the practices of feudalism can be revealed as flawed in such analysis. Capitalist development is presumed to be nested within the means of appropriation specific to feudalism, thereby assuming the very processes that need to be demonstrated and explained. There are assumptions about the centrality of trade and markets, from their earliest manifestations to modern capitalism, which fail to account for the specific social forms and property relations of capitalism as distinct from feudalism. 'Capitalism is simply more trade, more markets, more towns, and, above all, a rising "middle class"' (Wood, 1991: 7). This example of focusing on trade-centred impulses behind the transition to capitalism raises serious 'question-begging' assumptions about capitalism and the forces that shaped the sovereign states system (Wood, 2002a: 70).

Immanuel Wallerstein in his analysis of the modern world system relates the emergence of both capitalism and the modern states system to the 'long sixteenth century' and the establishment of a world market. At the centre of world systems analysis is a conceptualisation of state identity and its relationship to capitalist development. In tracing the origins of the modern states system, Wallerstein explicitly focuses on the feudal system of social organisation in order to trace changes in agricultural production that were the prelude to the expansion of capitalism in sixteenth-century Western Europe. Feudalism consisted of the social organisation of agricultural production based on a form of exploitation that involved the relatively direct appropriation of the surplus produced by peasants within a manorial economy run by the nobility (Wallerstein, 1974a: 36). The crisis of feudalism – representing a combination of secular trends, cyclical patterns and changes in the physical environment – led to a new form of surplus appropriation within a capitalist world economy based, not on direct appropriation of agricultural surplus in the form of tribute or feudal rents, but on more efficient and expanded productivity by means of a *world market* mechanism supported by expanded territorial state sovereignty (Wallerstein, 1974a: 36). In delineating the *differencia specifica* of capitalism, then, a social division of labour is highlighted in world systems analysis in different regions or zones of the world economy in tandem with distinct state structures. Within this theory of capitalist development 'the essential feature ... is production for sale in a market in which the object is to realise the maximum profit' (Wallerstein, 1979: 15). So the origins of capitalism are linked to an expanding world market as 'a capitalist mode is one in which production is for exchange; that is, it is determined by its profitability on a market' (Wallerstein, 1979: 159).

The onset of modern state formation in Europe, it is argued, also proceeded at this time, resulting in the rise of absolutist monarchies in Western Europe that 'is coordinate in time with the emergence of a European world-economy' and thus *both* cause *and* consequence of capitalism (Wallerstein, 1974a: 133). As a result, 'the development of strong states in the core areas of the European world was an essential component of the development of modern capitalism' (Wallerstein, 1974a: 134). Thus, Wallerstein ties the varied pursuit of national societies and the development of variegated patterns of *raison d'état* to different processes of accumulation stemming from the structural division of labour within the world economy and the distribution of 'strong' states in the core and 'weak' states in the periphery, complemented by semi-peripheral states in between. The world market coexists with multiple, territorially defined political entities, i.e. states. States in the core are characterised by monopolised production, which yields larger levels of profit in a 'free trade' system characterised by unequal exchange with countries in the semi-periphery and periphery. Once these leading production sectors have lost their monopolised privilege, they are shifted to countries in the periphery, where the market in these products is characterised by free competition and, as a result, lower levels of profit. 'Given the unequal power of monopolised products *vis-à-vis* products with many producers in the market, the ultimate result of exchange between core and peripheral products was a flow of surplus-value (meaning here a large part of the real profits from multiple local productions) to those states that had a large number of core-like processes' (Wallerstein, 2004: 18).

Fragmented political authority and the world market are, thus, closely related to each other. 'Capitalism and a world-economy (that is, a single division of labour but multiple polities and cultures) are obverse sides of the same coin. One does not cause the other. We are merely defining the same indivisible phenomenon by different characteristics' (Wallerstein, 1974b: 399, 2004: 23). In other words, capitalism requires an international system of multiple states. The alternative, a world empire with a unified political authority, would imply the end of capitalism. It 'would in fact stifle capitalism, because it would mean that there was a political structure with the ability to override a priority for the endless accumulation of capital' (Wallerstein, 2004: 58). Understanding political structures in this way, however, indicates Wallerstein's focus on the external relationship between state and market. Moreover, the spatial analysis of 'core' and 'peripheral' geographies is highly state-centric. As Robert Cox (1981: 127) detailed in his critique of world systems analysis, 'states and inter-state relations are the political structures that maintain in place the exploitative core–periphery relationship of economies.' This reduction of state attributes to geographical location leads to another type of warmed-up geographical determinism – a case of 'bad latitude' – that is inattentive to the internal relation of both 'core' and 'periphery'. For example, the uneven geographical expression of the social relations of production in the same space (e.g. contemporary Silicon Valley and Detroit in the United States) should not be understood through a fixation on state attributes as defining geographical place (as argued by Cox, 1987: 328; Smith, 2004: 189).

Giovanni Arrighi, in turn, distinguishes several hegemonies of historical capitalism or consecutive 'systemic cycles of accumulation' (Arrighi, 1994). Within each cycle, there is first an expansive phase during which capitalists invest money in commodities and production for trade. This implies that any kind of trade, in which goods are bought cheaply and sold more expensively, is a capitalist relation. Unsurprisingly, Arrighi dates the start of capitalism back to the thirteenth and fourteenth centuries, when medieval Italian city states were involved in long-distance trade. When trade does no longer yield sufficient returns, capitalists then switch to financial expansion, concentrating on making profits through investment. Eventually, it is argued, this will result in an even bigger crisis, leading to the establishment of a new systemic cycle. 'Financial expansions are thus seen as announcing not just the maturity of a particular state of development of the capitalist world-economy, but also the beginning of a new state' (Arrighi, 1994: 87). Very similar to Wallerstein, the different hegemonic cycles of accumulation are closely linked to specific dominant states. 'Inter-state competition has been a critical component of each and every phase of financial expansion and a major factor in the formation of those blocs of governmental and business organisations that have led the capitalist world-economy through its successive phases of material expansion' (Arrighi, 1994: 12). Whether it was the medieval system of Italian city states, Hapsburg Spain, the Dutch United Provinces of the early seventeenth century, England/Britain or the United States, their world hegemonic position underpinned specific systemic cycles of accumulation. Arrighi then identifies two logics, a capitalist and a territorialist logic, which relate to each other in different ways at different times.

Capitalism and territorialism as defined here . . . do represent alternative strategies of state formation. In the territorialist strategy control over territory and population is the objective, and control over mobile capital the means, of state- and war-making. In the capitalist strategy, the relationship between ends and means is turned upside down: control over mobile capital is the objective, and control over territory and population the means. (Arrighi, 1994: 34)

In sum, Arrighi defines capitalism as follows: 'An agency of capital accumulation is capitalist precisely because it reaps large and regular profits by investing its stock of money in trade and production or in speculation and the credit system' (Arrighi, 1994: 230). Capitalism is, thereby, not defined as a social relation, but through the existence of 'capitalists' in a market economy and their particular control or lack of control over the state, i.e. the way the capitalist logic is externally related to the territorialist logic (Arrighi, 2007: 332). While Arrighi focuses here on the external relations between the political and the economic, what he does not analyse are the internal relations between state and market.

There are clearly commonalities across these three perspectives. First, the emergence of capitalism is explained as a result of the growth of the market and the related growth of trade and rise of towns and cities. 'Capitalism resides here in the "logic of circulation" or in the political relations of distribution' (Teschke, 2003: 139). Nonetheless, it needs to be remembered that a focus on the commercialisation of trade, for example between Italian city states and the Far East, took place predominantly in luxury items such as silk for the elites and was based on buying products cheap in one place and selling them dear in another. The wealth with which these products were bought was accumulated within a dominant feudal mode of production, in which surplus extraction was politically enforced by the ruling nobility on the peasantry. Further, world systems analysis does not regard class struggle as the *basis* for capitalist development but its *expression*: constantly displaced and renewed as a consequence of strategies of exploitation. The approach therefore ends up 'assuming away the fundamental problem of the transformation of class relations', by assimilating the emergence of markets and merchants within the trade-centred impulses of commercial development (Brenner, 1977: 39). There is, therefore, an in-built failure to specify the particular, historically developed class relations through which processes of capitalist expansion and state formation worked themselves through in the transition from feudalism to capitalism (Aronowitz, 1981; Goldfrank, 1975; Skocpol, 1977). By default, the account of the onset of a capitalist dynamic of development and its relationship to the modern states system, in terms of causes and timing, is inherently indeterminate, obscured within 'a transhistorical assumption of capitalism' (Teschke, 2003: 137). Finally, two different logics confront each other (territorialist and capitalist) to become externally related in the development of successive hegemonies or systemic cycles of accumulation. The internal relationship between the 'economic' and the 'political' within capitalism is, however, overlooked. Therefore the task remains to provide: 1) a historical account of the emergence of capitalist social relations of production; and 2) a conceptualisation of the relationship between the geopolitics of modern state sovereignty and the outward expansion of capitalism through passive revolutions of capital linked to conditions of uneven and combined development.

Social Property Relations and the Political Map of Europe: 'Hurrah for England'?

Robert Brenner rejects the explanation of the emergence of capitalism as a result of the growth of market relations and increased trade centred in the rise of towns and cities (Brenner, 2001: 171). In order to understand the dynamics of capitalism, he turns the focus to underlying social property relations. Of course, the prior existing world market has shaped capitalism and capitalism, in turn, has completely transformed the world market, but in itself the world market alone cannot explain the transition from feudalism to capitalism. 'As the feudal monarchies of Spain and Portugal were to discover, the wealth plundered during the mercantile period did not fuel an industrial revolution on the Iberian Peninsula precisely because social relations were not transformed' (Ashman, 2010: 194). Under feudalism, the social property relations viewpoint holds that agrarian property was privately controlled by a class of feudal lords who extracted a surplus from the peasants by politico-legal relations of compulsion: 'extra-economic' coercion was articulated through means of labour services, rents in kind or customary dues owed to the individual lord by the peasant. Feudalism therefore involved a fusion of the juridical serfdom and military protection of the peasantry by a social class of nobles exercising a monopoly of law and private rights of justice within a framework of fragmented sovereignty (Anderson, 1974a, 150–1; 1974b, 404–7). Accordingly, what distinguished the feudal mode of production in Europe was the specific organisation of seigneurial and serf classes in a vertically articulated system of parcellised sovereignty and scalar property. 'It was this concrete nexus', notes Perry Anderson (1974b: 408), 'which spelt out the precise type of extra-economic coercion exercised over the direct producer'.

Under capitalist social relations of production, by contrast, the direct extraction of surplus is accomplished through 'non-political' relations associated with different forms of social power. As detailed in Chapter 1, in capitalist social forms surplus extraction is indirectly conducted through a contractual relation between those who maintain the power of appropriation, as owners of the means of production, over those who have only their labour to sell, as expropriated producers. The direct producers are thus no longer in possession of their own means of subsistence but are compelled to sell their labour power for a wage in order to gain access to the means of production (Brenner, 1986: 34; Rosenberg, 1994: 124; Wood, 1995: 31–6). Said otherwise, direct producers have access to the means of production only through the sale of their labour power in exchange for a wage, which is mediated by the purely 'economic' mechanisms of the market. The market, in this focus on social property relations, does not therefore represent an opportunity but a compulsion to which both appropriators and expropriators (capital and labour) are subjected, through the imperatives of competition, profit maximisation and survival (Wood, 2002a: 96–8, 102). As Marx argued, just as 'capital further developed into a coercive relation', compelling producers to offer for sale their labour power as a commodity to reproduce subsistence *and* do more work than is socially necessary, then so too does it compel the owners of the means of production to extract the maximum surplus value to compete (Marx, 1867/1990: 270–2, 424, 531–2).

The origin of capitalism – the displacement of 'politically' constituted property by 'economic' power – depended on an historical process of *primitive accumulation* signifying the reconstitution of peasants in possession of the means of subsistence into propertyless individuals compelled to sell their labour. This was 'the historical process of divorcing the producer from the means of production', leading to a situation in which 'capitalist production stands on its own feet' (Marx, 1867/1990: 874–5). This process of primitive accumulation also induced changes in the social position of women, so that the sphere of reproduction also became a source of value creation and exploitation (see Federici, 2004, and our expanded discussion in Chapter 6 on social reproduction feminism). Importantly, as Jairus Banaji reminds us, modes of production have historically been characterised by a multiplicity of forms of labour exploitation. The existence of wage labour in itself does not indicate that we have a capitalist mode of production. Wage labour was clearly present in the ceramics industry within the tributary mode of production in China in the eleventh century and also 'widespread in the Roman economy' (Banaji, 2010: 29–30, 117), generally based on slavery. In turn, capitalism still works through a variety of forms of exploitation today not least in the form of bonded labour within wage labour conditions, undocumented human trafficking for forced migrant and sex work and various usages of modern slavery. Hence the importance behind rethinking the history of capital to recognise the existence of *historical capitalism* – referring to certain social relations that could be attributed to capitalism – prior to the consolidation of capitalism as a *mode of production* (Banaji, 2010: 13). This 'facilitates the construction of an account of peripheral social development within which non-Western experiences can be liberated from the burden of correspondence with a predefined Western trajectory' (Tansel, 2015a: 67). As Alexander Anievas and Kerem Nişancıoğlu argue, 'a distinction must be made between "capital" and "capitalism." While capital – as we have seen – refers to a social relation defined by the relation between capital and wage-labour, capitalism refers to a broader configuration (or totality) of social relations oriented around the systematic reproduction of the capital relation, but irreducible – either historically or logically – to the capital relation itself' (Anievas and Nişancıoğlu, 2015: 218; Tansel 2015a: 82–5). Hence, capitalism implies that the capital relation around the private ownership of the means of production and 'free' wage labour has become the predominant and, therefore, determining form of labour exploitation within a particular mode of production.

In response to a 'general crisis' of the European economy during the seventeenth century, the ensuing class confrontations resulted in three totally divergent paths of subsequent social and economic development across the feudal agrarian societies of Western and Eastern Europe. First, in Central and Eastern Europe, faced with a relatively weak and disorganised peasantry, lords politically reconstituted themselves through a greater concentration of power within large serf estates (magnates) alongside the growing centralised states. Absolutist monarchies, as in Russia and Prussia, tended to advance the power of the large serf-owning magnates 'because their victory over Estates and similar institutions generally meant the weakening of the lesser nobles ... and of the towns, and the relative strengthening of the smaller groups of magnates who gathered round the ruler's Court' (Hobsbawm, 1965: 35). This led to the consolidation of serf estates and the accumulation of agrarian produce for export sale rather than subsistence crop consumption. In this second serfdom, 'in Europe east of the Elbe we have the familiar story of the lords entirely overwhelming the peasantry, gradually reducing through legislation peasant personal freedom, and ultimately confiscating an important part of peasant land and attaching it to their demesne' (Brenner, 1985a: 35–6). This eastern area was 'servile' because it was largely a food- and raw-material-producing 'dependent economy' of Western Europe. As early as the fifteenth century, Eastern Europe was required to export, among other products, cereals and wood to countries such as Holland, England and the Iberian Peninsula. Eastern Europe therefore played the role of raw materials producer within feudal social relations of production for the industrialising West in exchange for manufactured goods, notably textiles and other luxuries.

Second, in France, by contrast, there was a modification of old social property relations signified by the relative strength of peasant possession against declining seigneurial powers alongside continued surplus extraction by extra-economic means through the centralised tax/office structure. To cite the historical analysis of Engels:

While the wild battles of the ruling feudal nobility filled the Middle Ages with their clamour, the quiet work of the oppressed classes had undermined the feudal system throughout western Europe, had created conditions in which less and less room remained for the feudal lord. (Engels, 1884/1990: 556)

Absolutism involved 'consolidating the grip of the state as a gigantic landlord', a centralised apparatus of surplus extraction (Rosenberg, 1994: 135). According to Brenner (1985b: 264, original emphasis), 'the growth of *centralised surplus extraction* served to reorganise the aristocracy: it brought the lesser lords into dependence on royal office and induced the greater ones to come to court and ally themselves with the monarchy.' The absolutist state would develop in conflict with forms of seigneurial extraction while absorbing into state office those lords who were undermined by the eroding feudal system. Peasant proprietorship of land therefore continued but in mutual dependence upon the absolutist state, creating a very different class structure in the countryside revolving around a distinct triumvirate of (free)peasant/landlord/centralising state. The latter established rights to surplus extraction from peasant production while limiting landlords' rents to facilitate increased taxes. With land cultivated in small parcels by peasant tenants, the transition to capitalism was halted as land was not consolidated, peasants were not exposed to market imperatives and the likelihood of agricultural innovation and improvement was reduced. Absolutism 'led to a repetition of the

established medieval pattern of declining productivity leading to population and production crisis', illustrative of the seventeenth century
(Brenner, 1985b: 226).

Third, in England in the late fifteenth century, peasantries won freedom from landlords by ending the lords' capacity to extract an economic
surplus in the form of feudal rents, but were unable to establish freehold
rights over the land. Landlords, in contrast, were unable to reinstate
serfdom, but did respond by adopting economic rents that stripped the
peasants of traditional customary guarantees to their holdings, reducing
them to commercial tenants or agricultural wage labourers. Consolidated
holdings would therefore be leased out to large capitalist tenants who
would in turn farm them on the basis of wage labour and agricultural
improvement. These holdings would be secured through the enclosures
of commons, 'decrees by which the landowners grant themselves the
people's land as private property, decrees of expropriation of the people'
(Marx, 1867/1990: 885). As a consequence, direct producers no longer
possessed their full means of production and were compelled to produce
systematically for the market, resulting in competition, cost-cutting, specialisation, improvement and agricultural transformation through capitalist tenancy (Brenner, 1985a: 49–53). What would emerge would not be
peasant agriculture 'but a class of agricultural entrepreneurs, the farmers,
and a large agrarian proletariat' alongside the so-called domestic or put-
ting-out system, in which the merchant brought the products to handi-
craftsmen and part-time non-agricultural labour of the peasantry, for sale
in wider home markets (see Hobsbawm, 1962: 13–22). The agrarian
situation would become uniquely transformed through the monopolisa-
tion of land by commercially minded landlords, cultivated by tenant-
farmers employing the landless proletariat. A 'tripartite capitalist
hierarchy' would therefore become established between commercial
landlord/capitalist tenant/wage labourer through which the landed classes
had no need to revert to direct 'extra-economic' compulsion to extract
a surplus (Brenner, 1985b: 298).

What is significant is that the increasing reliance on purely 'economic'
modes of appropriation, the productive and competitive utilisation of
land rather than direct coercive surplus extraction, was central to creating
the conditions under which the primitive accumulation of capital could
proceed. Hence, the nascent ruling class of landlords could largely
depend on the 'impersonal' logic of 'economic' processes of exploitation
by capitalist tenants of relatively free wage labourers, leading to greater
intra-capitalist competition throughout the economy as a whole (Katz,
1993/1999: 71–2). This had significant consequences for the constitution
of the 'political'.

The political corollary of these distinctive economic relations was a formally autonomous state which represented the private 'economic' class of appropriators in its public, 'political' aspect. This meant that the 'economic' functions of appropriation were differentiated from the 'political' and military functions of rule – or to put it another way, 'civil society' was differentiated from the state – while at the same time the state was responsive, even subordinate to civil society. (Wood, 1991: 28)

Civil society therefore becomes equated with individual rights and private interests and 'appears as a framework external to the individuals, as a restriction of their original independence' (Marx, 1843/1975: 164). Hence, 'by the end of the seventeenth-century the English evolution towards agrarian capitalism had brought about the end of the age-old "fusion" of the "economic" and the "political", and the emergence of an institutional separation between state and civil society' (Brenner, 1985b: 299). From a social property relations viewpoint, state formation and capitalist development in England went hand in hand as the social transformations that brought about capitalism were the same that characterised the apparent separation of state and civil society, leading to the constitution of the capitalist state. Hence, the rather laconic but astute summarising of this account from Immanuel Wallerstein (1992: 594) as a 'hurrah for England' explanation of the emergence of the modern state. Returning to our critique of naïve idealism in Chapter 3, there is the argument that a focus on a set of Eastern inventions and resource portfolios (ideas, technologies, institutions) enables a breakout from the cul-de-sac of Eurocentrism (Hobson, 2011). But this position overlooks the subtle point made by Ellen Meiksins Wood (1995: 37, original emphasis) that:

The crucial issue is not the presence or absence of private property in land as such. China, for example, had well-established private landed property from a very early stage ... The important point is the relation between private property and political power, and its consequences for the organisation of production and the relation between appropriator and producer. The unique characteristic of Western development in this respect is that it is marked by the earliest and most complete transfer of political power to private property, and therefore also the most thorough, generalised and direct subservience of production to the demands of an appropriating *class*. (see also Brenner and Isett, 2002)

In addition to England, however, Robert Brenner also identifies the Low Countries, and here in particular the northern part, as an area where capitalist social relations of production emerged in the sixteenth century. While peasants had been driven off the land in England in processes of primitive accumulation around enclosures of common land, ecological degradation of agricultural land in the northern Low Countries undermined arable farming and, thus, subsistence production of Dutch farmers. In order to survive, these farmers (still owning their land) had to move into areas such as dairy farming and cattle production, in which they could maintain a competitive position in the market (Brenner, 2001: 208). They became, thus, subject to competitive market pressures, the characteristic of capitalist social relations of production. 'Having been rendered market-dependent producers who were obliged to buy their basic needs on the market, they were compelled to specialise, accumulate and innovate in order to survive in the face of competitive pressure' (Brenner, 2001: 218).[1] Urban industries, in turn, were heavily dependent on rural development for the supply of raw materials and labour. 'Powerless to control the countryside politically, the bourgeoisie sought to extend their reach by economic means. This led to forms of "proto-industrial" development, in which urban merchant entrepreneurs invested directly in rural industries as peasant production became increasingly geared toward the world market' (Anievas and Nişancıoğlu, 2015: 183). As a result, wage labour became increasingly characteristic of the Dutch economy. 'By the mid-sixteenth century, more or less market-dependent forms of wage-labour had become a structural feature, albeit a geographically uneven one, of the Dutch economy' (Anievas and Nişancıoğlu, 2015: 183).

With capitalism as a mode of production, having emerged in Europe and here England and the Low Countries first, the question then remains: how to conceptualise the emergence and expansion of capitalism in its relations to the geopolitics of the states system? The challenge is to do so without simply associating each condition as spheres externally related to each other. The fact that capitalism emerged within an already existing international states system is crucial in that one dynamic underlying this outward expansion has been interstate rivalry. Once established in England and fuelling the industrial revolution, Britain then exerted strong pressures on other states due to its much more successful and dynamic economy. 'From the late eighteenth-century and especially in the nineteenth, Britain's major European rivals were under pressure to develop their economies in ways that could meet this new challenge' (Wood, 1999: 7). Other states, foremost Germany and France in the late nineteenth century, also established capitalist social relations of production.

---

[1] Identifying the Low Countries as a birthplace of capitalism is controversial in the literature (Anievas and Nişancıoğlu, 2015: 180). Ellen Meiksins Wood, for example, a strong supporter of the Brenner thesis, is sceptical. For her, market dependence in the Low Countries was driven by opportunities, but, unlike in England, not by 'market imperatives, the imperatives of competition and profit/maximisation by means of increasing labour productivity' (Wood, 2002b: 76).

'The "industrialisation of war" in the nineteenth-century gave every state an interest in the promotion of capitalist economic relations in order to produce domestically the high technology weapons and transport systems on which military success now depended' (Callinicos, 2010a: 20).

The spread of capitalism, however, was not only the result of geopolitical rivalry. As outlined in Chapter 2, capitalism is characterised by periodic crises of overaccumulation. Capitalist expansion along lines of uneven and combined development has, therefore, also been the consequence of attempts to overcome its crisis-ridden nature. Rosa Luxemburg (1913/2003: 323) recognised that capitalism constantly has to expand outward and incorporate new, non-capitalist spaces in order to overcome crises resulting from limited expansive capacity of demand from within capitalism (Bieler et al., 2016). Famously, in *The Accumulation of Capital*, by analysing the creation and expansion of the hothouse conditions for capital accumulation in non-capitalist environments, Luxemburg concluded that 'from the very beginning, the forms and laws of capitalist production aim to comprise the entire globe as a store of productive forces' (Luxemburg, 1913/2003: 401). Luxemburg's first focus is on processes of primitive accumulation in dispossessing peasant producers to create a reserve of labour power based on the wage system in non-capitalist territories. In Chapter 7 on Global Capitalism, we discuss how millions of Chinese migrant workers have left their land in the inner parts of China and moved to booming coastal areas in search for wage labour employment. Second, militarism was also famously traced by Luxemburg (1913/2003: 419) as 'the executor of the accumulation of capital', as a province of the expansion of capital in gaining possession of the means of production and labour power through colonialism and imperialism (Luxemburg, 1913/2003: 367). As historical examples, Luxemburg mentions British policy in India, French policy in Algeria and the extension of commodity relations by European powers in China (Luxemburg, 1913/2003: 367). When analysing Global War and the attention to the Iraq War in Chapter 8, we refer back to Luxemburg's focus on militarism as a source of capital accumulation and the way this dynamic was played out not only during the conflict itself but also during the period of postwar reconstruction. Finally, Luxemburg discussed the role of international loans and the credit system, the role of the built environment and fixed capital, as an essential spatial arrangement for the absorption of surplus value (e.g. through railroad building, roads, dams, irrigation systems, warehouses, schools, hospitals, universities). In Chapter 9 on Global Crisis, we again discuss how loans to European peripheral countries played a crucial role in the build-up to the Eurozone crisis and the way the expansion of capitalist surplus accumulation is currently being reconstituted in countries such as Greece and Portugal.

Nevertheless, accounts of the emergence of capitalism in Europe and its subsequent outward expansion to the whole globe are often accused of Eurocentrism. 'It is therefore crucial to reflect further on whether an account of the rise of capitalism and the modern state can avoid the perils of Eurocentrism' (Morton, 2005: 517).

The Multilinear Dialectic of Uneven and Combined Development

It is beyond the purpose of this book to deliver any resolution to the debates on the spectre of Eurocentrism that has curbed recognition of the role of non-European states in the constitution of capitalism and the states system (see Anievas and Matin, 2016; Anievas and Nişancıoğlu, 2015; Bhambra, 2007; Chakrabarty, 2007; Chibber, 2013; Nişancıoğlu, 2013; Tansel, 2015b, 2016). Nevertheless, the critique of 'Eurocentric diffusionism', the problem of examining capitalism through the notion of uneven and combined development as a wave of diffusion unfolding outward from Western Europe to the non-European periphery (Blaut, 1993), has to be addressed. In other words, granting a privileged focus on the spatial system of Europe without making connections between inter-twined histories that lie both within and beyond the European context is considered problematic. While the periphery of non-Europe is often portrayed in social property relations accounts as a passive recipient of diffusions from the European core, the modern expansion of capitalism is presented largely in terms of internal, immanent forces (Blaut, 1999: 130–2). In order to overcome Eurocentrism, the goal is to avoid positing the non-West as ontologically exterior to the constitution of capitalism (Tansel, 2015b: 78).

In the following, we respond to the charge made against the social property relations approach as Eurocentric in two ways. First, we con-tribute to busting the myth that Marx projected a linear causality or progressive movement from capital's becoming in one specific temporal and spatial instance to its universalisation throughout the world. Second, we empirically illustrate how the emergence and outward expansion of capitalism from England and the Low Countries was heavily conditioned by their insertion within 'the international'. As for the former, there is a strong multilinear understanding of social development directly evident in Marx that reveals the wider geographical scope of his critique of political economy (Anderson, 2010: 197). Equally, 'deprovincialising Marx entails not simply an expanded geographic inclusion but

a broadening of temporal possibilities unchained from a hegemonic unilateralism' (Harootunian, 2015: 2). This endeavour pivots on a rereading
of Marx's statement that 'the country that is more developed industrially
only shows, to the less developed, the image of its own future' (Marx,
1867/1990: 91), which is interpreted as having a form of unilinear determinism built into it (Shanin, 1983: 4). However, Derek Sayer and Philip
Corrigan (1983: 79, original emphasis) have argued that the comparative
analysis here is between England and Germany.

Since Germany is a society in which capitalism has taken root already, its 'normal
development' can reasonably be expected to follow an 'English' path. But this in
no way implies any necessity for societies in which capitalist production is *not*
already established to do the same.

A multilinear theory of history is therefore evident here that contains
a focus on the dialectical unity of the inneraction of particularity and
universality within social development that needs to be recovered within
and for historical materialism (Anderson, 2010: 178–9). This is evidenced very well in Marx:

It would therefore be unfeasible and wrong to let the economic categories follow
one another in the same sequence as that in which they were historically decisive.
Their sequence is determined, rather, by their relation to one another in modern
bourgeois society, which is precisely the opposite of that which seems to be their
natural order or which corresponds to historical development. The point is not the
historic position of the economic relations in the succession of different forms of
society ... [r]ather, their order within modern bourgeois society. (Marx, 1858/
1973: 107–8)

Envisioning capitalism as creating a form of unevenness that combines
the general and the particular is also of a piece with provincialising Europe
and deprovincialising Marx (Chakrabarty, 2007; Harootunian, 2015).
For Harry Harootunian this entails emphasising the process of unevenness embedded in capital's continuous expansion across heterogeneous
temporalities and spaces. Referring to Marx on the lever of primitive
accumulation:

The history of this expropriation assumes different aspects in different countries,
and runs through its various phases in different orders of succession, and at
different historical epochs. Only in England, which we therefore take as our
example, has it the classic form. (Marx, 1867/1990: 876)

Hence, this is not to argue that such expropriations outside Europe follow
a linear causality, a singularly progressive movement, in the expansion of
capitalism as a mode of production. 'Attention to the different ways
capitalism developed in singular and specific sites affirms Marx's decision

to privilege the global theatre reflected in the formation of the world
market as the principal organising principle in envisioning any possible
world history' (Harootunian, 2015: 19–20). Capital's process of becoming, through its own spatial and temporal expansion, was therefore an
uneven developmental process that absorbed and combined previously
non-capitalist elements within and across the peripheries of Euro-
America. Trajectories of state formation are therefore embedded in the
uneven worldwide spread of capitalism *combined* with the condition of
differently constituted preceding political forms and social relations.
Trotsky recognised this multilinear causality when he developed the
notion of uneven and combined development. 'It is false that world
economy is simply a sum of national parts of one and the same type ...
In reality, the national peculiarities represent an original combination of
the basic features of the world process' (Trotsky, 1929/2004: 23).
'Unevenness', in his regard, 'is the most general law of the historic process
[that] reveals itself most sharply and complexly in the destiny of the
backward countries' (Trotsky, 1936/1980: 28). Due to the unevenness
of the developmental process, features appropriate to different historical
periods become combined within the character of a social formation.
Therefore a 'peculiar mixture of backward elements with the most modern factors' arises within a social formation confronted with insertion into
the expanding system of capitalism (Trotsky, 1936/1980: 31–2, 36, 72).

Alex Anievas and Kerem Nişancıoğlu demonstrate well how the emergence of capitalism in England and the Low Countries and its subsequent
outward expansion cannot be explained by referring exclusively to these
countries', or more generally Europe's, internal dynamics. Rather, both
the constitution and outward expansion of capitalism has to be understood by the way these countries relied on relationships with non-
European space along lines of uneven and combined development.
First, English capitalism was heavily conditioned by the Atlantic expansion following Columbus' invasion of the Americas in 1492. 'If it were not
for the specifically international conditions created by Europe's expansion into the Atlantic, it is likely that capitalism would have been choked
off by the limits of English agrarian capitalism' (Anievas and Nişancıoğlu,
2015: 152). The American colonies provided both markets for surpluses,
which could not be sold in Britain, as well as super-profits resulting from
plantations based on slave labour for reinvestment into the industrial
revolution. 'In the late eighteenth-century, income from colonial properties in the Americas was equal to approximately 50 per cent of British
gross investment. Since much of this would have been reinvested in
British industries, it provided a significant input into British industrialisation' (Anievas and Nişancıoğlu, 2015: 164). In other words, the full

establishment of the capitalist mode of production in England was conditioned by the opportunities afforded through the Atlantic expansion and the combination of wage labour in England with slave labour overseas (Anievas and Nişancıoğlu, 2015: 169). As for the Dutch case, the very emergence of capitalism was conditioned by 'the international'. Farmers in the northern parts of the Low Countries could switch to milk and dairy production for the market only because they gained access to cheap grain imports from the Baltic area from the mid fifteenth-century onward (Anievas and Nişancıoğlu, 2015: 181), where production was based on feudal social relations, as argued earlier. In the late sixteenth century, then, Dutch agriculture was increasingly characterised by large farms worked by wage labour. 'Crucially, one outcome of this process was an increase in the demand for labour-power concomitant with a reduction in its supply in the seventeenth-century, as population growth could not keep pace with economic growth' (Anievas and Nişancıoğlu, 2015: 226). Unlike in Britain, this bottleneck was not overcome through rapid technological innovation. Instead, Dutch capitalism drew on the availability of labour power in Asia in its expansion. 'By incorporating labour-power on a global scale, Dutch capital acquired a power of expansion it hitherto did not possess' (Anievas and Nişancıoğlu, 2015: 227). Importantly, rather than occupying territory and levying taxes as feudalist Spain and Portugal did in Latin America, Dutch capitalism focused on controlling production processes. 'Dutch preponderance rested on intervening and eventually establishing control over production and thus also labour-power. The integration of intra-Asian trade, therefore, 'facilitated for the first time the organisation of 'a hierarchy of capitals connecting a dispersed mass of labour-power' on a "global" scale' (Anievas and Nişancıoğlu, 2015: 234–5, citing Banaji 2010: 274). Localised resistance was crucial in the way this process played out. In order to get a foothold in South Asia, Dutch capitalism either integrated into existing networks or relied on blistering violence. At times, surplus labour was provided for free as in the case of clove production in Moluccas, while rebellions against clove production elsewhere were suppressed with brutal force.

Clearly, outward capitalist expansion and the full development of capitalism in Britain and the Netherlands was conditioned by the opportunities offered in the Americas and East Asia. Nevertheless, the fact that it was these two states, rather than Spain or Portugal, where capitalism was first fully established, indicates that the prior reconfiguration of the social relations of production around wage labour and the private ownership of the means of production in Britain and the Netherlands was crucial for their ability to absorb the opportunities offered in other areas of the world. 'Those countries where protocapitalist relations were emerging or had already emerged – Holland and England – made much more productive use of the bullion than did Spain, which was set on a course of empire-expanding geopolitical accumulation congruent with its feudal relations of production' (Anievas and Nişancıoğlu, 2015: 248). In short, the origin of capitalism is spatially a European phenomenon based on the emergence of a particular set of social property relations in England and the Netherlands, but one which was conditioned in its emergence and outward expansion by opportunities and resistances it encountered elsewhere.

These aspects are absent from Justin Rosenberg's projection of uneven and combined development as a transhistorical phenomenon and, thus, as intrinsic to the historical process itself (Rosenberg, 2006: 309). This is contrary to Trotsky's own stance that capitalism gains mastery over inherited unevenness through *methods of its own* through seeking new territories and economic expansion (Trotsky, 1928/1970: 19–20). Overlooked is Neil Smith's argument that 'uneven development is the systematic geographical expression of the contradictions inherent in the very constitution and structure of capital' and thus unique to capitalism (Smith, 1984/2008: 4). As Kees van der Pijl (2015: 61–2) clarifies, uneven and combined development is valid only for capitalism. Following Neil Smith (2004: 182):

A law that explains absolutely 'everything in the world' explains nothing, and the fact that 'nothing develops evenly', used as a philosophical justification for such a law, reduces it to triviality. Dressed in such pretence, it tells us absolutely nothing specific about capitalism, imperialism or the present moment of capitalist restructuring.

To argue, as Rosenberg does, that the theory of uneven and combined development itself 'captures at a general level the sociological character-istics of *all* development' (Callinicos and Rosenberg, 2008: 80, emphasis added) and that it can meet Kenneth Waltz's requirements for a general theory of IR (Rosenberg, 2013a: 185) indicates a misplaced envy of positivism and constitutes a departure from historically specific analysis of modern capitalist political space. Following our analysis elsewhere (Bieler, 2013; Morton, 2010b: 215–16, 2011/2013: 242–3), the specific character of uneven and combined development can be fully grasped only through an understanding of capitalist social relations of production, as we analyse in relation to current capitalist development in Part III of this book. Importantly, uneven and combined development does not only characterise the historic expansion of capitalism and the incorporation of non-capitalist space into capitalist social relations of production. Our argument is that uneven and combined development continues to shape the reconfiguration of social relations between different areas within global capitalism today, as Chapter 7 indicates in relation to the integration of China within the global political economy and Chapter 9 demonstrates on the plight of Greece and other peripheral countries within the Eurozone crisis.

When analysing the constitution and outward dynamic of capitalism along uneven and combined lines, it is essential to grasp the spatio-temporal dynamics and causal effects of state and class agents in the making of capitalist modernity. This is, however, missing from the literature to date. For example, Justin Rosenberg (2013b) references the spatio-temporal character of uneven and combined development without examining the organisation of space, the spatial logistics of state power or the contradictions of space. Space is 'there' but redundant and unexplored, a mere happenstance of developmental unevenness and combination. Addressing the spatial dynamics in capitalism's outward expansion is, however, crucial for the understanding of the wide variety of processes through which capitalism has become constituted in different geographical locations around the world. Otherwise, the framework of uneven and combined development can collapse into an impoverished historical geography of capitalism unable to explain the involvement of states and classes in processes of production and surplus appropriation (Rioux, 2013: 108). It was Michael Burawoy (1989: 793) in his illusive statement that recognised 'where Trotsky's horizons stop, Gramsci's begin'. Or, in David Harvey's (2003b: 101) usage, 'the molecular processes of capital accumulation operating in space and time generate passive revolutions in the geographical patterning of capital accumulation.' In what follows, then, we present passive revolution as capable of providing a lateral field of causality to address state and class forms of agency with the structuring conditions of uneven and combined development. This will allow us to capture spatial diversity in the making of capitalist modernity within the structuring conditions of uneven and combined development, emphasising the internal relations between the agency of social class forces and the structuring conditions of capitalism, as conceptualised in Chapter 2.

The Passive Revolutionary Road to Capitalist Modernity

With reference to the Italian Risorgimento – the movement for Italian national liberation that culminated in the political unification of the country in 1860–1 – Gramsci introduced a cluster of terms to capture the contradictory outcome of the crystallisation of this state formation process. These terms, he admitted, were difficult (sometimes impossible) to translate into a foreign language given their situatedness in Italian historico-political discourse, but they, nevertheless, had entered common circulation throughout 'Europe and the world' to address a category referring to the creation of modern states that 'was not restricted to Italy'. The Risorgimento therefore represented a fragile combination of *Rinascimento – Rinascita – Rinascenza*, literally meaning 'renaissance' and 'rebirth' or a triptych of revival, rebirth and reawakening. However, in the same note from the *Prison Notebooks*, Gramsci states that 'all of these terms express the concept of a return to a condition that had already existed before: that is, the concept of an aggressive *"ripresa"* (*"riscossa"*) of the nation's energies or of a liberation from a state of servitude in order to return to pristine autonomy (*riscatto*)' (Gramsci, 1996: 387, Q5§136). All these terms express an amalgam of revolt, insurrection or awakening (*riscossa*), as well as that of revival or renewal (*ripresa*) in relation to the state formation process of the Italian Risorgimento and its territorial, spatial and geographical patterning within wider uneven and combined developmental conditions. The Risorgimento was as much a rebirth, or revolution, as a restoration in which there was 'the acceptance, in mitigated and camouflaged forms, of the same principles that had been combatted' (Gramsci, 1996: 389, Q5§138, 1996: 389, Q5§139). But, given that Gramsci (1971: 220, Q13§27) recognised that 'restorations *in toto* do not exist', how are the contradictions of revolution and restoration conjoined in a way that offers a lateral field of causality to the conditioning situation of uneven and combined development? What is the *essential form* conveyed by these contradictions of revolution and restoration impacting on state formation processes beyond the mere *form of appearance* in time and space in the case of the Italian Risorgimento?

On the *form of appearance* of these contradictions in the case of Italy, it was the failure of the 'Jacobins' in the Partito d'Azione led by Giuseppe Mazzini and Giuseppe Garibaldi, among others, to establish a programme reflecting the demands of the popular masses and, significantly, the peasantry that came to mark the Risorgimento. Instead, challenges were thwarted and changes in property relations accommodated due to the Partito Moderato, led by Vincenzo Gioberti and (Count) Camillo Benso Cavour, establishing alliances between big landowners in the Mezzogiorno and the northern bourgeoisie, while absorbing opposition in parliament through continually assimilated change (or *trasformismo*) within the current social formation.

The Moderates do not acknowledge the agency of a collective force ... in the Risorgimento; they only recognise single individuals, who are either exalted so that they can be appropriated or slandered in order to rupture collective ties. (Gramsci, 1996: 110, Q3§125)

The essential form sustaining the appearance of the Risorgimento, though, was the concept and condition of passive revolution that can be defined as referring to various concrete historical instances when aspects of the social relations of capitalist development are either instituted and/ or expanded, resulting in both a 'revolutionary' rupture and 'restoration' of social relations. 'The problem', as Antonio Gramsci (1971: 219, Q13§27) states, 'is to see whether in the dialectic of "revolution/restoration" it is revolution or restoration which predominates'. A passive revolution therefore represents a blocked dialectic (Buci-Glucksmann, 1980: 315), or a condition of rupture in which sociopolitical processes of revolution are at once partially fulfilled and displaced (Callinicos, 2010b: 498). According to Gramsci, after the French Revolution (1789), the emergent bourgeoisie there 'was able to present itself as an integral "state", with all the intellectual and moral forces that were necessary and adequate to the task of organising a complete and perfect society' (Gramsci, 2007: 9, Q6§10). In contrast to the instance of revolutionary rupture in France, other European countries went through a series of passive revolutions in which the old feudal classes were not destroyed but maintained a political role through state power. As a result, such 'restorations are universally repressive' (Gramsci, 1996: 40, Q3§41). Hence:

[The] birth of the modern European states [proceeded] by successive waves of reform rather than by revolutionary explosions like the original French one. The 'successive waves' were made up of a combination of social struggles, interventions from above of the enlightened monarchy type, and national wars ... restoration becomes the first policy whereby social struggles find sufficiently elastic frameworks to allow the bourgeoisie to gain power without dramatic upheavals, without the French machinery of terror ... The old feudal classes are demoted from their dominant position to a 'governing' one, but are not eliminated, nor is there any attempt to liquidate them as an organic whole ... Can this 'model' for the creation of the modern states be repeated in other conditions? (Gramsci, 1971: 115, Q10II§61).

At issue here is not the question of the historical validity of the examples deployed. After all, as Gramsci himself noted, 'historians are by no means of one mind (and it is impossible that they should be) in fixing the limits of the group of events which constitutes the French Revolution' (Gramsci, 1971: 179–80, Q13§17). Equally, it was acknowledged that there can also be a 'system of interpretations of the Risorgimento' (Gramsci, 2007: 382, Q8§243). Nevertheless, it was concluded that:

The important thing is to analyse more profoundly the significance of a 'Piedmont'-type function in passive revolutions – i.e. the fact that a state replaces the local social groups in leading a struggle of renewal. It is one of the cases in which these groups have the function of 'domination' without that of 'leadership': dictatorship without hegemony. (Gramsci, 1971: 105–6, Q15§59)

The significance of the French Revolution was highlighted in terms of its geopolitical impact on the states system, 'which spilled over into the rest of Europe with the republican and Napoleonic armies – giving the old régimes a powerful shove, and resulting not in the immediate collapse as in France but in the "reformist" corrosion of them which lasted up to 1870' (Gramsci, 1971: 119, Q10§19). The Italian form of passive revolution in the appearance of the Risorgimento 'was a question of stitching together a unitary state' (Gramsci, 2007: 77, Q6§89). 'The concept of passive revolution, it seems to me', Gramsci (1996: 232, Q4§57) accordingly stated, 'applies not only to Italy but also to those countries that modernise the state through a series of reforms'.

There are at least two different but linked processes defining the *essential form* of the condition of passive revolution. It can refer to:

1) a revolution without mass participation, or a 'revolution from above', involving elite-engineered social and political reform that draws on foreign capital and associated ideas while lacking a national popular base. Passive revolution here describes the 'historical fact of the absence of popular initiative in the development of Italian history' (Gramsci 2007: 252, Q8§25) and how issues such as agrarian reform were 'a way of grafting the agrarian masses on to the national revolution' (Gramsci, 2007: 257, Q8§35); and

2) how a revolutionary form of political transformation is pressed into a conservative project of restoration in which popular demands of class struggle still play some role. It refers here to 'the fact that "progress" occurs as the reaction of the dominant classes to the sporadic and incoherent rebelliousness of the popular masses – a reaction consisting of "restorations" that agree to some part of the popular demands and are therefore "progressive restorations", or "revolutions-restorations", or even "passive revolutions"' (Gramsci, 2007: 252, Q8§25).

In the latter sense, passive revolution is linked to insurrectionary mass mobilisation from below while such class demands are restricted so that 'changes in the world of production are accommodated within the current social formation' (Sassoon, 1987: 207; see Femia, 1981: 260 n.74). As Gramsci (1996: 360, Q5§119) notes in the case of the Risorgimento, 'the bourgeoisie did not lead the people or seek its help to defeat feudal privileges; instead, it was the aristocracy that formed a strong party made up of people opposed to unbridled exploitation by the industrial bourgeoisie and to the consequences of industrialism.' In Italy, the ruling class systematically prevented the emergence of a 'new structure from below' and ever since 'has made the preservation of this crystallised situation the raison d'être of its historical continuity' (Gramsci, 2007: 121–2, Q6§162). Perhaps for that reason, it was noted that there was a 'congenital incapacity' within the Partito d'Azione to exercise leadership while the Partito Moderato resorted to a form of 'political-economic neo-Malthusianism' to block substantive agrarian reform (Gramsci, 1996: 181, Q3§125). The contradictory combination of revolution–restoration that is emblematic of a passive revolution is therefore that of an insurrectionary force domesticated (Morton, 2010a: 330). Or, to turn to the primary source, the theory of passive revolution as revolution–restoration refers to a 'domesticated dialectic' within the struggle-driven process of historical development (Gramsci, 2007: 372, Q8§225, 2007: 253, Q8§27). This does not mean that passive revolutions are consciously made by capitalists themselves; rather the emphasis is shifted to the effects of transformations constituting capitalism as a mode of production and the consolidation of modern state power (Callinicos, 1989: 124). The forms of appearance that passive revolutions may take do not imply inert, literally passive, processes. Everyday forms of passive revolution can be violent and brutal, the outcome neither predetermined nor inevitable. Hence, beyond the *form of appearance* of the Italian Risorgimento, a chain of passive revolutions called forth by capitalist modernity throughout the nineteenth and twentieth centuries may be identified, marking passive revolution as an *essential form* in the historical sociology of state-making processes. It indicates a description of capitalist modernity where there is a structural inability of the bourgeois political project to realise fully the practice of hegemony, delivering an incomplete process that becomes more the rule rather than the exception of state formation (Thomas, 2009: 154, 2013: 25). Albeit without the direct intent of a bourgeois class, these processes of state formation have often culminated in the persistence of old regimes in the latter half of the nineteenth century and, in the twentieth century, the failure of hegemony in peripheral capitalist modernity notwithstanding the partial molecular absorption and redefinition of class interests from below (Endnotes, 2015: 86, 100; Mayer, 1981/2010; and, for example, Allinson and Anievas, 2010; Chodor, 2015; Gray, 2010; Hesketh, 2017a; Munck, 2013; Roberts, 2015; Webber, 2016).

Regardless of the form of appearance *or* the essential content of a passive revolution, it is crucial to appreciate the role of class struggles over the political form of the state. The developmental unevenness of social property relations is open-ended rather than closed or ensnared within the structures of passive revolution and its logic of absorption. 'The thesis of the "passive revolution" as an interpretation of the

Risorgimento', Gramsci acknowledged, 'and of every epoch characterised by complex historical upheavals … [is in] danger of historical defeatism … since the whole way of posing the question may induce a belief in some kind of fatalism' (Gramsci, 1971: 114, Q15§62). Two factors can therefore be underscored to account for social change or contradictions and conflict within the theory of passive revolution. First, the concept of passive revolution 'remains a dialectical one – in other words, presupposes, indeed postulates as necessary, a vigorous antithesis which can present intransigently all the potentialities for development' (Gramsci, 1971: 114, Q15§62). This means emphasising the very contradictions of revolution–restoration and the role of popular masses in shaping the form and content of passive revolutions against state classes. The flow of organic and conjunctural movements within the structures of passive revolution is ultimately conditioned by the 'relations of forces' between contending class factions (Gramsci, 1971: 177–85, Q13§17). Second, in developing the theory of passive revolution, Gramsci (2007: 357, Q8§210) posed himself the following question: 'Should one regard as "revolutions" all those movements that describe themselves as "revolutions" in order to endow themselves with dignity and legitimacy?' In response, passive revolution is offered not only as an analysis of the specificity of Italian historical development (form of appearance) but also as a consideration of state formation conditions (essential form) through a method of historical analogy as an interpretative criterion (Gramsci, 1971: 54 n.4, Q25§2, 1971: 114, Q15§62). Gramsci's analysis of the specificity of Italian historical development and its form of appearance of passive revolution is thus developed 'not as a programme … but as a criterion of interpretation, in the absence of other active elements to a dominant extent' (Gramsci, 1971: 114, Q15§62). The explicative power of this method of interpreting state formation and the contradictions of class struggle therefore lies in 'the method of historical analogy as an interpretative criterion' (Gramsci, 1971: 54 n.4, Q25§2). As argued elsewhere (Morton 2007b: 604–5), Gramsci derives certain principles of historical research linked to the circumstances of Italian state formation while comparing – through historical analogy – different historical processes and, therein, the particular configuration of class struggles over the political form of state and capitalist modernity. Within the conceptualisation of passive revolution, then, lies an alternative interpretative theory of the history of modern state formation, the making of revolutions and the contradictions of class struggle. As a summing up of the internally related dimensions of uneven and combined development and passive revolution, Chris Hesketh (2017b: 15) states, 'the universal pressures generated by capitalist geopolitical competition are acknowledged but the geographical seats of class articulation remain the priority for analysis.'

Our argument, then, is that it is now possible to appreciate the concept and condition of passive revolution as a lateral field of causality to the structuring condition of uneven and combined development. This means that the concrete consideration of instances of passive revolution brings forth an engagement with state and subaltern class forces as agents that have been crucial in the making of modern states and transitions to capitalism. The concept of passive revolution offers a mode of theorising *both* the inner dynamics of capitalist modernity within states across space and time *and* how these processes of developmental catch-up are internally related to the geopolitical pressures of the states system. Passive revolutions are therefore a working through of pre-established sovereignties that may both transform (revolution) and sustain (restoration) the change-inducing strains brought about by a transformation in social property relations. Hence we can:

propose the category of passive revolution as an equivalent political form to a production process that privileged suborning what was useful at hand to serve capital's pursuit of surplus value and along the way produce continuing economic unevenness [that] modern nation-states were pledged to eliminate. (Harootunian, 2015: 131)

The challenge, accordingly, is to appreciate 'processes of passive revolution as *specific* instances of state transition that are internally related through the *general* world-historical conditions of uneven and combined development' (Morton, 2007a: 71, original emphasis).

Conclusion: Passive Revolution as the Political Rule of Capital

Through a critical engagement with theorisations of capitalism based on the emergence of a world market, we have crafted in this chapter our definition of capitalism as a mode of production based on the private ownership of the means of production and wage labour. While we draw extensively on Robert Brenner's and Ellen Meiksins Wood's work on social property relations in this respect, in response to the charge of Eurocentrism we acknowledge that the emergence and outward expansion of capitalism along uneven and combined developmental lines needs to be understood as conditioned by the inneraction with 'the international'. It cannot be explained by solely referring to internal developments within England and the Low Countries. Moreover, we engage with the criticism of existing conceptualisations of uneven and combined development for having been reluctant to deliver concrete accounts of the changing dynamics of developmental unevenness across space and time. For that reason the chronotype of passive revolution – a category functioning across space and time – has been presented in this chapter as a concept and condition that has an affinity with the theory of uneven and combined development but without the erasure of agency. Said otherwise, uneven and combined development and passive revolution are affinal concepts addressing the conditioning situation of how capitalist development unfolds and how class struggles between state and subaltern agents have produced and transformed space across time throughout variegated cycles of revolution and restoration. Passive revolution therefore provides a lateral field of causality or way of working through the internal dialectical relation between inherited processes of state formation and those ensuing class struggles that result from transformations in social property relations. How the force of capital – through its uneven and combined expansion on a world scale – comes to change the meaning of the production of space and place through variegated passive revolutions is therefore significant in attempting to address the different functions of capitalist space across time (Morton, 2017b). Instantiations of passive revolution are not part of a transhistorical universalisation but are, rather, part of a historically specific set of processes that exist within particular and local conditions. For that reason, this chapter has underscored the multilinear dialectic of uneven and combined development and the passive revolutionary road to modernity as internally related aspects of the same whole. The particularities of the form of appearance of passive revolution in producing and transforming space within local conditions, as part of the generalising essential form of passive revolutions marking state formation processes within uneven and combined developmental circumstances, are therefore significant internally related aspects of capital's entrance into modernity. As Gramsci (2007: 357, Q8§210) stated, writing in 1932, 'the whole of historical materialism is a response to this question', namely, 'whether the processes of nature and history are invariably "evolutionary" or could also include "leaps"'. Passive revolution is therefore the essential form of this expression of historical geographical restructuring that illuminates the spatial and temporal practices of state and class agents. Having dealt with the emergence of capitalism within a prior existing interstate system in this chapter, we now turn to the question of how we can conceptualise this inneraction between global capitalism and the geopolitics of the interstate system.

5   The Geopolitics of Global Capitalism

The role of the state in the global political economy or the relationship between the interstate system and globalisation has been the focus of scholarly debate for some time. Within mainstream international relations (IR) and international political economy (IPE) theories, however, these discussions have run out of steam. On one hand, neorealists such as Waltz (2000) and state-centric comparative political economists (Hirst and Thompson, 1999; Weiss, 1998) argue that globalisation mainly implies an increase in cross-border flows and, therefore, does not change fundamentally the interstate system. On the other hand, so-called hyperglobalists make the point that globalisation has drastically changed the international system with non-state actors, especially transnational corporations (TNCs), increasingly taking over core functions traditionally carried out by states (Strange, 1996). In turn, states become mere conduits, adjusting national economies to the requirements of global capital, to wither away as increasingly powerless actors (Ohmae, 1990, 1995) or to become restructured as competition states within the global economy, as transformationalists and others argue (Cerny, 2010; Held et al., 1999). The main bone of contention between these understandings is then whether and to what extent the state has lost authority vis-à-vis non-state actors in the global economy. Posing the question strictly in these terms, though, fails to comprehend the historical specificity of capitalism and the related consequences for the relationship between the interstate system and global capitalism, as it takes the separation between the economic and the political as a starting point of investigation.

As argued in Chapter 1, it is through the philosophy of internal relations that we can comprehend the historical specificity of capitalist social relations and the way this results in the apparent separation of 'state' and 'market', the 'political' and the 'economic'. The philosophy of internal relations implies that the character of capital is considered a social relation in such a way that the internal ties between the means of production, those who own them and those who work them, as well as the realisation of value within historically specific conditions, are all understood as

107

relations internal to each other (Ollman, 1976: 47; see also Bieler and Morton, 2008: 116–17). Hence, the apparent separation of the political and the economic arises precisely as a result of the process of reification and the alienation of labour under capitalism and the way production is organised around wage labour and the private ownership of the means of production. The purpose of this chapter is to construct a historical materialist perspective on the conceptualisation of capitalist and geopolitical dynamics. This assists the endeavour to understand the internalisation of the state within the fabric of capitalist modernity, or how the changing logics of capital are subsumed within the state (Teschke and Lacher, 2007: 578). In turn, this approach paves the way for the empirical analysis of the Iraq War undertaken in Chapter 8. In outlining the interdependence of the interstate system and capital accumulation, Christopher Chase-Dunn highlights three pertinent points for a historical materialist understanding of geopolitics and capitalism. First, the reproduction and expansion of the interstate system in Europe *required* the institutional forms and dynamic processes of capitalist accumulation. Second, the persistence of the interstate system is important for the continued viability of capitalism. Third, the dynamic of uneven development undercuts the possibility for global state formation, thus reproducing the interstate system (Chase-Dunn, 1989: 141–2, 147). These comments are crucial pointers to grasping the historical relationship between the interstate system and capitalism, as well as contemporary debates on the geopolitics of global capitalism that come to the fore in what follows.

The next main section discusses the question of state-centrism within historical materialist accounts of capitalist geopolitics and investigates in what way these accounts fall short in their conceptualisation of more recent changes in uneven and combined developmental logics of geopolitics and the interstate system. The subsequent section then proceeds with a critical engagement with the transnational state debate as a prelude to proposing an alternative historical materialist approach based on an appreciation of the *internal relation* of the interstate system and global capitalism. This is where we draw explicitly from the work of Nicos Poulantzas in order to theorise the inneraction between global capitalism and the multiple political authorities of the interstate system. Receiving renewed attention in recent years (see e.g. Bieler and Morton, 2003; Bruff, 2012; Hirsch and Kannankulam, 2011; Panitch, 1994), our argument is that Poulantzas offers fresh insight on the internalisation, or induced reproduction, of transnational capitalist class interests within different forms of state linked to the extension of global capitalism.

A Historical Materialist Convergence towards State-centrism

Alex Callinicos and the Sword of Leviathan in Shaping Capitalism

Commencing with his analysis of bourgeois revolutions and the emergence of capitalism as a mode of production (Callinicos, 1989), Alex Callinicos has in more recent years proffered an alternative approach to understanding state power and capital accumulation. His way forward is to think in terms of 'two logics of power, capitalistic and territorial, or two forms of competition, economic and geopolitical' (Callinicos, 2009: 74). He suggests to introduce, in line with Marx's own methodology, a new determination in a non-deductive way. Thus, 'the state system is treated as a dimension of the capitalist mode of production' (Callinicos, 2009: 83). In his focus on the classical bourgeois revolutions in England and France, as well as those 'revolutions from above', as in Germany, or passive revolutions, in Italy and Japan, where the central features of capitalism are brought about by the state, Callinicos is attentive to these two distinct, but related logics or registers, that is the interplay of both socio-economic and political transformation embedded in the 'transitional forms' of pathways to capitalism (Callinicos, 1989: 135–6). These two distinct but related registers then come to the fore in his more recent theorising about how capitalism is present geopolitically in rivalries between states, or what he terms the role of 'the sword of Leviathan' in shaping capitalism (Callinicos, 2003a, 2009). He states that 'the present system embraces geopolitics as well as economics, and that the competitive processes that threaten such destructive consequences involve not merely the economic struggle for markets, but military and diplomatic rivalries among states' (Callinicos, 2003a: 50). Here the 'logic of capital', based on exploitation and competitive accumulation, 'embraces the geopolitical rivalries among states', so that military power is embedded in the same logic. Any analysis of geopolitics and the states system has, thus, to source itself within the contradictions of capitalism. 'Capitalist competition takes the form not merely of economic rivalries between firms but also of geopolitical conflicts among states' (Callinicos, 2003a: 64, 66).

The tendency of uneven and combined development is considered a fundamental dynamic behind the maintenance of the system of territorial states. In the historical development of capitalism, high productivity complexes developed as a result of the way competition compelled capitals at the cutting edge of new technology and products to constantly innovate in order to stay ahead of competitors. Hence, Callinicos concludes:

The tendency of capitalist development to generate spatially concentrated economic complexes creates very powerful centrifugal forces that would strongly work to sustain the political demarcation of the world into territorial states. Capitalists in such a complex would have an interest in preserving the existing state to which they had privileged access; equally state managers would be reluctant to surrender the control they currently exercised over the resources of this complex. (Callinicos, 2009: 91)

In other words, the international states system is 'a necessary concomitant of the capitalist mode of production' (Callinicos, 2009: 88). Hence, Callinicos analyses the forms in which geopolitical and economic competition have become interwoven in modern capitalism without collapsing these analytically distinct dimensions into one another. 'I see economic and geopolitical competition as two forms – each with their own distinct and changing structure – of the more general logic of capitalist competition, forms that may mutually reinforce each other, but can also come into conflict' (Callinicos, 2003b: 146 n.19).[1] Overall, then, Callinicos considers 'two logics of power, capitalistic and territorial, or two forms of competition, economic and geopolitical' with the states system treated as a dimension of the capitalist mode of production, within a nondeterministic framework (Callinicos, 2009: 74, 83).

While clearly a significant engagement with the problematic of how to conceptualise the interplay between global capitalist and geopolitical dynamics, Callinicos' assessment does not go beyond the external relations between these two sets of dynamics. Thus, there is a hypostatisation of the two logics of capitalism and geopolitics in this account of imperialism, which are conceived as always-already analytically separate elements that are *then* subsequently combined.[2] The assessment of the

---

[1] In tracing the historical geography of uneven development, David Harvey (2003b: 30) has similarly mapped 'two distinctive but intertwined logics of power', namely a territorial logic of state power and a capitalist logic seeking spatio-temporal fixes for accumulation. For critical engagements, see the symposium in *Historical Materialism* edited by Ashman (2006), as well as the contribution of Lee, Wainwright and Glassman (2017).

[2] In *Deciphering Capital*, Callinicos conceptually asserts the relationality of capital, which pivots on a double relation of 1) the separation of workers from the means of production, giving rise to the exploitation of wage labour by capital, and 2) the dynamic, competitive struggle among capitals themselves (Callinicos, 2014: 17–18, 296–7, 321). But the threads of this inner connection are cut loose when it comes to assessing how these conditions of capital have relationality with the plurality of the states system. At best, the offering is that the underlying concepts have to be recast to take into account the movements of capital with the *interactions* of the states system but without delivering on this recasting (Callinicos, 2014: 323). At worst, the separation of this interaction is reinforced when stating that competition at the global level has 'continued to take economic as well as geopolitical forms' (Callinicos, 2014: 290). Relationality is conceptually asserted but unrealised, resulting in a collapse into the always-already separate and combined realms of the 'economic' and the 'geopolitical'.

peculiarities of U.S. imperialism enforces this view of separation by high-lighting: 1) the historical ability of the United States to establish hege-mony over the Americas through military dominance; 2) the role played by the structure of American capitalism based on the vertical organisation of TNCs; 3) the fact that this was supported in the post-1945 period by running a large balance of payments surplus, allowing the United States to export capital on a vast scale; and 4) that this was backed up by military supremacy evidenced by a permanent arms economy (Callinicos, 2003b: 16–18). The steps in this argument follow the beat of two separate, syncopated, rather than synchronous, rhythms: military, economic, eco-nomic, military. When assessing contemporary inter-imperialist rivalries, the summary is that 'the major capitalist states are bound together in relations and institutions that involve a complex and constantly shifting balance between cooperation and competition' (Callinicos, 2003b: 126). Elsewhere, evaluating the role of the United States, Callinicos writes that 'the U.S. remains by comparison with any other power, well ahead in both economic and military capabilities' (Callinicos, 2009: 225). A neorealist would not express it differently and it is not surprising that Callinicos argues himself that 'there is, necessarily, a realist moment in any Marxist analysis of international relations and conjunctures: in other words, any such analysis must take into account the strategies, calculations and interactions of rival political elites in the state system' (Callinicos, 2010: 21). As Gonzalo Pozo-Martin (2006: 236, 238) has highlighted, after departing from mainstream neorealist analyses, Marxism seems to be returning to a neorealist 'moment' and its dubious virtues in separating out territorialist and capitalist logics. Ray Kiely (2012: 237) extends this point about neorealism further by stating that Callinicos 'replicates that particular theory's weaknesses, as he replaces realism's ahistorical logic of international anarchy with an over-generalised account of geopolitical competition'. This book, in contrast, makes the case for a necessarily historical materialist moment of dialectics to consider the geopolitics of global capitalism.

Open Marxism: Global Capital and the Persistence of State-centrism

Elsewhere, Open Marxists explain the historical specificity of capitalism through an analysis of the underlying social relations of production. In a capitalist productive system based on wage labour and the private ownership of the means of production, the extraction of surplus value is not directly politically enforced, but the result of indirect economic pressures. 'The worker is not directly subject physically to the capitalist[;] his subjection is mediated through the sale of his labour power as a commodity on the market' (Holloway and Picciotto, 1977: 79). The 'economic' and the 'political' therefore appear as distinct, particularised forms of domination in abstraction from capitalist relations of production. In short, the emphasis on an analysis of the social relations of production – that we fully share – allows one to understand the state and the market as two different forms or expressions of capitalist relations and thus a particular historical form of class struggle. It also enables one to understand capitalism as a historical phenomenon and directs analysis towards an investigation of the internal relationship between the political and the economic. This includes, for example, an analysis of the role of the state and how, while appearing separate from the market, it ensures capitalism through a guarantee of the institution of private property (Burnham, 1995: 145). For Open Marxism, a crucial consequence of the separation of the 'economic' and the 'political' is the obscuring of the social class antagonism between capital and labour and the related class struggle. 'Class struggle is ... the daily resistance of the labouring class to the imposition of work – a permanent feature of human society above primitive levels' (Burnham, 1994: 225). Therefore, the historical process of class struggle in and against exploitation between capital and labour is key to the particular social form of the capitalist state. Class antagonism is thus regarded as a primary social relationship within which structures are instantiated and internally related to struggle (Bonefeld, 1992: 113–14). Class struggle is by definition also seen as open-ended, which promotes enquiry beyond the economic determinism of base/superstructure explanations (Burnham, 1994: 225). In sum, class struggle has 'to be brought back in to allow for a proper critical reassessment of the form of the state, its social constitution, role and purpose' (Bonefeld, 2008: 64).

However, when relating this understanding of the internal relationship between the 'political' and the 'economic', 'state' and 'market', and the role of class struggle in shaping these particular social forms to recent developments in the global political economy, Open Marxists exhibit a similar state-centrism to Callinicos. While the character of the accumulation of capital and, thus, class struggle is considered global in substance (Holloway, 1994: 30), the conditions of exploitation are standardised at the national political level. The form of class struggle at the global level is, therefore, the interaction of states, which 'are interlocked internationally into a hierarchy of price systems' (Burnham, 1995: 148). For example, Holloway (1994: 34) argues that 'the competitive struggle between states is ... to attract and/or retain a share of world capital (and hence a share of global surplus value).' Similarly, according to Peter Burnham (1995: 149):

[T]he dilemma facing national states is that, whilst participation in multilateral trade rounds and financial summits is necessary to enhance the accumulation of capital on the global level, such participation is also a potential source of disadvantage which can seriously undermine a particular national state's economic strategy. The history of the modern international system is the history of the playing out of this tension.

Thus, this tension is presupposed to be a competitive struggle between states, and state rivalry is, therefore, the expression of class struggle at the international level. As Burnham classically put it, 'growing competition among the bourgeoisie indicates that conflict and collaboration is the norm in the global system and is manifested in national terms as a struggle between states' (Burnham, 1998: 196). There is present here, again, a neorealist moment within a Marxist perspective that valorises a focus on states competing with each other for military and economic resources.

This state-centrism is then also reflected in empirical analyses by Open Marxists.[3] Notably Burnham has focused on the political economy of post–World War II reconstruction to argue that Britain did not simply submit to U.S. hegemony. Rather, in relation to the Korean War, 'the British decision to rearm was not an example of the UK bowing to American pressure, but was a decision taken by the government to show the United States that Britain had attained independent economic status in Western Europe and would not be treated as just another necessitous European nation' (Burnham, 1990: 12). While interesting as such, this is not a class analysis, but reverts to the state-centrism so characteristic of mainstream IR. More recently, various contributors have also been assessing forms of depoliticisation within British economic policymaking through a focus on the role of state managers in removing core aspects of economic policy from the discretionary control of the state.[4] But the central thread defining such analysis of processes of depoliticisation is the displacement of a concern with class relations by a preoccupation with state managers' perceptions and preferences: the focus is exclusively on the state management of governing strategies.

In addition, Werner Bonefeld has argued that the emergence of the international states system and capitalism have been part of the same process. For example, he states that 'both, the establishment of the national state and the world market, were products of the same social struggles that revolutionised feudal social relations' (Bonefeld, 2008: 67).

---

[3] Significant additional lines of criticism and points of engagement are raised in Bieler, Bruff and Morton (2010), Bieler and Morton (2003), Bruff (2009) and Tsolakis (2010).
[4] See Burnham (2003), Kettell (2004), Rogers (2009, 2013), Sutton (2015) and, with a partial but inadequate response to criticisms, also Dönmez and Sutton (2016).

In other words, both states and markets are considered logical complementary parts of capitalism, one requiring the other. As Ian Bruff (2009: 340) remarks, this assumption rests on two highly questionable positions: 'that capitalist social relations and the world system of national states emerged contemporaneously and in a complementary manner'. Nevertheless, not all state forms have been historically constituted as a moment of the capital relation. As discussed in Chapter 4, Benno Teschke makes a clear case that the international states system of absolutist states existed *before* the emergence and spread of capitalism. 'Plural state formation, creating the distinction between the domestic and the international, and capitalism, creating the distinction between the political and the economic, were not geographically and temporally co-constitutive. Multiple state formation came first' (Teschke, 2003: 74; see also Lacher, 2006). Although more recent attempts have been made to move beyond methodological nationalism, the focus on the uneven development of globally determined forms fails to address the plural constitution of state formation prior to capitalist development (see Charnock and Starosta, 2016; Fitzsimons and Starosta, 2017). This means that there is a shortcoming in Open Marxist work to develop a theory of 'the international', or how the prior existence of territorial states and the presence of a system of states shaped the subsequent geopolitical unfolding of capitalism.

Moreover, the preceding historical materialist analyses by Callinicos and the Open Marxists all overlook the processes related to global restructuring since the early 1970s. As Robinson has noted, 'globalisation represents an epochal shift; that is, fundamental worldwide changes in social structure that modify and even transform the very functioning of the system in which we live' (Robinson, 2004: 4). Especially noticeable here are the restructuring processes related to the transnationalisation of production and finance. Large parts of global production have increasingly been organised across borders. Outflows of foreign direct investment (FDI) rose from $88 billion USD in 1986 to $1,187 billion in 2000 as peak year (Bieler, 2006: 50). A period of recession led to a decline in FDI flows from 2001 to 2003, but four years of consecutive growth led to a new all-time high of FDI outflows of $1,996.5 billion in 2007 (UNCTAD, 2008: 253). Overall, there were 78,817 TNCs with 794,894 foreign affiliates in 2007 (UNCTAD, 2008: 212). Unsurprisingly, FDI flows have again declined since the onset of the global financial crisis in 2008, but even slightly lower levels contribute to the continuing build-up of FDI stocks over time, indicating the ever more important role played by TNCs. While outward FDI stocks had been $2,091,496 million in 1990 (UNCTAD, 2013: 217), they were

$7,460,522 million in 2000 and $26,159,708 million in 2016 (UNCTAD, 2017: 226). Robinson (2008: 30) additionally highlights as empirical indicators of the increasing organisation of production across borders 'the phenomenal increase in cross-border mergers and acquisitions; the increasing transnational interlocking of boards of directorates; the increasingly transnational ownership of capital shares; the spread of cross-border strategic alliances of all sorts; and the increasing salience of transnational peak business associations'. The implications of these figures have been contested. Drawing on the same data, Paul Hirst and Grahame Thompson (1999) assert that despite an increase in financial flows across borders, states are still in charge of the global economy and we should speak of internationalisation instead of globalisation.[5] Nevertheless, they overlook the qualitative implications of this increase in FDI. Unlike portfolio investment, for example, FDI through the acquisition of production facilities, to be integrated with production facilities in other countries, has a more long-lasting effect in that it reorganises the way production is structured. In other words, FDI should not simply be mistaken for financial flows across borders. Rather, it is a key indicator for production structures being integrated at the transnational level.

Importantly, the increasing transnationalisation of production, which implies a 'centralisation of command and control of the global economy in transnational capital' (Robinson, 2004: 15), has gone hand in hand with greater decentralisation and fragmentation of the production process itself through processes of outsourcing along the value chain. Thus, transnational production is increasingly organised in global commodity chains also referred to as global value chains (GVCs) (Robinson, 2008: 27). Tightly controlled by TNCs, we can distinguish buyer-driven GVCs such as those producing goods for Walmart stores and producer-driven GVCs as, for example, the value chain underpinning the production of Apple products (see Gereffi, Humphrey and Sturgeon, 2005). Accordingly, Martin Hart-Landsberg identifies contract manufacturing, part of GVCs, as a new phenomenon in the transnationalisation of production. In this process, TNCs 'began dividing the production process into ever finer segments, both vertical and horizontal, and locating the separate stages in two or more countries, creating cross-border production networks' (Hart-Landsberg, 2013: 91). In these networks, TNCs no longer own the various production sites along the GVC, but rely on

---

[5] For the expression of similar criticisms of FDI as an indicator of transnationalisation, see Anievas (2008: 196–7) and Weiss (1998); for a response to Hirst and Thompson as well as to Weiss, see Bieler (2006: 50–4).

'independent contract manufacturers to procure the necessary parts and components and oversee their assembly into final products' (Hart-Landsberg, 2013: 92). In other words, TNCs still superintend the process but their strategy has significantly changed. From owning cross-border production structures, they have moved to co-ordinating GVCs. As confirmed by the UN, 'TNC-coordinated [GVCs] account for some 80 per cent of global trade. Patterns of value added trade in [GVCs] are shaped to a significant extent by the investment decisions of TNCs' (UNCTAD, 2013: xxii). In general, these developments highlight again the increasing transnationalisation of production and the rising importance of TNCs in the global political economy. 'To the extent that participating firms are not themselves transnational, it means that TNC dominance over international economic activity is greater than previously stated. And to the extent that these firms are themselves transnational, it means that contemporary capitalist accumulation dynamics have given rise to a hierarchically structured, interlocking system of TNCs' (Hart-Landsberg, 2013: 20).

Hence, class struggle does not take place only between capital and labour at the national level but also between national and transnational class fractions. Core industries have spread their production networks across a range of developed and developing countries. The surplus value extracted is not automatically allocated within the territory of one particular state. While capital as such has become more centralised, production processes themselves are increasingly fragmented. In other words, the new landscape of capitalist accumulation does not reflect any longer a situation in which concentrated economic complexes are located within one specific country or even region (Callinicos, 2009: 91). Alex Callinicos' (2009: 203) conclusion, that 'the idea, then, that capital has broken free of its geographical moorings remains a myth', is an inadequate and rather outdated reflection on global capitalist development. Burnham's (1998: 197) assertion that 'the proletariat conducts its daily struggle in local-cum-national settings' but not beyond is no longer valid in a growing context of transnational solidarity. The specific characteristics of global capital and labour have changed and it is not enough to assess these simply as 'the recomposition of labour/capital relations expressed as the restructuring of relations of conflict and collaboration between national states' (Bonefeld, Brown and Burnham, 1995: 31). The most serious historical materialist challenge to understanding global capitalism has therefore come in the form of a periodisation that asserts a focus on the emergence of a transnational state form. The next section now looks in more detail at transnational state theorising, its periodisation of capitalism and how it accounts for the geopolitical structure of capitalist space and its fragmentation into a polity of states.

Confronting the Transnational State

Drawing on the work of Antonio Gramsci, among others, a different set of historical materialist approaches has emerged over the past four decades (see Bieler and Morton, 2004; Morton, 2007a). Highlighting changes in the production structure since the early 1970s, Robert Cox (1981: 147) concluded early on that 'it becomes increasingly pertinent to think in terms of a global class structure alongside or superimposed upon national class structures.' Social class forces are identified as key collective actors through an investigation of the production process. 'If we want to gain an understanding of the class structure of a particular society at a particular moment in history, we would do well to start with an analysis of the economy and the social production relations that prevail' (Robinson, 2004: 38). Importantly, as a result of transnational restructuring 'a new class fractionation, or axis, is occurring between national and transnational fractions of classes' (Robinson, 2004: 37) and 'transnational capital has become the dominant, or hegemonic, fraction of capital on a world scale' (Robinson, 2004: 21). Hence, through this focus on social class forces as the main agents engendered by the relations of production, it is possible to incorporate recent changes in the global political economy within a historical understanding of capitalism.

Nevertheless, William Robinson has established a unique position within historical materialist debates on globalisation. According to Robinson, globalisation as a new epoch within capitalism is characterised by four factors: 1) a new global production and financial system; 2) the rise of the transnational capitalist class (TCC); 3) the emergence of the transnational state (TNS); and 4) new relations of inequality not along geographical lines, but consisting of transnational social and class inequalities (Robinson, 2014: 2). While we agree with his understanding of the transnational restructuring of production and finance and the related emergence of the TCC as the dominant capital fraction, we disagree with his identification of the emergence of a TNS, regarded as a guarantor of capital accumulation at the global level, in transcending the pitfalls of neorealist analysis of global capitalism (see Robinson, 2003, 2004, 2007a, 2008).[6] As Robinson puts it, 'the TNS does not

---

[6] This focus is different from a theory of world state formation given that arguments on the subject enforce a 'two logics' approach – with the 'logic of anarchy' bracketed from the 'logic of capital' – in proposing the inevitability of a global Weberian state (see Wendt, 2003).

attempt to control territory per se but rather to secure the conditions that allow capital to freely accumulate in and across all territories' (Robinson, 2014: 68). The singular feature of this 'global capitalism' thesis, then, is the bold argument that 'in the emerging global capitalist configuration, transnational or global space is coming to supplant national space', with the attendant view that the nation state as an axis of world development is becoming superseded by transnational structures, leading to the emergence of a TNS (Robinson, 2001a: 532, 2003: 19–20, 2008: 6–7, 2011: 742). Thus, the nation state is no longer regarded as a 'container' for the processes of capital accumulation, class formation or development (Robinson, 2001a: 533, 2004: 89). In its stead is the constitution of a TNS defined as 'a particular constellation of class forces and relations bound up with capitalist globalisation and the rise of a transnational capitalist class, embodied in a diverse set of political institutions' (Robinson, 2003: 43, 2004: 99). Or, as the argument goes, 'a loose network comprised of inter- and supranational political and economic institutions *together with* national state apparatuses that have been penetrated and transformed by transnational forces' is emerging without acquiring a centralised form (Robinson, 2008: 34, original emphasis). In sum, it is argued that a key feature of the epoch of globalisation is not only the transformation of the state but its *supersession* as an organising principle of capitalism by a TNS apparatus. With reference to capitalism and its relation to the multiple states system, Robinson concludes that 'if capitalism's earlier development resulted in a geographical (spatial) location in the creation of the nation-state system, then its current globalising thrust is resulting in a general geographical dislocation' (Robinson, 2004: 98).

One of the central problems with the theory of global capitalism and the TNS thesis is that states are rather uncritically endorsed as transmission belts, or 'filtering devices', of proactive instruments in advancing the agenda of global capitalism (Robinson, 2003: 45–6). Stated directly, 'national states remain important, but they become transmission belts and local executers of the transnational elite project' (Robinson, 2003: 62). In other words, Robinson's view is that 'the inter-state system is no longer the fundamental organising principle of world capitalism and the principal institutional framework that shapes global social forces or that explains world political dynamics' (Robinson, 2011: 742). States do not disappear in this process of adjustment. 'Rather, power as the ability to issue commands and have them obeyed, or more precisely, the ability to shape social structures, shifts from social groups and classes with interests in national accumulation to those whose interests lie in the new global circuits of accumulation' (Robinson, 2004: 109). This process is regarded as one enforced by the disciplinary power of global capitalism (Robinson, 2004: 50). In other words, states may retain their institutional form, but they lose their traditional function of securing the conditions for successful capital accumulation. They 'are no longer the point of "condensation" of sets of social relations within a country. They are no longer nodal points for organising those relations with regard to another set of relations between the country and an international system of nation-states' (Robinson, 2004: 143). By way of example, one can take the so-called transitions to democracy, here understood as the promotion of polyarchy, referring to 'a system in which a small group actually rules and mass participation in decision-making is consigned to leadership choice in elections carefully managed by competing elites' (Robinson, 1996: 49). Transitions to 'polyarchy', in this argument, are therefore characteristic of states acting as transmission belts of capitalist globalisation. The problem here is that such broad claims neglect the differentiated outcome of specific class struggles within forms of state through which the restructuring of capital and socio-spatial relations are produced. The straight diffusion, or imposition, of transnational capital and polyarchic political structures needs to be considered much more critically in relation to struggles over the restoration and contestation of class power in specific forms of state (see Burron, 2012; Morton, 2011/2013). At the centre of the argument of the state as transmission belt is also a disaggregation of politics and economics so that 'class relations (and by implication, struggle) are viewed as external to the process of [global] restructuring, and labour and the state itself are depicted as powerless' (Burnham, 2000: 14). This leads to the identification of external linkages between the state and globalisation while the social production of globalisation within and by social classes in specific forms of state is omitted (Bieler et al., 2006: 177–8).

A further problem of the TNS thesis is that national restructuring during times of globalisation is generally conceptualised as a uniform process, integrating all states in the same way into the global political economy. 'The TNS thesis therefore offers a flattened ontology that removes state forms as a significant spatial scale in the articulation of capitalism, levels out the spatial and territorial logics of capital accumulation, and elides the class struggles extant in specific locations' (Morton, 2007a: 148). The point is not to take the dominance of one spatial scale over another as a given but to appreciate the manner in which capitalism operates through nodal rather than dominant points. This means appreciating states as political nodes in the global flow of capital, while eschewing claims that the global system can be reduced to a struggle between states (Bieler et al., 2006: 162, 191). The TNS thesis, however, assumes the unitary effect of capitalism, involving worldwide progression towards and diffusion of the presence of a TNS. Stated most clearly, by Robinson, the 'particular spatial form of the uneven development of capitalism is being *overcome* by the globalisation of capital and markets and the *gradual equalisation of accumulation* conditions this involves' (Robinson, 2004: 99, 2007a: 82, emphasis added). Behind this view of the gradual equalisation of accumulation conditions lies the core weakness at the heart of the TNS thesis. It is one that fails to keep in tension the contradictory tendencies of *both* differentiation entrained within state territoriality *and* simultaneous equalisation through the conditions of production induced by global capital. As Neil Smith (1984/2008: 122, original emphasis) elaborates:

Space is neither levelled out of existence nor infinitely differentiated. Rather, the pattern is one of *uneven development*, not in a general sense but as the specific product of the contradictory dynamic guiding the production of space. Uneven development is the concrete manifestation of the production of space under capitalism.

Whether it is the absolute space of state territoriality, or the partitioning of private property, 'capital does not succeed in eliminating absolute space altogether' (Smith, 1984/2008: 122). As Alexander Anievas (2008: 197, 199–203) asserts, 'there remains a continuation, if not acceleration, of the hierarchies of uneven development immanent to the capitalist mode of production. This persistent developmental tendency of capitalism acts as a centrifugal force against the emergence of the type of global capital postulated by Robinson.' Equally, as Fred Block (2001) indicated early on, Robinson underestimates the difficulties for transnational capital to achieve class unity, while Philip McMichael (2001) importantly pointed out that globalisation is always contested and constantly reformulated. Thus the spatial form of the state has a basis rooted within a given territoriality that is differentiated by the condition of uneven development while subjected to the levelling of such differences through the universalising tendency of capital and the equalisation of production. To concur with Paul Cammack (2007: 12), the phantom of the TNS is thus an unnecessary theoretical construct.[7]

To be fair, Robinson does not argue that uneven development is no longer important. For example, he outlines how in developing countries,

---

[7] It is noteworthy that a recent restatement of the TNS thesis contends that 'breaking with nation-centric analysis does not mean abandoning analysis of national-level processes and phenomena or inter-state dynamics. It does mean that we view transnational capitalism as the world-historic content in which these play themselves out' (Robinson, 2015: 17). But observe in this passage how the TNS is absent from the commentary, reinforcing its status as an unnecessary theoretical construct.

'glittering malls replete with the latest the global economy has to offer, fast-food chains, beckoning recreational centres and well-guarded residential neighbourhoods that would be the envy of any first world centre stick out as lagoons of wealth and privilege surrounded by oceans of poverty and mass misery, often divided only, and literally, by the very best security systems that social control and technology can buy' (Robinson, 2001b: 558). In fact, Robinson argues that uneven development occurs within and across states in increasingly transnationalised capitalist social relations of production. The problem, however, is that he delinks uneven development from the interstate system, or a geographical understanding, and instead attaches analysis to different social groups. In Robinson's (2001b: 558) words:

There is no theoretical reason to posit any necessary affinity between continued uneven development and the nation-state as the particular territorial expression of uneven development. The concepts of centre and periphery (uneven and combined accumulation), of development and underdevelopment, may be reconceived in terms of global social groups and not nations in which core-periphery designates social position rather than geographic location.

In other words, the fact that uneven development was linked to inequality between nation states was the result of how capitalism had initially developed historically. Conceptually, therefore, 'differentiation and equalisation as spatial phenomena are a social relation whose particular territorial or geographic expression is historical, contingent, and not predetermined to be international' (Robinson, 2014: 116). Thus, he accepts that capitalist accumulation is characterised by uneven development. 'This movement of values through space or the appropriation of surplus by some social groups may be immanent to capitalism, but what is not is that this space is by definition national space' (Robinson, 2014: 113). For Robinson, within globalisation, uneven development is reflected in inequalities between classes along transnational lines.

However, as noted in Chapter 4 on the emergence of capitalist social relations of production, capitalism was born into an anterior international system of state territoriality. The overriding problem in Robinson's global capitalism thesis is the absence of an adequate historical theory of capitalism and its unfolding through conditions of uneven and combined development that prevents a realisation of how global capital is (re)produced through the spatial scale of state power and how multiscalar relations are inherent to capitalism. For example, he explicitly argues that 'the nation-state, or inter-state system ... is an historical outcome, the particular form in which capitalism came into being based on a complex relation between production, classes, political power and territoriality' (Robinson, 2007a: 82). Akin to Open Marxists, as discussed in the previous section, this position is culpable in treating the relation between state and capital as 'immanent' by assuming the parallel development of capital and the territorial state. The result is a non-history of capitalism that misses the point that capitalism was born into a prior system of territorial states, or that the territorial state system has non-capitalist origins (Wood, 1997: 552, 2007: 155–7).[8] Nowhere is this more evident than in the global capitalism account of the onset of capitalist development, which shares the position of world systems analysis on the emergence of a world market and its expansion over the past 500 years (Robinson, 2011: 725; Wallerstein, 1974a: 36, 1979: 15, 159), correctly dismissed in our view for its submission to a transhistorical (or pan-capitalist) description of the commercialisation of trade (Brenner, 1977: 39). As a consequence, the point is overlooked that state power often plays a major role in offsetting crisis conditions in the accumulation of capital by providing a temporary 'spatial fix' for surplus value extraction (Harvey, 1985: 324–31). As Ellen Wood (2002a: 180, 2007: 156) surveys, '"global" capital ... will continue to profit from uneven development, the differentiation of social conditions among national economies.' In sum, the TNS thesis is unsuccessful in avoiding a non-history of capitalism and a unilinear trope about the state's demise, again peculiarly reminiscent of mainstream IR preoccupations about state capacity (see Brenner, 1997: 274–5; Evans, 1997: 62–98; McMichael, 2001: 203–5).

To elude this pitfall, it is important to reiterate that historically there was no necessary link between capitalism and a state system of multiple political entities at the onset of capitalist social property relations. As Joachim Hirsch and John Kannankulam (2011: 21) assert along this line, 'capitalism did not cause the territorially fragmented system of states to come into being, but it does not follow that this system is not necessary for the reproduction of capitalism.' Affirming the continuity of the inter-state system does not imply that changes and transformations in the

---

[8] We are in accord with Ellen Meiksins Wood's account of capitalism, marked by a specific set of social property relations and the ongoing importance of the state and the interstate system within global capitalism, so that 'the empire of capital depends upon a system of multiple states' (Wood, 2003: 14). As she elaborates, 'a military doctrine, then, has been evolving in the U.S. to deal with the contradictions of global capitalism. Its first premise is that the U.S. must have such a degree of military supremacy that no other state or combination of states, friend or foe, will be tempted to contest or equal it. The purpose of this strategy is not simply to deter attack but above all to ensure that no other state will aspire to global or even regional dominance' (Wood, 2003: 159). However, by contrast, our focus on the philosophy of internal relations ensures that we do not succumb to a state-centric narrative when analysing the global role of U.S. military force, as Chapter 8 corroborates.

geopolitical system of multiple states are not possible. New states have emerged during the history of capitalism; others have disappeared. 'As a result of the contradictions and conflicts that are inherent in the capitalist mode of societalisation, the concrete configuration of the state system changes constantly' (Hirsch and Kannankulam, 2011: 23). One need only think of the break-up of former Yugoslavia and the Soviet Union, or the formation of the republics of North Sudan and South Sudan in recent history. 'But the forces tending to prolong the historic connection between capitalism and the nation-state are very powerful, indeed rooted in the very nature of capitalism' (Wood, 2002c: 29). Hence, the task is not to analyse whether the interstate system has been replaced by a TNS, but to conceptualise the internal relationship between a continuing states system and the changing configuration of global capitalism in relation to the more recent transnationalisation of production processes.

The Internal Relation between the Interstate System and Global Capitalism

As alluded to previously, an alternative way of conceptualising the dynamics of capitalism and geopolitics can be constructed through a historical materialist focus on the philosophy of *internal relations*. Geopolitical relations linked to the states system are interiorised within the conditions of modernity as part of the composition of capital. Put differently, in the modern epoch the geopolitical states system is internally related to capitalist relations of production. In other words, the challenge is to conceptualise the state as a condensation of class forces in a way that emphasises its internal relations with social property relations, with the wider interstate system and with global capitalism.

Such an understanding can be developed by starting with Antonio Gramsci's notion of the integral state, as introduced in Chapter 1. Gramsci viewed the state not simply as an institution limited to the 'government of the functionaries' or the 'top political leaders and personalities with direct governmental responsibilities'. The tendency to concentrate solely on such features – common in much mainstream debate – was pejoratively referred to as 'statolatry': it entailed viewing the state as a perpetual entity limited to actions within political society (Gramsci, 1971: 178, Q13§17; 268, Q8§130). Instead, Gramsci holds that the state presents itself in two different ways through the 'identity-distinction' of *both* political society *and* civil society and not their separation (see Gramsci, 2007: 317, Q8§142; Morton, 2013: 136–43). Beyond the political society of public figures and top leaders, this approach views the state as 'the *entire complex of practical and theoretical activities* with which the ruling class not only justifies and maintains its dominance, but manages to win the active consent of those over whom it rules' (Gramsci, 1971: 244, Q15§10, emphasis added). This additional aspect of the state is referred to as civil society. The realms of political and civil society within modern states are inseparable so that, taken together, they combine to produce a notion of the integral state (Gramsci, 1971: 12, Q12§1; cf. Gramsci, 1994b: 67; Thomas, 2009: 137–41). Hence, the state is understood as the form of a particular condensation of class forces as well as the terrain within which and through which these social class forces struggle to achieve hegemony. It is then through the social relations of production that the internal relations between the 'political' and the 'economic', 'state' and 'market', manifest themselves.

At the same time, Gramsci was a fastidious student of 'the international', the world circumstances of hegemony, and argued that while the 'national' sphere remained the starting point to eliminate class exploitation and private property, capitalism was a world-historical phenomenon within conditions of uneven development (Gramsci, 1977: 69–72). A focus on the 'national' dimension as a point of arrival in understanding processes of capitalist expansion therefore affords analysis of the concrete development of the social relations of production and the relationship between politics and economics which is inscribed in the struggle over hegemony within a state, while remaining aware that 'the perspective is international and cannot be otherwise' because 'particular histories always exist within the frame of world history' (Gramsci, 1971: 240, 14§68; 1985: 181, Q29§2; Ives and Short, 2013; Morton, 2007b: 614–19). As Mark Rupert (1995: 35) has established, 'it is entirely consistent with this perspective to argue that interstate competition and warfare have had historically significant effects on the relation of capital and labour in the sphere of production, as well as upon state–society relations.' The next question is, then, how to combine this emphasis on state theory with a focus on 'the international' and emerging transnational class forces without lapsing into a state-centric account, or a TNS conceptualisation, which are both plagued in their own different ways by a two-logics emphasis on exterior relations between the political and the economic. It is here that we now draw on the work of Nicos Poulantzas in more detail.

Poulantzas' understanding of the state shadows Gramsci's definition of the integral state. Rather than their separation, both political society and civil society are viewed, as Peter Thomas highlights, as a dialectic of identity/distinction (Poulantzas, 1969: 77; Thomas 2009: 97). In the early 1970s, Poulantzas investigated the dynamics of what he identified as a new phase of imperialism since the end of World War II. He did not focus much on the changing relations between countries in the core capitalist spaces and countries in peripheral capitalist spaces, but the relations between states in the former and in particular the way a new imperialist world context was emerging through a rearrangement of the global balance of forces between the United States and an ever more integrated European Union (EU). In his analysis, he rejected explanations of Kautskyite 'ultra-imperialism' for underestimating the continuing inter-imperialist contradictions resulting from uneven development. Equally, he dismissed assessments of the EU as an emerging European supranational state contesting the dominance of U.S. capital (Poulantzas, 1974/2008: 221–2). Instead, he identified new rearrangements in the dominance of U.S. capital – reflected in an increase in FDI, non-portfolio investment, predominantly to locations in Europe, and the increasing centralisation and concentration of capital, as well as the closely related centralisation of U.S. money capital – that ensured the induced reproduction of foreign (international or, in today's parlance, transnational) capital within the various European state forms (Poulantzas, 1974/2008: 228–30). 'It is this induced reproduction of American monopoly capitalism within the other metropoles and its effects on their modes and forms of production (pre-capitalist, competitive capitalist) that characterises the current phase and that equally implies the extended reproduction within them of the political and ideological conditions of the development of American imperialism' (Poulantzas, 1974/2008: 227).

This relates closely to Poulantzas' understanding of the state. He emphasises that 'the basis of the material framework of power and the state has to be sought in the relations of production and social division of labour' (Poulantzas, 1978: 14). Thus, the political field of the state is present in the constitution and reproduction of the social relations of production. 'The position of the state vis-à-vis the economy is never anything but the modality of the state's presence in the constitution and reproduction of the relations of production' (Poulantzas, 1978: 17). Further, class bias is inscribed within the very institutional ensemble of the state as a social relation of production which not only permits a radical critique of liberal ideology but also promotes interest in the class pertinence and practices of the state as a strategic site of struggle (Poulantzas, 1973: 63–4). Social classes do not therefore exist in isolation from, or in some exterior relation to, the state. The state is present in the very constitution and reproduction of the social relations of production and is thus founded on the perpetuation of class contradictions. In short, by relating state institutions back to the social relations of production, Poulantzas is able to conceptualise the internal relation between state and market. As a result, the way American capitalism is then being reproduced within European state forms changes these state forms in the process. 'The modifications of the role of the European national states in order to assume responsibility for the international reproduction of capital under the domination of American capital and the political and ideological conditions of this reproduction bring about decisive transformations of these state apparatuses' (Poulantzas, 1974/2008: 254–5).

This leads to enquiry about the institutional materiality of the state or the various class interests that support the economic, political and ideological dimensions of capitalist social relations.

The establishment of the state's policy must be seen as the result of the class contradictions inscribed in the very structure of the state (the state as a relationship). The state is the condensation of a relationship of forces between classes and class fractions, such as these express themselves, in a necessarily specific form, within the state itself. (Poulantzas, 1978: 132)

The state, then, is not a simple class instrument or a subject, or 'thing' that directly represents the interests of dominant classes. Dominant classes consist of several class fractions that constitute the state, which thereby enjoys a *relative autonomy* with respect to classes and fractions of classes (Poulantzas, 1975: 97, 1978: 127). Yet, lest the meaning of this phrase is misunderstood, it should be made clear that relative autonomy *does not* mean a distancing from capitalist social relations of production but solely that the state experiences relative autonomy vis-à-vis the classes and fractions of classes that support it (Poulantzas, 1973: 256). Thus, the state has to mediate between the specific interests of different class fractions of capital, which may involve a decision against the interests of a particular fraction in view of securing capitalist reproduction in the medium to long term. Additionally, the state organises hegemony by imposing certain concessions and sacrifices on the dominant classes in order to reproduce long-term domination (Poulantzas, 1978: 184; see also Gramsci, 1971: 161, Q13§18; 245, Q6§81; 254–7, Q14§74–6). 'The state concentrates not only the relationship of forces between fractions of the power bloc, but also the relationship between that bloc and the dominated classes' (Poulantzas, 1978: 140). Returning to the increasing internationalisation of u.s. capital, the focus is then on how, since the 1970s in Europe, 'the states themselves assume responsibility for the interests of the dominant imperialist capital in its extended development actually within the "national" formation, that is, in its complex interiorisation in the interior bourgeoisie which it dominates' (Poulantzas, 1974/2008: 245).

In short, capital is not simply represented as an autonomous force beyond the power of the state but is embodied by classes or fractions of classes *within* the very constitution of the state. There are contradictory and heterogeneous relations internal to the state, which are induced by class antagonisms between different fractions of (nationally or transnationally based) capital. Hence 'foreign' capital, represented by TNCs or 'footloose' investment, does not simply drain 'state power' (Poulantzas, 1975: 170). Instead, stemming from the expansion of U.S. hegemony and the *internationalisation* of American capital in the 1970s, Poulantzas argued, through a process of *internalisation*, there was an 'induced reproduction' of capital within different states. This means that the internationalisation, or transnationalisation, of production and finance capital does not represent the expansion of different capitals outside the state but signifies a process of internalisation during which interests are translated between various fractions of classes within states (Poulantzas, 1975: 73–6). 'The international reproduction of capital under the domination of American capital is supported by the various national states, each state attempting in its own way to latch onto one or other aspect of this process' (Poulantzas, 1975: 73). The phenomenon referred to as *globalisation* therefore represents the transnational organisation of production relations which are internalised *within* states to lead to a modified restructuring (but not retreat) of the state in everyday life. Poulantzas understood that 'internationalisation was not a process influencing the state from the outside, but a development internal to it' (Wissel, 2011: 216).

In sum, the historical dimension of the formation of specific forms of state in their different ways needs to be taken into account when analysing the internal relations between the interstate system and globalisation. Global restructuring and the emergence of transnational class fractions does lead to forms of state restructuring. New transnational class forces of capital do not, however, confront the state as an external actor, as a TNS, but are closely involved in the class struggle over hegemonic projects within the state form. The exact way this is played out and the extent to which the interests of transnational capital become internalised within individual state forms needs to be empirically assessed and is likely to differ from state to state depending on the different configurations of social class forces and institutional set-ups at the national level in line with different historical trajectories of national state formation (Bieler and Morton, 2003: 485–9). At the same time, 'national states become more complex and contradictory as the growing heterogeneity of the bourgeoisie is internalised within and across them, crystallising in the form of (potentially destabilising) modified policies, institutional arrangements and apparatuses' (Bruff, 2012: 185). Seen in this way, globalisation and the related emergence of new transnational social forces of capital and labour have not led to a retreat of the state, a strengthening of the state or the emergence of a TNS. Instead, a restructuring has unfolded through an internalisation within different state forms of new configurations of social forces expressed by class struggles between different (national and transnational) fractions of capital and labour.

Conclusion: The Unity of Global Capitalism and Geopolitics

While there has been a lack of further development in the discussion of the role of the state and the interstate system in relation to globalisation within mainstream IR/IPE literature, recent debates within historical materialism have shown significant vibrancy. Nonetheless, even within historical materialist approaches, we have identified a continued attachment to analysing the external relations between 'state' and 'market', the 'political' and the 'economic', be it through a focus on two different logics, or be it through the emphasis on a '(neo)realist moment' in analysis. Unsurprisingly, assessments of globalisation have collapsed into state-centrism, insensitive to the transnationalisation of the social relations of production since the early 1970s. Alternatively, TNS theorising has taken into account recent developments in the reorganisation of capitalism. The focus here, though, does re-establish the separate appearance of the 'political' and the 'economic', albeit at a different scalar level. The emphasis on states as transmission belts overlooks the continuing importance of state forms and class struggle in the organisation of global capitalism. It therefore flattens our understanding of capitalist development and neglects the significance of processes of uneven and combined development.

Instead, this chapter offers a different historical materialist account based on the philosophy of internal relations. Individual state forms are the expressions of the materiality of the underlying social relations of production as well as conditions of class struggle articulated within and through them. Hence, attention needs to be cast towards examining how changing social relations of production internally shape a particular state form. More precisely, by drawing on Gramsci and Poulantzas it was established that in order to understand the internal relationship between the interstate system and capitalist accumulation, contemporary analyses need to examine the extent to which the interests of transnational capital have become internalised in specific forms of state. Variegation in the internalisation of the interests of transnational capital in specific state forms should not, however, overlook the fact that these national developments are situated within a global political economy characterised by uneven and combined development. Nor should it lead to a neglect of geopolitical rivalries between states, which are also part of the overall structure of class struggle. Finally, the fact that class struggle itself takes place not only within state forms but also within 'the international' needs to be reiterated. Importantly, as Jens Wissel (2011: 225) points out, 'the U.S. is also penetrated by transnational relations of forces and even in the U.S. the national bourgeoisie has lost influence ... thus the national basis of this concept of imperialism can no longer be maintained.' Yet figures such as Leo Panitch and Sam Gindin (2012) in their seminal publication still hold to the homogeneity of U.S. capital when reflecting on the political economy of American empire. As Chapter 8 demonstrates, the focus on the philosophy of internal relations will be drawn on further to contest this position in order to understand the relation between global capitalism and geopolitics with reference to the Iraq War. Moreover this will be done by drawing attention to class fractions within the U.S. form of state, connecting geopoliticians to capital circuits within arms manufacturing and the built environment of construction that shaped the mobilisation for war in and beyond 2003, and addressing different aspects of organic intellectuality (or intellectuals of statecraft), as raised in Chapter 3.

In relation to this chapter, instead of drawing insights from Gramsci and Poulantzas and slavishly applying them to a context very different from their time, we lay great stress on the constant need to adjust concepts in order to make them appropriate for the analysis of contemporary developments. As Bob Jessop argues, Poulantzas focused on the national state as the continuing scale at which political class domination is organised, which made him overlook the possibility of the supranationalisation of state forms. 'In focusing on the role of national states in contemporary imperialism, he failed to note how far the growing multiscalar interpenetration of economic spaces ... also implied a major rescaling of state apparatuses and state power' (Jessop, 2011: 54). According to Hans-Jürgen Bieling (2011), for example, as a result of a continuing process of constitutionalisation within the EU, it is increasingly possible to think in terms of a European form of state, a European statehood. The manner in which the interests of transnational capital have become internalised within individual EU member states has to be analysed. This thread is developed in Chapter 9 with reference to our analysis of the Eurozone crisis. Importantly, the focus here is on the social content of European integration and the way or extent to which the interests of transnational capital have become internalised within the EU form of state interacting with struggles over policy directions in the various EU member states. This allows us to grasp the internal relationship between the emergent geopolitics of the EU state form and the transnational relations of global capitalism and also includes a focus on the seemingly increasing occurrence of authoritarian neoliberalism, based on intensified state control over every sphere of socio-economic life within an unfolding period of capitalist crisis (Bruff, 2014).

Before moving to the empirical analyses in this book, however, having assessed the structuring conditions of global capitalism in Chapters 4 and 5, we now turn to the conceptualisation of class agency from a historical materialist perspective in Chapter 6. Only once this task has been completed will we be in a position to investigate instances of class struggle over Global Capitalism, Global War, Global Crisis.

6   Exploitation and Resistance

Previous chapters in this book have outlined what we have termed an *emergentist* theory of class composition and struggle that avoids a static notion of capitalist productive relations from which classes and class consciousness are seen to derive directly and correspond (see Chapter 1). Instead, our emphasis, as detailed in the focus on agents and structures (see Chapter 2), recognises emergent processes of class formation through which particular communities experience new structures of exploitation and points of antagonistic interest as a process of becoming. Recall that this emergentist theory of class derives, among others, from E. P. Thompson, who does not 'see class as a "structure", nor even as a "category", but as something which in fact happens (and can be shown to have happened) in human relationships' (Thompson, 1968: 8). Elsewhere, Antonio Gramsci, in his focus on the *ensemble of social relations*, similarly emphasised the struggle for hegemony as a dialectical process of 'becoming' defining the contradictions between state–civil society. 'If history', he wrote, 'is taken to mean, precisely, "becoming" in a "concordia discors" [discordant concord] that does not have unity for its point of departure but contains in itself the reasons for a possible unity', then the historical development of these processes has to be identified 'in the system of explicit and implicit "private and public" associations that are woven together in the "state" and in the world political system' (Gramsci, 2007: 186–7, Q7§35). Our argument is that this emphasis is carried forward in E. P. Thompson's focus on the positionality and situatedness of class processes when he writes that 'in any given society we cannot understand the parts unless we understand their function and roles in relation to each other and in relation to the whole. The "truth" or success of such a holistic description can only be discovered in the test of historical practice' (Thompson, 1978: 133; see also Cox, 1987: 355). From that basis, the focus on class identity – as an emergent process of becoming – has been advanced in the earlier chapters of this book from our internal relations perspective to argue that society is structured in class ways through historical and social processes. Class eventuates as people live and experience determinate situations within the ensemble of relations. This focus on class as a relationship – an emergentist process of becoming – means that no theoretical dualism is posited between structure and agency but rather an emphasis on the relational tie of structured processes with human agencies, as Chapter 2 demonstrated. Moreover, the shift to asserting class in internal relationship to underlying relations of production means recognising the antagonisms that generate conflicts and struggles through which class identity emerges in rupture with additional identities. As Ellen Meiksins Wood (1995: 98) elaborates:

> The notion of class as 'structured process' ... acknowledges that while the structural basis of class formation is to be found in the antagonistic relations of production, the particular ways in which the structural pressures exerted by these relations actually operate in the formation of classes remains an open question to be resolved empirically by historical and sociological analysis.

Our thematic chapters in the second part of this book have thus far initiated this sort of panoramic historical sociology. Hence a focus on the historical emergence of the international states system and the rise of capitalism through the structuring conditions of uneven and combined development and class strategies of passive revolution (see Chapter 4). Equally, there was then a focus on the relation of interiority between the geopolitics of the interstate system and the unfolding of global capitalism in regard to more recent dynamics surrounding the restructuring of globalisation (see Chapter 5). The purpose here was to construct a historical materialist perspective on the conceptualisation of capitalist and geopolitical dynamics and assist in endeavours to understand the internalisation of the state within the fabric of capitalist modernity, or how the changing logics of capital are subsumed within the state through global restructuring. Before addressing the empirical aspects of the internal relations of Global Capitalism, Global War, Global Crisis in Part III of this book, the purpose of the present chapter is to expand further our prism of class struggle by unravelling the social relations of race, gender, ecology and sexuality as internally constitutive of class, rather than external to it (see also McNally, 2015). The main question animating this chapter is therefore: how are the social processes of identity construction to be conceived in their internal relation and relevance to the conditions that produce them? Also, how can the conditions of exploitation and resistance be conceptualised in such a way so as to ensure that such a vantage point is not reductionist but open to struggles and identities beyond class relations in the workplace?

It was Antonio Gramsci, engaging in debates on the labour process in his own time, who recognised the notion of an 'extended factory' in order to assess variegated processes of production in nuanced ways (Gramsci, 2007: 220–1, Q7§96). Beyond the fixity of production associated with a spatial configuration (e.g. a factory, building or city), recognition of the extended factory for him meant referring to both artisanal and industrial forms of production, as well as the railroad and transportation industries more broadly, through which material practices in the production of space were revealed to be richly textured and complex. As Gramsci notes with reference to these instances of the extended factory, 'in terms of territorial organisation or technical concentration, these industries are dispersed, and this has a certain impact on the psychology of the workers' (Gramsci, 2007: 221, Q7§96). Of course, Gramsci developed this further through an acute sensitivity towards the gendered social reproduction of capitalism within 'Americanism and Fordism' and the new methods of the time that demanded 'a rigorous discipline of the sexual instincts . . . and with it a strengthening of the "family" in the wide sense . . . and of the regulation and stability of sexual relations' (Gramsci, 1971: 300, Q22§11; see Morton, 2007a: 103–4). In terms of widening an emphasis on spaces of class struggle, to assert a relational view that allows for diversity in the social construction and production of space, then, the first point to make is that the debates on class formation are as long-standing as the very practices themselves, which are regarded as constitutive of them. Therefore, our argument takes three main steps. First, due to the significance of its contributions to anti-reductionist debates within the historical materialist tradition and for providing the theoretical and epistemological conditions for a decentred political economy, the class-theoretic commitments coming out of the over-determinist theory of the Rethinking Marxism collective are introduced. Second, following our engagement with and against these new departures in class theory, we then develop our perspective on the extended factory. Importantly, this focus on class struggle around exploitation and resistance does not assume that other forms of identity involved in struggle such as gender, race, ecological or sexual forms can be subsumed within a logic of concordant unity. Rather, the contested nature of all identities is such that division and rupture have to be foregrounded and combatively insisted upon as part of a radicalised dialectics that is cognisant of the violent, antagonistic and contradictory open-ended dimensions of struggle (Ciccariello-Maher, 2017). Rejecting a *concordant unity*, then, we posit the relations of race, gender, ecology and sexuality as internally constitutive of class so that they are held in *combative unity*. It is by focusing on the combative unity of political identities as a process of becoming (held within the contradictions of a dynamic and opposing 'concordia discors') that a radicalised dialectics of political identity can be cast without displacing the centrality of class. Our argument is therefore that work and workers have to be understood in a broad sense and that class struggle goes beyond the traditional workplace and the mere confrontation between wage labour and employers, which is illustrated by weaving together brief commentary on key examples in the third section of this chapter. A focus on the 'social factory' (Cleaver, 1979/2000) and the increasing reorganisation of social space structured in view of capital accumulation but dependent on unwaged reproductive labour asserts an important feminist perspective on radicalised dialectics, which also comes to the fore in our focus on resistance to conclude this book (see Chapter 10).

Deconstructing Capitalism

In response to forms of economic determinism, the Rethinking Marxism group of scholars has made a major contribution to Marxist theorising. In order to develop an anti-determinism, these scholars have focused on 'an overdeterminist Marxism as a new social theory enabling a new kind of Marxist class analysis' (Resnick and Wolff, 2006: 5). For Louis Althusser, in *Reading Capital* and elsewhere, the concept of over-determination meant rejecting a linear planar space of causality in favour of recognising deep and complex forms where determination of practices within a whole social formation and their contradictions is constituted by the structure as a whole, shaping each practice and contradiction (Althusser, 1968/2005: 253; Althusser et al., 1965/2015: 342-3). Over-determination thus refers to an infinity of determinants none of which can be definitively allocated causal centrality or significance. Hence, capital-ism is perceived as decentred and constituted by a variety of practices, processes and events. 'From the perspective of overdeterminist theory', state some of its key advocates, 'the dialectic entails not only the co-implication of political, economic, natural and cultural processes in every site of occurrence but also the resultant openness and incomplete-ness of identity/being' (Gibson-Graham, Resnick and Wolff, 2001: 4). Over-determination thus eschews an emphasis on designating causal priority among aspects of political economy and is characterised by an emphasis on the relative autonomy and mutual constitution of class processes regarded as complexly interrelated (Gibson-Graham, 1996/2006: 16, 45; Ruccio, 2009: 150). The frontiers of radical political economy are also such, then, that any 'logic' driving the accumulation of capital is denied, with the assumption that capitalism has no necessary trajectory so that its conditions of reproduction are entirely contingent phenomena (Ruccio, 2011: 5, 11).

Further, due to a focus on economic representations and socio-spatial landscapes of economic difference, sites of the economy are regarded as discursively produced. For David Ruccio (2011: 40) this means that 'it is possible to accord discursive centrality to the accumulation of capital without attributing to it a priority in some kind of causal hierarchy of the myriad economic and noneconomic conditions of existence.' However, this does not imply that this perspective avoids a normative position on why one particular 'truth' may be preferable to others. 'Marxian theory affirms the relativity of truths to their respective over-determined theoretical frameworks, while at the same time taking up a clear, partisan attitude toward these truths' (Resnick and Wolff, 2006: 19). The normative consequences resulting from the adoption of one particular perspective are therefore held as decisive in deciding which particular 'truth' to privilege. In the words of David Ruccio (2011: 11):

Instead of relying on a notion of absolute truth, a Marxian approach was better characterised as a partisan relativism: relativism, in the sense that it involved a recognition that different truths were produced within different discourses, and there was no way of stepping outside the realm of knowledge to declare one or another theory to be the correct one; and partisan, because different knowledges had different social consequences, and arguing on behalf of one theory over others represented a stance in favour of one set of social consequences over others.[1]

As a result, Rethinking Marxism scholars do not reduce identities to class as the most significant category for identifying social groups. Class is just one process next to several others. 'This choice is understood to be over-determined by both class and non-class aspects of social life. No choice is determined by only theoretical or only cultural, political, or economic aspects of social life' (Resnick and Wolff, 2006: 50). In other words, 'an overdeterminist class analysis examines some of the ways in which class processes participate in constituting and, in turn, are constituted by other social and natural processes' (Gibson-Graham, 1996/2006: 55). Thus, space is opened up to other identities beyond class and their involvement in struggles against exploitation.

Based on this over-determinist position, J. K. Gibson-Graham and colleagues develop their criticism of 'capitalocentrism', which in their view unduly re-enforces the apparent strength of capitalism and downplays

---

[1] There is a resonance here with the 'strategic essentialism' raised by Gayatri Spivak (1987/2006), despite her later disavowal of the term, as well as the 'militant particularism' advocated by David Harvey, leading to his notion of the *insurgent architect* as an embodied person, occupying an exclusive space for a certain time, existing within a spatio-temporal context, who can 'translate' between cultures while nevertheless striving to necessitate transformative action (Harvey, 1996: 19–45, 2000: 233–5, 244–6).

the possibilities of resistance and non-capitalist economic forms. 'When we say that most economic discourse is "capitalocentric", we mean that other forms of economy (not to mention noneconomic aspects of social life) are often understood primarily with reference to capitalism: as being fundamentally the same as (or modelled upon) capitalism; as being the complement of capitalism; as existing in capitalism's space or orbit' (Gibson-Graham, 1996/2006: 6; see also Gibson-Graham, 2001: 166–7, and Ruccio, 2011: 254–7). In order to go beyond capitalism, it is important, they assert, to supplant 'the discourse of capitalist hegemony with a plurality and heterogeneity of economic forms' (Gibson-Graham, 1996/ 2006: 11). 'When capitalism exists as a sameness, noncapitalism can only be subordinated or rendered invisible (like traditional or domestic economic forms)' (Gibson-Graham, 1996/2006: 43). Focusing on the plurality of economic forms and a broader variety of class struggles allows us to question the assumed all-encompassing power of capitalism and open up ways of thinking about, and moving towards, concrete alternatives beyond capitalism and forms of alternative economy organising – or more recently workers' self-directed enterprises – without assuming the complete transformation of capitalism. 'If we can divorce our ideas of class from systemic social conceptions, and simultaneously divorce our ideas of class transformation from projects of systemic transformation, we may be able to envisage local and proximate socialism. Defining socialism as the communal production, appropriation and distribution of surplus labour, we could encounter and construct it at home, at work, at large' (Gibson-Graham, 1996/2006: 264; Wolff, 2013: 11–13). As Chris Hesketh (2016: 882–4) adeptly points out, opening up space for thinking about alternatives is one of the key contributions made by this reading of class and its decentred approach to critiquing capitalocentric discourse and its focus on non-capitalist class processes. The endeavour to reinvent class and highlight capitalism as more fragmented and dispersed through a realisation of an economy of difference and divergence is a crucial contribution of this anti-essentialist form of analysis.

How class processes are central to the production, appropriation and distribution of surpluses is also an important departure point for rethinking development and the critique of political economy (Resnick and Wolff, 1987; Ruccio, 2011). These perspectives, importantly differentiate between fundamental and subsumed classes. 'To underscore the importance of this distinction, we will henceforth refer to the extraction of surplus labour as the fundamental class process and to the distribution of surplus labour as the subsumed class process' (Resnick and Wolff, 2006: 94). This allows Stephen Resnick and Richard Wolff to include state functionaries as well as unwaged labour in the household in their class analysis. Both areas are part of subsumed classes, which do not produce surplus value, but are important to facilitate the production of surplus value by others. 'State and household involve social processes which are conditions of existence for the extraction of surplus-value upon which capital accumulation is premised. Our analysis thus shows how each social process both encourages and discourages the reproduction of capitalist exploitation' (Resnick and Wolff, 2006: 112). The distinction between fundamental and subsumed classes is then linked to the differentiation between productive and unproductive labour. Subsumed classes consist of unproductive labour, 'which produces neither value nor surplus-value. Its wages are defrayed by the transfer to it of a portion of surplus-value extracted by capitalists from productive labourers' (Resnick and Wolff, 2006: 101), i.e. fundamental classes. Building on these distinctions, J. K. Gibson-Graham, in turn, identifies 'two distinctive moments within any class process, the exploitative class process, where surplus labour is produced and appropriated, and the distributive class process, where appropriated surplus labour is distributed to a variety of social destinations' (Gibson-Graham, 1996/2006: 54). Overall, it is therefore argued that 'we reserve the notion of class struggles, then, to specify struggles over either the processes of surplus labour extraction or surplus labour distribution' (Resnick and Wolff, 2006: 116).

There are, however, a number of problems with the way such decentred and over-deterministic approaches attempt to overcome class essentialism. First, there is the claim that there is no 'logic' driving the accumulation of capital that problematically disavows the imperatives that compel *both* workers to sell their labour power to the capitalist on a continuous basis in order to subsist *and* capitalists to engage in profit maximisation and competition through surplus value production and realisation. As our previous chapters have highlighted (see Chapter 1, especially), the way the social relations of production are organised in capitalism around wage labour and the private ownership of the means of production induces a form of compulsion that capitalists impose upon workers and on each other so that there is an overall 'law of capital as enforced against both' (Marx, 1867/1990: 1056). However, J. K. Gibson-Graham argue differently in the following citation.

We may no more assume that a capitalist firm is interested in maximising profits or exploitation than we may assume that an individual woman wants to bear and raise children ... When we refer to an economy-wide imperative of capital accumulation, we stand on the same unsafe ground (in the context of the anti-essentialist presumption of overdetermination) that we tread when we refer to a maternal instinct or a human drive to acquisition. If we define capitalist sites as involving the appropriation and distribution of surplus-value, we cannot make any invariant associations between this process and particular structures of ownership, or distributions of power (or anything else), just as when we identify women by the wearing of dresses, we cannot draw any necessary conclusions about what's in the mind or under the skirt. (Gibson-Graham, 1996/2006: 16)

But this is a questionable analogy in that assumptions about the essence of 'woman' are always ever problematic in that they deny the proliferation of socially constructed difference. By contrast, our argument is that assumptions about the non-essence of capitalism in the form of exploitation would deny the very conditions of existence of capitalism itself. Put differently, our point is that a capitalist firm would not continue to exist, it would be eliminated, without the compulsion of competition and the appropriation of surplus value deriving from capitalism based on the condition of existence of exploitation. However, a 'woman' would still continue to exist, survive and thrive in terms of identity difference and plurality, without recourse to an essential definition grounded in motherhood or gender. A non-essential definition of 'woman' can continue to exist outside motherhood; a non-essential definition of capitalism cannot exist outside exploitation and the production of surplus value as well as its appropriation and then transformation into surplus capital. 'Accumulation for the sake of accumulation, production for the sake of production: this was the formula in which classical economics expressed the historical mission of the bourgeoisie in the period of its domination' (Marx, 1867/1990: 742).

Second, drawing from Jim Glassman, there is a clear difference to be drawn between an emphasis on contradictions and relations that are *over*-determined – involving complex underlying structures, rather than simple monocausal forces – and contradictions and relations that are over-*determined* – having a discrete number of such structures, the relative causal efficacy of which can be practically judged in given contexts (Glassman, 2003: 680). Hence the importance of insisting on the ruptural conditions constituting identities that exist within a combative unity and have to be foregrounded and insisted upon rather than subsumed within a reconciliative logic of concordant unity. Rescuing a theory of dynamic oppositions within which the dialectics of class warfare is present, through an internal combinatory of diverse identities and difference, inclusive of the decolonisation of race, is therefore at the crux of radical political economy rather than be consumed by an uncritical multiplicity of deconstructive manoeuvres (Ciccariello-Maher, 2017: 13). If class is defined as a process of becoming as 'situatedness or positionality in relation to processes of capital accumulation', then as David Harvey (1996: 359–60) attests, 'only through critical re-engagement with political economy, with our situatedness in relation to capital accumulation, can we hope to re-establish a conception of social justice to be fought for as a key value within an ethics of political solidarity built across different places.' Harvey therefore draws a qualitative difference between focusing on social *processes* of identity construction and the *conditions* producing identities. 'A politics which seeks to eliminate the processes which give rise to a problem [based on the conditions that produce them] looks very different from a politics which merely seeks to give full play to differentiated identities once these have arisen' (Harvey, 1996: 363). Hence the importance of focusing on the concrete conditions of uneven development that create the determined relations and variegated terrains of space, place and environment without occluding class pertinence. Returning to Glassman (2003: 691, original emphasis):

From a dialectical perspective ... unevenness is not the basis for privileging the *over*determined character of social processes but rather for understanding the connection between this and the over*determined* character of these processes, that leads to specific struggles in particular times and places being more powerful and important than others in relation to specific outcomes.

The spatial matrix of capitalism therefore weaves together the loom of inside and outside through specific determinative conditions of uneven development crystallised through relations of class, race, gender and ecology. 'The uneven development of capitalism', argues Nicos Poulantzas (1978:112), 'fastens on to those stoppages that are the diverse state formations; the rhythm of uneven development peculiar to each formation (in the economic, the political and the ideological, and among all three) fastens on to the moments of the state'. It is to these moments of condensation of class relations and wider points of rupture in Global Capitalism (Chapter 7), Global War (Chapter 8), Global Crisis (Chapter 9) that the chapters in the following section of this book address while also turning to reflect on their mutual relation to new counter-spaces of resistance to conclude this volume (Chapter 10).

Meanwhile, third, as discussed in detail in Chapter 3, we find equally problematic the focus on rethinking the economy through deconstruction and discourse. As Resnick and Wolff (2006: 24) formulated it, 'any change in the thinking process, thought-concretes, change the concrete-real in two ways: a change in thinking is a change in one component process of the social totality, and, on the other hand, any change in thinking has impact on all the other social processes, thereby changing them. In turn, a changed social totality reacts back upon the thinking process to change it in the ceaseless dialectic of life.' Similarly, Gibson-Graham (1996/2006: 15) uphold that 'alternative economic discourses become the sites and instruments of struggles that may subvert capitalism's provisional and unstable dominance.' This is most recently lauded as one of the benefits of attending to nuance, diversity and over-determined interaction within the positive frame of reference they claim as *weak theory*. In contrast, *strong theory* organises events into understandable and seemingly predictable trajectories, such as the master frame of reference that is capitalocentrism (Gibson-Graham, 2014: 148–9). But these claims can be found problematic on the following two counts, one epistemological and the other ontological. In relation to the former, there can be a no more epistemologically robust, consistent and resolute approach than that of the tremendously *strong theory* offered by the Rethinking Marxism perspectives. A set of powerful discourses revolving around a commitment to over-determinism, contingency and the critique of capitalocentrism organises non-capitalist activities into understandable articulations. There is no better exemplar of this *strong theory* than the commitment to 'take back the economy' by demystifying everyday economic life in order to create a post-capitalist world (Gibson-Graham, Cameron and Stephen Healey, 2013). Further, as already signposted, there is a clear granting of discursive priority and centrality to the accumulation of capital, a discursive move that belies the claim that over-determinism avoids a privileging of any causal hierarchies (see Ruccio, 2009: 149–50, 2011: 40). The critique of capitalocentrism is therefore a *strong theory* that retains as its object knowledge taking place entirely in thought to produce a purely cognitive appropriation of the economic world, which we have already critiqued in its cognate forms earlier in this book (see Chapter 3). The violent abstractions of classical political economy are substituted by the critique of capitalocentrism for the indeterminate general abstractions of total contingency.

At the ontological level, in addressing issues of class analysis there is a focus on the practices of performing and appropriating surplus labour in the form of surplus value as part of the capitalist fundamental class process. The distribution of surplus labour across a myriad of activities by diverse agents is then referred to as a subsumed class process within capitalism, while also recognising the role of non-class payments (Ruccio, 2011: 223–4). However, if the commitments to over-determinist theory are in any way meaningful, beyond a suggestive reference to class process as complex constitution, then this approach to surplus labour needs to be questioned in terms of, first, reading *Capital* and, second, *Reading Capital*. In the first instance of reading *Capital*, Marx states clearly that to transform money into capital there has to be 'annexed surplus-value' to thereby 'valorise value' (Marx, 1867/1990: 268). Subsequently, there is the distinction made between absolute surplus value (in the form of the lengthening of the working day) and relative surplus value (in the form of increasing the productivity of labour by revolutionising the labour process for the production of a commodity, cheapening the commodities that are inputs). Henceforth, returning to the theme of compulsion:

The law of the determination of value by labour-time makes itself felt to the individual capitalist who applies the new method of production by *compelling* him [*sic*] to sell his goods under their social value; this same law, acting as a coercive law of competition, forces his competitors to adopt the new method. (Marx, 1867/1990: 436, emphasis added)

The production of absolute surplus value (the prolongation of the working day) is then related to the *formal subsumption* of labour under capital and the production of relative surplus value (necessary labour and surplus labour based on a shorter time for producing the equivalent of the wage of labour) is related to the *real subsumption* of labour under capital or the productivity or intensity of labour (Marx, 1867/1990: 645). 'All surplus-value', states Marx (1867/1990: 672), 'whatever particular form (profit, interest or rent) it may subsequently crystallise into, is in substance the materialisation of unpaid labour-time'. In the second instance of *Reading Capital*, where the articulation of over-determination theory is introduced and presented, this emphasis on surplus value within the structure of capitalism as a mode of production is strongly evident. First, the generalised expression of capitalism as a mode of production is outlined through the identity of concrete labour (determining the use value of commodities) and abstract labour (determining their value), with abstract social labour regarded as the foundation of the theory of value (Althusser et al., 1965/2015: 108). Second, these tendencies specific to capitalism, existing as structural laws within a mode of production, are held as linking both the phenomena of capitalist competition and the motives of capitalists, which become individually internalised (Althusser et al., 1965/2015: 129). The focus here is therefore on labour creative of surplus value that explicitly avoids obscuring the formation of surplus value and thus capitalism as a determinate historical relation of production. Our point is that beyond a suggestive association with over-determination there is very little engagement with reading *Capital* – involving a commitment to reading the text itself on the issue of surplus value, returning to the text on class process – nor *Reading Capital* – having recourse to its method of double reading in order to give rise to differential sharpenings on understandings of surplus value beyond the class issues of mediations and determinations of everyday life.

Fourth, the distinction between productive and unproductive labour is not unique to the Rethinking Marxism tradition. As John Smith, for example, recently argued, 'the social wealth that is consumed by the nonproduction labourers derives from the surplus labour of the production labourers, that is, the labour they perform in excess of what is required to replace their own consumption, what Marx calls necessary labour' (Smith, 2016: 63). It is in the process of production proper in which living labour is incorporated as an *agens* (effective force) into capital and it is this surplus value that is then appropriated by capital and partly redistributed to unproductive labour for the services they render in the process of selling goods on the market (Marx, 1867/1990: 1018). The distinction between productive and unproductive labour is crucial in that it highlights that any 'profits' from financial market activities, some would argue speculations, ultimately need to be secured in processes of productive labour. Investment bubbles ultimately burst at the moment when investors realise that the promised profits cannot be realised in the industrial economy. From a focus on class struggle and resistance, however, it is dangerous to pit productive against unproductive labour, potentially creating unhelpful divisions between workers. As ecofeminists such as Maria Mies (1986/2014), Ariel Salleh (1997/ 2017) and social reproduction feminists such as Mariarosa Dalla Costa (2008), Lise Vogel (1983/2013) and Silvia Federici (2012) have recognised, the sphere of reproduction as a source of value creation and exploitation is pivotal in transcending the dichotomy between class and patriarchy so that 'gender should not be considered a purely cultural reality, but should be treated as a specification of class relations' (Federici, 2004: 14). Further, the focus on 'reproductive labour is a metabolic bridging of human and natural cycles', enabling a privileging of the body attentive to race, sexuality and environmental habitat that is not class innocent (Salleh, 2003: 64, 1997/2017). Capital did not only respond to the global crisis in the 1970s through the transfer of production to cheap labour locations in the Global South. It also restructured, Harry Cleaver argues, 'the rest of the social factory in order to expand the imposition of the work of reproducing labour-power' (Cleaver, 1979/2000: 109). When thinking about capitalist social relations as a whole, and the implicated reality of exploitation and resistance, it is, therefore, in our view more useful to think in terms of a 'social factory' which encompasses productive and unproductive wage labour as well as non-wage labour in the production, appropriation and distribution of surplus value. After all, 'the calling into question by capitalism of the forms of wage-labour opens up a path of rupture with the wage condition' (Endnotes, 2008: 98). Going beyond struggles at the workplace is essential, then, when assessing the possibilities of resistance against exploitation.

We now explore these conditions of the social factory further in developing a contribution to feminist perspectives on radicalised dialectics where gender, race, ecology and sexuality are held in combative and ruptural relations but also as 'a political signifier of class relations, and of the shifting, continuously redrawn boundaries which these relations produce in the map of human exploitation' (Federici, 2004: 155).

Class Struggle in the Social Factory of Capitalism

Trade unions' self-image in advanced capitalist states after World War II has been that their actions were at the forefront of securing real material gains for workers and society more widely through the establishment of welfare states. Unsurprisingly, analyses of resistance, including Marxist accounts, have tended to focus on class struggle at the workplace and the conflict between trade unions and employers' associations within the wider social formation. Importantly, trade unions' activities in these struggles have not always been progressive. Operating within institutions of social partnership with employers and the state, trade unions have frequently dropped their initially more radical demands and become reformist in ideological outlook and programme (see Humphrys and Cahill, 2016). Concordant with Colin Barker (2013: 52),

as the 'labour movement' has emerged as a recognised and licensed agency of working-class representation, it has also commonly narrowed its ideological agenda. Trade unions appear as agencies of both struggle for and containment of workers' demands.

As we discussed in Chapter 4, revolutions occurred in the twentieth century where there was not the full efflorescence of capitalism but, rather, where capitalist development had only recently been extended through uneven and combined developmental expansion. In the words of Gramsci, 'in periods of crisis, it is the weakest, most peripheral segment that reacts first' (Gramsci, 1992: 130, Q1§43). More commonly, subaltern class demands were only at best partially fulfilled and more often narrowed, simplified or redefined in a series of passive revolutions, giving rise to capitalist development, albeit without direct intent (see also Endnotes, 2015: 100). Nevertheless, we can also agree with Barker (2013: 52), who points out that '"trade unionism" is not a fixed quality.' Just because trade unions have become co-opted into capitalist structures does not by default imply that they cannot be otherwise. Inadvertently, too narrow a focus on the workplace and trade unions has also resulted in a pessimistic understanding of a decline in the power of labour. 'The premise of decline was based on a mistaken identification of the working class with manual workers in industry, rather than all those whose subsistence is based upon the sale of their labour power' (Radice, 2015: 33). Here, again, we find ourselves in agreement with the view that criticises an uncritical acceptance of a focus on class struggle, equated with an invariant workers' identity linked to unionism as a programme to be realised. The defeat of such programmatism is then regarded as the defeat of the activity of workers and the impossibility of the liberation of labour (Endnotes, 2008: 155). Unsurprisingly, too, this critique of 'classism' has wider resonances based on 'the forward drive of the working class as a class within capitalist society, where its organisations came to occupy as much social space as possible' (Endnotes, 2008: 146). In order to overcome these limitations, a broader definition of labour is required that is cognisant of the increasing reorganisation of territory, the body and nature as social spaces structured in view of the needs of production, reproduction and capital accumulation (Federici, 2012: 7). As David Camfield argues,

society is produced by human beings. Work, understood in the broad sense of creative practice, is the basis of social organisation. 'Work is all-constitutive.' Here it is very important to heed the feminist insistence that work is much more than what is done for wages. Much human labour is unpaid, including the unpaid domestic labour, largely carried out by women. (Camfield, 2002: 42)

As we discussed in Chapter 2, for Marx it is in the hidden abode of production where exploitation takes place, masked by an apparent political equality within liberal representative democratic practices and institutions. 'Inequality and exploitation are not merely the result of the legacies of feudalism or the (perhaps correctable) inadequacies of the less fortunate; they are rooted in the relations of production that he identifies' (Radice, 2015: 35). Drawing on the notion of the hidden abode of production, Nancy Fraser in her conceptualisation of capitalism extends it into additional spheres. 'In order to discover capitalism's secrets', she states, 'I shall seek production's conditions of possibility behind that sphere, in realms that are more hidden still' (Fraser, 2014:57). In addition to the separation between the 'economic' and the 'political' in capitalism, as discussed in detail in Chapter 1, Fraser first points to 'the institutional separation of "economic production" from "social reproduction", a gendered separation that grounds specifically capitalist forms of male domination, even as it also enables capitalist exploitation of labour power and, through that, its officially sanctioned mode of accumulation' (Fraser, 2014: 67). Women working in the sphere of social reproduction are essential for capitalist accumulation, but this social position is commonly hidden by their condition of unwaged labour in the household that is actually the foundation of surplus value extraction. 'They appear to stand only in some private relation to the male wage earner but not to capital' (Cleaver, 1979/2000: 155). Moreover, for Fraser, there is the identification of a further separation, which is 'the ontological division, pre-existing but massively intensified, between its (non-human) "natural" background and its (apparently non-natural) "human" foreground' (Fraser, 2014: 67). Thus, in many ways in line with Marx's own assessment of exploitation, by referring to capitalism's hidden abodes, Fraser is able to link struggles over gender and the environment into struggles against capitalist exploitation. In a next step, though, she then separates these struggles from the capitalist economy, understood in a rather narrow way. 'Unlike the crisis tendencies stressed by Marx, however, these do not stem from contradictions internal to the capitalist economy. They are grounded rather, in contradictions between the economic system and its background conditions of possibility – between economy and society, economy and nature, economy and polity' (Fraser, 2014: 71). The danger here is one of falling back into a conceptualisation that separates and exteriorises the relations between the capitalist economy and these background conditions rather than regarding these different struggles as internally related expressions of resistance to capitalist exploitation. The structuring conditions of capitalism and here especially its expansionary tendency underline exploitation in these various abodes. Hence, in response to Fraser, while accepting this idea of hidden abodes across the spaces of political economy we want to understand capitalism much more broadly to encompass precisely all these abodes in relation to their unity-in-diversity as forms in radical tension and, at times, combat (see Endnotes, 2015: 85; McNally, 2015: 143). 'There is no labour (or work) outside of gender, race or ability', as Susan Ferguson (2016: 55) reminds us, 'just as there is no gender, outside of race, labour or sexuality'. Retained within our definition of capitalism, then, is the point that 'structure and struggle are no longer conceived as externally related. All who labour are present from the beginning because work is recognised as constitutive of society. This includes wage-labour, domestic labour and other forms' (Camfield, 2002: 44). It is Harry Cleaver's (Cleaver, 1979/2000) notion of the 'social factory', then, that specifically enables us to conceptualise capitalist social relations of production in such a way that it configures identities in and through combative differences that are internally related.

When reflecting on the increasing number of struggles of the late 1960s and 1970s, Cleaver asserts that 'the reproduction of the working class involves not only work in the factory but also work in the home and in the community of homes . . . the working class had to be redefined to include nonfactory analysis' (Cleaver, 1979/2000: 70). Assessing what he called the 'social factory' allowed Cleaver to take into account all the other forms of unwaged activities that are necessary for the reproduction of capital but take place outside the workplace. Yet it is Silvia Federici (2012: 35–6) who extends this by stating that 'the time we consume in the "social factory", preparing ourselves for work or going to work, restoring our "muscles, nerves, bones and brains" with quick snacks, quick sex, movies, all this appears as leisure, free time, individual choice.'[2] Therefore, waged labour at the workplace not only hides the surplus value appropriated by capitalists but it also hides all the other labour outside the 'factory', necessary for the reproduction of workers (Cleaver, 1979/2000: 71). As for unwaged work,

the most closely analysed aspect of this is the work involved in the training and upkeep of labour-power itself – work performed by the wage worker but also by unwaged household workers – mainly wives and children. Other formally unwaged work includes such things as travel to and from the job, shopping, and those parts of schoolwork, community work, and church work that serve to reproduce labour-power for capital. (Cleaver, 1979/2000: 84)

Drawing on the work of Mario Tronti, among others, Cleaver also concluded that 'the identification of the leading role of the unwaged in the struggles of the 1960s in Italy, and the extension of the concept to the peasantry, provided a theoretical framework within which the struggles of American and European students and housewives, the unemployed, ethnic and racial minorities, and Third World peasants could all be grasped as moments of an international cycle of working-class struggle' (Cleaver, 1979/2000: 73). This requires a new definition of 'worker', beyond the direct employee–employer relationship, in order to incorporate the whole 'social factory' of capitalism. In short, in agreement with Camfield, 'theorising structure and struggle as internally related through the constantly contested process of capitalist social reproduction puts class, gender and other social struggles at the centre of analysis' (Camfield, 2002: 49). More widely, Federici (2012: 122) elucidates the implications for ruptural cycles of struggle and revolution:

The feminist movement's lesson has been that not only is reproduction the pillar of the 'social factory', but changing the conditions under which we reproduce ourselves is an essential part of our ability to create 'self-reproducing movements'.

This notion of the extended factory, or social factory, is pivotal to developing a feminist perspective on radicalised dialectics by understanding

---

[2] This vitiates the claim that Federici enforces a strict division between the 'labour question' and the 'identity question' on issues of reproductive work; see Endnotes (2013: 88–9).

the reorganisation of reproductive work, housing, public space and the family as a labour question and not just an issue of identity politics.

This conceptualisation does not imply, of course, that exploitation along class, race or gender lines, for example, is simply unique to capitalism. Nevertheless, the particular form these ruptures of identity take is specific to capitalist class processes. It is important to note in this respect that capitalism is indifferent to social identities and exploits people regardless of their particular individualities while nevertheless heightening antagonisms by condemning difference to demonisation, inferiority, discrimination or violence at specific conjunctures. As Ellen Meiksins Wood (2002d: 279) makes clear, 'if capitalism derives advantages from racism or sexism, it is not because of any structural tendency in capitalism toward racial inequality or gender oppression, but on the contrary because they disguise the structural realities of the capitalist system and because they divide the working class' (Wood, 2002d: 279). Hence, capital may deploy social identities around race, nation or gender to fragment and divide class interests (Harvey, 1982/2006: 383). 'It is only by dividing and pitting one group of workers against another that capital can prevent their dangerous unity and keep the class weak enough to be controlled' (Cleaver, 1979/2000: 113). Of course, some trade unions too have at times employed a discourse of gender or race, on immigration in order to protect their white male membership on secure permanent contracts (see Ledwith, 2006: 98–9). Interestingly, while this may provide white, male workers with some short-term advantage, ultimately it is capital and the system of patriarchy that gains overall.

Patriarchal gender relations also exist because male privilege gives those who have it a material interest (mediated by class relations, which make this interest much greater for ruling-class men than working-class men, given the magnitude of the former's stake in capitalism) in maintaining gender oppression. As a result, male gender interests often converge with the class interests of capital. (Camfield, 2016: 498)

At the same time, ethnicity may be an important factor in mobilising collective class agency, whether that be in relation to Black Lives Matter or, as Davide Però illustrates, in relation to the Latin American Workers' Association (LAWAS) and its organising in London. LAWAS embedded its activists 'in a solidarity circuit where class and ethnicity are interwoven, making them feel stronger and cared about' (Però, 2014: 1164). Race, gender and other identities are, therefore, often closely involved in moments of class struggle albeit within a combative rather than simply concordant unity. Indeed, 'it is difficult to conceive of a society that perpetuates class exploitation without using existing racial and gender differences (and etching new ones) as channels for that exploitation' (Smith, 2000: 1026). At the same time, resistance against these forms of exploitation along gender or racial lines must not overlook the point that the fundamental dynamics of exploitation are rooted in the way capitalist social relations of production are organised. 'The strategic implications are that struggles conceived in purely extra-economic terms – as purely against racism or gender oppression for example – are not in themselves fatally dangerous to capitalism, that they could succeed without dismantling the capitalist system but that, at the same time, they are probably unlikely to succeed if they remain detached from an anticapitalist struggle' (Wood, 2002d: 281). In other words, these forms of exploitation must be situated within a radicalised dialectic of combative social struggle that does not occlude the social relations of production but envisions class, gender, decolonial, ecological and sexuality concerns all as combinations of internally related instances rather than instances in exteriority. 'Feminism that speaks of women's oppression and its injustice but fails to address capitalism will be of little help in ending women's oppression' (Holmstrom, 2002: 2).

Racism, in turn, acquires a unique connotation as a result of capitalism. 'It was precisely the structural pressure against extra-economic difference which made it necessary to justify slavery by excluding slaves from the human race, making them non-persons standing outside the normal universe of freedom and equality' (Wood, 2002d: 280). At the same time as women were treated with hostility, a war of violence was conducted against colonial slaves, so that wage labour in Europe was refined as an instrument of accumulation – within the hidden abode – coeval with both the racial hierarchies of slave labour and the exploitation of female unpaid labour (Federici, 2004: 104). The conditions of primitive accumulation, analysed earlier in our expansive and panoramic historical sociology (see Chapter 4), therefore directly ensured not only the persecution of indigenous peoples through colonisation, racism and slavery but also and at times simultaneously the degradation of women through access to women's bodies, their labour, to gain control over the most basic means of reproduction and place the female body, the uterus, at the service of the accumulation of labour power (Federici, 2004: 181). As Silvia Federici documents in *Caliban and the Witch*, rather than a decolonised dialectic that subsumes race (or class) to gender, there has to be a focus not only on a radicalised dialectic of decolonisation but also on how race is linked through its relation of interiority to gender, class, sex and ecology. In her words, 'if "femininity" has been constituted in capitalist society as a work-function masking the production of the work-force under the cover of a biological destiny, then "women's history" is "class history",' which is also of a piece with colonial history (Federici, 2004: 14). She then traces how primitive accumulation at the dawn of capitalism involved not only the expropriation of land from the peasantry and the subjection of nature to capital, not only the extirpation and enslavement of indigenous peoples in the Americas, but also profound transformations in the reproduction of labour power and the social position of women, including control over and free access to women's bodies and their sexuality within the confining bonds of marriage and procreation. Extirpation, enslavement and entombment of indigenous peoples as part of the prehistory of capital is therefore of a piece with the extirpation, enslavement and enwombment of women as part of the disposable human material of the transition to capitalism (Federici, 2004: 184; Marx, 1867/1990: 915). In her own words, 'the advent of capitalism in Europe – land privatisation and the Price Revolution', resulted in 'the construction of a new patriarchal order', defined as the patriarchy of the wage, and 'the production of racial and sexual hierarchies in the colonies', which all formed subsequent terrains of solidarity and confrontation (Federici, 2004: 86).

Of course, racism in itself, aligned with gender or ecology, is not a function of capitalism and ending discrimination, oppression or despoliation need not mean ending exploitation, as struggles in South Africa against apartheid would attest (see Bond, Desai and Ngwane, 2013). Equally, ecological struggles against the dialectical relation between human and extra-human natures – or capitalism-in-nature – linking paid work and the appropriation of unpaid work and energy need not in themselves threaten capitalism. As Jason Moore (2015: 172) verifies, 'shut down a coal plant and you can slow global warming for a day; shut down the relations that made the coal plant and you can stop it for good.' Hence, the elements in the accumulation and displacement of primary carbon offsetting mechanisms, such as the Clean Development Mechanism (CDM) established under the Kyoto Protocol, can actually provide a new spatial 'fix' for states and for capital, seeking to continue burning fossil fuels while establishing profit from carbon trading (see Bryant, 2018). By 'fixing' a socio-spatial divide between advanced capitalist states, where carbon credits are consumed, and peripheral states, where carbon credits are produced, CDMs displace the costs of responding to climate change to those affected by projects that are 'fixed' within particular local communities in the Global South (Bryant, Dabhi and Böhm, 2015). As David Harvey points out, environmental groups 'can either ignore the [capitalist] contradictions, remain within the confines of their own particularist militancies – fighting an incinerator here, a toxic waste dump there, a World Bank dam project somewhere else, and commercial logging in yet another place – or they can treat the contradictions as a fecund nexus to create a more transcendent and universal politics' (Harvey, 1996: 400). Overcoming capitalism's internalisation of planetary life and processes therefore means that challenging social and environmental injustices also directly has to target the conditions dictated by the era of the Capitalocene, referring to the current age shaped by relations privileging the endless accumulation of capital. Struggles over the *oikeois* – referring to the connection of human and extra-human natures – are thus class struggles over world ecology dialectically combining the internalisation of biospheric relations within capitalism and value relations in reproduction that have racialised, gendered and ecological consequences stemming from the appropriation of nature (Moore, 2015: 144–5; see also Mies, 1986/2014; Salleh, 1997/2017). In line with the overarching focus of our book on the internality of dialectics, or the philosophy of internal relations, the combative struggle between and for class, race, gender, sexuality and ecology have all to be put squarely at the centre of analysis in relation to capitalist relations of production and social reproduction. In what follows we now turn our attention to four threads that flow from our expanded understanding of class struggle to think beyond the workplace within the wider nexus of the 'social factory' to encompass informal labour, the biosphere and female labour struggles positioned within the context of race and gender dynamics.

Linking the Social Factory and Expanded Forms of Class Struggle

First, alongside a clear recognition of the internal connection between production and reproduction (Cox, 1987: 252, 351), it was Robert Cox who argued that workers experiencing conditions of restructuring within globalisation have become fragmented along two principal lines. In addition to the division between national labour working in production sectors organised within a country and transnational labour working in transnational production sectors, he identified the division between established labour, workers on permanent contracts in the core of the economy, and non-established labour. The latter, also referred to as unprotected workers, 'have insecure employment, have no prospect of career advancement, are relatively less skilled, and confront great obstacles in developing effective trade unions' (Cox, 1981: 148; also see Davies and Ryner, 2006; Harrod 1987). As part of the transnationalisation of production, we have experienced not only a centralisation of command in the global political economy but also a fragmentation with many aspects of the transnational production process outsourced and subcontracted to other companies. Together with a huge population influx into urban areas, particularly in the Global South, this has led to an increasing casualisation and informalisation of the economy, in which permanent, full-time employment contracts have to a large extent become a feature of the past. In a way, 'it is no longer accurate today', Dan Gallin argues, 'to describe the informal sector as "atypical"' (Gallin, 2001: 228). This has always been the case in developing countries, but informalisation more and more also affects developed countries in the Global North (Standing, 2011), where employers are on the offensive and demand a flexibilisation of the labour market based on the argument that this would be necessary in order to retain competitiveness. Once again the silent and dull conditions of compulsion to accumulate come to the fore in which profit and growth maximisation can only result from surplus value production and realisation while 'direct extra-economic force is still of course used' as well (Marx, 1867/1990: 899). All these factors can therefore become evident through the notion of unprotected workers, where a layering of conditions of exploitation may coalesce various patterns of social relations of production, for example, as in the case of sex work combining unpaid domestic labour and the redefinition of female sexuality as work alongside debt bondage, where sex work, sex trafficking and sex tourism carry deeply racialised assumptions (Federici, 2006). For various reasons, trade unions have found it extremely difficult, if not impossible, to organise unprotected workers. Hence the need to think beyond traditional trade union organising of workplaces within the social factory where novel types of organising may be required. StreetNet International is one good example of a non-union organisation mobilising new types of unprotected workers.[3] Organisations which directly mobilise street vendors, market vendors and/or hawkers, i.e. workers without a direct employer counterpart, can affiliate with StreetNet International. The goal is to exchange information on how best to organise people within the peripheries of the labour market so that they can represent their interests in the most effective way through local, national and international campaigns. Coordinating members especially from Africa, Latin America and Asia make StreetNet International a truly transnational organisation.[4] More recently in the United Kingdom, we have witnessed the emergence of new, smaller and more flexible trade unions in London, successfully engaging in the organising of precarious cleaners, often with a migrant background (Però, 2014). Avoiding large, bureaucratic unions in these instances has allowed

---

[3] StreetNet International, www.streetnet.org.za/; accessed 31 May 2011.
[4] For an overview of other successful examples of organising informal workers and the potential involvement of trade unions, see Bonner and Spooner (2011).

such movements to focus more on the concrete issues of daily exploitation that they face.

Second, 'as this relationship is being replaced by a variety of more diffuse and indirect but nonetheless dependent relationships in the process of production, trade union organising can no longer focus primarily on the employment relationship' (Gallin, 2001: 233). Trade unions as member organisations, therefore, need to reach beyond the workplace. The Argentine Workers' Central Union (Central de Trabajadores de la Argentina, CTA), for example, organises workers across the social factory inclusive of social movements such as environmental groups and activists, which can affiliate even if they are not workers in a traditional understanding.[5] Community unionism is another way of reaching beyond the workplace and into the sphere of social reproduction. The term 'community unionism' is used conceptually and practically in a number of different ways. In general, however, 'community unions identify with the broader concerns of their ethnic, racial and geographical communities. The organisations view housing or civil rights or immigration issues as connected to their core mission around worker organising and issues of class and race, class and place, class and gender, and class and ethnicity are joined in this model' (Stewart et al., 2009: 8). Community unions reach back historically to a tradition when it was normal for trade unions to be involved with issues of working-class communities beyond the workplace (Greenwood and McBride, 2009: 201). Amanda Tattersall's (2009) analysis of a coalition between a teachers' union and a parents and citizens' initiative in Sydney, Australia, in the early 2000s illustrates well how community unionism can be very successful at influencing policy-making, especially when it succeeds in rallying around issues of common concerns, in this particular instance in relation to small class sizes. In turn, this has made it easier for teachers to demand an increase in salaries. The moment trade unions connect with issues of relevance beyond their own direct workplace, there is a good chance of being more successful. Against the background of the global financial crisis since 2008, and declining power at the point of production, British trade unions have also more generally started to emphasise a community-organising approach outside the traditional industrial arena. Campaigning has often involved the struggle against austerity cuts, reaching into the sphere of social reproduction as a result. Different types of community organising include close cooperation with civil society organisations such as

---

[5] Presentation by Bruno Dubrosin, CTA delegate at the tenth Congress of the Southern Initiative on Globalisation and Trade Union Rights (SIGTUR) in Perth, Australia (4 December 2013).

Unison's cooperation with Citizens UK, as well as the setting up of community-based branches as in the case of the trade union Unite. Focusing on issues such as a living wage, community organising in the United Kingdom has successfully bridged the sphere of employment relations with the sphere of social reproduction (Holgate, 2015).

Another attempt to situate struggles across the social factory and outside the narrowly construed workplace has been made by Kees van der Pijl. He argues that neoliberal capitalism is characterised by the fact that capitalist discipline has now also been further extended within the entire process of social reproduction, involving the exploitation of the social and natural substratum, dovetailing well with the world ecology perspective introduced earlier and its understanding of nature as a matrix of dialectical relations of capital accumulation, reproduction and human/extra-human nature (Moore, 2015). In response to the commodification of social services and the intensified destruction of the biosphere, as well as the disruption of traditional life, a whole range of new, progressive but also nationalist right-wing social movements has emerged to defend the environment and sphere of social reproduction (van der Pijl, 1998: 46–8; see also Bakker and Gill, 2003; Rupert, 2000). This is analysed as class struggle as much as exploitation and resistance to it in the workplace. In other words, the struggle of social movements against neoliberal globalisation, for example, can also be conceptualised as class struggle. The European Citizens' Initiative (ECI) on Water as a Human Right, a broad alliance of user groups and trade unions, as well as environmental organisations, represents a good example of a progressive alliance across the whole social factory against exploitation (Bieler, 2017). On one hand, there is the interest of trade unions in keeping water provision in public hands, as working conditions are generally better in the public than in the private sector. On the other hand, user groups are supportive of universal access to affordable, clean water and environmental groups of sustainable management of water resources instead of treating water as a commodity. It is again this inclusion of issues across the social factory and beyond the workplace, the right to access clean water, which has allowed these trade unions to link up with other social movements and thereby broaden the social basis for resistance and form bonds of solidarity. We return to this example in Chapter 10 in more detail.

Finally, adding to the perspective of social reproduction feminism, Chandra Mohanty argues that analysis of capitalist exploitation needs to be grounded in the experience of the most exploited workers in the global economy, i.e. female workers, often working from home in developing countries. 'Any analysis of the effects of globalisation needs to centralise the experiences and struggles of these particular communities of women and girls' (Mohanty, 2003: 235). It is from this perspective that capitalist exploitation of workers can be understood in its gendered and racial dimension and the way related discourses to fragment the working class can be deployed in such circumstances. 'Management exploits and reinforces these ideologies by encouraging women to view femininity as contradictory to factory work, by defining their jobs as secondary and temporary, and by asking women to choose between defining themselves as women or as workers' (Mohanty, 2002: 167). Moreover, 'the explanation also lies in the specific definition of Third World, immigrant women as docile, tolerant, and satisfied with substandard wages' (Mohanty, 2002: 169). Equally, it is especially women who are most affected by current cuts to public sector jobs and services, partly because the workforce in the public sector is predominantly female and partly because women are more likely to have caring responsibilities or be lone parents (Abramovitz, 2002). As Jacqui True (2016: 53) cogently argues, 'the impact of the financial recession and austerity measures has disproportionately affected women with respect to loss of homes, unpayable debt, public sector job losses, and cuts to services.' Hence, when analysing exploitation and resistance in times of austerity, analysis can also be grounded in the experience of women in industrialised countries. When thinking in terms of resistance by the most exploited women in the global political economy, the Self-Employed Women's Association (SEWA) in India, registered as a trade union, but organising predominantly female homeworkers, is one of the most successful cases (Mohanty, 2002: 175).[6] Through initiatives such as its green livelihoods strategy, SEWA has protected the livelihoods of many of its 1.3 million female members (Sahoo, 2012). SEWA also provides an excellent example of how these novel forms of organisation can be integrated in formal global labour institutions. In 2006, it was accepted as an affiliate by the International Trade Union Confederation. Not all is well, though, for as Dan Gallin points out, this 'was largely a symbolic achievement. The new International had neither a "department" nor a "desk" for informal workers, nor was the informal workers' agenda any part of the priorities of the new organisation' (Gallin, 2012: 11). Nevertheless, these developments point to encouraging directions in organising transnational solidarity within the social factory in the current context of the structuring conditions of global capitalism.

---

[6] SEWA, www.sewa.org/; accessed 14 June 2012.

Conclusion: Towards Global Capitalism, Global War, Global Crisis

In tracing the spatial reorganisations of capitalist crises, David Harvey has surmised that 'workers' control or community collectives in relatively isolated production units can rarely survive – in spite of all the hopeful *autonomista, autogestion* and anarchist rhetoric – in the face of a hostile financial environment and credit system and the predatory practices of merchant capital' (Harvey, 2012: 122–3). Rather than this capitalocentric refrain and dismissal, we prefer his own more expansive emphasis on the linkages he establishes between the exploitation of living labour in work-based struggles and popular forces at the neighbourhood or community level organising against the recuperation and realisation of surplus value in peoples' everyday living spaces through the reorganising and socialising of work in the home, the neighbourhood and the city. Therefore, citing Bill Fletcher and Fernando Gapasin (2008: 174),

a community-based organisation rooted in the working class (such as a worker's centre) that addresses class-specific issues is a labour organisation in the same way that a trade union is. (as cited by Harvey, 2012: 135)

From our discussion, it should be clear that asserting the significance of the social factory is pivotal in order to understand the reorganisation of territory as a social space that is increasingly structured according to the needs of capital accumulation. At the same time, this expansive notion of the social factory provides a persuasive assessment of exploitation and resistance beyond the capitalocentric confines of the discipline of capital and workerist programmatic organising. Additionally, it is through the notion of the social factory that a feminist perspective on radicalised dialectics can be asserted that is able to combatively articulate the tensions and connections between class, gender, race, sexuality and ecology without assuming these forms exist within an anodyne and concordant unity. The dialectical internal relations perspective we have offered in this chapter has projected the unity-in-diversity of these identity dynamics in order to offer a radical, open-ended understanding of class struggle. As Silvia Federici affirms:

The extension of the commodity-form to every corner of the social factory, which neoliberalism has promoted, is an ideal limit for capitalist ideologues, but it is a project not only unrealisable but undesirable from the viewpoint of the long-term reproduction of the capitalist system. Capitalist accumulation is structurally dependent on the free appropriation of immense areas of labour and resources that must appear as externalities to the market, like the unpaid domestic work that women have provided, on which employers have relied for the reproduction of the workforce. (Federici, 2012: 140)

Whether social movements shaped in and through the social factory and engaged in anti-capitalist alternatives can reorganise territory as a social space and move from organising in and *dominating place* towards *commanding space* in transcending their own militant particularisms remains a question for future struggles (on these fecund distinctions, see Harvey, 1996: 324). Meanwhile struggles over territory, land, resources, living labour, basic subsistence, reproductive work, racist discrimination, contemporary war and humanity-in-nature abound. Moreover, 'the division between the still regularly employed and the fractions of the surplus population is becoming the key division within struggles, today' (Endnotes, 2015: 164; also see Endnotes, 2010: 20–51; Soederberg, 2014). In order to unravel the dynamics of Global Capitalism, Global War, Global Crisis, the historical method of 'postholing' is now employed in Part III of this book that tries to depict the sweep of historical forces and at the same time some of the richness of detail which comes from delving into a specific moment. Recall from Chapter 1 that the historical method of postholing invites theory about why historical change occurs and demands a theoretical perspective on history beyond explanations of immediate contingencies or sheer chance (Sennett, 1977/2002: 42). The postholing method deployed in the chapters that follow therefore warrants a focus on the sweep of the historical forces of Global Capitalism, Global War, Global Crisis in relation to the specificity of the uneven and combined developmental expansion of capitalism in relation to Brazil, Russia, India, China and South Africa (the BRICS), and especially China (Global Capitalism in Chapter 7); the Iraq War, in order to try and reveal details in this case of U.S. imperium (Global War in Chapter 8); and the political economy of the Eurozone (Global Crisis in Chapter 9) – all linked to the wider dynamics of global restructuring. A focus on the cohered differences of class struggle from the perspective of radical dialectics and the philosophy of internal relations facilitates the empirical interventions that follow across the social factory.

Part III

Empirical Interventions

7   Global Capitalism and Rising Powers

The phenomenon of the rise of the so-called BRICS (Brazil, Russia, India, China and South Africa) has been discussed since 2001. 'Problematising it as related to the decline of American dominance and the rise of global China (and other emerging markets), a Goldman Sachs team selected some useful "non-Western others" and narrated them as being low risk with high growth potential' (Sum and Jessop, 2013: 443). It was alleged that the economic core of the global political economy was slowly but steadily moving from the traditional industrialised countries in Europe, Japan and North America towards rapidly industrialising and developing emerging markets elsewhere in the world. In this chapter, we assess the significance of these changes in the global political economy through a historical materialist analysis based on the philosophy of internal relations. This will help us to grasp the internal relations between changes in global capitalism with the dynamics of geopolitical rivalry parsing the ways in which the rise of the BRICS within global capitalism is of a piece with processes of state transformation engendering potential new forms of geopolitical tension. 'Much of the discussion about the rise of the BRICS is actually really a discussion about one BRICS country, that of China' (Kiely, 2015: 10). Our focus in this chapter is, therefore, on China. In line with the postholing method, introduced in Chapter 1, this allows us to capture some of the empirical richness of capitalist transformation in detail, while understanding at the same time the broader sweep of historical forces.

Many mainstream attempts have been made to analyse the 'rise' of China in the global political economy. Neorealists stress the potential rivalry especially between the United States and China. China's recent New Silk Roads or One Belt, One Road strategy – a cluster of large infrastructure projects linking China with Europe, for example – is discussed in terms of a 'defensive' or 'offensive' grand strategy along these lines (Leverett and Bingbing, 2016: 110–11). John Mearsheimer, in turn, who identifies the United States as a regional hegemon in the Americas, concludes that 'my theory says that the ideal situation for any great power is to be the only regional hegemon in the world' (Mearsheimer, 2006: 161). Hence, the United States is expected to do everything possible to prevent China from becoming a regional hegemon in Asia. 'The United States can be expected to go to great lengths to contain China and ultimately weaken it to the point where it is no longer capable of ruling the roost in Asia' (Mearsheimer, 2006: 162). In short, great power conflict is inevitable. Liberal approaches, by contrast, focus on economic cooperation between the two states and highlight China's peaceful integration into the global economy exemplified, for example, in its accession to the World Trade Organization (WTO) in 2001. John Ikenberry agrees that China is on the rise. Nevertheless, 'China does not just face the United States; it faces a Western-centred system that is open, integrated, and rule-based, with wide and deep political foundations ... today's Western order, in short, is hard to overturn and easy to join' (Ikenberry, 2008: 24). China will rise, in other words, but it will be within a Western order characterised by Western rules. 'The overall system is dense with multilateral rules and institutions – global and regional, economic, political, and security-related. These represent one of the great breakthroughs of the postwar era. They have laid the basis for unprecedented levels of cooperation and share authority over the global system' (Ikenberry, 2008: 30). Joseph Nye, moreover, emphasises the complex interdependence tying the United States and China together in the global economy. Unlike some neorealists, he does not regard the fact that China holds enormous reserves of up to $2.5 trillion USD of foreign exchange, mainly in U.S. Treasury securities, as an indication of a power shift from the United States to China. 'China could threaten to sell its holdings of dollars and damage the U.S. economy', he asserts, 'but a weakened U.S. economy would mean a smaller market for Chinese exports, and the U.S. government might respond with tariffs against Chinese goods' (Nye, 2010: 149). In other words, while the United States depends on China to maintain high levels of dollar reserves, China depends on the U.S. market for the export of its goods. In sum, in contrast to neorealist approaches, liberal perspectives do not argue that the rise of China will inevitably result in great power conflict. Cooperation, from which both sides tend to benefit, is much more likely. While these approaches assess the implications of China's rise differently, they have in common that they take the separation of the 'state' and 'market', the interstate system and the global economy (or the 'political' and the 'economic') as their ahistorical starting point of analysis.

Equally, the debate between those who argue that the rise of China is due to its integration with the neoliberal global political economy of the Washington consensus and those who credit the role of the authoritarian

Chinese state with this success succumbs to the same shortcoming. In other words, the debate about whether the rise of the BRICS is the result of a triumph of the West, because the BRICS adjusted to neoliberalism, or a challenge to the West based on state-led development (Kiely, 2015: 33–44, 65), is also beset by this separation of the 'economic' and the 'political'. Market-centric understandings of development, for example, completely overlook that neoliberalism itself is also always based on political regulation. Yet such separations can even creep into more self-declared historical materialist accounts of rising powers and global capitalism. Witness Matthew Stephen (2014: 914) arguing, for example, that 'rising powers therefore face a dilemma in their orientations towards liberal global governance. On the one hand, rising powers are increasingly functionally dependent on the existing institutional frameworks of global governance to oversee a transnationally integrated global economy. On the other, their statist forms of capitalist development put them into tension with the market-making and individualist (liberal) tenets of global governance.'

As discussed in Chapter 1, state and market within capitalism attain the appearance of separation due to the particular way the social relations of production are organised around the private ownership of the means of production and wage labour and how, as a result, surplus value is extracted through extra-political means based on the sale of labour power by those who do not own their own means of production (Wood, 1995: 29, 34). Ultimately, however, in our historical materialist perspective both the 'political' and the 'economic' are simply differentiated forms of the same underlying social relations of production. They are not relegated to *spatially separate spheres*. Instead, the social constitution of the economy is understood as embodied in juridical-political and ideological forms, as expressed, for example, by the state guarantee of private property. Hence, only a focus on the social relations of production allows us to comprehend these internal relations and, thus, the historical specificity of capitalism.

In other words, analysing the emergence of the BRICS through the philosophy of internal relations makes clear that this rise cannot be an issue of different state policies, nor a binary issue of great power rivalry versus cooperation. The 'economic' is always internally related to the 'political' and differences in the forms of these internal relations are due to a variety in the configuration of the social relations of production underpinning specific state forms. As discussed in Chapter 5, the extent to which the interests of transnational capital are internalised within specific forms of state differs from country to country, as does the particular form of capitalist restructuring. Hence, in order to grasp the internal relations between the interstate system and global capitalism, our analysis has to start with an assessment of the social relations of production and the way production in China is integrated into the global political economy. In a second step, then, we assess in this chapter the changing form of state in China and analyse the way different configurations of social class forces are expressed at the state level. Before moving to this analysis, however, we first address alternative historical materialist accounts of the rise of China and the BRICS to assess whether they can overcome the shortcomings of the mainstream debate.

Alternative Historical Materialist Accounts

Within historical materialist assessments a variety of different conclusions can be derived. Authors including Samir Amin and Giovanni Arrighi contend that China provides a progressive alternative to the way capitalism inheres elsewhere. In Arrighi's words, 'the failure of the Project for a New American Century and the success of Chinese economic development, taken jointly, have made the realisation of [Adam] Smith's vision of a world-market society based on greater equality among the world's civili-sations more likely than it ever was in almost two and a half centuries since the publication of *The Wealth of Nations*' (Arrighi, 2007: 8). Importantly, Arrighi here distinguishes between industrial revolution in the West, based on new machinery, and industrious revolution in Asia, relying much more on large numbers of workers. He highlights positively the role township and village enterprises (TVES) play in expanding domestic demand and developing rural agriculture. The 'observation that in the TVES the intensive cultivation of small plots of land is combined with industrial and other forms of non-agricultural work, and with investments in the improvement of the quality of labour, confirms the validity of the [industrious revolution] thesis' (Arrighi, 2007: 365). In short, Arrighi identifies in China a different development path from advanced industrialised countries in the West, a path deemed more promising in terms of social equality and more peace-ful in relation to the geopolitical order.

If the reorientation succeeds in reviving and consolidating China's traditions of self-centered market-based development, accumulation without dispossession, mobilisation of human rather than non-human resources, and government through mass participation in shaping policies, then the chances are that China will be in a position to contribute decisively to the emergence of a commonwealth of civilisations truly respectful of cultural differences. (Arrighi, 2007: 389)

Elsewhere, Samir Amin bases his assessment on the appropriation of ground-rent and, in his view, how agricultural land has not been commodified. Farmers and village communes have certain usufruct rights including the renting out of land to others, but they are not allowed to sell land, as it is not their private property. 'This "Chinese specificity" – whose consequences are of major importance – absolutely prevents us from characterising contemporary China (even in 2013) as "capitalist" because the capitalist road is based on the transformation of land into a commodity' (Amin, 2013b: 16). Hence China has not chosen once and for all the 'capitalist road', accelerating its integration into contemporary capitalist globalisation, based on 'catch-up' in terms of per capita income comparable to the West (Amin, 2013a: 64). Amin observes a sense of continuity from Mao's China in 1950 to today in the establishment of state capitalism. 'The Maoist construction put in place the foundations without which the opening would not have achieved its well-known success' (Amin, 2013b: 23). The result is a state capitalism that is different from 'free market' capitalism. From this viewpoint, China has not integrated into financial globalisation because state capitalism 'is the preliminary phase in the potential commitment of any society to liberating itself from historical capitalism on the long route to socialism/communism' (Amin, 2013b: 20). The success of this strategy is not automatic. Nonetheless, the current stage of Chinese state capitalism includes, at least for Amin, the potential for a successful transition to socialism as soon as the forces of production are developed enough.

These assessments, however, are obviously not without problems. Arrighi, coming from a world systems analysis position and its commercialisation viewpoint on capitalist development (see Chapter 4), fails to understand the key dynamics underpinning the rise of China. As he argues, 'the capitalist character of market-based development is not determined by the presence of capitalist institutions and dispositions but by the relation of state power to capital. Add as many capitalists as you like to a market economy, but unless the state has been subordinated to their class interest, the market economy remains non-capitalist' (Arrighi, 2007: 332). Even if a domestic capitalist class had come into existence (with Arrighi unsure that this has actually happened), it would still depend on whether this class has seized the control of the state to turn China into a capitalist country (Arrighi, 2007: 369). As already discussed in Chapter 4, Arrighi thereby falls back on an understanding that treats the 'market' (here capitalists) as separate from the 'state'. According to this view, as long as the latter remains dominant, we do not have a capitalist system. The focus on the external relations between the Chinese state on one hand and economic development in China on the other therefore produces an ahistorical analysis similar to the mainstream analyses mentioned earlier. By abstracting an analysis of 'state' and 'market' from the social relations of production, Arrighi is unable to understand the character of capital as a social relation and the cluster of internal relations organised around wage labour and the private ownership of the means of production.

Amin's assessment is problematic too in the way he contrasts state capitalism with free market capitalism, emphasising the external relationship between the 'political' and the 'economic'. Precisely because peasants have not held a title to their land, but only user rights, it has been easy to dispossess them, asserts David Harvey. 'As many as 70 million farmers may have lost their land in this way over the past decade. Commune leaders, for example, frequently asserted de facto property rights over communal land and assets in negotiations with foreign investors or developers' (Harvey, 2005: 146). Private property has not been fully established in China. Nevertheless, 'by separating usage rights from ownership, pragmatic leaders effectively legitimised the transfer of land for commercial uses in the absence of de jure privatisation' (Peck and Zhang, 2013: 372). Considering the increasing proletarianisation of a large migrant workforce plus the decisive role the transnational capitalist class (TCC) plays in the organisation of Chinese production and, to a lesser extent, the emergence of a Chinese capitalist class (see later in this chapter), Chinese development is just one of the latest expressions of neoliberal restructuring including accumulation by dispossession with Chinese people being expropriated and driven from their land. This shows 'that we are not confronting any simple "export" of neoliberalism from some hegemonic centre. The development of neoliberalism must be regarded as a decentred and unstable evolutionary process characterised by uneven geographical developments and strong competitive pressures between a variety of dynamic centres of political-economic power' (Harvey, 2006a: 31). In short, in line with our definition of capitalism around the social property relations perspective, we analyse the BRICS phenomenon through an examination of the social relations of production and the particular way Chinese production has become integrated into the global political economy. The structuring condition of outward expansion around uneven and combined development, discussed in Chapter 4, will be essential in this respect. In the next section, the emergence of the BRICS and here in particular China is assessed against the background of the global economic crisis since the 1970s and in particular the pursuit of a spatial fix, in which labour-intensive manufacturing production has been shifted from industrialised to developing countries.

The Rise of the BRICS and the New International Division of Labour

The post-1945 period in industrialised countries was characterised by enormous growth rates and increasing wealth. National class compromises between capital and labour underpinned the post–World War II economic recovery. While labour accepted capital's prerogative over the means of production and the way production is organised, capital in turn agreed on workers participating in growing wealth through a steady increase in wages and improvement in working conditions. In tripartite relationships, the state supported this compromise through Keynesian, demand-led economic policies guaranteeing full employment in a system of mass employment and mass consumption. Additionally, the state lent its support through an expanding welfare state establishing universal access to services such as healthcare and education. Observers often speak of a golden capitalist age when commenting on the post-war period. Nevertheless, as discussed in Chapter 2 in relation to the structuring conditions of capitalism, while the social relations of production are enormously dynamic as both labour and capital have to reproduce themselves in competition on the market, capitalism is also crisis ridden. In the late 1960s and early 1970s, the global political economy entered a crisis of over-accumulation, manifested in a declining rate of profit (Robinson, 2014: 131). Economic growth was no longer strong enough to ensure both capitalist super-profits and rising wages for workers. Unsurprisingly, the late 1960s and early 1970s saw increasing levels of industrial conflict across the industrialised world.

In response, capital renounced the national class compromise and re-established and reorganised production across the global political economy through the search for a combination of various 'fixes' to the economic crisis. First, a technological fix, characterised by drastic innovation in production processes at the capital-intensive end in industrialised countries, was combined with a spatial fix, transferring labour-intensive parts of manufacturing such as in the textile industry to cheap labour locations elsewhere in the global political economy (Silver, 2003: 64–6). As John Smith makes clear, it is a form of global labour arbitrage, 'the substitution of relatively high-wage workers in imperialist countries with low-wage workers in China, Bangladesh, and other nations in the Global South' (Smith, 2016: 188), which has allowed capital to continue reaping super profits since the major economic crisis of the 1970s. According to Marx, 'it is only in the actual process of production that *objectified labour* is transformed into capital by absorbing living labour and hence it is only then that *labour transforms itself into* capital' (1867/1990: 994–5, original emphasis), with this role now

increasingly performed by living labour in the Global South. This development has been further supported by a product fix and the shift towards new
industrial sectors including the semiconductor industry, employment and
producer services, as well as the education industry (Silver, 2003: 123).
In short, in the transnationalisation of production, such processes have been
increasingly organised across borders with the manufacturing process
located in various countries. As discussed in Chapter 5, transnational corporations (TNCs), organising global value chains (GVCs), have emerged as
a key presence in these processes. Additionally, a financial fix, often referred
to as financialisation, revived growth potentials in that the financial sector
itself was transformed into an area of capitalist accumulation in its own right
through the introduction of ever more new financial products and investment opportunities. Within capital, power shifted from manufacturing to
finance capital. As David Harvey (2006a: 24) argues, 'the general effect was
that financial interests (the power of the accountants rather than the engineers) gained the upper hand within the ruling classes and the ruling elites.
Neoliberalism meant, in short, the financialisation of everything and the
relocation of the power centre of capital accumulation to owners and their
financial institutions at the expense of other fractions of capital.'

These developments, however, could not have occurred without an
enormous increase in the global workforce. Richard Freeman (2010)
shows that the integration of China, India and the former Soviet Union
during the 1980s and 1990s doubled the global proletariat to almost
3 billion by 2000. As David Coates correctly noted, 'the enhanced global
mobility of capital in the last three decades has social rather than technical
roots. Capital is more geographically mobile than it was in the past
because it now has more proletariats on which to land' (Coates, 2000:
255). The emergence of the BRICS and the rise of China, in short, have to
be seen as part of these developments of reorganising capitalist accumulation at the global level. In the following subsections, we now first assess
the location of Chinese production in the global political economy before
looking more generally at the so-called rise of the Global South.

Chinese Production in the Global Political Economy

It was Marx (1894/1991: 364–5) who stated that, 'if capital is sent
abroad, this is not because it absolutely could not be employed at
home. It is rather because it can be employed abroad at a higher rate.'
As discussed in Chapter 4, capital's outward expansion is characterised
by the dynamic of uneven and combined development. The integration
of new forms of state into the global political economy has proven to be
no exception in this respect. First, development in China is combined

with development in advanced industrialised countries, dependent to a large extent on foreign direct investment (FDI) by TNCs. In 1987, the state committed itself to export-led development (Harvey, 2005: 128), followed by the decision in 1992 to open up the economy more centrally to market forces and foreign capital. Since then, Chinese exports have been dominated by foreign TNCs. By 2003, foreign TNCs and joint ventures 'accounted for almost 80% of China's exports of industrial machinery, 90% of computers, components, and peripherals[,] and 71% of electronics and telecommunications equipment' (Panitch and Gindin, 2014: 152). This tendency has intensified in recent years. 'TNCs produce approximately 85 percent of China's high technology exports. Moreover, the share of China's high technology exports produced by wholly foreign owned TNCs continues to grow, from 55 percent in 2002 to 68 percent in 2009, suggesting a tightening of foreign control' (Hart-Landsberg, 2015: 5).

Second, however, Chinese development is highly uneven in comparison with development in advanced, industrialised countries. Chinese production is predominantly based on cheap labour, necessary for assembling the various parts into final products for export to North American and European markets. 'Chinese leaders have, like the leaders of most other countries, consciously pursued a low-wage growth strategy for some time' (Hart-Landsberg, 2015: 14). Unsurprisingly, it is these foreign TNCs which reap super-profits from exploiting Chinese workers. Foxconn, assembling products for Apple, is a clear example in this respect. It 'made $2.4 billion in profits in 2010, or $2,400 per employee, compared to $263,000 in profits reaped by Apple for each of its 63,000 employees (43,000 of whom are in the United States)' (Smith, 2012: 90). When observers talk about the dramatic rise of China, they tend to refer to the increase in Chinese exports. 'China's share of global exports was just 1.9% in 1990, compared to 8.5% for Japan, 11.6% for the U.S. and 12.1% for Germany. By 2005, the comparable figures were 7.3% China, 9.4% Germany, 5.7% Japan and 8.7% the U.S. By 2010, post-crisis, the figures were 10.6% China, 8.1% Germany, 5.2% Japan and 8.6% the U.S. By 2010 then, China had emerged as the world's biggest exporter' (Kiely, 2015: 69–70). However, an analysis of how Chinese production is predominantly integrated into the social relations of production globally provides a more accurate picture of the situation. In manufacturing especially, we need to look at Asia as a whole if we want to understand the location of Chinese production. 'Developing Asia occupies the leading position in the new international division of labour. The region's share in total world exports of manufacturers grew from 11.1 percent in 1996–1997 to 33.8 percent in 2009/2010. Its share of total third world exports of manufactures increased from 68 percent to 76 percent over the same period' (Hart-Landsberg, 2015: 4). Within Asia, China mainly operates as the regional assembly platform. 'It is China's unique position as the region's production platform that enabled the country to increase its share of world exports of IT products from 3 percent in 1992 to 24 percent in 2006, and its share of electrical goods from 4 percent to 21 percent over the same period' (Hart-Landsberg, 2013: 34). In turn, these products are mainly destined for markets in North America and Europe integrating East Asia within the global political economy, but also making it dependent on continuing demand in the Global North (Hardy, 2017: 195). In sum, 'since the region's trade activity largely involves an intraregional trade of parts and components culminating in China-based exports aimed primarily at the United States and the European Union, the reality is that Asia has become ever more tightly integrated and dependent on exporting to developed capitalist markets, especially the United States' (Hart-Landsberg, 2013: 36). Thus, China's production is mainly based on cheap labour and labour-intensive activities, dominated by foreign TNCs and highly dependent on access to markets elsewhere. The focus on Chinese export levels clearly distorts the picture, as it does not take into account the amount of imports of prefabricated parts, which are then assembled in Chinese production sites. Moreover, because of the focus on cheap labour, the value-added captured in China is comparatively low. As Ernest Mandel once argued, 'on the world market, the labour of a country with a higher productivity of labour is valued as more intensive, so that the product of one day's work in such a nation is exchanged for the product of more than a day's work in an underdeveloped country' (Mandel, 1975: 71–2). This is the 'second-wind' of uneven development as ultra-modern advances in technology ensure that peripheral spaces come to accept a new form of specialisation, emerging as a producer of capital goods, but still lagging behind advanced capitalist centres (Amin, 1976: 190; Bieler and Morton, 2014).

In other words, due to the transnationalisation of production and its spatial fix, large parts of labour-intensive manufacturing have moved towards the Global South, reorganising the integration of peripheral space into the global political economy along the lines of uneven and combined development. At the same time, however, such uneven and combined development has meant that industrialised countries have continued to focus on high-value-added manufacturing, ensuring that this has remained in the Global North. As Ray Kiely (2012: 239–40) indicates:

In 1970, 18.5 per cent of the total exports from the developing world were manufactured goods; with the phenomenal rise of China since the early 1990s, this figure had increased to over 80 per cent by the end of the 1990s. However, at the same time, since the liberalisation of the 1980s, developed countries' share of manufacturing exports fell (from 82.3 per cent in 1980 to 70.9 per cent by 1997), but their share of manufacturing value added actually increased over the same period, from 64.5 per cent to 73.3 per cent.

Unsurprisingly, despite Chinese 'catch-up', the gap between China and industrialised countries has remained enormous. 'In 2010 (even after the aftermath of the crisis and recession) China's GDP was $5.9 trillion – only 40 percent of the U.S.'s $14.6 trillion. Translated into GDP per head this gap is even starker: China's $4,260 was only 9 percent of the U.S.'s $47,240' (Hardy and Budd, 2012). As Neil Davidson concludes, 'although China develops more dramatically than any of the countries, like India, with which it is usually bracketed, it is unlikely on any remotely foreseeable scenario, to "catch up" with the West in any overall sense' (Davidson, 2006: 226). Especially a shift towards more high-value-added production has proved illusory to a large extent. There are some more high-value-added facilities in the area around Shanghai (Bieler and Lee, 2017), but in general China has not been able so far to escape the labour-intensive location in the global political economy. 'Indeed, China has not managed to develop a global brand-leader with a global market and procurement system' (Saull, 2012: 326; see also Kiely, 2015: 46–8). China, the leading member of the BRICS, continues to be far behind industrialised countries in absolute political-economic terms. 'China's population is 24% higher than that of all the high income countries put together, but its income is only one-fifth that of those countries' (Kiely, 2015: 125).

Importantly, Chinese development has been highly uneven and combined not only globally, but also locally. Domestic unevenness, first, is the result of China's cheap-labour, export-oriented strategy. As most export production is based on cheap labour, China must ensure a continuing supply of workers willing to work for low wages. This has been secured partly as a result of the privatisation of state-owned enterprises (SOEs) in the mid-1990s, which resulted in the redundancy of some 60 million workers (Chan and Selden, 2014: 601), and partly due to the growing group of migrant workers, which amounted to 277 million workers by early 2016, coming from the countryside to the new production powerhouses in the coastal areas (Chan and Selden, 2017: 259). Second, the unevenness of Chinese internal development is also reflected in workers' falling share of GDP, which 'fell from approximately 53 percent of GDP in 1992 to below 40 percent in 2006. Private consumption as a percent of GDP also declined, falling from approximately 47 percent to 36 percent over the same period' (Hart-Landsberg, 2013: 50; see also Qi, 2014).

The Chinese government has started to stimulate domestic consumption since the 2008 financial crisis in the expectation that increasing domestic purchasing capacity will boost consumption. Nonetheless, 'China's level of consumption, at 36 percent of GDP, is much lower than the world average, which measures in at 60 percent of GDP' (Hsu, 2015). Third, China's development model has led to enormous levels of inequality, further confirming the underlying unevenness inside China. 'Inequality has risen rapidly and the Gini co-efficient has risen from 0.28 in the early 1980s to 0.48 in 2008. It has been estimated that 0.1% of households have 45.8% of total household wealth – that is, 1.3 million people hold almost half of the household wealth of 1.3 billion people' (Kiely, 2015: 134). Hypermodern coastal regions are counterpoised to backward, inner rural areas. 'According to one estimate, the "winners" of the economic reforms – the state administrators, managers, private entrepreneurs, professionals and technicians – amount to approximately 9 per cent of the entire population. The losers, on the other hand – the production workers, service workers, farmers, the unemployed and underemployed – amount to about 82 per cent of the population' (Gray, 2010: 460).

In turn, the agricultural sector has played a crucial role in the Chinese development model, indicating the way industrialisation in coastal areas has been combined with a different form of agricultural production in rural areas. In practice this has ensured the supply of cheap labour in that it provides a separate stream of income especially for the dependents of migrant workers left back home. This facilitated the super-exploitation of migrant workers themselves. As John Smith (2016: 197) outlines, Marx discussed three different forms of increasing the exploitation of workers: 1) absolute surplus value through measures such as the lengthening of the working day; 2) relative surplus value by increasing labour productivity through the introduction of new technology in the production process; and 3) forms of super-exploitation in which wages are reduced below the value of labour power. Super-exploitation is thereby closely linked to global labour arbitrage.

Global labour arbitrage-driven outsourcing is driven by lust for cheaper labour, and corresponds most directly to the 'reduction of wages below their value'. In other words, global labour arbitrage, the driver of the global shift of production to low-wage nations, is the third form of surplus value recognised by Marx as a most important factor. (Smith, 2016: 238–9)

As workers' wages are pressed below the value of labour power, something else must ensure their survival, with agricultural production often acting as a 'shock absorber' to the capitalist process (Morton, 2011/2013: 58). Agriculture is thus closely linked to industrial production in that 'agriculture and the rural society provide the conditions for the reproduction of labour power. For rural households, agriculture in most cases is merely one of their income sources. Rural households are semi-proletarianised as they are participating in both household-organised agricultural production and wage employment' (Qi, 2014). In short, combined development in China is reflected in the way agriculture has facilitated the super-exploitation of Chinese workers below the rate of subsistence. As Andrew Higginbottom argues, 'systemic oppression to force the price of labour power below its value is not at all archaic; rather it is the principal factor offsetting the declining rate of profit in modern imperialism. The same idea is better termed super-exploitation' (Higginbottom, 2011: 283–4). In China, this super-exploitation is ensured through the way agriculture continues to support the reproduction of cheap labour for exploitation by foreign TNCs.

The Rise of the Global South?

Thinking about the BRICS more generally, there has been a lot of discussion over the rise of the Global South, often justified through a focus on a drastic increase in South–South trade, 'which accounted for less than 9% of world trade in 1960 but as much as 42% in 2008' (Kiely, 2015: 160). Nevertheless, rather than comparing countries of the Global South as independent units and adding up their various trade levels, our approach – in line with Philip McMichael's (1990) method of 'incorporated comparison' – is to understand how the various countries are differently integrated into the global political economy as a totality. We have already seen how China has developed into a regional assembly hub in Asia, where prefabricated products are put together into final goods, which are then exported for sale on North American and European markets. 'Around 22% of exports of the main East Asian countries to each other are for final demand, while 60% is destined for final demand in the U.S., Europe and Japan. Seen in this way, the rise of South–South trade reflects less the rise of the South and more its continued dependence on the markets of the North' (Kiely, 2015: 88). Africa and Latin America, furthermore, have mainly participated in global trade through exporting primary commodities to China in its relentless demand for more resources.

While Latin American and sub-Saharan nations have long specialised in the export of primary commodities, developing Asia, especially China, has now replaced core capitalist countries as their main export market. China has surpassed the United States as the world's largest consumer of major metals and agricultural commodities. In 2011, it consumed approximately 20 percent of all non-renewable energy resources, 23 percent of major agricultural crops, and 40 percent of base metals. (Hart-Landsberg, 2015: 6)

In line with the crucial role of the state in Chinese development (see later in this chapter), access to these primary commodities has partly been secured through outward FDI by large Chinese SOEs, 'accounting for approximately 80% of Chinese cumulative investment stock' (Deng, 2013: 519; see also UNCTAD, 2017: 31). In the sub-Saharan region, widespread deindustrialisation has accompanied this process. 'One important reason that the region's high rate of growth did not produce meaningful improvements in majority well-being is that growth driven by primary commodity exports generally creates few formal sector jobs' (Hart-Landsberg, 2015: 15). Moreover, deindustrialisation has gone hand in hand with exploitative working conditions. Common trends in Chinese companies in Africa include 'tense labor relations, hostile attitudes by Chinese employers toward trade unions, violations of workers' rights, poor working conditions, and unfair labor practices' (Jauch, 2011: 52). In turn, as Kiely points out, 'Latin America is a major exporter of primary commodities to China, with copper ore, soybean, soya oil, iron ore, crude oil, and refined copper leading the way in terms of exports ... ; if we combine primary goods and resource based manufactures, then in 2008 87.7% of Latin American exports were in these sectors, compared to 53.6% for the rest of the world' (Kiely, 2015: 160).

In sum, South–South trade is not an autonomous engine of growth for developing countries but, rather, mainly consists of the export of primary commodities to China and the trade in parts in Asia towards China, where they are assembled for export to the Global North (Hart-Landsberg, 2015: 15). While states in Africa and Latin America heavily depend on continuing demand for primary commodities in China, the latter and other states in Asia, which are part of GVCs, rely on healthy consumer markets in North America and Europe. 'Despite their large trade volumes', Alfredo Saad-Filho writes, 'China and the other East Asian [developing economies] have little scope to drive growth in the South, because their trade is heavily integrated into regional production chains and their net exports are geared to [advanced economies'] markets, which capture most the value created along the chain, leaving little available for circulation within the South' (Saad-Filho, 2014: 588). India has become integrated into the global economy in a slightly different way. While China developed through a focus on cheap-labour manufacturing, 'in India it has been the services sector which has led, accounting for 59% of GDP at factor cost in 2011/12, compared with industry's share of 27% and only 14% for agriculture' (Vanaik, 2014: 20). Overall, however, this has not resulted in general developmental 'catch-up' either. 'The modernity and wealth of India's software hubs sits very uncomfortably with a rural and small town landscape that continues to be defined by its poverty, underdevelopment, and stagnation that blights the lives of millions and which continues to pose limits on India's enthusiasm for further global integration' (Saull, 2012: 332).

Unsurprisingly, a general developmental 'catch-up' of the Global South with advanced industrialised countries cannot be identified. 'There has been a small shift towards a decrease in inequality between countries in recent years, but also a trend of growing inequality within countries over the last thirty years, offset lightly by a partial reversal in some countries in the 2000s' (Kiely, 2015: 136). In terms of competitiveness based on productivity, none of the BRICS has managed to move towards the top. 'For 2013–14, the U.S. stood at number 5 in the world, behind Switzerland, Singapore, Finland and Germany. China, however, stood at 29, South Africa at 53, Brazil at 56, India at 60 and Russia at 64. In 2010–11, Brazil ranked 42nd, Russia 57th, India 39th and China 26th in the world' (Kiely, 2015: 185). In short, there can be no question of developmental 'catch-up', not for China or any other country in the Global South. Inequality between the Global South and the Global North remains vast. '149 million of the global absolute poor and global insecure live in the developed countries, while 5,172 million live in the global South' (Kiely, 2015: 150). Instead, polarisation (the construction of centre/periphery contrasts) is immanent to the uneven development of capitalism. 'This polarisation eliminates the possibility for a country from the periphery to "catch up" within the context of capitalism' (Amin, 2013a: 78).

Considering this rather shaky political economy for China and the BRICS more generally, what are the internally related geopolitical implications? To start, an analysis with a focus on the social relations of production is essential for understanding the relations between the 'political' and the 'economic', the 'state' and 'market', including the internal relation of geopolitics and global capitalism. Nevertheless, a focus on the social relations of production identifying China as a part of global capitalism does not automatically lead to a uniform analysis. As demonstrated in Chapter 5, various historical materialist approaches evaluate these changes in the social relations of production associated with globalisation differently. William Robinson's analysis of the BRICS, on one hand, emphasises the way rising powers have become integrated into the transnational state (TNS). 'The picture that emerges is less one of the state controlling capital or of the old state capitalism than of transnational capital colonising the state in new ways' (Robinson, 2015: 7). In turn, these states then do transnational capital's bidding. 'The Brazilian government's aggressive programme of agricultural trade liberalisation, waged through the World Trade Organisation (WTO) ... is not in defence of "Brazilian" interests against Northern or imperial capital but on behalf of a transnationalised soy agro-industrial complex. The Brazilian state acted in the way we would expect as a component of the TNS' (Robinson, 2015: 9). Nevertheless, while the BRICS have become increasingly integrated into the global political economy, this does not automatically imply the integration of capitalist classes into the TCC. As Matthew Stephen asserts, 'there is little sign of the hegemonic integration of the state classes amongst the BRICS, despite their strong integration into transnational production' (Stephen, 2014: 927). Also as a result of geopolitical security tensions, Saull adds, the integration of the BRICS into the neoliberal bloc has been limited (Saull, 2012: 333). As we argued in Chapter 5, the peculiarities of different forms of state continue to play a distinctive role in the global political economy and the extent to which the interests of transnational capital have become internalised into specific forms of state needs to be assessed on a case-by-case basis.

By contrast, Leo Panitch and Sam Gindin, although they agree on the capitalist character of Chinese development, emphasise the continuing centrality of the U.S. state in global capitalism, in line with their general argument discussed in Chapter 8 below. Rather than a weakness, they assert, 'the U.S. trade and credit "imbalances" were actually indicative of the extent of China's integration into the American-led global capitalist order. U.S. imports from China provided low-cost inputs for businesses and cheap consumer goods for workers, while China's march to capitalism at home was characterised by the largest inflow of foreign capital and technology as well as the greatest export dependence of any late developer in history' (Panitch and Gindin, 2014: 147). In short, in a rather statecentric analysis, they simply assert 'the central role that the American state continues to play in reproducing global capitalism' (Panitch and Gindin, 2014: 154). Nevertheless, the United States should not be mistaken for a unitary actor. In Chapter 8 on the Iraq War, we identify two different class fractions around transnational capital, on one hand, and national capital, on the other, struggling over which course the U.S. form of state would take in relation to that conflict. Equally, in view of the rise of China, a number of different class alliances have emerged struggling with each other over which line the U.S. state should pursue. As James Petras (2015) outlines, there are the IT TNCs such as Apple and IBM who would lose out if the United States adopted a more confrontational stance and they, therefore, lobby Washington to adopt a course of cooperation. They are confronted by a nationalist-military complex, bent on intensifying tensions with China, while Wall Street finance would prefer pressuring China to deregulate its financial markets further, rather than provoking China into a confrontational stance. These class alliances are shifting. What they outline, however, is that we cannot simply leave such relations unclarified, as Panitch and Gindin do.

Our own analysis is different from these positions – both the state-less focus of the former and the U.S. state-centric focus of the latter – that both equally re-establish an emphasis on the external relations between geopolitical and capitalist logics. While Robinson discusses how the economic is reconstituted at the global level overcoming the interstate system, Panitch and Gindin reassert the centrality of the U.S. state form but without unpacking the class contradictions and struggles therein. In line with our argument in Chapter 5, we argue, by contrast, that the state still has to be analysed as a nodal point in the organisation of capitalist accumulation. Understanding the state as a condensation of material relations in line with Nicos Poulantzas makes clear that state-level class struggles over the organisation of the social relations of production continue to be key in understanding the changing global political economy. As Ian Taylor clarifies, integration of social class forces in the TCC does not necessarily contradict the continuing importance of states. 'Policy elites in the emerging economies have progressively entered the ranks of the transnationalising ruling classes, although this process is ongoing and incomplete, and contra the transnational capitalist class thesis, this has not been incompatible with state sovereignty and territoriality' (Taylor, 2017: 14). Integration into forms of transnational capital does not imply the absence of conflicts or contradictions. It does, however, indicate that there is no fundamental challenge to the dominant, neoliberal order. 'Integration into the transnational structures of production and exchange of neoliberal globalisation is a fundamental determinant of the orientations of the rising powers vis-à-vis global governance' (Taylor, 2017: 39). Even the global financial crisis did not result in a fundamental break with neoliberalism by the BRICS (Schmalz and Ebenau, 2012: 497–8). This integration at the global level, however, has to be analysed through the way and extent to which the interests of transnational capital have become internalised within the different forms of state constituting the BRICS. Taylor expresses this well when he argues that 'analysis of global restructuring then has to capture the transnational reorganisation of the social relations of production and account for class struggles that take place, entangling national and transnational class fractions and operating from inside and through national expressions of the state' (Taylor, 2017: 203). In the next section, following our use of the method of postholing, we assess the changing Chinese form of state and its role in neoliberal restructuring. In this way, the internal relations between the integration of rising powers into global capitalism and the new geopolitical challenges of the global order can be comprehended.

Transforming China: Class Struggle and the Road towards Neoliberalism

Liberal analyses treat civil society as a progressive force. This is the realm where democracy works and individual groups are given the possibility of participating in policymaking. 'The private sphere (i.e., civil society as distinct from and opposed to the state in the liberal scheme of things) . . . is regarded as the terrain where freedom is exercised and experienced' (Buttigieg, 1995: 5). At the international level, many regard civil society actors as the agency re-establishing political authority and control over the economy, which has outgrown the confines of states and national systems of democratic accountability. The re-regulation of the market at the international level is linked to Karl Polanyi's (1944/1957: 130–77) idea of a double movement: after a period of *laissez-faire*, a phase of political regulation follows. Nevertheless, analysing civil society separately from the social relations of production, these approaches, first, indulge in theoretical dualism (similar to Polanyi himself; see our discussion in Chapter 1), in which the state re-establishes control over the economy from the outside. Second, these approaches cannot take into account the different levels of structural power available to individual actors. An employers' association organising capital in a transnational production sector with a considerable amount of structural power is treated equally in such analysis to an environmental non-governmental organisation (NGO) unable to muster any kind of structural power (Bieler, 2011: 165–6). Liberal perspectives do not therefore understand that 'civil society is not some kind of benign or neutral zone where different elements of society operate and compete freely and on equal terms, regardless of who holds a predominance of power in government' (Buttigieg, 1995: 27).

Hence, when analysing the Chinese form of state, we draw on a historical materialist understanding of civil society. Importantly, for Gramsci the form of state consists of 'political society', i.e. the coercive apparatus of the state more narrowly understood including ministries, the police and other state institutions, and 'civil society', made up of political parties, unions, employers' associations, churches, etc. (Gramsci, 1971: 257–63, 271). Understanding the 'integral state' as political society plus civil society allows Gramsci to theorise the modern state in its internal relations, as demonstrated in Chapter 1. For Gramsci, civil society is the sphere of hegemonic struggle over the purpose of a particular state form. Linked back to the social relations of production, it is clear that different social class forces operate within and through a form of state to establish their particular interests as part of the national interest. Some liberal analyses argue that the concept of civil society could not be applied to the Chinese form of state as China is not a liberal representative democracy and is therefore without a fully functioning civil society. However, the notion of the integral state does not necessarily assume a representative democracy but considers state institutions as part of political society and forms of voluntary organisations as part of civil society.

The Chinese Form of State: A Case of Passive Revolution?

Analysing capitalist restructuring in China, Kevin Gray (2010) highlights the important role of the state in a class strategy of passive revolution, as introduced in Chapter 4. Recall in that chapter that we defined a passive revolution as an emergent class strategy that either institutes and/or expands aspects of the social relations of capitalist development, resulting in both a 'revolutionary' rupture and a 'restoration' of social relations. In China, since there was no dominant class fraction or class alliance in support of restructuring, state officials have been crucial in sustaining the conditions of restructuring, especially from the late 1970s and early 1980s onwards. Following our twofold classifications in Chapter 4, rather than the passive revolutionary road of capitalist transformation in China involving a revolutionary form of political transformation in which popular demands of class struggle have played some role, what has unfolded has been more a 'revolution from above', involving elite-engineered social and political reform that draws on foreign capital and associated ideas while lacking a national-popular base. Therefore, Gramsci's framework, Gray asserts, 'can help to address the issue of the role of the state in facilitating the restoration of capitalism, and how this "revolution from above" has been embedded within broader processes of transnational accumulation and inter-state rivalry' (Gray, 2010: 455). Thus, the Chinese state plays a crucial role in the country's development, combining an authoritarian regime of labour subordination at the domestic level with an active geopolitical role of ensuring the supply of oil and raw materials for the economy, especially through its active engagement with countries in sub-Saharan Africa. The authoritarianism of China's labour regime 'is not a surprising development as it follows the logic of China's enmeshment into the global political economy as a final stage low value-added manufacturer' (Gray, 2015: 143).

A number of key features are characteristic of the emergence of capitalism in China: 1) the gradual development of capitalism; 2) the crucial role of the state; 3) a regionalisation of economic decision-making authority; 4) continuing state control of finance; and 5) integration into the global political economy through WTO membership in 2001. First, the integration of China into the global political economy was a gradual process. Initially in 1978, the intention was simply to instil competition between SOEs. No master plan or blueprint for change existed (Breslin, 2009: 46). The fact that China pursued a strategy of export-led growth driven by inward FDI is also very much the result of changes in the global political economy at the time. China's opening in 1978 coincided with the new strategy by large companies to transnationalise their production structures and look for cheap labour in the Global South in order to overcome economic recession and declining profitability levels in industrialised countries. Had China opened up during the 1950s or 1960s, when production in industrialised countries had been based on national class compromises, the development of Chinese capitalism might have taken a completely different direction. Second, in line with a class strategy of passive revolution, the Chinese state was crucial in shaping policies to introduce competition in SOEs, from the late 1970s and into the early 1980s, when agriculture was restructured. In fact, 'the state's de-collectivisation of agriculture in the early 1980s played a key role in bringing about the semi-proletarianisation of the rural workforce to supply the export-oriented sector in the coastal areas' (Gray, 2015: 139). Equally, to decide on an export-led growth strategy in 1987, to privatise SOEs during the 1990s and to open up to FDI by TNCs, as well as to grant local government the right to organise decentralised accumulation, were all decisions taken by the state class cadre as part of China's passive revolution strategy. Third, Chinese growth dynamics were based on a combination of political centralisation with economic regionalisation. During the 1980s, 'the developmental enthusiasm of local states was enabled/encouraged by fiscal decentralisation, which selectively devolved decision-making power to local governments, tying revenue growth to the career progression of local officials and spawning a unique form of "local state corporatism"' (Peck and Zhang, 2013: 376). The Chinese state, as a result, has become to a considerable extent fragmented, Shahar Hameiri and Lee Jones affirm. 'Since the reform era began in 1978, the Chinese state has experienced considerable disaggregation, the divestment of power and control to semi- and fully private actors, and the devolution of authority and resources to subnational agencies. These changes were designed to insert China into a global division of labour, and the consequent transnationalisation of production and investment has further spurred state transformation' (Hameiri and Jones, 2016: 82; see also Hameiri and Jones, 2015). In other words, increasing regional autonomy as the result of political decisions by the Chinese state cadre has driven capitalist competition and growth dynamics and is, therefore, a key aspect of the transformed Chinese form of state. This also became important in China's response to the global financial crisis in 2008, when the central government relied on local governments to make up funding of new fiscal initiatives of up to $586 billion. 'Local governments were being told to take their share in boosting the economy without being given the resources to do so – but with controls on bank lending relaxed. Although local governments were not formally legally allowed to directly borrow from the banks to fund projects, they did so indirectly through various forms of locally owned companies known as development investment platforms' (Breslin, 2011b: 192).

This points to a fourth key feature of Chinese capitalism in addition to decentralisation, namely state control of the financial system. 'Despite moves towards marketisation of sorts, the financial system has allowed the state to retain effective (and profitable) control over those economic sectors that are deemed essential to the functioning of the economy, and to retain a strong influence over the rest of the economy' (Breslin, 2014: 997). Ultimately, there is an underlying confidence that the state will bail out failing financial institutions. Finally, capitalist transformation was anchored externally in WTO membership in 2001. 'The importance of exports as an engine of economic growth meant that guaranteeing access to the U.S. market in particular, and those of the developed world in general, was essential for job creation' (Breslin, 2009: 95). WTO membership promised to deliver on this objective and has underpinned a situation in which Chinese development has rested heavily on FDI by foreign TNCs. Hence, it is not appropriate to talk about a Chinese alternative to Western capitalism. Rather, as Taylor (2017: 186) maintains, 'China is both an active participant and tacit co-manager of the established global order. Through this, Beijing lends credibility to the system whilst at the same time serving to play an important role as an intermediate actor bridging the ongoing world system, dominated as it is by the capitalist heartland and emerging "rising" actors.' While China's path to capitalism is distinctive, it does not justify the idea of a separate, alternative Beijing model of capitalism, Shaun Breslin asserts. 'If the China model is thought of as being abnormal and deviating from the dominant norm of (neo)liberal development (as it is in some areas), then this simply ignores the normality of strong state developmentalism over history' (Breslin, 2011a: 1323). Rather than thinking about a specific model, we should clarify what China is not: 'it is not big bang reform and shock therapy; it is not a process where economic liberalisation necessarily leads to democratisation; it is not jettisoning state control over key sectors; it is not full (neo-) liberalisation (particularly in financial sectors); it is not being told what to do by others' (Breslin, 2011a: 1338–9).

China's class strategy, or the way capitalist restructuring was implemented within conditions of passive revolution, required careful balancing within the national form of state and broader class struggles, which is now dealt with in more detail.

Passive Revolution and the Control of Labour

The state has played a clear role in the capitalist transformation of China's passive revolution. More recently, however, a capitalist class system has emerged in China. Capital is mainly represented by forces of transnational capital behind the large amounts of FDI flowing into China. More and more, though, these class forces have been joined by a Chinese capitalist class. Stephen (2014: 925) speaks about emerging 'red capitalists', which 'are adept at exploiting party–state relations in tandem with global export manufacturing'. They were partly created from the ranks of the party-state bureaucracy, especially during the process of the privatisations of SOEs during the 1990s. Partly, such 'red capitalists' are present in the remaining SOEs in key sectors of the national economy, including 'banking; power generation and distribution, oil, coal, petrochemicals and natural gas; telecommunications; armaments; aviation and shipping; machinery and automobile production; information technologies; construction; railroads; insurance; grain distribution and the production of iron, steel and non-ferrous metals' (Peck and Zhang, 2013: 371). Although still state-owned, these companies follow clear capitalist strategies. 'SOE executive bonuses are tied to financial performance, while inter-local competition and "GDPism" increasingly constitute the foundations both for resource allocations and party advancement' (Peck and Zhang, 2013: 372). Moreover, these companies have become heavily involved in overseas investment (UNCTAD, 2017: 30–8), which is why Jerry Harris speaks about a statist TCC in China. 'Its investments have merged Chinese economic interests with other statist TCC fractions as well as private TCC sectors' (Harris, 2012: 18). There may be capitalist competition between various TNCs, but Chinese state-owned TNCs are no fundamental challenge to neoliberalisation as such, rather they are pretty much part and parcel of it. In short, 'statist transnational capitalism is as much a part of global capitalism as western private TNCs' (Harris, 2012: 25). There are close links between these 'red capitalists' and the

Communist Party, often leading to a description of networked capitalism, meaning 'linkages between the state and the nascent capitalist class were largely achieved through a corrupt relationship between private entrepreneurs and party cadres, with many cadres themselves becoming entrepreneurs' (Gray, 2015: 140). In other words, 'there is a symbiotic relationship (at the very least) between state elites and new economic elites. They have effectively co-opted each other into an alliance that, for the time being, mutually reinforces each other's power and influence, not to mention personal fortunes' (Breslin, 2009: 79). The relationship between the Chinese Communist Party (CCP) and capital was formalised in 2002 when entrepreneurs were invited to become party members. In the following year, the state was officially put in charge of protecting private property (Breslin, 2009: 71).

In the process of capitalist transformation, the Chinese workforce has also been transformed. Initially, workers in the large SOEs did not go quietly. Nevertheless, their resistance post-redundancy did not put enough pressure on the state to change course. As Pringle (2013: 191) argues, 'during the spring of 2002, large-scale protests by laid-off oil workers in northeast China came to an end. I regard the defeat of the oil workers' three-week occupation of Iron Man Square in Daqing as marking the end of the traditional danwei-based working class as a distinct organising force.' This does not imply, however, that labour unrest has ended in China. Opposing transnational capital and Chinese domestic 'red capital', there is the large force of 277 million super-exploited migrant workers. While the state's initial task within the class conditions of passive revolution has been to hasten hothouse fashion capitalist processes, it now has to manage the struggle between transnational capital and migrant labour. Due to the super-exploitation in cheap labour production facilities, a wave of strikes and demonstrations has taken place since the late 2000s.

Official statistics show that in 1996, 48,121 labour disputes were accepted for arbitration, the total rising sharply to 120,191 in 1999, involving more than 470,000 aggrieved laborers as numbers soared in the context of massive layoffs of state sector workers. The upward trend continued from 2000, reflecting widespread incidences of rights violations as the private sector expanded. Labour cases further skyrocketed to 693,465 involving more than 1.2 million labourers nationwide in the economic crisis of 2008. These were disputes over wage and insurance payments, illegal layoffs, and inadequate compensation payments. (Chan and Selden, 2014: 607)

According to a research report (*China Labour Bulletin*, 2014: 17), from the beginning of June 2011 to the end of December 2013, 470 strikes and protests by factory workers were recorded across the country. The bulk of

China's factory protests occurred in the manufacturing heartland of Guangdong, and especially in the Pearl River Delta (PRD), where a large part of the cheap labour production facilities is located.

Unsurprisingly, the state is heavily involved in organising civil society in China. In view of these protests, the Chinese state has revived the role of the official All-China Federation of Trade Unions (ACFTU). In China, there is no right to free association and 'the right to strike was removed entirely from the 1982 constitution and has not been reinstated' (Gray, 2015: 149). Instead, the ACFTU functions as part of a state corporatist system, in which its focus is not on the independent representation of workers' interests, but on mediating between workers and capital in order to ensure social harmony. Unsurprisingly, the ACFTU cannot pursue strategies and objectives which contradict state policies. Thus, 'the CCP has attempted to restructure civil society so that social organisations such as trade unions serve to mediate social tensions, and their revival as part of a wider legalisation of industrial relations can be seen as a key element of the CCP's passive revolution' (Gray, 2015: 142). This focus on mediation is also in line with the more general strategy of an interventionist, 'activist state', which has increasingly directly interfered in labour disputes since 2008, emphasising informal settlement through mediation at various levels. 'This hands-on approach to labour conflict resolution involved intra-government coordination to manage the two sides, encourage compromise, threaten extremists or leaders with repression, and buy off disputants whenever possible in the hopes of an early, peaceful resolution' (Gallagher, 2014: 90). Ching Kwan Lee and Yonghong Zhang (2013: 1503–4) describe this strategy of mediation through depoliticising industrial conflicts and an emphasis on material concessions to pacify workers as 'bargained authoritarianism', but they also point to the fragile nature of these resolutions. 'When state-society bonds are commodified and depend so heavily on market-like exchange of compliance for benefits, there is no authority in authoritarianism, no noncontractual elements of contract, and arguably no durability beneath the façade of stability. A fiscal crisis, a recalcitrant and principled protest leadership, or any unexpected derailment of the bargaining process can provoke the state's repressive machinery, politicising state-society interaction' (Lee and Zhang, 2013: 1505).

In parallel to these official efforts of structuring civil society, a whole range of more informal labour NGOs have emerged in recent years as a form of support and organisation of Chinese workers (Bieler and Lee, 2017), with some of them operating as 'organic intellectuals', mobilising workers and organising them for collective action against super-exploitation (Hui, 2014: 211–15). The Chinese state's position on these informal NGOs is ambiguous. At times, they tolerate them as long as they focus on assisting individual workers in obtaining their rights such as the payment of wages. At other times, however, especially when these informal labour NGOs become more active in strike organisation and collective bargaining attempts, they are oppressed, indicating the limits of 'bargained authoritarianism'. Between June 2012 and October 2012, the Chinese government came down hard on labour NGOs in the area of Shenzhen, part of the PRD (Zhang, 2012), triggering a group of scholars (more than 140) from the outside world to sign an open letter to the Guangdong Municipal to express their grave concern at the Guangdong government's repression of grassroots labour NGOs (Sacom, 2012). The same happened again on 3 December 2015, when authorities detained twenty labour activists in Guangdong Province (Pringle, 2015). 'All of these activists are associated with four grassroots labour NGOs in the Pearl River Delta.'[1] In general, the Chinese state as part of the class strategy of passive revolution has increasingly resorted to coercion when responding to labour unrest. 'Government spending on internal security (policing and domestic surveillance) now exceeds the size of the country's defense budget' (Peck and Zhang, 2013: 384).

Nevertheless, the class strategy of passive revolution within the case of China's state transformation is not only characterised by coercion. More recently, 'the Chinese state has been changing from forcefully engineering the passive revolution into constructing capitalist hegemony' (Hui, 2016a: 70). This does not eliminate class struggle, but it has succeeded in ensuring that some workers at least have accepted capitalist common sense and values. For example, in order to avoid collective action, the CCP has favoured the establishment of an individual-based legal framework for worker rights. In other words, 'the party-state now tries to contain labour unrest within the economic arena and acquire workers' allegiance to the capitalist moral and ethico-political leadership' (Hui, 2016a: 71). The labour law system provides workers with a way of officially pursuing their individual grievances. In turn, this has fostered a sense of legitimacy of the current system among workers. In short, the 'labour contract system introduced in the reform period has concealed class exploitation by breaking up the working class as a collective force into political "individual persons" and "subjects of law" so as to reduce their bargaining power and pre-empt the formation of a self-conscious class; workers, as individuals, are thought to be on an equal footing with employers from a legal point of view' (Hui, 2016b: 442). The party-state

---

[1] For further details, see www.ipetitions.com/petition/scholars-opposing-the-abuse-of -state-power; accessed 16 December 2015.

efforts of establishing capitalist hegemony are further aided by 'a range of consensus-building activities under the umbrella of the "Chinese Dream" discourse. Most prominent amongst these is the "Core Socialist Values" campaign, which lays out the CCP's vision through four goals at each of the national, societal, and citizenship levels' (Gow, 2017: 93). This campaign is rolled out across civil society through the material structure of ideology consisting of intervention in schools, colleges, universities, the various media outlets, religious organisations, NGOs and trade unions, as discussed in Chapter 3. As Michael Gow highlights well, the CCP attempts to anchor this campaign in a broad, common-sense understanding of Confucian values. 'The CCP aims to imbricate its Core Socialist Values within established beliefs, values, dispositions, and social conventions. In doing so, it seeks to encourage conduct which is already viewed as culturally and socially desirable' (Gow, 2017: 109). Materially, an attempt is made to integrate disadvantaged workers through specifically devised consumption strategies. As Ngai-Ling Sum outlines, so-called Diaosi, highly precarious and super-exploited workers, have been discovered by capital as a potentially growing market in times of falling demand for luxury items, binding these workers in turn to the dominant capitalist system (Sum, 2017: 304–8).

Foreign transnational capital has not really gained direct political influence over state institutions (Schmalz and Ebenau, 2012: 493). The power of transnational capital is of a more structural nature. Especially in times of crisis, the state finds it difficult to enforce higher working standards in view of economic recession. Most recently, the global financial crisis impacted the Chinese political economy. 'The highly export-driven Chinese model in particular came to face serious difficulties, whereby coastal provinces like Shanghai and Guangdong were hit the hardest. In the quarter of 2008, about 670,000 factories went into bankruptcy' (Schmalz and Ebenau, 2012: 494). This had dramatic implications for employment levels. 'In January 2009 for example, following a third consecutive monthly fall in exports, a year on year monthly decline of 17.5% was recorded, and in this period an estimated 20 million migrant workers in the export sector lost their jobs' (Kiely, 2015: 121). Equally, when wages increase, be it as the result of a rise in the minimum wage by the state, or due to labour shortages, capital is able to relocate production to sites with cheaper labour. As Gray (2010: 463) reports, 'there are already signs that this is happening.' Similar, to our discussion of Nicos Poulantzas in Chapter 5, Chan and Hui (2017) argue that the state needs to be understood as a field and condensation of class struggle enjoying relative autonomy vis-à-vis various capitalist class fractions and dominated social forces. Hence, during the economic crisis the compulsion and competitive pressures of global capital induced the Chinese state towards reducing the protection of workers. In the wake of economic recovery, however, workers started to reassert themselves in a wave of radical ruptures (see Chapter 10). To ensure the overall continuation of capitalist accumulation the state had to intervene in relation to demands around collective bargaining and company contributions to social insurance systems.

Conclusion: The Continuation of Capitalist Contradictions

There are few signs suggesting either that China is replacing the United States as the next global hegemon or that the BRICS, including China, or the Global South as a whole are in the process of developmental 'catch-up' with advanced industrialised countries. The rise of the BRICS, ultimately, can be unmasked as a discourse artificially created by Goldman Sachs economists and further spread by international organisations and investment bankers to ensure a continuation of capitalist accumulation through three overlapping narratives of the BRICS as excellent locations for investment; the BRICS as excellent places for consumption as a result of a rising middle class; and the BRICS as an important lender, i.e. 'as drivers of recovery in the context of the North Atlantic Financial Crisis' (Sum and Jessop, 2013: 440). Overall, the rise of the BRICS has to be situated within wider restructuring processes of neoliberalisation, responding to the crisis of over-accumulation in the 1970s. 'In short, core country TNCs initiated a complex restructuring of global patterns of production and trade. The process, aided by governments, has knitted together third world economies in ways that reflect the interests of leading core and third world country capitalists as well as their allies' (Hart-Landsberg, 2015: 7).

Nevertheless, the global, and therefore also the Chinese, political economy remains crisis prone. The moment there is a crisis of demand in the United States and, for that matter, Europe, the Chinese export-led growth strategy is under pressure. In response to the global financial crisis, China implemented a stimulus package of $586 billion in 2008 and 2009. Highly praised at the international level and regarded as proof of the narrative of China as a lender able to lead the global political economy out of crisis, the way it was structured had dramatic implications at the national level. Because local governments were asked to provide matching funds for central government investment, the result was an 'increasing commodification of land as a means to generate income' (Sum and Jessop, 2013: 457). A staggering construction boom with most of the investment going to the creation of built environments, urbanisation and physical infrastructure followed. As David Harvey (2016) reports, between 1990 and 1999, the United States consumed 4,500 million tonnes of cement, while China consumed 6,500 million tonnes of cement between 2011 and 2013. Thus, in three years the Chinese consumed nearly 45 per cent more cement than the United States had consumed in a decade. Construction, in other words, absorbed surpluses of capital and labour resulting from the crisis in other sectors. In turn, this had social implications. 'Land sales and property development became important investment and speculative activities with consequences such as a property bubble, forced displacement from land, peasant riots, state terror, dispossession of the already vulnerable (e.g. migrant children) and increasing inequalities' (Sum and Jessop, 2013: 463). Unsurprisingly, the housing market in China has been overheating. 'Housing prices are reported to have risen by 140 percent nationwide since 2007, and by as much as 800 percent in the main cities such as Beijing and Shanghai over the last five years' (Harvey, 2012: 58). Jane Hardy (2017: 194–5) explains well how China's response to the global financial crisis is based on a fundamental contradiction. On one hand, the government intends to boost domestic demand through higher wages and domestic investment into infrastructure to become less dependent on exports to North America and Europe; on the other, however, it needs to keep wages low to ensure increasing productivity and continuing competitiveness, on which large parts of Chinese exports are based. It is, therefore, not surprising that private consumption as a percentage of GDP has not increased. In 2012, it was still at 35 per cent (Hart-Landsberg, 2015: 14).

Surplus capital, however, has not only been invested in property and construction projects at home. China's One Belt, One Road project, first announced in 2013 and rolled out in 2015, is equally a response to the crisis of over-accumulation, with China becoming the second largest country of outward FDI with an increase by 44 per cent to $183 billion in 2016 (UNCTAD, 2017: 54, 222–5). The initiative covers six major international economic corridors from China to Europe. It is 'a massive anticipated development of connective infrastructure from Western China across much of Eurasia' (Leverett and Bingbing, 2016: 126). The project is clearly intended to absorb the overcapacity, overproduction and excess commodities of the Chinese political economy and here in particular steel and coal resources (Wei, 2016: 3, 15). Against the background of Chinese foreign exchange reserves of almost $4 trillion in June 2014, the Chinese government started to search 'for alternative investment opportunities abroad for companies in China (predominantly state-owned enterprises, SOEs) that have been engaged in extensive infra-structural projects across the country for a decade or more' (Ferdinand, 2016: 951). It is still early days. Nevertheless, this renewed expansion of capitalism will most likely intensify tensions around uneven and combined development in the region. While it will assist in overcoming the crisis of over-accumulation within China, this solution through outward expansion can always only be temporary.

Moreover, parallel to this crisis of over-accumulation around China, a crisis of over-accumulation continues at the global level. 'According to Federal Reserve data from late 2010, companies in the United States held $1.8 trillion in uninvested cash, more than at any time since 1956 (adjusted for inflation) – a powerful indicator of the persistence of over-accumulation' (Robinson, 2014: 157). A lot of private finance in a desperate search for profitable investment opportunities has been invested in property assets in the BRICS and other Global South countries, fuelling asset bubbles that are in danger of bursting at any moment, resulting in yet further global crisis. For example, 'in China the share of foreign investment in real estate increased from 10% in 2006 to 23% in 2010' (Kiely, 2015: 118). Hence, there is a close link between crisis at the global level and crisis within various BRICS and indeed, in other parts of the global political economy, as we see in Chapter 9 and our analysis of the Eurozone crisis set against the background of the global financial crisis.

To conclude, based on the historical materialist approach and philosophy of internal relations animating this book, this chapter has raised doubts about notions of China as an alternative to neoliberalisation. Although the state has played an active role in the capitalist transformation of China, ultimately Chinese production and development has become highly integrated into the general neoliberalisation dynamics of the global political economy. Equally, notions of China as a new economic giant have been shown to be misplaced. Instead, based on cheap labour and the super-exploitation of workers, China occupies a rather fragile position focusing on the assembling of export products in capitalist global production. The spatial fix it provides for capitalism's global crisis of over-accumulation is, however, only temporary. Capitalist crises can never be permanently resolved. Equally, modes of domination constantly need to be reasserted. Saull (2012: 33) identifies the increasing unevenness within the BRICS as a major fault line of further crisis. 'It is the unevenness within countries such as India and particularly China – evident in the dramatic differences in levels of development between different regions and in the staggering inequalities between cities and the countryside' – where the continued reproduction of neoliberalisation is more vulnerable. There is, therefore, a fundamental volatility in these countries and, for some, 'it is in this inherent instability that the possibilities for permanent revolution lie' (Davidson, 2010: 17–18). As demonstrated earlier, Chinese workers have become increasingly militant in recent years and unwilling to accept further conditions of super-exploitation. The case of the BRICS and here, again, especially China indicates that workers are not only victims of capitalist exploitation but also have the agency of resistance and are fighting back. The conclusion to this book returns to these moments of contestation and resistance in more detail (see Chapter 10).

8   Global War and the New Imperialism

The invasion of Iraq in 2003 was waged by the so-called Coalition of the Willing. How to conceptualise the connections between capitalist dynamics and interstate war has bedevilled historical materialist geopolitics for some time. There is an agreement that interstate war cannot simply be read off from the economic necessities of capitalist accumulation. Access to diesel may have played a part in the U.S. push for the attack on Iraq, but it would be too simple to argue that this was the single cause driving the decision. As Alejandro Colás and Gonzalo Pozo (2011: 219) have recognised in their attempt to develop a Marxist geopolitics, 'the centrality of space will depend on the degree to which it is marked by the particular social infrastructure, class constitution, and commodification of territory in different geographies and historical contexts.' But as critics have suggested, precisely *where* one would expect detailed analysis of such contexts, *how* the analysis avoids a mechanistic geo-economic position and *what* the specific focus on political agency is are all lingering problems in the examination of capitalist geopolitics (Agnew, 2011; Black, 2011; Guzzini, 2011). To focus on a 'gearbox of imperial control' that enables the structures of contemporary imperialism, through different modes of foreign relations, to manage postcolonial states is equally problematic (van der Pijl, 2011). Economic determinist analyses of this type cannot illuminate the complex dynamics of class struggle underlying contemporary geopolitics, such as the invasion of Iraq.

Following the framework set out at the beginning of this book, the purpose of this chapter is to deliver a historical materialist perspective on the internal relationship of the state and geopolitics through an analysis of U.S. imperium in relation to the Iraq War. To recap, the argument in Chapter 1 detailed the philosophy of internal relations that distinctively marks historical materialism as a theory of history. Summarily put, the dialectical emphasis of historical materialism stresses the priority of the internal relationship of content and form where generative processes of capital formation are prioritised rather than different moments (events, things or entities) (Harvey, 1996: 74–5). This means two things in relation to the argument of this chapter. First, in developing an account of Global War through the Iraq War it is important from a historical materialist perspective to internally relate geopolitics to processes of capital accumulation in order to analyse the dynamics underlying the invasion. Referring back to the need for a necessarily historical materialist moment in international theory, this means highlighting the content of the form of the geopolitics of global war or how both state geopolitical and capital formation dynamics underpin the material practices and discursive modes of political economic power. Second, as David Harvey (1996: 269) argues, 'any recourse to a philosophy of dialectics or internal relations leads, either explicitly or implicitly, to a relational view on space and time.' In the context of the empirical interventions of Part III of this book, this means drawing on the postholing method (introduced in Chapter 1) in order to relate the sweep of historical forces of Global Capitalism, Global War, Global Crisis to the specificity and richness of detail of the 'new imperialism' in Iraq. As Marx (1857–8/1973: 408) stated in the *Grundrisse*, 'the tendency to create the *world market* is directly given in the concept of capital itself. Every limit appears as a barrier to be overcome.' Hence an examination of 'new imperialism' on the basis of the method of postholing in this chapter in order to assess how the barriers to the expansion of capitalist production were overcome through Global War in Iraq. This then enables a focus on conditions of Global Crisis in Chapter 9 with the aim of understanding the uneven and combined developmental contradictions currently existing within contemporary capitalism.

The argument in this chapter proceeds by engaging with classical Marxist debates on imperialism between the perspectives on inter-imperialist rivalries (Lenin, Bukharin) and ultra-imperialism (Kautsky). This analysis is then linked to a discussion of key contemporary examples of authors pursuing these different lines of thinking. After all, imperialism is 'a rather loose concept which in practice has to be newly defined with reference to each historical period' (Cox, 1981: 142). The first section thus links the classic analyses of world capitalist expansion, war, conflict and imperialism by V. I. Lenin and Nikolai Bukharin to the work of Alex Callinicos and his focus on renewed inter-imperialist rivalry, in which the United States is seen as wanting to secure its access to and control over Middle East oil in relation to intensifying competition with China and other capitalist powers. The second section stretches the focus on contemporary reflections on geopolitics organised through inter-imperialist alliances to the work by Leo Panitch and Sam Gindin as well as Ray Kiely and how this relates back to Karl Kautsky's notion of ultra-imperialism. Here, the United States as the hegemonic power is assumed to lead other capitalist states in the reorganisation of the global economy. Ultimately, it is argued that both sets of approaches only examine the external relations between the separate but linked logics of state geopolitics and capital. The third section, in turn, critically analyses William Robinson's contemporary work on the emergence of a transnational state (TNS) and how this results in an analysis of the Iraq War, which overlooks the continuing importance of state forms as nodal points in the organisation of global capitalism, building on our engagement in Chapter 5.

In the fourth and fifth sections, we develop an alternative approach to understanding capitalist expansion. In line with earlier discussions of structure and agency in Chapter 2, we first conceptualise the structuring conditions of capitalist expansion in line with Rosa Luxemburg's spatial account of the accumulation of capital and expansion into non-capitalist spaces through ongoing processes of primitive accumulation, detailed in Chapter 4. Our argument emphasises how the political expression of the expansion and extension of capital proceeds in terms of the geopolitical spatial organisation of capital's violence. In the instance of the Iraq War, the spatial organisation and geographical expansion of the accumulation process is established through the contemporary power of the United States within which and through which national and transnational capital operate. Hence, drawing on our conceptualisation of the internal relations between the interstate system and global capitalism and the related focus on struggles over the internalisation of transnational capital's interests in national forms of state as developed in Chapter 5, in the fifth section we move then to the analysis of agency and in particular the processes of class struggle within the U.S. form of state and how they are related to wider struggles over spaces of imperialism and the invasion of Iraq in 2003. This then furthers our overall argument within this book that historical materialism distinctively delivers an assessment of the internal relations of Global Capitalism, Global War, Global Crisis to establish a necessarily historical materialist position or moment within international theory.

The Realist 'Moment' in Historical Materialist Geopolitics

At the centre of Lenin's *Imperialism: The Highest Stage of Capitalism* was a focus on the export of capital as the typical feature of modern imperialism. This itself was embedded in conditions of uneven development between economically 'advanced' and 'backward' countries. As a result, three essential features can be traced marking this account of the expansion of capitalist imperialism. First, despite capitalism's expansion on a world scale, inherent divisions remain. 'However strong the process of levelling the world, of levelling the economic and living conditions in different countries', states Lenin (1916/1964: 259), 'considerable differences still remain.' Second, added to this, is the hint of a territorialist logic to the expansion of capitalism. There is 'the inevitable striving of finance capital to extend its economic territory and even its territory in general' (Lenin, 1916/1964: 83). The expansion of finance capital therefore heightens the unevenness and contradictions inherent in the world economy and reinforces the territorial division of the world. Third, inter-imperialist rivalries and the spatial expansion of capitalism are extended through bellicose geopolitical relations on a world scale. 'The question is: what means other than war could there be *under capitalism* to overcome the disparity between the development of productive forces and the accumulation of capital on the one side, and the division of colonies and spheres of influence for finance capital on the other?' (Lenin, 1916/1964: 275–6).

For Bukharin, there is an *anarchic structure of world capitalism* that finds expression in constant capitalist competition despite the growth of economic interdependence.

The anarchic character of capitalist society is expressed in the fact that social economy is not an organised collective body guided by a single will, but a system of economies interconnected through exchange, each of which produces at its own risk, never being in a position to adapt itself more or less to the volume of social demand and to the production carried on in other individual economies. This calls forth a struggle of the economies against each other, a war of capitalist competition. (Bukharin, 1917/1929: 115)

This anarchic structure of the world economy expresses itself in two facts: capitalist crises and the perpetuation of wars. 'War in capitalist society is only one of the methods of capitalist competition, when the latter extends to the sphere of world economy' (Bukharin 1917/1929: 54). Capital is described as a *horror vacui*. 'It rushes to fill every "vacuum", whether in a "tropical", "sub-tropical", or "polar" region' (Bukharin, 1917/1929: 58). Within the anarchical structure of capitalist competition, war is clearly heralded as the chief means in the reproduction of relations of production for imperialist interests. Following a period of conflict, the role of fixed capital formation is signalled as pivotal in increasing the growth of centralisation and concentration of capital accumulation. This is described as a 'feverish process of healing the wounds' of war, through the reconstruction of railways, factory plants, machinery, transportation hubs, allied with the expansion of the military, the extending of state power and the centralisation of finance capital (Bukharin, 1917/1929: 149). In vernacular

terminology we define this process as a strategy of Bomb-and-Build
through which capitalism expands, combining extensive processes of geographical expansion (spreading over territories) and intensive processes of
spatial concentration (deepening conditions of exploitation). As a result,
'capitalist society is whirling in the mad hurricane of world wars'
(Bukharin, 1917/1929: 158).

To a large degree, Alex Callinicos extends these insights to argue that
capitalist imperialism should be understood as the intersection of economic and geopolitical competition. 'Conceiving imperialism as the
intersection of two logics of power or forms of competition avoids economic reductionism' (Callinicos, 2009: 72). He thus identifies 'two logics
of power, capitalistic and territorial, or two forms of competition, economic and geopolitical' (Callinicos, 2009: 74).[1] The international states
system is thereby treated as a dimension of the capitalist mode of production. From the outset, Callinicos attempts to distance himself from (neo)
realist accounts in international relations (IR) (Callinicos 2009: 83).
Nevertheless, as already demonstrated in Chapter 5, this understanding
of the states system as a distinct determination with its own logic of
geopolitical competition still implies a rather state-centric focus, especially when analysing developments in international politics. 'One implication of this point is that there is, necessarily, a realist moment in any
Marxist analysis of international relations and conjunctures: in other
words, any such analysis must take into account the strategies, calculations and interactions of rival political elites in the state system'
(Callinicos, 2010a: 21). This conceptual position also has implications
for Callinicos' empirical analysis of developments in the global economy.
Despite globalisation, various national capitals remain dependent on the
support of their specific state. 'Capitals involved in increasingly global
networks of trade and investment depend on different forms of support,
ranging from tariff and subsidy to the assertion of military power, from
their nation-state' (Callinicos, 2005: 2). At the international level, this
results, then, in competition of a plurality of major capitalist states, each
defending the interests of its particular national capitalist class. Related to
the war in Iraq, the U.S. position in favour of invasion is then understood
as a way of asserting its dominance vis-à-vis other capitalist rivals, be they
in Western Europe or among emerging economies such as China. 'Seizing
Iraq would not simply remove a regime long obnoxious to the U.S., but
would both serve as a warning to all states of the costs of defying American
military power and, by entrenching this power in the Middle East, give

---

[1] Different versions of a 'two logics' account of the new imperialism can be found in Harvey
(1985, 2003b), as well as Arrighi (1994), as detailed in Chapters 4 and 5.

Washington control of what Harvey calls "the global oil spigot" on which potential challengers in Europe and East Asia are particularly dependent' (Callinicos, 2005: 7; Harvey, 2003b: 25).

There are, however, several problems with this analysis. First, conceptually, Callinicos' analysis is problematic because his focus on two distinct logics, a geopolitical and an economic logic, implies analysing the external relation between the two. To broaden the optic for a moment, this results in a rather similar position to Sandra Halperin's (2011) analysis of the Iraq War that also separates analysis into two 'moments': one shaped by the military-industrial conglomerate of Anglo-American interests; the other shaped by the concentration of the political economy of global restructuring. Likewise, Doug Stokes (2005: 218, 230; Stokes and Raphael, 2010: 35–8) hypostatises two 'dual' logics, a 'national' logic and a 'transnational' logic, at the heart of American empire that too easily becomes a binary opposition with a focus on external relations, in attempting to trace the continuities and contrasts of imperialism. Although richer theoretically and empirically, the assessment of 'Open Door' imperialism by Bastiaan van Apeldoorn and Naná de Graaff, into a division of 'corporate affiliations' on one hand and 'policy-planning networks' on the other hand, also succumbs to a two-logics approach (van Apeldoorn and de Graaff, 2014; de Graaff and van Apeldoorn, 2011). Returning to our argument in Chapter 1, by overlooking the internal relationship between the two logics, however, there is a danger of reifying the appearance of transnational outcomes linked to nationally based struggles within state security policies and thus the geopolitical dynamic reflected in state strategies. According to Bertell Ollman (2003: 80), 'Marx refers to mistaking appearance for essence as "fetishism".' Indeed, the aforementioned work does fetishise the state (or a military-industrial moment, or a policy-planning logic) as distinct and separate from world capitalism (or global restructuring, or transnational capital). Instead, as outlined in the first chapter of this book, we articulate a philosophy of internal relations when conceptualising the interstate system and global capitalist accumulation. As discussed in Chapter 5, we avoid understanding the essence of the apparently independent and separate position of the 'market', or capitalism, outside of its internal relation with the 'state', or geopolitics, linked to the underlying social relations of production.

Related to the understanding of the market and the state as relations internal to capitalism, Simon Bromley makes clear in his analysis of the invasion of Iraq that the United States has been in no position to control the oil market with or without invasion (Bromley, 1994: 34). Building on his earlier analysis of Middle East politics that has always avoided a monocausal focus on oil in favour of analysing world market conditions (see Bromley, 1994: 96–100), he goes on to state that:

It remains the case that three-fifths (and rising) of the world's oil is traded on highly integrated markets across national borders and the rest moves on national or regional markets in which prices are aligned with international movements. The actual route travelled from well-head to final consumption by any given barrel depends primarily on economic decisions and circumstances beyond the control of governments. (Bromley, 2006: 429)

In other words, the invasion of Iraq could never simply have been a move to gain exclusive control over oil at the expense of imperialist rivals. Hence, 'to the extent that u.s. power, including military forces, is successfully deployed to meet the ends of expanding and diversifying supplies, it serves the interests of all oil-consuming countries that are dependent on the world market' (Bromley, 2006: 420; see also Bromley, 2005: 254). This understanding indicates that a rethinking of u.s. hegemony and informal empire is necessary.

Rethinking U.S. Hegemony and Informal Empire: Towards Ultra-imperialism?

One of the tensions that arose in classical Marxist debates on imperialism was the instant dismissal of the theory of 'ultra-imperialism' as sketched by Karl Kautsky. Kautsky queried whether imperialism is 'the last possible phenomenal form of capitalist world policy' and if capitalism 'may still live through another phase ... a phase of ultra-imperialism?' (Kautsky, 1914/1970: 44, 46). In contrast to Lenin and Bukharin, Kautsky conjectured as to whether the violent explosions of imperialism might be replaced by a 'holy alliance of the imperialists' through which the expansion of capitalism might be secured (Kautsky, 1914/1970: 46). Lenin dismissed this as 'ultra-nonsense'.

Kautsky's utterly meaningless talk about ultra-imperialism encourages, among other things, that profoundly mistaken idea which only brings grist to the mill of the apologists of imperialism, i.e., that the rule of finance capital *lessens* the unevenness and contradictions inherent in the world economy, whereas in reality it *increases* them. (Lenin, 1916/1964: 272)

The rivalries of national capital were held to endure and these antagonisms of conflict and struggle would be constant in shaping the advanced stages of capitalist development rather than an imaginary hope of permanent peace. Equally, Bukharin dismissed the theory of ultra-imperialism and its focus on the centralisation of capital as a thesis of 'peaceful capitalism'. For sure, 'the great stimulus to the formation of an international state ... is given by the internationalisation of capitalist interests', but, 'significant as this process may be in itself, it is, however, counteracted by a still stronger tendency of capital towards nationalisation, and towards remaining secluded within state boundaries'. Once again, the antagonistic interests between states understood in military terms will prevail over any 'world capitalist organisation' in the form of a world state (Bukharin, 1917/1929: 137–8).

Contemporary rethinking of imperialism can be similar to Kautsky's arguments. Leo Panitch and Sam Gindin argue that the making of global capitalism was superintended by American empire as the ultimate guarantor of capitalist interests globally. It is, therefore, 'wrong to assume an irresolvable contradiction between the international space of accumulation and the national space of states' (Panitch and Gindin, 2012: 4, 10–12). Capturing this sentiment, Ray Kiely also states that 'the process of internationalisation did not lead to a new era based on competing national blocs of capital, as theorised by Bukharin, but rather a reorganisation of U.S. hegemony and an intensification of international integration, or what came to be called (economic) globalisation' (Kiely, 2010: 141). The so-called Volcker Shock from 1979 to 1982 is crucial for such analysis. At one point, U.S. interest rates were increased to more than 19 per cent in 1981. It not only facilitated economic restructuring but also shifted the balance of class forces in order to break the militancy of U.S. labour. 'It simply involved limiting the growth in the money supply and allowing interest rates to rise to whatever level – and at whatever short-term economic cost – was necessary to break the back of inflation and the strength of labour' (Kiely, 2010: 146; Panitch and Gindin, 2005a: 61). The Volcker Shock also reconstituted the material basis of American empire, inducing, as an 'unintended side effect', the debt crisis in Latin America with debtors' net interest payments in the region skyrocketing from 33 per cent to 59 per cent of total export income between 1979 and 1981 (Panitch and Gindin, 2012: 179, 214). In and beyond Latin America, two principal routes enabled this emerging form of U.S. hegemony to extend abroad. First, U.S. capital invested heavily in Europe, especially from the 1970s onwards. According to Panitch and Gindin, 'this penetration of Europe by American corporations and banks meant the implantation of American capital as a class force inside European social formations', thereby transforming European social relations in the American image (Panitch and Gindin, 2005a: 53). Second, the United States extended its informal empire through what Kiely calls 'free trade imperialism', enforcing neoliberal restructuring upon other countries by obliging them to open up their economies to free trade (see Gallagher and Robinson, 1953; Kiely, 2007: 30–9, 2010: 51, 188).

From this perspective of free trade imperialism, it is then also clear that the invasion of Iraq was mainly about maintaining an open international market for oil, as discussed earlier. The divisions between France and Germany, on one hand, and the United States on the other, over the invasion of Iraq, would thus be seen as exaggerated and certainly not assessed as expressions of inter-imperialist rivalry. Instead, 'the disputes over Iraq were more about tactics and strategy over how to police a rogue state, rather than a manifestation of systemic geopolitical rivalries. Indeed ... these disagreements were as sharp within the U.S. state as they were between the U.S. on the one hand, and France, Germany and Russia on the other' (Kiely, 2010: 163). As Kiely further argues, 'these tensions coincided with substantial cooperation over the conduct of the war. This included collaboration on the part of French and German intelligence services with the U.S., the use by U.S. forces of European airspace during the war, and collaboration with the CIA over flights carrying alleged terrorists to secret torture centres' (Kiely, 2010: 233). In short, through neoliberal globalisation, the United States re-established its leading role within the global political economy in close cooperation with other capitalist countries. 'While there is considerable evidence of conflict for the "Leninists" to emphasise, there is much to back the "Kautskyite" view which emphasises cooperation' (Kiely, 2010: 234).

Unsurprisingly, then, the debate here is sandwiched between an emphasis on conflictual rivalry between capitalist states (Callinicos) or the stress on cooperation through the joint management of global capitalism (Kiely, Panitch and Gindin), mirroring in some respects the classical debate over inter-imperialist rivalry versus ultra-imperialism. This can lead to the view that the underlying dynamics of international politics are still shaped through conflict/cooperation, unintentionally reproducing mainstream state-centric tendencies holding the United States as a unitary actor (see Kiely, 2010: 242, 245–7; Panitch and Gindin, 2005a: 47). The position that the American state superintends global capitalism certainly adds more nuance. However there is a reticence to offer an analysis of the role of specific class fractions within the American state that facilitate the superintendence of capitalism at the global level, leaving the relationship of the 'two logics' of state power and capital accumulation unclarified (Panitch and Gindin, 2012: 7–12). This has three consequences. First, the focus on the implantation of American capital inside European social formations reveals how their analysis reduces transnational capital solely to the agency of U.S. hegemony (Panitch and Gindin, 2005a: 53). Second, although there is an attempt to examine the forces within the American economy – notably the

U.S. Treasury and Federal Reserve – impelling informal empire, Panitch and Gindin miss a full-scale analysis of the contradictory class interests within the United States shaped by the intertwining of both financial and military vectors. Finally, third, just as Suzanne de Brunhoff (1978: 115) once quipped that 'what was happening in the United States' was largely left out of Nicos Poulantzas' theorisation of imperialism, 'because American capital is presented in an abstract and static manner' of pure empirical description, then equally missing in Panitch and Gindin's account of the making of global capitalism is a focus on the military determinations of formal American empire allied with the class interests of informal empire linked to finance within the U.S. state. As Panitch and Gindin (2005b: 115) state, 'the asymmetries of empire need to be factored into the interpenetration and evaluation of exchange rates, trade accounts, fiscal deficits, capital flows, international debt'. American empire is reduced to finance and its informal characteristics (Panitch, 2000; Panitch and Gindin, 2003).

The dominant tendency across the rethinking of U.S. imperialism is therefore to neglect (Callinicos) or misconstrue (Panitch and Gindin) the role of transnational capital and the implications this has for the international states system. To expand, both empirically misunderstand the fundamental dynamics of globalisation linked to the transnationalisation of production and the related implications for the international states system. As discussed in detail in Chapter 5, as a result of these restructuring processes linked to globalisation, we have witnessed the emergence of a transnational capitalist class (TCC). Hence, it is no longer possible simply to speak in terms of a rivalry between 'German' capital, 'French' capital or 'American' capital etc. The next section now looks at William Robinson's reflections on the Iraq War in view of his conceptualisation of the TCC and the rise of the TNS.

Transnational State Formation: Ultra-imperialism Regnant?

Drawing on and engaging with Leslie Sklair's (2001) work on the TCC, William Robinson starts his assessment of the changes in the global economy through a focus on the social relations of production.[2] As outlined in Chapter 5, it is this starting point that allows him to conceptualise the implications of globalisation since the early 1970s. As a result of the transnationalisation of production, he argues that

---

[2] For the beginnings of this work, see Robinson and Harris (2000), and for recent scholarship on the TCC, including contributions by Sklair and Robinson, see Struna (2015).

'transnational capital has become the dominant, or hegemonic, fraction of capital on a world scale' (Robinson, 2004: 21). Moreover, Robinson states that we are witness to the emergence of a transnational state (TNS), regarded as a guarantor of capital accumulation at the global level. He thus makes the bold claim that 'in the emerging global capitalist configuration, transnational or global space is coming to supplant national space', with the attendant view that the nation state as an axis of world development is becoming superseded by transnational structures, leading to the emergence of a transnational state (Robinson, 2003: 19–20, 2008: 6–7).[3]

In relation to the post–World War II era, Robinson argues that the project of transnational capital is beginning to eclipse U.S. hegemony within the global political economy. Instead, the United States has been integrated into the TNS and its military power made available to this emerging world social form serving the interests of transnational capital.

As the most powerful component of the TNS, the U.S. state apparatus defends the interests of transnational investors and of the system as a whole. Military expansion is in the interests of the TNCs. The only military apparatus in the world capable of exercising global coercive authority is the U.S. military. The beneficiaries of U.S. military action around the world are not 'U.S.' but transnational capital groups. (Robinson, 2007a: 89)

The war in Iraq is regarded as precisely one such conflagration through which the interests of transnational capital have been expanded. Robinson concurs with Panitch, Gindin and Kiely that divisions between France and Germany, on one hand, and the United States, on the other, are simply disagreements about how best to maintain the global capitalist system. However, disagreement unfolds about the identification of a shift from American hegemony to the dominance of transnational capital through the TNS. In Robinson's view, 'as the most powerful component of the TNS, the U.S. state apparatus attempts to defend the interests of transnational investors and the overall system and to confront those political forces around the world that, in one way or another, threaten those interests or threaten to destabilise transnational capitalist processes' (Robinson, 2014: 103). Military engagements, thus, are simply a way of extending this new form of global capitalism. 'The "war on terrorism" provides a seemingly endless military outlet for surplus capital, generates

---

[3] Although in more recent analysis it is argued that 'breaking with nation-state-centric analysis does not mean abandoning analysis of national-level processes and phenomena or inter-state dynamics. It does mean that we view transnational capitalism as the world-historic content in which these play themselves out' (Robinson, 2015: 17). Of note here is how the organising centrality of the transnational state falls out of the window, as noted in Chapter 5.

a colossal deficit that justifies the ever-deeper dismantling of the Keynesian welfare state and locks neoliberal austerity in place, and legitimates the creation of a police state to repress political dissent in the name of security' (Robinson, 2007a: 92). Hence a theory of global capitalism that distances itself from the notion of ultra-imperialism, or the 'peaceful' cooperation among capitals, collapses here into a conflict-driven view of competitive pressures in the global political economy superintended by the transnational state (Robinson, 2004: 61).

As we highlighted earlier in Chapter 5, the transnational state thesis offers a flattened ontology that removes state forms as a significant spatial scale in the articulation of capitalism, levels out the spatial and territorial logics of capital accumulation and elides the class struggles extant in specific locations. Hence, Robinson overlooks the continuing importance of states as nodal points in the global accumulation of capitalism as well as the uneven and combined developmental dynamics of global capitalism. Robinson misses the point that 'the real push for change comes from the TCC inside the national structure, with the process conditioned by the local balance of political and economic forces' (Harris, 2006: 55). By underestimating the continued importance of the state form as nodal within global capitalism, Robinson neglects ongoing struggles within the U.S. state between nationalist and globalist fractions of the ruling class, linked to the military-industrial-academic complex (Harris, 2005: 145). Robinson overlooks the point that rather than simply supporting the interests of transnational capital, there has been a clear intra-class conflict within the United States over the decision to invade Iraq. In order to unravel the economic and geopolitical dynamics linked to the invasion of Iraq, then, there is a need to focus on dynamics of class struggle within the U.S. form of state. As developed in Chapter 5, it is through this focus on intra-class struggle that the internal relation between capital and territory can be grasped dialectically in that both are internally related forms or expressions of the same underlying configuration of the social relations of production.

How can the spatial effects of the concentration of capital accumulation be understood within the circumstances of present-day geopolitical conditions while drawing from past concerns about imperialist expansion? How is it possible to integrate an analysis of transnational class agency into the dynamics of the interstate system? In line with our historical materialist position on agency–structure, developed in Chapter 2, the next section first discusses the structuring conditions of global capitalist social relations, thereby extending the argument of the thematic considerations in Chapter 4 and here in particular our discussion of Rosa Luxemburg's and Leon Trotsky's work. This provides the setting within which, in the subsequent section, our analysis of the TCC and its involvement in struggles over strategies of capitalist expansion in the Iraq War is placed. The latter focuses on the internal dynamics of class struggle in the United States, the social formation at the very core of capitalist social relations of production on a global scale.

The Iraq War and Militarism as a Province of Accumulation

It was Theda Skocpol (1979: 19) who noted 'the international states system as a transnational structure of military competition was not originally created by capitalism. Throughout modern world history, it represents an analytically autonomous level of transnational reality – interdependent in its structure and dynamics with world capitalism, but not reducible to it.' Similarly, Hannes Lacher (2006) and Benno Teschke (2003) have demonstrated that capitalism emerged within a prior existing international system of absolutist states. As discussed in Chapter 4, once capitalist social relations of production had, however, emerged in England, state formation and capitalist development went hand in hand as the social transformations that brought about capitalism in England were the same that characterised the apparent separation of state and civil society leading to the constitution of the capitalist state (Wood, 1991: 26).

As introduced in Chapter 2, several key structural dynamics can be identified as a result of how capitalist social relations of production are set up around the private ownership of the means of production and 'free' wage labour. First, because capital, similar to labour, also has to reproduce itself through the market, individual capitalists are constantly in competition with each other. It is the resulting innovative impetus which makes capitalism such a dynamic mode of production (Marx, 1867/1996: 739). Second, capitalism is also prone to periodic crises, as this dynamic development inevitably results in a crisis of over-accumulation, when unemployed workers and surplus profits can no longer be brought together in a meaningful way (Harvey, 1985: 132). In response to the crisis tendencies of capitalist social relations of production there is an inherent structural dynamic of outward expansion along uneven and combined developmental lines as first conceptualised by Leon Trotsky (1936). Initially, this dynamic brought non-capitalist space into capitalist social relations of production. Over time, however, outward expansion along uneven and combined development also occurred through the way the relations between the core and periphery in the global economy were reconstituted along novel lines, first in the way labour-intensive manufacturing was transferred to countries in the Global

South after World War II but especially from the 1970s onwards, then currently in the way peripheral countries are being restructured through incorporation into an expanded free trade system, including not only the trade in goods, but also services, public procurement, trade-related invest-ment measures, intellectual property rights and investor-state-dispute-settlement mechanisms (Bieler and Morton, 2014). Rosa Luxemburg (1913/2003), in turn, asserted that militarism was one of the key dynamics underlying this outward expansion of capitalism. As outlined in Chapter 4, she understood the military as 'the executor of the accumulation of capital' and militarism as such as a source of capital accumulation (see Bieler et al., 2016). Here, the

money, which capital has set circulating, first fulfils its primary function in the exchange with labour power, but subsequently, by mediation of the state, it begins an entirely new career. As a new purchasing power, belonging with neither labour nor capital, it becomes interested in new products, in a special branch of produc-tion which does not cater for either the capitalist or the working class, and thus it offers capital new opportunities for creating and realising surplus value. (Luxemburg, 1913/2003: 444)

Militarism provides a new sphere of accumulation out of the wages of workers. It is also, as Luxemburg notes, a superior source of accumula-tion. 'In the form of government contracts for army supplies the scattered purchasing power of the consumers is concentrated in large quantities and, free of the vagaries and subjective fluctuations of personal consump-tion, it achieves an almost automatic regularity and rhythmic growth' (Luxemburg, 1913/2003: 446).

David Harvey critically points out that Luxemburg sees the imperative of the accumulation of capital solely in terms of the violent subjection of non-capitalist spaces to imperialist rivalries, ignoring other means whereby capitalism creates fresh room for accumulation through a variety of strata-gems in actual historical situations. In particular, new rounds of accumula-tion by dispossession are also a way for capital to continue the accumulation of surplus, including, for example, the current pressures for the privatisation of public services (Harvey, 1975/2001: 260–1, 1982/2006: 437, 2003b: 147–8). Nevertheless, he does affirm, albeit with caution, that militarism as a constitutive moment in the structural dynamics of capital accumulation (whereby military expenditures and the deployment of war are means through which the global spatial integration of capitalism is ensured) has critical purchase on the present. In a moment when 'peaceful' expansion of capitalism has become ever more difficult, Robinson too argues that militarism, as discussed by Luxemburg, plays a crucial role in securing the continuation of capital accumulation on a global scale. Militarism has become:

an instrument for prying open new sectors and regions, that is, for the forcible restructuring of space in order to further accumulation, either on the heels of military force or through the state's contracting of corporate capital for the production and execution of social control and war. The train of neoliberalism became hitched to military intervention and the threat of coercive sanctions as a locomotive for pulling forward the train of global capitalism. Wars, interventions, and conflicts unleash cycles of destruction and reconstruction and generate enormous profits. We are now living in a global war economy that goes well beyond 'hot wars' such as those in Iraq or Afghanistan. (Robinson, 2014: 149)[4]

The finances involved in war capitalism, to keep the war machine well oiled, are staggering. 'The Pentagon budget increased 91 percent in real terms between 1998 and 2011, and even apart from special war appropriations, it increased by nearly 50 percent in real terms during that period' (Robinson, 2014: 148). As Table 8.1 reveals, the overall cost of the Iraq War to the United States was $823.3 billion over a ten-year period. Britain, as a second-rate power, maintains the fourth biggest military budget in the world (after the United States, China and France) and its total spend in the Iraq War, drawing from the same data set, was £8.3 billion. Furthermore, over a ten-year period, Iraqi arms imports have totalled nearly $2.8 billion and Iraqi oil revenue exports have totalled $393.6 billion. Total Iraqi civilian deaths during the Iraq War have been calculated to be 121,292 (between 2003 and 2013). The significance of Iraq, then, embraces different aspects of capital accumulation. It concerns the military and oil-service industries, but also the creation of physical infrastructure in the built environment through fixed capital. This comes to the fore as temporary relief from the problems of over-accumulation and the crisis tendencies in the general rate of profit raised by the contradictions of capitalism. After all, 'capitalist development has to negotiate a knife-edge path between preserving the values of past capital investments in the built environment and destroying these investments in order to open up fresh room for accumulation' (Harvey, 1975/2001: 274). As David Harvey (1982/2006: 431) goes on to attest, the problems of capitalism cannot 'be resolved through the instant magic of some "spatial fix"', but temporary relief can be enacted through allying militarism with the significance of oil, the

---

[4] This emphasis has been extended in a novel approach to the drug wars to understand the war on drugs in the context of struggles over territory, land and resources and how it has bolstered a war strategy through dispossession and terror in order to expand the capitalist system into new or previously inaccessible territories and social spaces; see Paley (2014: 15–16).

Table 8.1 *The Iraq War in figures*

	2003	2004	2005	2006	2007	2008	2009	2010	2011	2012
Iraqi Arms Imports	—	$72 m	$189 m	$305 m	$269 m	$308 m	$402 m	$455 m	$722 m	—
Iraqi Oil Revenue Exports	$5.1bn	$17.2bn	$23.3bn	$31.9bn	$61.2bn	$38.3bn	$39.2bn	$49.2bn	$82.9bn	$45.3bn
U.S. **Cost of the War**	$53bn	$75.9bn	$85.5bn	$101.6bn	$131.2bn	$142.1bn	$95.5bn	$71.3bn	$49.3bn	$17.7bn

Source: The Guardian, 'Iraq after the Invasion: A Decade Visualised' (14 March 2013), www.theguardian.com/news/datablog/2013/mar/14/iraq-ten-years-visualised

construction and reconstruction industries and fractions of finance capital. In everyday vernacular this can be summarised as a Bomb-and-Build strategy, linking militarism and reconstruction of the built environment to stave off capitalist crisis. Put differently, the 'extra-economic' conditions of warfare and militarism are therefore paramount – demonstrated by the U.S. cost of the war and the smaller but still significant level of Iraqi arms imports – in paving the way for new rounds of American-led dispossession and capital accumulation, including securing Iraqi oil exports, as evidenced in Table 8.1. Hence the accent given to *military neoliberalism* that is regarded as essential to the continued expansion of capitalism (Retort, 2005: 72–7).

The extension and concentration of demand brought about by conflict is also seen empirically in the United Kingdom by the fact that 'the additional net costs incurred on operations (for example in Afghanistan, Iraq, and Libya) are not paid for from the Defence Budget, but rather by the Special Government Reserve. Between 2001–2 and 2009–10, the Reserve has provided an additional £18 billion on top of the Defence Budget to cover operational costs.'[5] As the Ministry of Defence statement shows, capital can expand demand through conflict so that militarism, or the strategy of Bomb-and-Build, becomes a key source of accumulation that benefits the long-term interests of capital in general, not just those involved in the military-industrial complex.

Linked to this military spending is the continued success of both the United States' and Britain's globally competitive arms industry, the latter thriving despite the general weakness of British manufacturing. Britain, through entities such as BAE Systems with 100,000 workers and $18 billion in revenues, has 'maintained the largest and strongest military-industrial-scientific complex in Western Europe – a complex that retained its strength while other parts of the British economy and society fell apart' (Edgerton, 1991: 165). Within the United States, Boeing, Lockheed Martin, Raytheon and Northrop Grumman stand as the four largest monopolies within the defence industry. In general, it is not surprising that companies linked to war capitalism including arms manufacturers, construction companies and related service industries have been reaping extra profits since 9/11 and the global war on terror. 'The Spade Defense Index, a benchmark for defense, homeland security, and aerospace stock went up every year from 2001 to 2006 by 15 percent. In the decadent world of global capitalism, war, conflict, and instability

---

[5] Ministry of Defence, 'Defence Spending: Information about Key Areas of the Defence Budget', http://webarchive.nationalarchives.gov.uk/+/http://mod.uk:80/DefenceInternet/AboutDefence/Organisation/KeyFactsAboutDefence/DefenceSpending.htm; accessed 5 September 2011.

generate an environment for permanent accumulation' (Robinson, 2014: 153).

In short, our approach improves on extant conceptions of imperialism (*viz.* Callinicos) by explicitly attempting to internalise the dialectical relationship between the territorial logic of power and the spatial expansion of capitalism as discussed in Chapter 5. Additionally, we also emphasise, in line with our position on structure-agency developed in Chapter 2, that this approach to the accumulation of capital internally relates the *structuring* conditions of global capitalism towards constant outward expansion to the *agency* of transnational capital within these processes. Thus, our focus now turns to the intra-class struggles within the U.S. form of state, which is central to global capitalism. In other words, the *agency* of class struggles within the United States between different transnational and national fractions of capital has to be analysed within the *structural* context of the constant pressure for capitalist expansion.

Class Struggle in the U.S. Form of State and the Strategy of Bomb-and-Build in the Iraq War

To recapitulate a central argument of this book, in the modern epoch the geopolitical states system is internally related to capitalist relations of production. Therefore, we stress how there is an *internalisation* of class interests within the state – albeit through the transnational expansion of social relations – rather than assuming that states have become mere 'transmission belts' from the global to the national level (see Chapter 5). In other words, the challenge is to conceptualise dialectically the state form in a way that emphasises its internal relation with market conditions, with the wider interstate system and with global capitalist relations.

As Robinson develops (correctly in our view), the transnationalisation of production has led to the emergence of transnational capital as a new significant form of agency so that class struggle is no longer only between national capital and labour but potentially also between national and transnational class fractions of capital and labour. While splits between 'nationalist' and 'globalist' class fractions should not be exaggerated, dominant tendencies can be observed in the United States in relation to the war in Iraq. Commonly, the nationalist wing is seen as linked to the interests of U.S.-based military and defence industries, the oil industry and other 'internationally noncompetitive businesses' (Hossein-Zadeh, 2006: 4; Nitzan and Bichler, 2002: 208–12). In the political sphere members of this fraction might promote unilateralism, the unrivalled pre-eminence of U.S. military power, and notions of pre-emptive warfare as key strategies for the protection of the 'national interest', which more often than not means U.S.-based capital (Harris, 2005: 142). In this sense, it could be said that the nationalist wing of the U.S. elite was politically represented by the neo-conservatives who gained power with the election of George W. Bush in 2001 and for whom such strategies were of central importance. Meanwhile the globalist wing can be linked to 'nonmilitary transnational capital' representing the interests of the TCC (Hossein-Zadeh, 2006: 4). Generally, the globalist wing is much more loosely tied to notions of U.S. hegemony, which instead promote policies of coordination with allies to ensure stability within the international system in the interests of a fully functioning and integrated global economy (Harris, 2005: 142). However, it would be ill advised to overstate a complete division between nationalist and globalist fractions, or unilateral and multilateral positions, in relation to the Iraq War or more generally throughout U.S. foreign policy. As Frederick Tsai (2008: 48) usefully summarised, 'foreign policy initiatives have been multilateral if possible, but unilateral if necessary.'[6] In relation to Iraq, it was only when a multilateral strategy became impossible (prior to March 2003) that a rift then emerged between national and transnational capital fractions. Yet this struggle between different class fractions within the U.S. form of state is overlooked by Robinson and his assertion that the U.S. state apparatus is simply at the disposal of the TCC. If the TNS thesis was correct, one would expect the U.S. administration and other elites who were instrumental in promoting war in Iraq to have strong links to the globalist fraction and therefore be tied to the interests of transnational capital.

Yet Robinson's argument that the invasion of Iraq in 2003 was undertaken in the interests of the TCC is critically undermined by the fact that a dominant tendency expressive of the nationalist wing of the U.S. ruling elite had come to hold a hegemonic position during the build-up to war. It thus held influence not only over policy in the form of the neo-conservatives within the Bush administration but also over the wider discursive framing that served to justify the invasion. This discourse, manifest in the rhetoric of state officials as well as wider intellectuals of statecraft (or organic intellectuals) – the cornerstone of the focus on the material structure of ideology in Chapter 3 – emphasised the importance of increasing U.S. hegemony through the promotion of the use of unilateral, pre-emptive force, a policy which clearly ran counter to a globalist agenda. To this end, Iraq's vast oil reserves were seen in strategic political

[6] See also Anievas (2014: 114–15) on how unilateralism-multilateralism are always-already present moments, or internally related aspects, of the extension of capitalist accumulation, including the systematic use or threat of force and violence through formal and informal empire.

terms as much as in economic terms as a means by which the United States could increase its political power in the region. In the following, the capital links of the key intellectuals of statecraft (or the organic intellectuals as the architects of war) and their dominant ties with the national wing of U.S. capital – in particular to the defence and oil industries – are examined.[7]

In a critique of Robinson's thesis, Harris correctly notes that a military strategy which promotes 'hegemonic domination commanded by the nationalist wing of U.S. capitalism cannot be described as a transnational consensus' (Harris, 2008: 39). Protecting and promoting U.S. hegemony through the use of force has long been a strategy of the neo-conservatives who were at the heart of the Bush administration. It was most notably elaborated by the conservative intellectuals of statecraft William Kristol and Robert Kagan and their concept of 'benevolent hegemony' as discussed in an article published in *Foreign Affairs* in 1996 (Kristol and Kagan, 1996: 20). It was also evident in the work of the neo-conservative think-tank 'The Project for the New American Century', which was established in 1997 with the explicit goal of promoting 'American global leadership' (Project for the New American Century, 1997a). In its 'Statement of Principles', which was signed by prominent neo-conservatives Dick Cheney, Donald Rumsfeld and Paul Wolfowitz (all of whom came to hold high-level positions within the Bush administration), it advocates a strong military in order to 'meet both present and future challenges' as well as a 'foreign policy that boldly and purposefully promotes American principles abroad'. It goes on to urge the United States to meet its responsibilities as the global superpower in order to confront 'challenges to our fundamental interests' (Project for the New American Century, 1997b). A similar rationale permeated the National Security Strategy of 2002 that, as Noam Chomsky (2003: 3) notes, 'declared the right to resort to force to eliminate any perceived challenge to U.S. global hegemony'. In this document setting out the parameters of the 'war on terror', the Bush administration declared its intentions to use pre-emptive force to defend 'our interests at home and abroad by identifying and destroying the threat before it reaches our borders' (National Security Council, 2002). This discourse about pursuing U.S. hegemony was closely linked to ideas about American exceptionalism, perhaps most notably articulated in the neo-conservatives' unilateral foreign policy as set out in the Defense Planning Guidance draft of 1992, written under the

---

[7] See also the survey of foreign policy thinkers across the dyad of Realism and liberalism, covering Robert Kagan, Zbigniew Brzezinski, Robert Art and the outlier Thomas P. M. Barnett in Anderson (2013: 136–62; 2017).

supervision of Paul Wolfowitz, which strongly advocated the use of unilateral military force to secure the pre-eminence of the United States in
the post–Cold War era (Herring and Rangwala, 2006: 8–9).

This policy of a unilateral pursuit of u.s. hegemony was clearly at odds
with a globalist agenda, which favoured multilateralism. For example,
in May 2003 the French subsidiaries of eleven transnational companies
including Microsoft, IBM and McDonalds signed an open letter warning
about the economic consequences of the continuing rift between France
and the United States over policy towards Iraq.[8] Furthermore, the
Transatlantic Business Dialogue, led by the CEOs of Coca-Cola and
Unilever, identified diplomatic tensions between the United States and
Europe over Iraq as 'a mortal threat to further coordination of liberalisation, free trade and global economic growth' (Paul, 2007: 69).
However, with multilateralism at an impasse, the rhetoric of neo-
conservative unilateralism gained salience. A dominant discourse of u.s.
unilateralism at that time emerged, linked to the nationalist wing of the
u.s. elite, which retained firm roots within the military-industrial-
complex (MIC), the institution that has control over the u.s. military
machine and is therefore key to understanding some of the dynamics of
u.s. foreign policy. The MIC, initially identified by Senator William
Fulbright in the late 1960s (Giroux, 2007: 15), includes more than 150
military-educational institutions, with some directly linked to the MIC
such as the National Defense University and the Army's War College,
as well as 'hundreds of colleges and universities that conduct Pentagon-
funded research, provide classes to military personnel, [and] design pro-
grams specifically for future employment with various departments and
agencies associated with the warfare state' (Giroux, 2007: 18–19).
Consequently higher education in the United States has become increasingly militarised and linked to defence policy. For example, in a 2006
report, the Association of American Universities encouraged its members
to cultivate u.s. talent in order to 'fill security-related positions in the
defense industry, the military, the national laboratories, the Department
of Defense and Homeland Security, the intelligence agencies and other
federal agencies' (Association of American Universities, 2006).

With regard to the struggle between globalist and nationalist fractions
both within the MIC and the extended military-industrial-academic
complex, Harris goes on to note that the nationalists' strategy of unilateralism and pre-emptive aggression was made operational by the 'new
worldwide threat' of terrorism after the terrorist attacks of September 11,

[8] BBC News, '"Appeal for Peace" on U.S.–French Trade', http://news.bbc.co.uk/1/hi/busi
ness/2991995.stm; accessed 14 April 2009.

2001. The 'war on terror' provided the pretext for neo-conservatives, geopolitical realists and unilateralists within the MIC to create 'widespread internal support for their policies'. In this way, anti-globalist forces have rallied round the MIC to 'build a political bloc and to challenge the TCC' (Harris, 2005: 145–51). Darel E. Paul comes to a similar conclusion about the rise of the neo-conservative movement to establish a (temporary) hegemonic position, utilising the 'Caesarist moment' created by the attacks on September 11 (2001) to generate a 'new post 9/11 social bloc' (Paul, 2007: 65). It was by utilising this dominant position that the nationalist wing of the U.S. ruling elite was able to control and formulate the production of a prevalent discourse around policy towards Iraq, which was based on notions of benevolent U.S. hegemony, American exceptionalism and unilateralism and the need for pre-emptive military force.

Within this discourse of bolstering U.S. hegemony, Iraq's oil reserves became increasingly important. These oil reserves were not seen primarily as an economic prize, but rather as a political, strategic asset. The 'crucial issue' for the United States since 1945 in regard to the vast oil reserves of the Middle East 'has been control, more so than access or profit' (Chomsky, 2007: 38). As Michael Klare (2004: 62) notes, the U.S. desire to dominate the Middle East rests on more than just concerns about 'the safety of its future oil supply', with recognition of the 'political leverage' that control over this oil would give to the United States vis-à-vis other oil-importing countries. This was recognised in a 2004 report from the National Intelligence Council which states that 'growing energy demands ... will have a substantial impact on geopolitical relations' and identifies the increasing instability of traditional Middle Eastern suppliers as a central concern (National Intelligence Council, 2004: 59, 62). Following a similar logic, former national security advisor and key intellectual of statecraft Zbigniew Brzezinski (2003/4: 8) explains how:

America has major strategic and economic interests in the Middle East that are dictated by the region's vast energy supplies ... America's security role in the region gives it indirect but politically critical leverage on the European and Asian economies that are also dependent on energy exports from the region.

It is difficult to reconcile either the nationalist discourse or the policy of promoting U.S. hegemony which lay behind the invasion of Iraq with Robinson's argument that the principal goal of the invasion was to open the country up to transnational capital. This is not to deny that there were economic motivations behind the invasion of Iraq or that capitalist logics of power did not have a role to play. As Alan Cafruny and Timothy Lehmann (2012: 16) point out, 'Anglo-American firms – excluded from the country for decades – now control the lion's share of Iraq's oil and natural gas sectors. The U.S. retains significant over-the-horizon capabilities on Iraq's borders, through its archipelago of bases across the Gulf Cooperation Council states.' However, by examining the capital links of key architects of war, or intellectuals of statecraft,[9] within the Bush administration, one can see that the majority of these links were to U.S.-based defence and oil companies rather than to transnational capital.

This is certainly true of two of the most important architects of war, former Secretary of Defense Donald Rumsfeld and former Vice President Dick Cheney. Donald Rumsfeld had to sell off directly owned stocks in Lockheed Martin and Boeing (two major defence companies) before taking office, but was still part or complete owner of private investment firms 'that were devoted to defence and biotechnology stocks'. Dick Cheney meanwhile was CEO of Halliburton, a U.S.-based oil company, before becoming vice president, and retained hundreds of thousands of shares and unvested options as he entered the vice presidency (Klein, 2007: 311, 313). Other influential, if more informal, advisors to the Bush administration also had strong ties to oil and defence companies. Henry Kissinger, the former secretary of defence who not only remained close to the Bush administration but also became an important commentator and intellectual of statecraft contributing to the debate over Iraq (Woodward, 2004: 163), owns a company called Kissinger Associates which is reported to have represented a host of large corporations including Hunt Oil and Fluor, an engineering company that was 'one of the biggest reconstruction contract winners in Iraq' (Klein, 2007: 320). The Defense Policy Board, whose role it was to give independent advice to the secretary of defence, had nine of thirty members with links to defence companies, with four members being registered lobbyists (Politi and Verlöy, 2003). Meanwhile Richard Perle, who chaired the Defense Policy Board, a position which he used to 'argue forcefully in the press for a pre-emptive attack on Iraq', had recently set up a venture capital firm called Trireme Partners, 'which would invest in firms developing products and services relevant to homeland security and defense' (Klein, 2007: 320).

These links to oil and defence companies spread to groups that were set up by the Bush administration to argue the case for war. James Baker, who

---

[9] Intellectuals of statecraft are 'those intellectuals who offer normative and imperative rules for the conduct of strategy and statecraft by the rulers of the state' and can include a 'whole community of state bureaucrats, leaders, foreign policy experts and advisors' linked to the activities of statecraft, see Ó Tuathail and Agnew (1992: 193) and Ó Tuathail, Dalby and Routledge (1998: 8). The link is clear to Antonio Gramsci's notion of organic intellectuals as active mediators of struggles over hegemony between class forces, as discussed in Chapter 3 (Gramsci, 1971: 5–23, Q12§1).

was appointed co-chair of the Iraq Study Group, owned 'one of the leading oil and gas law firms in the world', a major client of whom was Halliburton. He also became an equity partner in the Carlyle Group, which is a 'defence-oriented equity firm' (Klein, 2007: 317). The Committee for the Liberation of Iraq, a pressure group established in 2002 to argue the case for war, also had strong links to the arms industry. Its convenor, Bruce Jackson, had only a few months earlier been vice president for strategy and planning at Lockheed Martin. Other representatives of Lockheed within the Committee included Charles Kupperman, Lockheed Martin's vice president for space and strategic missiles, and Douglas Graham, Lockheed's director of defence systems. George Schultz, who headed the committee, was a member of the board of directors of Bechtel, the largest engineering company in the United States, where he had earlier served as CEO, a company that would collect billions from reconstruction contracts in Iraq (Klein, 2007: 319). Beyond personal ties, oil and defence companies are economically and structurally closely linked to the U.S. government, and therefore retain a national tendency rather than transnational focus. Harris notes that the military industry is international rather than transnational, as it has investments, production and employment which remain 'in their country of origin and mainly access the global markets through exports', and relies heavily on state protectionism. For example, in 2001, 72 per cent of Lockheed Martin's sales 'came from U.S. government procurements'. Moreover, 75 per cent of all U.S. military foreign sales are processed by the Pentagon (Harris, 2005: 145–6). This means that including organisations such as Lockheed Martin in a register of corporations supposedly evidencing the dominance of transnational capital obscures their position as a fraction of capital linked to national policy planning (van Apeldoorn and de Graff, 2014: 45–6). Furthermore, in terms of the contractual reconstruction of the built environment in Iraq, the role forged in the early days by the U.S.-led Office of Reconstruction and Humanitarian Assistance (ORHA) in Iraq involved a main $680 million contract for the reconstruction of electrical, water and sewage systems, which was granted to the Bechtel Group. The senior vice president of Bechtel, Jack Sheehan, was a member of the Defense Policy Board, a Pentagon advisory group whose members were approved by Secretary of Defense Donald Rumsfeld. George Schultz, the former secretary of state, was also on Bechtel's board and chaired the advisory board of the pro-war Committee for the Liberation of Iraq. The contract was, at the time, the largest of an initial $1.1 billion reconstruction project headed by the United States Agency for International Development (USAID). It also led to further awards to Bechtel to repair airports, dredge and restore ports such as Umm Qasr, rebuild hospitals, schools, government ministries and irrigation systems and restore transport links, 'giving Bechtel an overwhelmingly important role in virtually every area of Iraqi society'.[10] A $7 billion contract for controlling oil fires was also awarded to Kellogg, Brown & Root, a division of Halliburton, once run by Vice President Dick Cheney.

Based mainly in the United States and profiting chiefly from government sales or government-aided procurements, these companies tend to constitute elements of the national wing of u.s. capital. Their close ties to the neo-conservatives within the Bush administration provide another explanatory factor in regard to the decision to invade Iraq, even in the absence of multilateralism. Andrew Flibbert criticises accounts of the war that place emphasis on domestic economic factors by arguing that business interests in the region could have been advanced without military action or invasion (Flibbert, 2006: 321). However, this critique is based on the assumption that 'business interests' are a homogenous and universal category, an assumption strongly contested by Jonathan Nitzan and Shimshon Bichler's concepts of dominant capital and differential accumulation. Their conceptualisation of capital rests on the assumption that dominant capital seeks as its priority differential rather than absolute accumulation, meaning that capital groups 'try not to maximise profit, but to beat the average and exceed the normal rate of return' (Nitzan and Bichler, 2004: 257). They note that arms companies and to a certain extent oil companies, as a potentially dominant capital group, have an interest in renewed conflict, particularly in the Middle East. Tension and war bring higher oil prices, leading to higher oil revenues and profits for the Organisation of Petroleum Exporting Countries (OPEC) countries and oil companies. Local governments then use this petroleum money to buy more weapons, in the meantime laying the groundwork for the next conflict. So 'if the oil and armament groups surrounding the Bush Administration have a broad interest here, clearly it is an interest in some measure of instability and war, not peace' (Nitzan and Bichler, 2004: 258). The u.s. nationalist class fraction was therefore much more likely to benefit from pre-emptive warfare in Iraq than the globalist strategy and the building of alliances between countries to create a stable global market. In short, an analysis of the intra-class struggle over the invasion of Iraq within the u.s. form of state makes clear that rather than the u.s. ideological state apparatus being at the disposal of the TCC, it was the nationalist fraction of capital which was shaping and

---

[10] *The Guardian*, 'Bechtel Wins Contract Prize' (18 April 2003), www.guardian.co.uk/wo rld/2003/apr/18/iraq.oliverburkeman1?INTCMP=SRCH; accessed 14 April 2009. See also Anievas (2008: 203).

constituting the strategy of Bomb-and-Build in Iraq, or the linkage of militarism and reconstruction of the built environment to stave off capitalist crisis.

Conclusion: Towards Global War and Bomb-and-Build on a World Scale?

In this chapter, it was argued that neither an approach focusing on inter-imperialist rivalry nor an approach emphasising multilateral cooperation under the leadership of the United States can adequately examine the internal relations between the geopolitical and capitalist dynamics underlying world order. Unsurprisingly, both sets of approaches produce rather state-centric accounts of the reasons behind the invasion of Iraq in 2003. The focus then moved to an assessment of the transnational state (TNS) thesis. While this can incorporate the changing social relations of production as a result of globalisation and thus the emergence of transnational capital as a new class fraction, there is a rather uncritical and unquestioning assumption at the heart of this thesis that the United States has simply been transformed into an apparatus at the disposal of the interests of transnational capital. The war on Iraq, according to the logic of this argument, was therefore a strategy of transnational capital that benefitted this specific class fraction. Having acknowledged, however, the continuing importance of the structured coherence that state forms grant to the spatial organisation of capitalism as well as the dynamics of uneven and combined development within the interstate system, we asserted the importance of focusing on the intra-class struggle within the U.S. form of state over the war in Iraq. It thus became clear that this conflict was actually shaped more by a nationalist tendency within the U.S. ruling class who were in a dominant position and were the primary intellectuals of statecraft behind the invasion and subsequent reconstruction. Summarily put, the discussions over unilateralism and multilateralism became important in relation to Iraq when it had become clear that a multilateral strategy based on a decision by the UN Security Council was not feasible. Divisions between national class fractions of capital and transnational fractions were not so much over going to war as such, but whether to proceed with war in a situation when multilateralism was not possible. Neo-conservative discourses were utilised by national capital on this occasion to justify a unilateral strategy at this historically specific juncture.

Unsurprisingly, when it came to the distribution of contracts for the reconstruction of Iraq after the war, it was not transnational capital that was the main beneficiary. Instead, the awarding of reconstruction contracts was largely focused on U.S.-based companies and capital groups. A 2003 report for Congress noted how, immediately after the invasion, a decision was made 'to limit the number of bidders for these [reconstruction] projects to a select few American companies' (Margesson and Tarnoff, 2003). The report goes on to describe how 'normal public bidding requirements were waived' when USAID began awarding contracts for reconstruction projects in February and March 2003, with specific companies invited to submit bids. Indeed it was two U.S.-based companies that were the biggest beneficiaries from reconstruction contracts. Halliburton was given a huge contract to run the Green Zone in Baghdad and was hired to help run the 'living support services' of the Coalition Provisional Authority (Chandrasekarn, 2006: 12). It was also given 'the exclusive United States contract to import fuel into Iraq' and in March 2003 'was awarded a no-competition contract to repair Iraq's oil industry', having already received more than $1.4 billion in work.[11] As noted earlier, the major U.S. engineering company Bechtel was given the first contract by USAID in April 2003, and was awarded a second contract in January 2004, tasked with providing 'a major program of engineering, procurement, and construction services for a series of new Iraqi infrastructure projects ... at a total value of up to $1.8 billion' (Bechtel, 2004). The contract included the provision of 'engineering, procurement and construction services in support of an Iraq Infrastructure Reconstruction Program', providing assistance in areas as wide ranging as 'electric power, water and sanitation services; transportation systems, selected public buildings, ports and waterways, and airports' (USAID, 2007).

Our account challenges the assumption of Panitch and Gindin that U.S. imperialism cannot be linked to class fractions or conditions of formal empire (Panitch and Gindin, 2012: 7). Moreover, our analysis demonstrates the importance of the creation of the physical infrastructure in the built environment through fixed capital within conditions of global war as one way of providing temporary relief from the problems of over-accumulation and the crisis tendencies in the general rate of profit raised by the contradictions of capitalism. This is the knife-edge path discussed earlier, which is navigated between preserving the values of past capital investments in the built environment and destroying these investments in order to open up fresh room for accumulation (Harvey, 1975/2001: 274). Hence it is through new imperialist interventions in Iraq and, perhaps,

[11] *New York Times*, 'High Payments to Halliburton for Fuel in Iraq', 10 December 2003, www.nytimes.com/2003/12/10/international/middleeast/10GAS.html; accessed 29 October 2008.

elsewhere (Afghanistan or Libya) that one can witness the spatial ordering of the built environment through militarism and other mechanisms of finance linked to specific fractions within the U.S. state form and thus the policy of Bomb-and-Build on a world scale.

The next chapter extends the main focus of this book on the conditions of Global Capitalism, Global War, Global Crisis into an analysis of the global financial crisis (GFC) and the contradictions inherent within the subprime mortgage crisis in the United States and its impact throughout the wider global political economy, including the Eurozone. Once again the postholing method is deployed that defines the empirical interventions in this book to reveal how the GFC has resulted from uneven and combined development across the global political economy while generating forms of resistance to conditions of austerity, which are addressed in Chapter 10.

9   Global Crisis and Trouble in the Eurozone

Since 2007 global capitalism has been gripped by its latest crisis. When the major investment bank Lehman Brothers declared bankruptcy on 15 September 2008 a year later, it had become clear that the financial crisis had exceeded worst expectations. What initially had started as a subprime mortgage crisis in the United States of America quickly spread through the financial markets around the world. At great cost, states in industrialised countries, including European Union (EU) members, shored up their private banking systems and injected money into the economy more generally to stem off recession. Governments around the world spent $11 trillion USD to bail out failing financial institutions and to repair the financial system in order to prevent a further downturn of the economy. In the United States, the sums spent on saving the financial system represented 25.8 per cent of GDP; in the United Kingdom, it was a staggering 94.4 per cent. In turn, however, against the background of high levels of uncertainty, financial markets froze. Banks and financial institutions ceased lending to each other as well as industrial companies. With liquid finance becoming scarce on global financial markets, peripheral Eurozone countries especially found it increasingly difficult to refinance their debts. Ever higher interest rates had to be offered to the financial markets in order to sell the necessary state bonds. While countries had been quick at bailing out ailing banks, they were reluctant to assist other countries. Thus, the Eurozone crisis goes right back to the global financial crisis (GFC), albeit played out in diverse trajectories in different countries. 'The sudden rise of public debt across the eurozone in the last couple of years has been purely the result of the crisis of 2007–9' (Lapavitsas et al., 2012: 40).

Ultimately, however, the GFC only triggered the Eurozone crisis. As we argue in this chapter, the crisis is much more fundamentally rooted in the conditions of uneven and combined development and capitalism's general tendency towards crisis, as discussed in Chapter 4, within the context of financialised relations of class power. In order to overcome the global economic crisis in the 1970s, capital first responded with a spatio-temporal fix transferring labour-intensive production to cheap-labour locations in the Global South. Chapter 7 delivered an assessment of how this underlies to a large extent the so-called rise of China. Second, capital responded with an alternate but coeval spatio-temporal fix through the development of more and more financial instruments and the transformation of mortgages, credit card debt, student loans, car loans and other debt for consumptive purposes into asset-backed securities as a central source of liquidity creation and growth. For Costas Lapavitsas, such financialisation, since the 1970s, has entailed: 1) the increasing involvement of non-financial enterprises in financial processes on an independent basis, undertaking financial market transactions on their own account; 2) banks focusing on transacting in open financial markets with the aim of making profits through financial trading rather than through outright borrowing and lending; and 3) individuals and households becoming increasingly reliant on the formal financial system to facilitate access to vital goods and services, including housing, education, healthcare and transport (Lapavitsas, 2013: 3–4). Elsewhere, Susanne Soederberg refers to such dispossessive strategies of neoliberalism as debtfarism, meaning the rhetorical and regulatory imposition of disciplinary mechanisms to reconstruct and normalise the growing dependency on high-priced credit to subsidise the basic subsistence needs of low-income and underemployed and unemployed workers (Soederberg, 2014: 46–7). The purpose of this chapter is to situate the wider conditions of financialisation and debtfarism within the context of the Eurozone crisis and its underlying dynamics of uneven and combined development (Bieler and Jordan, 2015). In line with our postholing method, we focus here more narrowly on the dynamics underpinning the Eurozone crisis in order to understand concrete details of the global financial crisis, while at the same time developing a broader theoretical understanding of historical change. Hence, the first section reveals the limits of several institutional and state-centric approaches to the Eurozone crisis, emphasising especially their reluctance to address the underlying social relations of production and thus the way variegated political economies of specific state forms are interlinked within the wider European scalar political economy. The subsequent two sections then assess, first, recent post-Keynesian interventions, which identify roughly the early 2000s and the introduction of the Euro as the starting point of the crisis. Second, by contrast, we argue that the Eurozone crisis goes back much further to the very moment when countries such as Greece and Portugal joined the EU, highlighting the importance of uneven and combined development as an analytical device and carried through our earlier consideration of the supposed rise of China (see Chapters 4 and 7, respectively). Analysing the Eurozone crisis as an instance of class struggle in this third section, in line with one of the major strands running throughout this book, our emphasis is on how such conditions of struggle have taken place within the emerging European form of state, assessing the extent to which the interests of transnational capital have become internalised and contested within the EU. Running ahead of the following sections, then, this chapter extends a focus on the inner tie of global crisis to the integration of states within the political project of Europe. The internal relations of the tie between global crisis and the trajectories of different territorial state forms within the emergence of the Eurozone will therefore assist in advancing our argument in this book about Global Capitalism, Global War, Global Crisis as all internally related aspects of the same whole.

Explaining the Eurozone Crisis: The Limits of Institutional Approaches

One set of explanations for the Eurozone crisis focuses on cultural arguments. Apparently 'lazy Greek workers' have been put forward in some circles as the cause of the crisis, despite the fact that Greeks are among those who work the most hours in Europe.[1] Another set of explanations pursues a state-centric line of enquiry. Simon Bulmer, for example, argues that it was the particular, German version of neoliberalism (or ordo-liberalism) that had been decisive in shaping the Eurozone crisis 'not least because Germany is the largest contributor to the Eurozone bailout mechanisms' (Bulmer, 2014: 1255). Similar state-centric analyses can be found in historical materialist scholarship. As Alex Callinicos maintains, 'Berlin's hard line over the Eurozone crisis arises from the effort to maintain an export model painfully reconstructed by German capital (with the pain felt by German workers) over the past decade' (Callinicos, 2011: 3). Domestic struggles between capital and labour within Germany are detected by Callinicos, but in line with his general position on the role of the state at the international level (see Chapter 5), states are largely treated as unitary actors within the Eurozone.

Robust mainstream analyses follow an institutionalist line of argument. Hyperglobalist, liberal analyses of globalisation had envisaged that countries subject to 'free market' competition would converge around one specific institutional model amenable to the interests of transnational

---

[1] See Charlotte McDonald, 'Are Greeks the Hardest Workers in Europe?', BBC News (26 February 2012), www.bbc.com/news/magazine-17155304; accessed 1 September 2014.

corporations (TNCs) and the global political economy. Related to the introduction of Economic and Monetary Union (EMU) and the Eurozone, 'it was deemed possible, given self-regulating markets, for the European periphery to import disinflation from the more "virtuous" countries at no social costs' (Simonazzi, Ginzburg and Nocella, 2013: 656). In other words, free market competition would result in a convergence of national political economies around the most efficient institutional set-up. Institutionalists, especially from within the Varieties of Capitalism (VOC) literature, pointed out early on that this convergence hypothesis was conceptually and empirically misguided and spoke about at least two ideal-type convergence trajectories, one around a liberal market economy and one around a coordinated market economy (Hall and Soskice, 2001). Transferred to the Eurozone crisis, this has allowed VOC scholars to highlight the role different national institutional set-ups, different national growth models, have played within the political economy of EMU. Peter Hall, for example, points out that the crisis has little to do with fiscal imprudence in Southern European countries. Rather, the form of crisis 'originated in the structural strains generated when different types of political economies were joined in a currency union' (Hall, 2012: 357). On one hand, the export-led growth models of Germany and other Northern European states, built on high levels of wage coordination, benefitted from EMU. 'Based on serious efforts to contain wage rates, countries in northern Europe such as Germany began to build up large balance-of-payments surpluses inside the eurozone' (Hall, 2014: 1228). On the other hand, southern demand-led growth strategies ran into difficulties. Cheap credit within the Eurozone as a result of northern surpluses allowed Southern European countries to continue their demand-led growth strategies for some time, but higher levels of inflation eventually led to an increase in prices and unit labour costs. As EMU made currency devaluations impossible, 'those countries saw their current-account balances deteriorate as their products became less competitive on world markets, just as competition from the emerging economies of Asia and Eastern Europe intensified' (Hall, 2014: 1228). In other words, national political economies with such different institutional growth models should never have been put together in one currency union. Elsewhere, Bob Hancké looks in more detail at wage formation institutions when explaining the crisis. While wage moderation was enforced in all European countries in the run-up to EMU, once the European Central Bank (ECB) had replaced independent national banks, wage formation diverted in the Eurozone into two blocs: 'a highly integrated northern block where coordinated wage bargaining keeps wage costs under control in all sectors of the economy, and the southern

European countries, where labour costs have risen relative to the north' (Hancké, 2013: 60). For instance, Germany and related countries, thanks to a strong set of wage formation institutions, continued to be able to generate wage moderation and ensure national competitiveness. However, countries without such institutions and an independent central bank fared less well. Especially in these latter cases, public sector unions used their new freedom and drove up wage increases, ultimately damaging competitiveness (Hancké, 2013: 63–7). A vicious circle ensued, resulting in higher levels of inflation and yet further higher wage demands. The ECB, at the same time, was in no position to affect wage formation in individual countries. Alison Johnston and Aidan Regan, in turn, emphasise the importance of different inflation levels in understanding the divergence in trade and external lending between different Eurozone countries. As they argue, 'we trace this divergence to the incompatibility of two distinct growth regimes that produce different inflation rates; high inflation-prone, domestic demand-led models, which predominate in the "mixed market" economies of southern Europe, and low inflation-prone, export-led models, which dominate northern co-ordinated market economies' (Johnston and Regan, 2016: 319). Although they focus on the role of different inflation levels, the argument is the same. Different growth regimes should have never been combined within EMU. The stickiness, the path-dependency of their different institutional set-ups, was unlikely to converge. EMU, however, prevented high-inflation, demand-led models from adjusting their national competitiveness by making exchange rate adjustments impossible. High-inflation countries drifted ever more into a non-competitive position.

VOC literature has greatly contributed to our understanding of the role of institutions in the Eurozone crisis. Ultimately, however, they fall into the trap of 'methodological nationalism', meaning 'an approach that conflates the society with the state and the national territory, and takes it as the unit of analysis' (Pradella, 2014: 181). While divergent economic performances are related back to institutional differences at the state level, what is not understood is the way economic performance in one country is closely related to economic development in other countries. These approaches not only disregard but also conceptually inhibit the ability to examine the underlying social relations of production of the European political economy cutting across national borders. As Ian Bruff (2011: 486) has made clear, by focusing on the varieties of capitalism, this literature overlooks how the different models of capitalism also represent varieties in capitalism. The institutional reductionism of these approaches, externalising institutions as relatively isolated and independent to each other, does not therefore allow such approaches to comprehend the historical specificity of capitalism. In line with our argument in Chapter 1 and the general focus on the philosophy of internal relations shaping our historical materialist analysis, while there are, of course, institutional differences between different national political economies, they are ultimately different varieties of the way the 'economic' has been apparently separated from the 'political' within capitalism and how the social relations of production are organised around the private ownership of the means of production and wage labour. Finally, by overlooking how various national political economies are connected with each other through the social relations of production, these approaches implicitly overlook that not everyone can pursue a low wage, export-oriented growth strategy. After all, the manner in which demand has been suffocated in Germany, through downward pressure on wages and growing precariousness of employment (see later in this chapter), cannot be replicated everywhere. Even if the 'right' wage-setting systems were in place to keep down unit labour costs, when some countries run large export surpluses, others will inevitably have to manage large trade deficits. In other words, the different political economies of different state forms need to be situated within the broader structuring conditions of European political economy as a whole.

In the next section, we discuss an array of post-Keynesian and some historical materialist analyses, identifying the unevenness inherent in the mutual dependence of export-led and debt-led growth models within the European political economy. While highlighting important dynamics across the European political economy, we argue that such arguments overlook the principle that unevenness is a result of the general structuring conditions of capitalism, not simply particular policies and institutional settings around EMU. Moreover, while some scholars capture the uneven nature of capitalist development, they overlook the combined dynamics within these processes. Hence in the subsequent section, we emphasise the centrality of class struggle in our historical materialist analysis of uneven and combined development across the EU.

Unevenness within the European Political Economy: Export-Driven versus Debt-Driven Growth Models

From the early 1990s to the first half of the 2000s, GDP growth rates have been comparatively high in Greece, Ireland, Portugal and Spain, often higher than in Germany as well as the wider Eurozone and EU averages (see Table 9.1). However, this growth proved unsustainable. When the GFC struck, economic growth quickly vanished, at least partly due also to

Table 9.1 *GDP growth rates, 1993 to 2013*

	Greece	Ireland	Portugal	Spain	Germany	Eurozone members	EU members
1993	-1.6	2.7	-2.0	-1.0	-1.0	-0.7	-0.1
1994	2.0	5.8	1.0	2.4	2.5	2.5	2.9
1995	2.1	9.6	4.3	2.8	1.7	2.5	2.7
1996	2.9	9.3	3.5	2.7	0.8	1.7	2.0
1997	4.5	11.2	4.4	3.7	1.8	2.7	2.8
1998	3.9	8.9	4.8	4.3	2.0	3.0	3.0
1999	3.1	10.8	3.9	4.5	2.0	3.0	3.0
2000	3.9	10.2	3.8	5.3	3.0	3.9	3.9
2001	4.1	5.8	1.9	4.0	1.7	2.2	2.2
2002	3.9	5.9	0.8	2.9	0.0	1.0	1.3
2003	5.8	3.8	-0.9	3.2	-0.7	0.7	1.3
2004	5.1	4.4	1.8	3.2	1.2	2.3	2.6
2005	0.6	6.3	0.8	3.7	0.7	1.7	2.1
2006	5.7	6.3	1.6	4.2	3.7	3.2	3.4
2007	3.3	5.5	2.5	3.8	3.3	3.1	3.1
2008	-0.3	-2.2	0.2	1.1	1.1	0.5	0.5
2009	-4.3	-5.6	-3.0	-3.6	-5.6	-4.5	-4.4
2010	-5.5	0.4	1.9	0.0	4.1	2.1	2.1
2011	-9.1	2.6	-1.8	-1.0	3.7	1.6	1.8
2012	-7.3	0.2	-4.0	-2.6	0.4	-0.9	-0.5
2013	-3.2	1.4	-1.1	-1.7	0.3	-0.3	0.2
2014	0.7	5.2	0.9	1.4	1.6	0.9	1.4
2015	-0.2	7.8	1.5	3.2	1.7	1.7	1.9

Created from World Development Indicators; www.databank.worldbank.org/data/;
accessed 30 August 2016.

the subsequent imposition of neoliberal austerity programmes.[2] For
example, in the case of Greece:

[2] Ireland is to some extent an exception in this respect. In summer 2016, the Irish GDP figure
for 2015 was actually upgraded to 26 per cent for 2015 after the inclusion of foreign
companies in the statistics (Inman, 2016). GDP has always been a contentious measure to
assess the economic performance of a country and this figure casts further doubt on the
usefulness of GDP within today's global political economy (Fioramonti, 2013). 'Despite its
claim to be a measure of product, GDP measures the results of transactions in the marketplace' (Smith, 2016: 262). For example, including contract manufacturing outside the
country, tax inversions by U.S. companies with their headquarters in Ireland, the relocating
of patents and transfer pricing as well as the re-domiciling of assets by the aircraft leasing
company Aercap, the Irish GDP figure for 2015 looks impressive, but may actually say little
about the actual strength of the Irish economy, estimated to have been around 5 per cent
(Taylor, 2016). Hence, we need to treat these data with caution and only take them as
an indication of a general tendency at best. However, considering that national and
European policymaking is itself justified with references to GDP levels, these data continue
to retain some relevance.

among the most important reasons is that it was largely driven by debt. Over the period 2001 to 2007, debt-financed private consumption averaged a high 85 percent of GDP and the government deficit averaged close to 6 percent of GDP. Investment remained generally weak except for the housing sector, which benefited from a debt-financed housing bubble. Perhaps most troubling, domestic demand was increasingly satisfied by imports. Greece's current account deficit exploded over the period, from 7.2 percent to almost 15 percent of GDP. As a consequence, Greek spending did little to strengthen the country's weak industrial base. The country's growth became ever more dependent on low interest loans from European banks, especially those from France and Germany. (Hart-Landsberg, 2016: 2)

Post-Keynesian analyses tend to identify the institutional set-up of EMU as the main cause of the crisis and thus uneven development across the European political economy. 'EMU came with an economic policy package that is rule bound and has proven exceptionally dysfunctional during the crisis' (Stockhammer, 2016: 366). Equally too Costas Lapavitsas (2013: 293) has highlighted a core and periphery dynamic within the Eurozone that 'has led to enormous indebtedness among peripheral countries, giving a particular form to peripheral financialisation' (see also Flassbeck and Lapavitsas, 2013). The related undermining of national policy autonomy in responding to economic crises is especially singled out as problematic (Stockhammer and Köhler, 2015: 38). With exchange rates between countries fixed as a result of the common currency and national fiscal policy severely restricted within the Stability and Growth Pact, the only way to increase competitiveness has been downward pressure on wages and work-related conditions (Bieler, 2006: 5–7; Lapavitsas et al., 2012: 158).

Thus, by default, the EMU has limited countercyclical state intervention in times of crisis and has relied from the beginning on downward pressure on wages for adjustment alongside the development of financialisation and the creation of national and personal debt for economic growth.

This has resulted in two distinct growth models, which are both unstable: debt-driven growth and export-driven growth. Both allow for growth, but are intrinsically unstable, because they require increasing debt to income ratios. In the case of the debt-driven model it requires domestic debt; in the case of the export-driven model it requires foreign debt of the trade partners. It is these rising mountains of debt that erupted in the crisis. (Stockhammer, 2016: 369)

Hence, the main problems of EMU from a post-Keynesian perspective are understood to be the result of insufficient demand and in particular the asymmetries in the formation of such overall demand across the European political economy as a whole (Patomäki, 2012: 79).

The uneven dynamic between the two different models is reflected in trade statistics. Export-driven growth models such as Germany have experienced an export boom in recent years, with almost 60 per cent of its exports going to other European countries (Trading Economics, 2013a). Germany's trade surplus around the start of the crisis was even more heavily focused on Europe with around 60 per cent of the surplus going towards other Eurozone countries and about 85 per cent of the surplus going to all the EU members if combined.[3] However, such a growth strategy cannot be adopted generally. Some countries also have to absorb these exports. This is what many of the peripheral countries now in trouble, such as Greece, Portugal, Spain and Ireland, have done. 'The net trade in goods between Germany and [Portugal, Ireland, Italy, Greece and Spain] amounted to some 2.24 per cent of Gross Domestic Product (GDP) in 2007, accounting for 27.5 per cent of Germany's trade account surplus' (Laskos and Tsakalotos, 2013: 86). The large profits resulting from German export success, of course, needed new points of investment to generate more profits. State bonds of peripheral countries seemed to be the ideal investment opportunity with guaranteed profits, backed by sovereign states. Thus, 'Germany has been recycling its current account surpluses as FDI and bank lending abroad' (Lapavitsas et al., 2012: 31, 2013: 293–5; see also Stockhammer and Köhler, 2015: 42). In turn, these credits to the periphery were used to purchase more goods in the core or to invest in non-tradable sectors such as construction. 'Trade imbalances have fuelled credit growth and bubbles in the credit-led economies as the current account surpluses of the export-led economies were flowing to credit-led economies and providing further liquidity' (Stockhammer, 2011: 10). Germany's export successes crucially hinged on the credit-led solutions to neoliberalism's aggregate demand problem (Bellofiore and Halevi, 2011). Ultimately, some post-Keynesians contend that the creation of credit goes back to increasing income inequality over past decades. Seeing their relative income decline, low-income households increasingly had to rely on credit in order to maintain their living standards. In aggregate terms, 'given the rise in inequality the credit expansion in the personal sector [was] both necessary for supporting aggregate demand and employment and at the same time unsustainable' (Sturn and van Treeck, 2013: 126). The introduction of the Euro and the related low interest rates in peripheral countries facilitated this financialisation of the European political economy, as it

---

[3] Sergio de Nardis, 'German Imbalance and European Tensions', Vox Policy Portal of the Centre for Economic Policy Research, http://voxeu.org/article/german-imbalance-and -european-tensions (2 December 2010); accessed 1 September 2014.

made cheap credit available in these countries. 'Confronted with the stagnant and export-oriented performance of the dominant country of the Eurozone, peripheral countries have adopted a variety of approaches. Spain and Ireland have had investment booms that were based heavily on real estate speculation and bubbles. Greece and Portugal, meanwhile, have relied on high consumption, driven by household debt' (Lapavitsas et al., 2012: 21; Lapavitsas, 2013: 293–5).

The export-driven growth model of Germany and the debt-driven models of countries such as Greece and Portugal are just as mutually dependent on each other as are the export-led Chinese economy and the credit-led u.s. economy at the global level. Firms in core countries would not have been able to pursue export-led growth strategies if global aggregate demand had not been supported by the real estate and stock market bubbles that occurred in the periphery. Peripheral countries, unable to compete with German productivity levels and strong export performance, ended up as countries with large account deficits. In the long run, such development strategies based on capital inflows were unsustainable.

The suggested solutions by the bulk of these arguments follow classical Keynesian lines. For example, Stockhammer (2011: 5) argues that:

[A]n active coordination of wage policy has to be at the centre of a new policy mix. This requires institution building and a very different role for labour unions in economic policy making. Wage policy has to ensure that wages grow with (national) productivity growth, that wage growth is consistent with (properly defined) price stability (on the European average), and with sustainable current account positions within the Eurozone. This implies that wages have to grow at substantially higher rates in Germany than in the deficit countries.

Hence, wage growth is regarded as essential for the stimulation of aggregate demand (Lavoie and Stockhammer, 2013: 4–5). A post-Keynesian proposal in this respect is the 'European wage standard', based on national collective bargaining that is coordinated at the European level and intended to cause a convergence at the European level of national wage shares, and, thereby, halt the fall of the wage share in Europe. As Emiliano Brancaccio (2012: 56) argued:

[A]bove the minimal level of growth, the standard would link the growth of nominal wages with respect to labor productivity to the balance of trade so as to foster a return to equilibrium between countries with trade surpluses and those with deficits. In particular, the countries characterised by systematic current account surpluses would be required to accelerate the growth of nominal wages with respect to labor productivity.

This focus on demand management through wage policy is complemented with calls to control finance more systemically by restructuring and shrinking the financial sector, introducing a tax on financial transactions and implementing mechanisms to redistribute wealth across the various regions of the EU as well as a fiscal policy with the goal to ensure full employment and reinvigorate the public provision of goods and services (Lapavitsas, 2013: 315–16; Stockhammer, 2016: 375–6). Other authors are less convinced that reflationary measures in Germany alone are sufficient to overcome the crisis. Hence, some recommend targeted industrial policies facilitating high-road strategies towards broader product diversity in Southern Europe (Simonazzi et al., 2013: 671–3). Politically, these policies are reflected in the proposals by the so-called EuroMemo Group.[4] Every year, this group of post-Keynesian economists meets for an assessment of the state of the EU and for developing proposals in view of the crisis. To date, the emphasis has been on 'mutualisation of debt (e.g., Eurobonds); EU-wide industrial policy; fiscal transfer payment and a larger EU budget; EU-wide capital controls, EU-wide wage co-ordination norms; a common expansionary fiscal policy; and external policies that require collective European agency' (Ryner, 2015: 288). The vision for the European future is clearly a federalist solution with a common economic and wage-coordination policy. Finally, from this viewpoint, a solution to the Eurozone crisis is embedded within a democratic global Keynesianism. As Heikki Patomäki argues, 'global Keynesianism aims to regulate global interdependencies in such a way as to produce stable and high levels of growth, employment and welfare for everyone and everywhere, simultaneously' (Patomäki, 2012: 175). Worldwide, a wage-led recovery should be based on a 'Global Keynesian New Deal', including a re-regulation of the financial sector, the reorientation of macroeconomic policies in export-led growth countries towards a stabilisation of domestic demand and 'the reconstruction of international macroeconomic policy co-ordination and a new world financial order' (Hein and Mundt, 2013: 175).

Nevertheless, there are at least two key flaws in these assessments and solutions. First, there is the assumption that capitalism can overcome crises successfully as long as the right state policies are adopted. This position overlooks the fundamental crisis tendency of capitalism and the uneven and combined developmental response of outward expansion. How different national political economies are tied together in uneven relations is correctly identified, but the dynamics resulting from the combined effects of development across the EU are overlooked. Thus,

[4] See EuroMemo Group, www.euromemo.eu/; accessed 30 June 2016.

unevenness across the European political economy is not only due to EMU, but has characterised the European political economy for much longer. Free trade policies, as initially embedded within the EU Customs Union since 1968 and then especially the Internal Market from the mid-1980s onwards – when free trade was extended from trade in goods to trade in services and finance – generally tend to deepen the inequality between countries, as advanced countries with higher levels of productivity benefit disproportionately from trade. Often, this may also involve a degree of deindustrialisation in less advanced countries, as industries in countries with lower productivity levels cannot compete with the higher productivity levels in partner countries. 'Unevenness is not . . . a result of market imperfections, but is in fact a product of the way competitive markets work in the real world' (Kiely, 2007: 18). Rather than simply focusing on the institutional set-up of EMU as responsible for unevenness across the European political economy, our argument is that there needs to be a focus on the fundamental role of capitalism in enhancing inequality and, thus, increasing and locking in contemporary forms of unevenness (Bieler and Morton, 2014: 41). The uneven and combined development of capitalism thus constitutes the geopolitical dynamic of the European integration project reflected within the variable adoption of different state strategies of accumulation and territoriality, building on our earlier discussion of the conditions of capitalist expansion within a prior states system in Chapter 4 in this book.

Second, the assumption that capitalism can overcome crises successfully as long as the right state policies are adopted relates the main cause of a decline in the share of wages in national income to the decline in the bargaining power of trade unions (Stockhammer, 2013). Therefore, in order to ensure wage growth, trade unions need to be empowered and play a clear role together with strong employers' associations, plus government involvement if needed, in national wage bargaining (Hein and Mundt, 2013: 178). In other words, the national institutions of the post–World War II class compromise are invoked, which had guaranteed steady wage increases and strong domestic demand levels in industrial countries such as Germany and Sweden up to the 1970s. Such a technocratic vision, however, completely misunderstands the dynamics underlying working-class gains in the post–World War II global political economy. As Stockhammer and Köhler admit themselves, such 'suggestions have strong normative elements with little regard for the political preconditions of its implementation' (Stockhammer and Köhler, 2015: 45). Asbjørn Wahl (2011) makes clear that strong bargaining institutions and the establishment of a welfare state were not an outcome deriving from the benevolence of employers or state policies but rather the result of successful class struggle. Hence, stronger wage growth will never be the result of a change in technocratic state policies. It can only come about as a result of class struggle and labour re-balancing the power of capital. In short, in order to understand the dynamics underlying the Eurozone crisis, we need to focus on class struggles over the continuation and contestation of capitalist exploitation (see also Pradella, 2014: 191). Once again this draws our attention to the internal relations between the structuring conditions of capitalism linked to the outward expansion of capitalism along uneven and combined developmental lines and state strategies of accumulation and territorialisation that are themselves caught up in the agent-driven circumstances of class struggle, as presaged in our arguments in Chapter 2.

Uneven and Combined Development in the European Political Economy

The Structuring Conditions of European Integration

Uneven and combined development between Northern and Southern European countries goes much further back than simply to the establishment of EMU in the early 2000s. Within the confines of EU membership, from the very beginning various states – Ireland in 1973 and Greece, Portugal and Spain during the 1980s – have been intricately locked into heightened relations of uneven and combined development. From the origins and evolution of the Portuguese capitalist state, 'the Portuguese economy, retarded and inefficient, remained largely dependent on foreign capital ... and despite the aura of political radicalism at home, republican ideals were generally undermined by conciliation and moderation with the bourgeoisie' (Chilcote, 2010: 27). In more recent times, unevenness has been further reflected throughout different productivity levels with peripheral European countries such as Portugal historically linked to labour-intensive sectors and states such as Germany mainly involved in capital-intensive sectors of global value chains (GVCs). For example, the Portuguese economy is characterised by low-technology, labour-intensive production structures, often poorly organised and based on human resources with low levels of qualification (Rodrigues and Reis, 2012: 198). The modernising strategies in the area of industrial production by several successive Portuguese governments have not worked, as Jamie Jordan (2016) demonstrates in a detailed analysis of the Portuguese textile and clothing (TC) and footwear industries as well as motor vehicles. While the former sectors actually expanded during the 1980s and 1990s, this was mainly based on small and medium-sized companies, which functioned as subcontractors to larger, international TNCs and focused on labour-intensive assembling of prefabricated parts. As for the latter, in 1995 a motor vehicle assembly plant was opened in Palmela near Lisbon as a joint venture with Ford and Volkswagen. Similar to the TC and footwear industries, although 50 per cent of components were produced nationally, the remaining 50 per cent, mainly capital-intensive production components, were imported from other countries such as Germany, France and the United Kingdom. 'Essentially then, the same configuration of hierarchy developed in the establishment of a new export-oriented production structure, in this case producing motor vehicles, as had developed in the case of the already present TC and footwear industries' (Jordan, 2016: 15). Considering that capital-intensive parts were generally imported from abroad, while Portuguese components and assembling depended on labour-intensive aspects of production, it is clear that Portuguese development was subordinated to requirements of the European political economy. Thus, where production does take place in capital-intensive industries, the foreign value-added content of the final exports is high. For instance, in 'Transport Equipment' the foreign content of Portugal's exports stood at 59 per cent, with the respective figure for 'Electrical Equipment' at 54 per cent, while the figures for Germany are markedly lower (35 per cent and 25 per cent, respectively) (OECD/WTO, 2014). This indicates that Portuguese firms are primarily involved in the final assembly of imported goods before they are exported, with the net value of such exports being low. The capital-intensive parts are unsurprisingly derived from European states. 'Nearly half of the total value of Portugal's exports of Transport equipment originated in other European countries', with key states being Spain, Germany and France (OECD/WTO, 2014).

In Greece's case, there is a similar form of dependent industrialisation, the recent history of which has been shaped by forms of industry based on low-level technology; a division of labour where labour productivity is kept low and highly skilled labour is reproduced in the countries elsewhere in and beyond Europe; and profits realised from the production of surplus value by labour power is expatriated (Poulantzas, 1976: 13–15). As Nicos Poulantzas further argued, the specific types of regime in dependent countries such as Greece played a particular role there due to the precise forms assumed by uneven development and the conjunctures of class struggle. Hence the *internalisation* of the contradictions of uneven development within the development of various social formations: 'there is really no such thing as external factors on the one hand, acting purely from "outside", and opposed to internal factors "isolated" in their own "space"' (Poulantzas, 1976: 21–2). In the present, this situation is even more dramatic due to an overreliance on exporting primary goods and non-tradable services. Greece's main exports are 'food (19 per cent of total exports), petroleum products (15 per cent), pharmaceuticals (5 per cent) and aluminium (4 per cent). Others include: olive oil, textiles, steel and cement' (Trading Economics, 2013b). Greece's domestic value added of gross exports stood at 77 per cent in 2009, which is higher than Germany at 73 per cent (OECD/WTO, 2014). However, the important difference is that much of this domestic content in Germany is exported through high-value-added tradeable manufacturing goods which are internationally competitive, while 'relatively high domestic value added in Greece's exports in part reflects its specialisation in services exports', for example non-tradeables, without any corollary manufacturing base due to lower levels of productivity and competitiveness (OECD/WTO, 2014). Greece too had attempted industrial transformation but it had actually experienced deindustrialisation from the moment it had joined the EU in 1981. Manufacturing in Greece had been unable to cope with the higher levels of competition within the EU free trade regime. Hence this overview of Greek exports since the 1990s indicates the predominantly labour-intensive activities.

In 1990, the top exporting industries in Greece were the TC and footwear sector (25.5 per cent of total exports), food products (17.9 per cent), chemicals and minerals (13.1 per cent), and metal products (7.5 per cent). By 2006, a significant shift had occurred with the chemicals and minerals contribution to total exports increasing to 16.2 per cent, followed by food processing (11 per cent), construction materials and equipment (11 per cent), with the TC and footwear share of exports standing at only 8.7 per cent. (Jordan, 2016: 16)

Where there is more capital-intensive production, this depends to a large extent on sourcing of 'foreign' capital-intensive parts imported into Greece, where they are assembled and re-exported. In short, production in both Greece and Portugal has been marked by dependent industrialisation and labour-intensive roles within GVCs, drawing similarly pessimistic conclusions about development possibilities as in the case of China in Chapter 7.

This vulnerable position has become more precarious since the integration of China during the 1980s and 1990s into the global political economy. The TC and footwear industries have, especially, lost out to cheaper labour locations in Asia. The rise of China has been precisely built on cheap-labour production, some of which was formerly carried out in the EU's southern peripheral countries (see Chapter 7). From the early 2000s onwards, then, even the more capital intensive parts of production have lost out to competitive pressure as a result of the end of the Cold War and the EU's eastward expansion to Central and Eastern Europe (CEE). The quest for national competitiveness and corresponding policy adjustments played an ever increasing role in EU policy during that period, including dominant forms of transnational capital within the internal structures of CEE states, while the EU's transfer payments failed to counter economic disparities even at a distributional level (Ó'Beacháin, Sheridan and Stan, 2012: 227; Shields, 2012). In fact, Western European corporations have benefitted greatly from this unevenness between the old EU member states and the new members from CEE. By integrating suppliers from low-wage CEE countries in their transnational production networks they reduced their wage costs considerably through whipsawing tactics that put subcontractors and workers from different locations in competition against each other. German multinationals profited most from the availability of a cheap and well-trained industrial labour force in its Eastern hinterland. German firms established themselves predominately in the Czech Republic, Poland, Hungary and Slovakia and used relocation threats to obtain concessions at home (Bohle and Greskovits, 2012; Meardi, 2013). This increased their international competitiveness significantly. 'The delocalisation of manufacturing to emerging Europe has actually helped to create jobs in the home country by sustaining productivity in manufacturing, while contributing to the sharp fall in Germany's relative unit labour costs' (Simonazzi et al., 2013: 660). This restructuring within European production networks and the eastward reorientation of German trade came, however, at a cost for Southern European countries, which were unable to find alternative export outlets and were increasingly unable to compete with China in their traditional production sectors. In response, a notable part of Southern Europe's low-cost industry moved to the EU's south-east (Sacchetto, 2007), where wage levels are as low as in China (Stan and Erne, 2014). Between 2003 and 2008, the flow of Italian and Greek direct investments in Romania and Bulgaria ($12.89 billion USD), for example, exceeded German investments in these two countries ($11.08 billion), noticeable especially if one bears in mind that the German GDP figures were about 40 per cent higher than the combined Italian and Greek numbers (UNCTAD, 2014). As long as cheap credit within the Eurozone guaranteed the necessary aggregate demand, despite ongoing wage moderation, the relatively high growth rates between the mid-1990s and up to 2007 in Europe's southern and eastern periphery seemed to indicate a 'catching-up' process with core EU countries. 'In 2008, the global financial crisis put an end to this and revealed the underlying unevenness in the European political economy' (Bieler and Erne, 2014: 159).

As discussed earlier, rather than succumbing to methodological nationalism, an analytical focus on class struggle is required for understanding the Eurozone crisis. David Harvey (2005: 16) has identified neoliberalisation as a strategy by transnational capital to re-establish its control over the production process and restore class power. Alongside ongoing austerity across the EU, European integration too can be understood as a class project by capital to strengthen its position vis-à-vis labour. As Panagiotis Sotiris (2017: 172) remarks, current European integration is above all 'a class strategy that represents the combined efforts of European capitalist classes to respond to the global economic crisis and to the particular crisis of the European "social model" by means of an offensive neoliberal strategy of capitalist restructuring'. Across the EU, employers abuse the crisis to cut back workers' post–World War II gains. The crisis provides capital with the rationale to justify cuts that it would not otherwise have been able to implement. In other words, unlike mainstream arguments, the historical materialist approach underpinning this volume focuses on class struggle as the main heuristic device of explanation. Rather than regarding struggles over how to handle the crisis as struggles between individual countries, e.g. Germany, the economic miracle, on one hand, Greece and Portugal, on the other, current conditions are understood as driven by struggles between capital and labour across, between, and within various national levels, including the wider space at the European level as a whole.

Class Struggle over the Future European Political Economy

As discussed in Chapter 4, Rosa Luxemburg argued that there is a constant expansive dynamic to accumulation, so that capital has to rely on the possibility of expansion into new geographical areas previously less central to its constitution. One key way of securing new overseas markets, is by extending international loans, which provide a dual function in this respect. First, they are an investment opportunity for accumulated surpluses in advanced capitalist centres. Second, they provide the finance with which additional products can be bought within capitalist peripheries. Luxemburg mentions the example of British loans to the newly independent countries in Latin America in the early nineteenth century, which were then used to purchase British goods (Luxemburg, 1913/2003: 403). Of course, peripheral countries ran into problems servicing these debts. In *The Accumulation of Capital*, Egypt's turn to cotton and sugar production in the nineteenth century is provided as an example. 'One loan followed hard on the other, the interest on old loans was defrayed by new loans, and capital borrowed from the British and French paid for the large orders placed with British and French industrial capital' (Luxemburg, 1913/2003: 414). Over time, the situation grew worse with every new rescheduling of debts and extension of new credit. Foreign powers moved into Egypt to take charge of the country's public finances (Luxemburg, 1913/2003: 416–17). Eventually, the whole country was taken over. 'The British military occupied Egypt in 1882, as a result of twenty years' operations of Big Business, never to leave again. This was the ultimate and final step in the process of liquidating peasant economy in Egypt by and for European capital' (Luxemburg, 1913/2003: 417).

Clearly, none of the countries currently experiencing trouble in the Eurozone, be it Greece, Portugal, Ireland or Spain, can be regarded simply as the 'constitutive outside' to capitalism, or a peripheral space directly correlative to Egypt. Nevertheless, some of the dynamics Luxemburg observed can be noted in relation to the expansion of capitalist surplus accumulation and how it is currently being constituted within the Eurozone under conditions of neoliberalisation, including: 1) the way loans from core capitalist spaces to peripheral spaces ensure a profitable mode of investing surplus capital; 2) the fact that such a strategy is not sustainable in the medium to long term; and 3) that the ultimate shift towards more authoritarian forms of government and the undermining of national sovereignty and democracy can be witnessed (Bieler et al., 2016: 433–6). Until the onset of the GFC in 2007, large financial flows from Germany and other export-oriented economies to countries in Southern Europe proved a highly profitable investment opportunity. More goods were purchased in Northern Europe and growth rates in Southern Europe itself remained high as a result of financialised debt-led growth. Nevertheless, this strategy was not sustainable and a shift towards a more authoritarian form of government took place, with the Troika, consisting of the European Commission, the ECB and the International Monetary Fund (IMF), imposing its conditions in exchange for bailout agreements. In May 2010 and March 2012, Greece received financial help, Ireland was bailed out in November 2010, Portugal in May 2011. In March 2013, it was the turn of Cyprus. Most recently, Greece was bailed out for the third time in the summer of 2015 under highly controversial circumstances surrounding a struggle between a centre-left Greek government led by the relatively new party Syriza and the Troika on behalf of the EU. Spain and Italy have also been heavily affected. Spanish banks required strong support by their government to stay afloat and Italy has found it increasingly difficult and expensive to secure new loans on international financial markets. While not having to succumb to a formal bailout package, Italy and Spain had to present austerity programmes, developed nationally, before the extension of loans from European institutions were made to recapitalise their banks.

For those under the 'guidance' of formal agreements, the bailout packages were made dependent on austerity policies including: 1) cuts in funding of essential public services; 2) cuts in public sector employment; 3) a greater push towards the privatisation of state assets; and 4) an undermining of industrial relations and trade union rights through enforced cuts in minimum wages and a further liberalisation of labour markets. In more concrete terms, first the EU's peripheral countries were obliged to cut back drastically fiscal spending. For example, 'the fiscal cuts imposed on Greece amount to 10.5 per cent of GDP for 2010 and 2011, and another 9.9 per cent until 2014. The consequence of this austerity has been a drop in GDP of 25 per cent since 2008, the bulk of which came after the memorandum agreement in 2010.'[5] But imposed austerity went also beyond direct cuts. 'At the same time [Greece] has been forced to introduce new legislation in labour markets and to engage in ambitious privatisation' (Lapavitsas et al., 2012: 120). Attempts to ensure both labour market deregulation and establish wage-setting as 'more efficient' are clearly directed against trade unions' involvement in social and economic decision-making at the national level (Erne, 2012: 232). As Steffen Lehndorff (2015: 165) points out, new labour market legislation in Greece included 'the priority of company agreements over sector agreements, the suspension of the extension procedure of collective agreements, and a 22 per cent cut in the statutory minimum wage (31 per cent for under-25s)'. Similarly, as part of the bailout package for Portugal, the government agreed to stop extending collective agreements automatically to the whole industrial sector in 2011. Unsurprisingly, collective bargaining coverage has fallen drastically. 'In 2010 a total of 116 industry level agreements ... were extended by government to cover all employees in the industry concerned. However, in 2011 this fell to 17 and in 2012 to 12.'[6] Hence, while in 2010, 1,309,300 employees were covered by collective industry-level agreements, in 2012 it was only 291,100 employees. There have also been amendments to the Labour Code with the aim of creating greater flexibility for firms, thereby allegedly enhancing competitiveness and wage moderation. These changes have included reduced 'pay for overtime by

---

[5] Crisis Observatory, 'Gross Domestic Product (Annual Percentage Change, 1990–2015)', http://crisisobs.gr/wp-content/uploads/2013/03/2.Gross-Domestic-Product1.pdf; accessed 1 September 2016.

[6] ETUI, 'Portugal – Key Facts: Collective Bargaining', www.worker-participation.eu/National-Industrial-Relations/Countries/Portugal/Collective-Bargaining; accessed 22 November 2013.

50 per cent'; further flexibilisation of fixed-term contracts by extending the 'probationary' period from six months to a maximum of three years; and the relaxing of rules for redundancy and dismissal, especially for reasons revolving around economic circumstances (Clauwaert and Schomann, 2012: 9, 11–12; Pine and Abreu, 2012: 25). In short, the crisis has been used by Troika officials to undermine the power of trade unions by cutting back their involvement in collective bargaining and industrial relations more generally while also creating more flexible labour markets, further enhancing the power of capital.

Additional pressure was put on peripheral countries to privatise key national assets in order to improve the balance sheets. This pressure often bypassed democratic procedures. In August 2011 in relation to Italy, Jean-Claude Trichet, then the president of the ECB, and Mario Draghi, who succeeded him in November 2011, urged '"the full liberalisation of local public services ... through large scale privatisations", ignoring the fact that 95.5 per cent of Italian voters had rejected the privatisation of local water services in a valid national referendum less than eight weeks earlier' (Erne, 2012: 229; see also Bieler, 2015a). This point is enhanced by the fact that Greece had initially put forward a proposal for only €3 billion worth of privatisation. Eventually, this was raised to €50 billion only months later due to the explicit dissatisfaction of Troika officials. However, privatisations have stalled in Greece, with projected revenues continually being adjusted to 2020. As the global political economy has stagnated, and Greece has been adversely affected, state-owned enterprises (SOEs) have simply been unattractive to international investors, even at deflated market prices. Against this background of sluggish privatisation, the most recent bailout agreement was used to impose even more stringent monitoring processes. As part of the agreement, Greece had to commit itself to transfer €50 billion worth of Greek state assets to a new fund. Initially, the fund was even supposed to be located in Luxembourg, i.e. outside the country and its influence. In the end, it was agreed that the fund would remain in Athens, but with similarly little influence exercised over it by Greek politicians.[7] One of the initial aims of privatisations in Portugal was to raise €5 billion. By April 2014, this target had been exceeded, reaching almost €9 billion with more still scheduled (European Commission, 2013a: 28). This has included various public utilities, with a particularly contentious privatisation being 'the planned sale of the state water supplier Aguas de

---

[7] *The Guardian*, 'Greece Bailout Agreement: Key Points' (14 July 2015); www.theguardian .com/business/2015/jul/13/greece-bailout-agreement-key-points-grexit; accessed online 15 July 2015.

Portugal' (Busch et al., 2013: 23). The SOEs which remain have been restructured [in other words entailing, redundancies and pay cuts] to bring down costs, and most have reached operational balance by the end of 2012' (European Commission, 2013b: 28). Again, the crisis has been used by capital to engage in state rollback and extend the marketisation of essential public services, while attacking labour unions, planning agencies, entitlement systems, public bureaucracies through funding cuts, downsizing organisations and privatisation. Of course, such neoliberalisation processes of market-oriented reform are also a form of re-regulatory restructuring to secure the rule of capital (Peck, 2010: 22–3).

Importantly, the class character of the agreements is also reflected in the fact that it was not the Greek, Portuguese, Irish or Cypriot citizens and their healthcare and education systems which have been rescued. Rather, it is banks that have organised the lending of export profits to peripheral countries which had been exposed to private and national debt in these countries. For example, German and French banks were heavily exposed to Greek debt, British banks to Irish debt.[8] By now, much of this exposure has been socialised through bond purchases by the ECB. 'As a result of the agreements, the share of bonds in Greek debt decreased from 91.1 per cent in 2009 to 20.7 per cent in 2014 and the share of loans increased from 5.2 per cent in 2009 to 73.1 per cent in 2014. At the end of 2014, the Greek government owed €317 billion, with approximately 78 percent owed to European Union governments, the ECB, and the IMF' (Hart-Landsberg, 2016: 5). In other words, 'the northern Europeans were essentially bailing out their own banks' (Hall, 2014: 1231). Hence, by the time of the negotiations of the third Greek bailout agreement, the European banking system was no longer vulnerable to Greek debt, which strengthened the hand of the Troika.

Arguably, the struggles over the most recent bailout agreement of Greece signify most clearly the dynamics of class struggle underpinning the Eurozone crisis. When the Greek parliament decided to hold a referendum over the Troika bailout proposals, the ECB decided no longer to provide additional emergency liquidity assistance to Greece, thereby indirectly forcing the Greek government to close the banks and stock market as well as to limit ATM withdrawals and transfers of funds.[9] During the negotiations, Troika officials had regularly dismissed any

---

[8] *The Guardian*, 'Greece Debt Crisis: How Exposed Is Your Bank?' (17 June 2011), www .theguardian.com/news/datablog/2011/jun/17/greece-debt-crisis-bank-exposed; accessed 18 June 2011.

[9] *The Guardian*, 'Greek Banks to Stay Closed on Monday' (29 June 2015), www.theguardian .com/business/2015/jun/28/greek-crisis-ecb-decide-emergency-funding; accessed 30 June 2015.

Greek counterproposals. While the Greek finance minister at the time, Yanis Varoufakis, attempted to explain rationally why further austerity could not result in a revival of the Greek economy, the Troika – relying on capital's superior structural power – simply imposed its conditions. 'Troika policy was not shaped by some "objective" interest in promoting European unity or well-being. Rather, it was motivated by a long-standing capitalist class project to weaken labour, privatise public assets, and liberalise and deregulate economic activity throughout Europe' (Hart-Landsberg, 2016: 11). As Panagiotis Sotiris (2017: 177–8) makes clear, these processes clearly limited sovereignty:

The basic disciplinary process imposed upon Greece has been that of evaluations and review. Representatives of the [Troika] established themselves inside ministries and demanded a say in most policy choices while simultaneously scrutinising the entire mechanism of Greek public administration and finance. At the same time, the loans were given in doses, each dose conditional upon positive evaluation of the progress made in implementing the Memoranda. Each round of evaluation was a hard negotiation with the representatives of the government usually ending up with offering new concessions to the Troika.

In sum, capital has used the crisis to push through restructuring it would have been unable to do otherwise. First, it secured private banks, which had been exposed to Greek debt in 2010; then it demanded further restructuring, changing the balance of power in favour of capital. Enforced directly by the Troika, countries in financial difficulties – in exchange for further loans to avoid bankruptcy – are asked to implement far-reaching restructuring measures of state rollback, including public sector cuts and privatisation of state-owned enterprises, as well as further deregulation and reregulation of labour markets. These are all measures which strengthen the position of capital vis-à-vis labour, facilitating a further intensification of exploitation. Returning to Luxemburg's analysis of the role of international loans, the foreign control of the exploitation of Southern European workers is strongly asserted. Yet, unlike Luxemburg's example of Egypt, where it was the imperial power of Britain that undermined local autonomy, within the Eurozone it is increasingly European institutions around the Troika which play this role. Nevertheless, it has not only been peripheral states that have been put under restructuring pressures. In core states such as the United Kingdom, too, capital has sought restructuring and austerity. The following section now analyses the wider restructuring of the European form of state and the way in which the interests of transnational capital have become internalised within the EU state form, thereby picking up on earlier discussions about how to conceptualise the internal relations between geopolitics and global capitalism, as discussed in Chapter 5.

The Internalisation of Transnational Capital's Interests in the EU Form of State

Interestingly, the European form of state plays a specific role in this respect. As discussed in Chapter 5, national state forms remain crucial nodes in the global organisation of capital accumulation. Since the early 1950s, an additional form of state and set of institutions have emerged at the European level with its own structural selectivity increasingly privileging the interests of capital over those of labour (Bieler, 2006: 179–82). This European state form has become a crucial player in ensuring that austerity has affected not only crisis countries in the Eurozone but all EU member states. Prior to the GFC, capital did not request any further institutional mechanism to enforce neoliberalisation. EMU, with its implicit emphasis on wages and working conditions as the only adjustment mechanism, was considered enough to ensure capital-friendly policies. From 2011 onwards, however, European-level state structures were further developed, internalising the interests of transnational capital at the expense of labour (Bieler and Erne, 2014: 150; Erne, 2015: 345).

Austerity in the form of wage cuts in the public sector and cuts in services, pensions and social benefits has not only been imposed on countries struggling with sovereign debt, but across the whole EU. Crucial here are the so-called Six-Pack and the Two-Pack, as well as the Fiscal Compact giving the Commission and Council the right to issue country-specific neoliberal recommendations. 'According to these six new EU laws that came into force after their publication in the EU's *Official Journal* on 23 November 2011, Eurozone countries that do not comply with the revised EU Stability and Growth Pact or find themselves in a so-called macroeconomic excessive imbalance position, can be sanctioned by a yearly fine equalling 0.2 per cent or 0.1 per cent of GDP respectively' (Erne, 2012: 228). The related surveillance procedures are organised in four, ever more intrusive stages: 1) the assessment of countries according to a scoreboard (European Commission, 2013b); 2) in-depth reviews; 3) corrective action plans; and 4) surveillance visits (Erne 2012: 231). The new surveillance powers of the Commission, re-enforced by the so-called Two-Pack of new EU laws in 2013 (Erne, 2015: 346), became visible on 15 November 2013, when the Commission announced its verdict on the planned budgets of sixteen EU member states, namely stage 2 in-depth reviews. While no country was asked to revise its budget and thus enter stage 3, it established several cases of substantial criticism, including a focus on Germany for its current account surplus. Italy and Spain were identified among others as being at risk of breaking the Stability and Growth Pact rules (Kelpie, 2013). These mechanisms have been enhanced by the 'Fiscal Compact', also referred to as the Treaty on Stability, Coordination and Governance in the EMU (TSCG), which came into force on 1 January 2013. The so-called balanced budget rule requires 'the national budgets of participating member states to be in balance or in surplus' (European Council, 2013). This enhances the fiscal pressure put in place by the Stability and Growth Pact (SGP) by deeming the goal 'to have been met if their annual structural deficit does not exceed 0.5 per cent of nominal GDP'. This is different to the fiscal deficit in that the structural position is assessed against what output 'would be' if economic performance was at its optimum, as opposed to the fiscal deficit, which is simply measured against current output. As Hugo Radice (2014) indicates, the economic measurements for this are highly contestable, but it ensures fiscal rectitude as the social content of such a policy. By submitting fiscal policy to the mathematical calculations of experts, it has become depoliticised, moved beyond democratic control 'towards construction of legal or constitutional devices to remove or insulate substantially the new economic institutions from popular scrutiny or democratic accountability' (Gill 1991, 1992: 165). If the balanced budget rule is breached, then an 'automatic correction mechanism' would be initiated to bring the 'deviations' in line over a fixed period. It is to be implemented in national law of binding force, ideally in the form of a constitutional amendment (EuroMemo Group, 2013: 19). Countries who do not observe these structural constraints are referred to the European Court of Justice, the rulings of which are legally binding (Degryse, 2012: 58). Clearly, European control over national fiscal policy has been tightened. Only changes to the no bail-out clause are an exception to the general direction and even they are linked to conditionality. 'The EU has, belatedly, set up a collective fund for member states that have lost access to market finance (European Financial Stability Facility and European Stability Mechanism). This fund gives loans to the countries that are misleadingly referred to as "rescue packages" and imposes conditionality that is similar in spirit (if not as far reaching) as IMF adjustment programmes' (Stockhammer, 2016: 372).

The power of labour has also been limited by such restructuring although not, however, through a direct imposition of new constraints. Rather, as Roland Erne (2015: 357) illustrates well, 'European trade unions' and social movements' difficulties in politicising European economic governance are best explained by the ability of the new supranational EU regime to nationalise social conflicts.' One of the eleven indicators used by the Commission as part of its scoreboard when assessing the economic performance of member states (see earlier in this chapter) is related to changes in nominal unit labour costs. 'Increases that go beyond the thresholds set out in the scoreboard trigger the regulation's prevention and correction mechanisms' (Erne, 2015: 347–8). In other words, the Commission is now empowered to intervene directly in national wage-setting systems through its role as overseer of the European political economy with the clear objective of reducing the power of trade unions and eroding wages and working conditions. 'The [European Commission] and ECB regard wage flexibility as the cure to economic imbalances. By this they mean downward wage flexibility (they have not called for higher wages in Germany)' (Stockhammer, 2016: 371). 'There is no doubt', Erne (2015: 354) concludes, 'that the new regime's league tables, [country-specific recommendations], corrective action plans, and potential fines for non-compliance are effectively eroding the bargaining autonomy of the social partners'. As this European-level policy is, however, enforced through individual national implementation rounds, it is extremely difficult for trade unions to contest this policy at the European level.

These changes in EU economic governance, internalising the neoliberal interests of transnational capital, can be related to a gradual deepening of depoliticisation in the form of 'authoritarian neoliberalism'.[10] Authoritarianism here does not refer to an order imposed by non-democratic means and brute force. Rather, it can 'be observed in the reconfiguring of state and institutional power in an attempt to insulate certain policies and institutional practices from social and political dissent' (Bruff, 2014: 115; see also Gill, 1992). This reconfiguration is generally passed by national parliaments within political systems of representative democracy, albeit by narrow majorities. As Tansel clarifies (2017b: 2), authoritarian neoliberalism 'reinforces and increasingly relies upon 1) coercive state practices that discipline, marginalise and criminalise oppositional social forces and 2) the judicial and administrative state apparatuses which limit the avenues in which neoliberal policies can be challenged'. In peripheral countries, the Troika together with parliamentary elites has controlled state budgets from the outside and thus disciplined state policymaking. Additionally, the economic governance system of the EU as a whole has been restructured along the lines of authoritarian neoliberalism, moving economic decision-making outside democratic accountability. Interestingly, these moves have especially empowered

---

[10] On authoritarian neoliberalism, two emerging developments are worthy of note. First, there is an overlap in the conceptualisation of this condition with the notion of authoritarian constitutionalism (see Oberndorfer, 2015). Second, there is an important consideration of the limits of the concept and condition of authoritarian neoliberalism due to its problematic periodisation (see Ryan, 2017).

the Commission as well as the ECB. The Commission may have lost some of its traditional agenda-setting role during the crisis, but, as Michael Bauer and Stefan Becker (2014: 216–25) reveal, its role in implementing social and economic policies as part of the new economic governance structure around the Six-Pack, Two-Pack and Fiscal Compact plus its membership in the Troika responsible for dealing with the Eurozone crisis countries has been significantly enhanced. This is exemplified in the way 'the Commission's fines apply automatically unless a qualified majority of national financial ministers veto them within a period of 10 days' (Erne, 2015: 347). In turn, the ECB, although it has lost a lot of citizens' trust as a result of its role in crisis management (Roth, Gros and Nowak-Lehmann, 2014), considering its role in the Troika and its management of the Euro in general, 'is the institution whose public salience increased the most during the Euro crisis and whose leverage in EU decision-making has increased' (Tosun, Wetzel and Zapryanova, 2014: 207). Overall, 'these reforms have been predominantly techno-cratic. They have boosted the role of the ECB as a lender of last resort and supervisor of the European financial system; they have strengthened the Commission in fiscal supervision' (Schimmelfennig, 2014: 326). In other words, the whole new economic governance of the EU form of state continues to reflect a turn to the depoliticising tendencies of authoritarian neoliberalism, limiting the possibilities of oppositional social forces.

Conclusion: The Success of Austerity

Through a focus on the current dynamics of uneven and combined development underlying restructuring in the EU and the inner ties to conditions of class struggle, this chapter has extended the philosophy of internal relations approach to Global Capitalism, Global War, Global Crisis as one of the key arguments of this book. In so doing, this chapter has maintained a focus on the inner connections between the uneven and combined developmental conditions of contemporary global capitalism and the response of different state strategies and class struggles to the global crisis. It has been conjectured that there is nothing inherent to capitalism that ensures the reproduction of uneven and combined development and thus no barriers or absolute guarantees against the further integration of states, 'as the European integration project testifies' (Teschke and Lacher, 2007: 579). However, despite tracking the changing configuration of the EU form of state, our argument has served to highlight how uneven and combined development is an entrenched and intrinsic aspect of contemporary global capitalism constituting state strategies of territoriality. The historical materialist philosophy of internal relations as a cornerstone of this chapter and this book as a whole thus conceives of the uneven and combined development of capitalism and the variable adoption of different state strategies of accumulation, territoriality and class struggle as integral elements related to one another as a whole. From the very beginning of its historical geographical sociology, capitalist expansion across the European political economy has been highly uneven, as discussed in Chapter 4. More recently, as argued in the present chapter, in relation to the founding of the EU across contemporary history, Southern European countries and Ireland have been further integrated along lines of uneven and combined development. The development of export-led economic growth models versus debt-driven economic growth models has been re-enforced by the institutions of EMU and the wider project of European integration. In other words, from the beginning of EU membership, Greece, Portugal, Ireland and also Spain have been embedded within relations of uneven and combined development, which has catapulted them towards a position of labour-intensive industries within wider European social relations of production. High economic growth rates in the early 1990s, facilitated by easy credit through membership in the Eurozone, were ultimately unsustainable. When the Eurozone crisis, triggered by the global financial crisis, threatened to undermine capitalist accumulation in Europe, capital used the crisis for further neoliberalisation, increasing its power vis-à-vis labour. In a further turn towards the depoliticisation of authoritarian neoliberalism, austerity was extended and imposed on countries in crisis through a removal of social and economic policies from democratic accountability at the general European level. Post-Keynesian analyses and politicians such as the former Greek finance minister Yanis Varoufakis correctly point out that, economically, austerity has failed. Nevertheless, as David Ruccio has demonstrated in relation to structural adjustment programmes in Latin America, such policies should actually be regarded as a success, when considered in relation to the way in which they have strengthened the class dimensions of capitalism. 'What may be a failure from the standpoint of achieving full employment, price stability, and balance-of-payments equilibrium can be considered successful in terms of promoting the widening and deepening of capitalist class processes' (Ruccio, 2011: 204). Related to the Eurozone crisis, understanding austerity as a capitalist project, it does not matter that Greece, for example, has gone ever further into economic decline. In strengthening capital over labour, in opening up Greek companies for privatisation by foreign capital, austerity has clearly been successful. Thus, it is no surprise that further neoliberal restructuring has continued to be the main response to the Eurozone crisis in Europe.

It is especially free trade policies, crucial in the way uneven and combined development has been deepened inside the EU, which the EU has promoted as a response to the crisis. Ferdi De Ville and Jan Orbie identify four distinctive free trade discourses employed by the Commission since the onset of the crisis in 2007–8:

i) warning against the threat of protectionism; ii) presenting further liberalisation as a contribution to recovery; iii) depicting trade as the only possible source of growth for the EU-in-crisis; and iv) modestly moderating the discourse by admitting that internally there needs to be attention to the demand-side of recovery and externally the EU's own liberal policies should be more reciprocated. (De Ville and Orbie, 2014: 162)

While there is a slight variation over time, what is clear is that there is a furtherance of the 2006 'Global Europe' strategy, characterised by an aggressive, neoliberal free trade policy based on the demand of reciprocity by partner countries (Bieler, 2013). 'The fact remains that in the crisis context free trade is widely seen as the only legitimate policy response, with those openly choosing not to conform facing widespread censure' (Siles-Brügge, 2014: 566). Ultimately, the danger is that this will exacerbate current problems 'by further exposing the peripheral economies to competition from low-wage economies with competitive export structures' (De Ville and Orbie, 2014: 162). Nevertheless, what may look unworkable from a general economic perspective can serve the interests of transnational capital, heavily dependent on free trade. In a way, the heavy emphasis on deepening free trade, visible especially in the negotiations of the Treaty on Trade and Investment Partnership (TTIP), would be another way of internalising the interests of transnational capital. As John Hilary (2014: 6) outlines, the main emphasis is on removing 'regulatory "barriers" which restrict the potential profits to be made by transnational corporations on both sides of the Atlantic'. The intended provisions for Investment-State-Dispute-Settlement mechanisms are especially aimed at strengthening the power of transnational capital vis-à-vis states, as they seek 'to grant transnational corporations the power to sue individual countries directly for losses suffered in their jurisdictions as a result of public policy decisions' (Hilary, 2014: 30). And while the TTIP is currently on hold as a result of increasing resistance across Europe, the Comprehensive Economic and Trade Agreement (CETA) between Canada and the EU, by many considered a Trojan horse for the TTIP, is being promoted for ratification within the EU.

'In October 2010', affirms Lucia Quaglia (2011: 666), 'the European Union adopted a directive regulating alternative investment fund managers (AIFMS), amongst which managers of hedge funds featured prominently'. At first sight, this tighter regulation of hedge funds in the EU seems to present a different path to strengthening neoliberalism in the wake of the financial crisis. Nevertheless, we need to remember that capital, of course, is not a homogenous actor. At times, the interests of different capital fractions may be in conflict. In such moments, the notion of the relative autonomy of the state comes into play. 'Capitalist law appears as the necessary form of a State that has to maintain relative autonomy of the fractions of a power-bloc in order to organise their unity under the hegemony of a given class or fraction' (Poulantzas, 1978: 91). Clearly, in the post-crisis period, capital was divided internally too and calls have been made to constrain the most risky financial practices deemed to have caused and intensified the crisis. Hence, by regulating hedge funds, the EU form of state ensured the continuation of capital accumulation and, thus, the general interest of transnational capital as a whole without questioning neoliberalisation.

The EU's social dimension has slowly withered away. From the very beginning, it had been part of a market-building process (Bieler, 2015b: 27–30). The marketisation of welfare services has further increased existing levels of inequality (Crespy, 2017). More recently, however, there have been signs that we see a kind of revival of the social dialogue between the European employers' association BUSINESSEUROPE and the European Trade Union Confederation (ETUC) initiated by the current president of the Commission, Jean-Claude Juncker, in March 2015. On 27 June 2016, Commission Vice President Valdis Dombrovskis and Commissioner for Employment, Social Affairs, Skills and Labour Mobility Marianne Thyssen signed together with the social partners a statement on a 'new start for social dialogue' (European Commission, 2016a). This followed the agreement between EU social partners for central government administration on 21 December 2015 (EPSU, 2015). These developments in the social dimension have been accompanied by a focus of the Commission on fiscal expansion. In its suggestion for a Council Recommendation on 16 November 2016, the Commission called for an 'overall positive fiscal stance contributing to a balanced policy mix, to support reforms and to strengthen the recovery through a fiscal expansion of up to 0.5% of GDP in 2017' (European Commission, 2016b: 6). As Poulantzas (1978: 31) has also argued, the leading forces of the power bloc have to make concessions to subordinated forces at times in order to ensure stability for capital accumulation. Perhaps the increasing contestation of European integration, reflected in resistance against austerity in Greece and Brexit in the United Kingdom, has reminded policymakers that they need to broaden again the social basis of the neoliberal hegemonic project in the EU. After all, hegemonic orders are never stable, but have constantly to be reaffirmed. In the context of intensified austerity, we have witnessed new forms of resistance across the EU. The final chapter of this volume now draws out the main lines of such resistance, complemented by an assessment of the general contestation of capitalist accumulation on a world scale.

Conclusion

10 Ruptures in and beyond Global Capitalism, Global War, Global Crisis

Earlier chapters in this volume have addressed the relation of interiority between Global Capitalism, Global War, Global Crisis through a set of arguments that have spanned *conceptual reflections* on class agents and structures alongside developing a historical materialist stance on the material structure of ideology in Part I; *thematic considerations* on uneven and combined development, geopolitics and the centrality of class struggle in Part II; and *empirical interventions* analysing a set of spatial dynamics in Part III, linked to the expansion of spaces of capital (Global Capitalism), the geopolitics of conflict and violence bolstering conditions of dispossession through forms of new imperialism linked to territory and social spaces (Global War) and expressions of the crisis conditions of capitalism shaping specific spatially geographical conditions in the Eurozone following the aftermath of the global financial crisis (Global Crisis). This concluding chapter has as its purpose two central aims. First, spatial dynamics are addressed by dedicating the central focus of this chapter to outlining a topography of connected class struggles that bespeak the combined manner of radical ruptures of resistance and their very interiority to the expression of spaces of Global Capitalism, Global War, Global Crisis. The radicalised dialectic at the centre of our approach means that a specific combination exists of elements of resistance and class struggle that are internal to Global Capitalism, Global War, Global Crisis, with this chapter treating the internal combinatory of such struggles over space and territory in a distinct manner in order to grant due regard to spaces of difference and resistance within the global political economy. Second, in addressing the spatial dynamics of class struggle the aim is also to demonstrate how the internal relationship of the three master themes of Global Capitalism, Global War, Global Crisis are themselves internally related. Although this has been asserted throughout this book across various chapters it is the purpose of this chapter to demonstrate how Global Capitalism, Global War, Global Crisis are themselves part of an internal combinatory and are thus related in constitution to each other, as opposed to their relation as instances in

249

exteriority. Hence, the first section of this chapter addresses how the internal relations of Global Capitalism, Global War, Global Crisis are understood within the parameters of this book and is completed by raising some reflections on spatial dynamics of resistance and processes of primitive accumulation. This is followed by three sections which discuss spaces of radical rupture within the global political economy. Drawing on the notion of the social factory introduced in Chapter 6, we contemplate the social factory in China, the social factory in Europe and the social factory as itself a forum of wider rupture to articulate three topographies of class struggle. In this way we conclude this whole book by reflecting on the social mediations of class struggle through the social factory in shaping the terrain of Global Capitalism, Global War, Global Crisis through resistance.

Spatial Dynamics

Throughout this book we have articulated the internal relationship of the three master themes of Global Capitalism, Global War, Global Crisis. This position can now be advanced in a little more detail to argue, first, that within the preceding chapters we have articulated a focus on the inner constitution of Global Capitalism through the *double unity* of uneven and combined development *and* the geopolitics of Global War, within which the contradictions and ruptures of spaces of class struggle endure, thereby viewing Global Capitalism and Global War as consubstantial. Second, we have interconnected a further *double unity* through the focus on the geopolitics of Bomb-and-Build Global War *and* conditions of Global Crisis, within which the contradictions of overproduction and surplus absorption exist as spaces of capital in tandem with spaces of resistance that again endure, thereby viewing Global War and Global Crisis as consubstantial.

As demonstrated in Figure 10.1, our original argument in this book is that there is a pattern of relationship between the three elements (Global Capitalism, Global War, Global Crisis) that is designated by a subset that has a unity and relative autonomy. Hence the conditions of Global Capitalism, Global War, Global Crisis are internally linked by both the double unity (or subset) of uneven and combined development and geopolitics and the double unity (or subset) of Bomb-and-Build expressions of new imperialism and crisis contradictions expressed by spaces of capital and spaces of resistance. The expression of Global Capitalism, Global War, Global Crisis is not, though, a simple derivative of the analysis of the two successive forms (or subsets) of connections that can be 'read off' as laws of motion. Instead, the analysis of Global Capitalism,

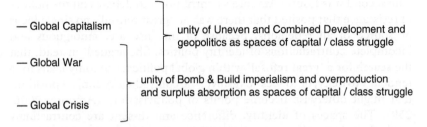

— Global Capitalism

— Global War

— Global Crisis

unity of Uneven and Combined Development and geopolitics as spaces of capital / class struggle

unity of Bomb & Build imperialism and overproduction and surplus absorption as spaces of capital / class struggle

Figure 10.1 The internal relations of Global Capitalism, Global War, Global Crisis

Global War, Global Crisis is made possible through the internal relations and combination of connections, which are contingent and have a relative autonomy. In this way our dialectical approach to unpacking Global Capitalism, Global War, Global Crisis advances beyond prevailing frames of reference in political geography, which we criticised for maintaining a 'two logics' position on the territoriality of the geopolitical conditions of the states system and the geoeconomics of global capitalism. These realms were held as always-already separate and then combined and thus the logics of state territoriality and global capitalism were grasped as relations of exteriority and combined only in an additive manner (see Arrighi, 1994; Chase-Dunn, 1989; or Harvey, 2003b; and, more recently, Lee, Wainwright and Glassman, 2017). Such approaches do not convincingly trace the linkages between the internal combination of geopolitics and global capitalism, as detailed in Chapter 8 on the Iraq War.

In Chapter 2, we established a focus on class struggle as the crucial method for appreciating the internal relations between the structuring conditions of capitalism and class agency. In this conclusion, we return to class struggle in order to comprehend spatial dynamics of resistance and processes of primitive accumulation. Two fascinating separate interventions, both with bold arguments, have appeared in recent decades to focus on the politics of resistance. The first was André Drainville's important, but still much overlooked, critique of the spatial coherence of the global political economy as projected within heterodox approaches. For Drainville, critical approaches have treated the global political economy and spatial dynamics with too much class coherence and thereby assumed the constitution of a distinct social space in the making of global capitalism. As a consequence, analysis 'must give way to more active sorties against transnational neoliberalism, and the analysis of concepts of control must beget original concepts of resistance' (Drainville, 1994: 125).

The second was Louise Amoore's contribution to debates on the politics of resistance that posited that there was no 'great refusal', no single locus or source of all rebellions, because of the insecure, ambiguous and incomplete contradictions of identity politics. She argued, instead, that the search for a 'great refusal' within global political economy leads to 'a tendency to deny, or to seek to resolve, the contradictory subject positions that might otherwise become points of politicisation' (Amoore, 2006: 259). The spaces of identity, difference and dissent are contrastingly marked, in her opinion, by interstitial ambiguities and contradictions where there is a lack of certainty which leads to an emphasis on complete contingency in shaping possible futures. There is clearly still a continued reluctance in some quarters to address issues of *both* global restructuring through integration *and* resistance through differentiated spatial dynamics (with the latter overlooked or inadequately treated in Overbeek and van Apeldoorn, 2012; Ryner and Cafruny, 2016; Shields, 2012; van Apeldoorn and de Graaf, 2016). Notwithstanding this neglect, a plethora of work now addresses original concepts of resistance, which our own research has consistently aimed to assert across varied spaces and territories inclusive of labour and social movements (e.g. Bieler, 2006, 2011, 2015a, 2017; Bieler and Erne, 2014; Bieler and Lee, 2017; Bieler and Lindberg, 2010; Bieler, Lindberg and Sauerborn, 2010; Bieler and Morton, 2003, 2004b, 2007; Hesketh and Morton, 2014; Morton, 2002, 2006, 2007a, 2011/2013). Looking back to the previous arguments in this book, of course, there is also a clear articulation in this volume of the need to avoid capitalocentrism to address, instead, ruptural conditions of class struggle and how this engenders differentiated social movements contesting space, territory and the state to try and reconfigure non-capitalist ways of producing and living (Chapter 6). It is also noteworthy that there is wider work precisely addressing the diversity and plurality of 'great refusal' resistances – covering decolonial and gender conflicts, struggles over sexuality rights, labour resistances and social movements constituting contested territories from Occupy, to the Zapatista Army of National Liberation (Ejército Zapatista de Liberación Nacional) (EZLN) in Chiapas, Mexico, to the Arab Uprising (see Lamas, Wolfson and Funke, 2017), as well as a plethora of work on the notion that class relations, specifically, are not a purely contingent affair and that in the repetition of exploitation there is a system to the production, appropriation and distribution of surplus value (e.g. Hesketh, 2017a). Looking back to the previous arguments in this book, again, we have consistently placed a clear emphasis on how class belonging is not *behind* identity formation in a pre-constituted manner but, rather, that class emergence itself is an outcome in the process of becoming that is *ahead* in the crucible of future struggles (Chapters 2 and 6). In framing our approach to ruptural conditions of class struggle, then, this chapter therefore shares the position that the spatial dynamics of variegated responses to capital accumulation are best regarded through a focus on struggles over *accumulation by extra-economic means* that flows from the violent appropriation of nature, territory, labour and the sphere of reproduction as a source of value creation and exploitation, especially regarding women's unpaid reproductive labour, as well as racial hierarchies resultant from colonial intervention.

Following Jim Glassman (2006: 617, 622), accumulation by extra-economic means is a fruitful way to consider the wider spatiality and geography of primitive accumulation referring to a panoply of forms of accumulation by means of expanded reproduction that have an extensive (geographical) and intensive (social) frontier. From Chapter 4, it should be recalled that primitive accumulation is the process Karl Marx considered as 'nothing else than the historical process of divorcing the producer from the means of production. It appears as "primitive" because it forms the pre-history of capital, and of the mode of production corresponding to capital' (Marx, 1867/1990: 875). Marx is therefore clear that primitive accumulation – transforming the social means of subsistence into capital – is not the result but the very point of departure in constituting capitalism (Marx, 1867/1990: 873). In a key passage, the blistering violence of the expansion of capitalism is thus described.

The discovery of gold and silver in America, the extirpation, enslavement and entombment in mines of the indigenous population of that continent, the beginnings of the conquest and plunder of India, and the conversion of Africa into a preserve for the commercial hunting of blackskins, are all things which characterise the dawn of the era of capitalist production. These idyllic proceedings are the chief moments of primitive accumulation. Hard on their heels follows the commercial war of the European nations, which has the globe as its battlefield. It begins with the revolt of the Netherlands from Spain, assumes gigantic dimensions in England's Anti-Jacobin War, and is still going on in the shape of the Opium Wars against China, etc. (Marx, 1867/1990: 915)

Yet, beyond the racial violence of exploiting the colonies where people have 'nothing to sell except their own skins', there is also a wider focus on alternative powerful levers mobilised for the concentration of capital (Marx, 1867/1990: 873, 918). Alongside the extinction of indigenous peoples, Marx gives clear consideration to how such policies might be accompanied by legislation to seize land violently; annex Church property and estates; induce famine conditions to forcibly expropriate the soil from peasant producers; enact the usurpation and dispossession of agricultural producers, such as through the clearing of estates in Scotland under the

Duchess of Sutherland just as the indigenous peoples of the Americas and Australia would be similarly cleared akin to the 'trees and brushwood'; engage in the practice of scalping of indigenous peoples, encouraged by the British Parliament that set the male, female and child rates for Native Americans in the Massachusetts Bay area of New England; establish both wage slavery and direct slavery as the pedestal for capital; draw on public debt as a means for the concentration of capital; utilise the international credit system as a way of concealing sources for primitive accumulation; and develop the system of taxation as an expropriating agent for capital (Marx, 1867/1990: chapters 26–33). This is not an exhaustive list. Elsewhere, with a comment on the recognition and contribution of women's unpaid labour to the rise of capitalism, Marx (1867/1990: 517, emphasis added) cogently stated:

> In England women are still occasionally used instead of horses for hauling barges, because the labour required to produce horses and machines is an accurately known quantity, while that required to maintain the women of the *surplus population* is beneath all calculation. Hence we nowhere find a more shameless squandering of human labour-power for despicable purposes than in England, the land of machinery.

As we discussed earlier (see Chapter 8), such policies and their contemporary correlates have been analysed as a process of accumulation by dispossession in David Harvey's assessment of the new imperialism, as a way for capital to continue the accumulation of surplus through contemporary means involving inter alia the commodification of land; changes in property relations; the appropriation of natural resources; and the use of national debt, the credit system and the inflationary process as an expression of class struggle, all of which are contingent upon the stance of the state (Harvey, 2003b: 145). Yet what is missing across the classical account (Marx) as well as its contemporary equivalent (Harvey) is how capitalism is dependent on *both* the sphere of social reproduction *and* the appropriation of nature as a source of value creation and exploitation, which a focus on ongoing struggles over accumulation by extraeconomic means connects. 'The worldwide increase in violence against women is basically concentrated on this "territory",' argued Maria Mies (1986/2014: 170) in her canonical statement, which is manifest in the social position and concealment of women in the reproduction of labour and the role of unpaid labour power in reproducing capital. The sequencing of the role of direct violence and the gendered architecture of contemporary war and conflict, the targeting and undermining of basic food subsistence by u.s. food assistance programmes, the destruction of infrastructure within the built environment through warfare and the provocation of a reproduction crisis that takes women as a primary target – for example within the femicides of drug war capitalism – can all be articulated as expressions of and struggles over accumulation by extra-economic means (Federici, 2012: 76–84; Paley, 2014: 15). Human metabolic interaction with nature is also in lockstep with this history of primitive accumulation, specifically if we consider the appropriation of fossil energy (past and present) by the development of commodity production. As Andreas Malm has documented, the primitive accumulation of fossil capital – the self-expanding value passing through the metamorphosis of fossil fuels into CO_2 – has freed up sources of energy flowing from nature (water) to establish a spatial logic of centralisation through 'coal enclosures' (steam). The result is a relational process springing from the expropriation of land and the internality of the exploitation of biophysical resources by the constitution of fossil capital. As coal was 'placed right under the driving fire of capital accumulation, as the fuel transmitting motion to the labour process, a spiral of growing fossil fuel combustion was ... integrated into the spiralling growth of commodity production' (Malm, 2016: 292). Equally, then – as Jason Moore makes clear – capitalist accumulation depends on the appropriation of cheap nature, nature's life-making capacities as unpaid work across the Four Cheaps: cheap labour, food, energy and raw materials. Hence, the expanded flow of cheap labour, food, energy and raw materials into the commodity system is also part of the history of primitive accumulation, the expansion of new frontiers of accumulation and, therefore, struggles over accumulation by extra-economic means (Moore, 2015: 98). This point is chiefly advanced through the constitution of *abstract social nature* as a blend of practices through which the mapping, identification, quantification, measuring and coding of nature is enacted to extend value relations beyond abstract labour (Moore, 2015: 194).[1] These historical processes of state and class measurement and mapping are precisely forms of struggle over accumulation by extra-economic means and the way capitalism brings

---

[1] Abstract social nature is a riff off both abstract labour (Marx) and abstract space (Lefebvre). As Henri Lefebvre (1974/1991: 348, original emphasis) stated, capitalism 'can achieve nothing but abstractions: money and commodities, capital itself, and hence abstract labour ... within abstract space' (Lefebvre, 1974/1991: 348, original emphasis). Abstract space embodies violence in structural terms constituted by the grids, nodes, networks of property, production and exchange through which the law of value exerts its abstract domination and corresponds to abstract labour and the general form of commodity production within capitalism (Lefebvre, 1974/1991: 307, 341, 404). So abstract space encompasses both direct state power and violence directed towards commanding space and the seemingly apolitical form of space – the space of economic infrastructure and technocratic planning – that functions to conceal violence, appearing as a neutral backdrop where 'contradictions ... are smothered and replaced by an appearance of consistency' (Lefebvre, 1974/1991: 363).

new frontiers into its realm. 'The dialectic of abstract social nature and abstract labour is at the heart of those *historical natures* that are cause, consequence and unfolding condition of successive long centuries of accumulation' (Moore, 2015: 194, original emphasis). Or, with Malm (2016: 301, original emphasis), 'capital *produces* abstract space, as a matrix of nodes and arteries that evolve not through their revealed biophysical attributes, but through the circuits of capital itself.'

Indeed, the European Social Forum (ESF) in Firenze/Italy in November 2002 is a pivotal embodiment of this sort of dialectical relation of interiority that we hold as so important to understanding the threefold internal development of Global Capitalism, Global War, Global Crisis (Bieler and Morton, 2004b). The main themes structuring the programme were 1) resistance to neoliberalisation, with some movements themselves at the ESF articulating this in relation to humanity's exploitation of nature; 2) opposition to the then-impending war in Iraq; and 3) demands for a new type of participatory democracy. Hence, spaces of class struggle shaped through mobilisations such as the Stop the War Coalition in the UK understood, whether implicitly or explicitly, neoliberal restructuring and the Bomb-and-Build strategy of the Iraq War as part of the same outward geopolitical expansionary dynamic of capital. With strong trade union support and wider social movement momentum, the Stop the War Coalition clearly articulated and critiqued the position that 'The world must be reordered along free-market capitalist lines, and Britain, because of its imperial past, has a particular part to play in this reordering' (Murray and German, 2005: 25). We turn now to consider in more detail three wider instances in the mediation of class struggle that are shaping the current terrain of Global Capitalism, Global War, Global Crisis through resistance. To sharpen our focus on such struggles over accumulation by extra-economic means in what follows, we draw on the notion of the social factory, developed in Chapter 6. This will enable us to weave together a threefold focus on class struggles within the social factory, respectively, in China and Europe, and then more broadly through a wider array of ruptural struggles, including world ecology struggles over the biosphere.

The Rise of China and the Social Factory

Set within the context that we discussed in more detail in Chapter 7, involving a crisis of overproduction, a declining rate of profit and increasing labour militancy, capital shifted labour-intensive production to countries in the Global South from the 1970s onwards. Beverly Silver clearly outlines this process to highlight how access to cheap and precarious or unprotected labour only ever offers a temporary 'spatial fix'. Where capital moves, collective resistance by labour follows. 'Each time a strong labour movement emerged, capitalists relocated production to sites with cheaper and presumably more docile labour, weakening labour movements in the sites of disinvestment but strengthening labour in the new sites of expansion' (Silver, 2003: 41). Unsurprisingly, all the BRICS countries (Brazil, Russia, India, China and South Africa) have been characterised by large-scale strikes encompassing movements engaged in reorganising geographic space and territories within and beyond the location of the traditional workplace. These territories of resistance therefore cover rural and urban social movements aiming to address spaces of difference, including gender relations and inequalities around unpaid labour, by seeking to establish, modify and further networks of solidarity, reciprocity and mutual assistance against neoliberalism. In Latin America, such movements have sought to affirm a territoriality based on use value in attempts to advance a new organisation of geographic space (Zibechi, 2012: 18). More specifically, Jörg Nowak (2015) discusses strike waves in the construction sector between 2011 and 2013 in Brazil, strikes in South African mining in 2012 and 2014 and labour militancy in the Indian automobile sector in 2011 and 2012 as key examples confirming that worker mobilisations are becoming increasingly organised throughout the BRICS against conditions of super-exploitation. Indeed, even more optimistically his argument is that it might be possible to identify moments of cross-national inspiration, potentially indicating a global strike wave (Nowak, 2016: 272). However, a cautionary tone needs to be raised about the programmatism of labour militancy, as discussed in Chapter 6, referring to struggles revolving simply around the wage form and the expansion of the workers' movement narrowly understood. As Immanuel Ness (2015) indicates in his analysis of large-scale strikes in China, India and South Africa, workers tend to concentrate their demands on basic rights, including the right to strike, the right to free association and the right to collective bargaining within capitalism, but not beyond. In what follows, we look at the situation of the social factory in China in more detail, encompassing the workplace and the sphere of social reproduction, to assess the increasing reorganisation of space structured in view of capital accumulation but dependent on unwaged reproductive labour.

As discussed in Chapter 7, the particular way in which the social relations of production in China have become integrated within the global political economy has clear implications for labour militancy, class struggles and the wider social factory. A straightforward increase in Chinese wages and improvement in working conditions might imply the danger that capital transfers production to other, even cheaper labour locations as a response. 'In this process, new "spatial fixes" put China's export industry under pressure and show the limits of social upgrading in the low value-added links of [global value chains]' (Schmalz, Sommer and Xu, 2017: 295). Alternatively, capital may increase productivity through the introduction of new technology to automate the production process needing fewer workers (see Lüthje and Butollo, 2017). Yet this does not mean that Chinese workers' struggles are without wider import. In line with Silver's expectations, we have witnessed a significant number of large-scale strikes by workers in China, resisting conditions of super-exploitation. According to Tim Pringle, the defeat of the traditional working class in the early 2000s during the process of privatisation and restructuring of state-owned enterprises did not imply an end to class conflict. Roughly at the same time, migrant workers started to make themselves heard in resistance to super-exploitation in the export-oriented processing industry (Pringle, 2013: 191). One of the most well-known large campaigns was the 2010 strike at the Nanhai Honda car plant in southern China. It was a turning point for Chinese labour more broadly due to a wider realisation that its collective resistance could result in more expansive economic and political gains (Friedman, 2014: 132). Other well-known examples of defiance by Chinese labour include the 2013 Yantian dock strike, when 'hundreds of gantry and tower crane operators lodged a non-union strike . . . and paralysed the world's biggest single-site container handling port in Shenzhen' (Cao and Meng, 2017: 272), as well as the strike by roughly 40,000 workers at the Yue Yuen shoe factory in Dongguan in April 2014 (Schmalz, Sommer and Xu, 2017). Equally noteworthy is the string of suicides by workers in Foxconn factories since 2010 in protest against their super-exploitative working conditions, resulting from direct pressure by Apple and its relentless focus on profit maximisation (Chan, Pun and Selden, 2013: 104–8). Importantly, however, it is not only the large industrial sites and companies with foreign links that are affected by labour militancy. In his analysis of class struggles in the southern province of Guangdong, Pringle also analyses in detail the mobilisation of the highly precarious and fragmented sanitation workers in Guangzhou and the way their collective struggle secured them larger compensation for contract termination in the autumn of 2014 (Pringle, 2017: 255). Overall, he argues, labour has emerged as a class against capital in Guangdong province, changing the relations of force and pushing capital and state into forms of collective bargaining. Jenny Chan and Mark Selden especially emphasise the role of second-generation migrant workers in these struggles, who focus on improving their lives in the cities of their workplace rather than returning home (Chan and Selden, 2017: 261).

Nevertheless, it is not only the young generation of migrant workers which has been involved in strike action. As Stefan Schmalz, Brandon Sommer and Hui Xu make clear, older migrant workers are prepared to take action if their retirement payments are endangered. Some 40,000 workers went on all-out strike at the Yue Yuen shoe factory in Dongguan in 2014, when it became apparent that their employer had not maintained payments legally required to cover social insurance contributions. In turn, this encouraged workers at other large industrial sites to go on strike due to similar social insurance disputes. 'For these employees, the stakes are high: they fear the potential loss of their pensions, especially if the minimum contribution time is not reached or if the company does not remit contributions according to the law' (Schmalz, Sommer and Xu, 2017: 295).

In attempting to ascertain the contingent possibilities for labour militancy two main sources have been identified: 1) associational power depending on collective organisations such as trade unions and political parties; and 2) structural power subdivided into two subtypes. 'The first subtype of structural power (which we shall call marketplace bargaining power) is the power that results directly from tight labour markets. The second subtype of structural power (which we shall call workplace bargaining power) is the power that results from the strategic location of a particular group of workers within a key industrial sector' (Silver, 2003: 13). The declining birth rate has increased the marketplace bargaining power of Chinese workers. As fewer younger workers are entering the labour force, the cheap labour development model comes under increasing pressure and workers can ostensibly be in a stronger position to demand wage increases, better working conditions or social benefits. The second noticeable source of power is workplace bargaining power. Across highly integrated global value chains (GVCs), a disruption in one segment of such a chain can result in huge losses for capital. 'With workers' growing awareness of the opportunities presented by the fact that giant corporations face pressures to meet quotas for new models and holiday season purchases, they have repeatedly come together at the dormitory, workshop, or factory level to voice demands or to stage protests' (Chan and Selden, 2017: 267). Workplace bargaining power is even more visible in the case of the Yantian dock strike. In this example, dockworkers enjoy a unique location given that the moment they engage in strike action there is the potential for the whole GVC to break down (Cao and Meng, 2017: 272). Furthermore, there are also new sources of power, logistical and symbolic/societal, available to workers (Webster, 2015). Societal power involves 'the struggle of "right" against "wrong", providing a basis for an appeal both to the public and politicians, as well as to allies in civil society' (Webster, Lambert and Bezuidenhout, 2008: 12).

Cao and Meng in their analysis of the Yantian dock strike identify this type of power within discourses on endangered health resulting from the way work in ports is organised. Logistical power, finally, has been available to dockworkers in the form of social media, allowing them to organise collectively outside of the workplace trade union, which was not the initiator of strike action (Cao and Meng, 2017: 280–1). In short, both old and new forms of resources have proved vital in the case of Chinese workers' struggle for better working conditions and social justice. This is also especially pertinent to struggles over the social exclusionary effects of policies such as the *hukou* (household registration) system of demographic control instituted under the Mao era but displaying a blend of neoliberal and authoritarian statism. The *hukou* institution classifies Chinese citizens according to their 'agricultural' or 'non-agricultural' residency, with the aim of constraining and excluding the more than 277 million 'floating' rural migrants from certain social welfare rights as well as attempting to restrict movement between rural and urban spaces. Therefore 'the *hukou* institution and the ability of the Chinese party-state to determine the territorial allocation of means of production jointly enabled for the enforced absorption of surplus value from rural residents' goes to the heart of the social factory and struggles against accumulation by extra-economic means (Lim, 2017: 259). Not having to provide social welfare to incoming rural migrants means that municipal governments can divert surplus capital from households to the built environment, mixing accumulation by extra-economic means through the deployment of the *hukou* institution with authoritarian neoliberalism in contemporary China.

Finally, it is reasonable to summarise associational power in the case of Chinese workers as rather weak. As discussed in Chapter 7, the official All-China Federation of Trade Unions (ACFTU) is pretty much a state organisation, not an independent trade union. To date, the ACFTU has refused to accept the international standards of the International Labour Organization. Thus, the ACFTU serves more as a transmission belt for state policies. It is still institutionally affiliated to the Chinese Communist Party (CCP), the union's leaders are not elected by shop-floor workers and, more importantly, the ACFTU does not have workers' support and hence does not and cannot represent the workforce in China. At times, often in response to labour militancy, the ACFTU mediates conflict on behalf of the state and protects workers' legal rights, but it is not an independent workers' organisation (Lambert and Webster, 2017: 315–21). Non-governmental organisations (NGOs) linked to informal labour, on the other hand, either focus on supporting workers through after-work and cultural programmes or they attempt to represent directly the individual and collective interests of workers, such as several NGOs in the Pearl River Delta (Bieler and Lee, 2017: 209–11). Thus small, informal labour NGOs can play a crucial role in securing workers' rights at times but are always in danger of facing authoritarian state repression. Wage levels and working conditions in China are a problem not only for Chinese workers but also affect workers around the world in that cheap Chinese labour puts downward pressure on wages in other parts of the world, i.e. the so-called China price (Lambert and Webster, 2017: 313). The challenge is, therefore, to establish links of transnational solidarity that can transcend the borders and spaces of differentiated social factories, in order to avoid a focus purely on labour movements within state space, which may then simply underbid each other in the competition for foreign direct investment (FDI) and jobs (Bieler et al., 2010: 249–53; see also Bieler and Lindberg, 2010). There is an argument that rather than engaging with the ACFTU and being co-opted into its close relationship with the CCP, the focus should be on strengthening Chinese civil society through support for those informal labour NGOs within the social factory of wider class struggle.

The Eurozone Crisis and the Social Factory

In the wake of the Eurozone crisis, whether in the countries of Europe's southern periphery or other EU member states pursuing variegated austerity policies, the conditions of capitalist exploitation were equally met with diverse forms of resistance. When a Syriza government came to power in January 2015, hopes were high that it would be able to break the deadlock of austerity in Greece, indicating a way forward also for other countries in the EU. While other political parties in Greece – especially the social democratic Panhellenic Socialist Movement (PASOK) and the Christian democratic New Democracy – had become compromised due to their involvement in the Eurozone crisis, Syriza emerged as a leading contender for political power from about 2010 onwards out of the milieu of local resistance movements and the so-called movement of squares in Greece (Sotirakopoulos and Sotiropoulos, 2013). 'Syriza's orientation as a mass connective party enabled it to attract growing numbers of supporters, some who joined the party and some who didn't, while strengthening its own democratic and emancipatory strategic vision' (Hart-Landsberg, 2016: 9). Syriza came to power in early 2015 on the basis of a promise to cancel the Memoranda, which had underpinned Greece's increasing economic hardship characterised by high unemployment levels of around 25 per cent with youth unemployment of more than 50 per cent as well as a collapsing healthcare sector, among others. During six months of intensive negotiations, it had, however, become clear that the Troika was in no mood to relent austerity measures, even in the face of a referendum on austerity on 5 July 2015, in which a majority of 60 per cent of the voters rejected the Troika's terms. If at all, the referendum hardened the position of the Troika and Greece ended up capitulating by accepting even harsher conditions for a third bailout only one week later. The hopes of the European left were seemingly dashed.

Of course, structural pressures were undermining the Greek position in the first half of 2015. Because of the way debt had been rescheduled from private banks towards the European Central Bank (ECB) and International Monetary Fund (IMF) in previous agreements, the European banking system was no longer in danger (see Chapter 9). The structural power of transnational capital was, moreover, reflected in the ECB's decision to stop providing additional emergency liquidity assistance to Greece, thereby indirectly forcing the Greek government to close the banks and stock market as well as to limit ATM withdrawals and transfers of funds. Nevertheless, observers also identify key problems in Syriza's strategy as causes for its failure. As discussed in Chapter 2, several strategies are always possible within a concrete setting of the structuring conditions of capitalism. Hart-Landsberg points out that the party's increasing focus on representative democracy instead of mass mobilisations linked to the social factory had weakened it in its dealings with the Troika. 'With negotiations their top priority, Syriza leaders became increasingly unresponsive to the solidarity economy, apparently discounting its potential for involving working people in building new institutions and relationships capable of helping them withstand Troika-induced economic pressures' (Hart-Landsberg, 2016: 14). A debt audit was never fully pursued and an ideological offensive against the class character of Troika policy was not enacted. Stathis Kouvelakis, in turn, argues that a crucial change in Syriza's strategy had already occurred in the wake of the June 2012 elections. First, people from the establishment and here especially PASOK were brought into the party. Then, 'turning Syriza into a leader-centred party was the second aspect of the process. The aim was to move from a militant party of the left, with a strong culture of internal debate, heterogeneity, involvement in social movements and mobilisations, to a party with a passive membership which could be more easily manipulated by the centre' (Kouvelakis, 2016: 49). In other words, the party transformed itself from a mass party rooted in social movements into a top-down electoral machine, prioritising the direct negotiations with the Troika towards an 'honourable compromise' within the limits of programmatic parliamentarism. The popular radicalisation of the social factory around the referendum had not been drawn on as a source for moving towards a more radical strategy that included 'default on the debt, nationalise the banks, impose capital controls and prepare for an alternative currency' (Kouvelakis, 2016: 60). Syriza retained political power in elections in September 2015, but has been involved ever since in managing severe austerity in line with Troika demands. Elsewhere, the left has not fared much better electorally. There were hopes with Podemos, a new party in Spain emerging out of increasing social movement activities around 15-M, or the *indignados* movement, and the occupation of large squares, to take power in Spain and move in a new, anti-austerity direction. In the end, however, Podemos too became more like an electoral machine revolving around a populist strategy (Antentas, 2016: 10). Ultimately, the party failed in its bid for power in the June 2016 elections, coming only third despite an electoral pact with the United Left Party.

The fact that the Greek alternative was defeated can indicate the desolate state of the European left. This is no more visible than in the failure of organised labour to stem neoliberal restructuring in the EU. Crucially, trade unions have accompanied neoliberal restructuring in Europe with their response mainly of a 'yes, but' variety towards neoliberalisation policies. Yes to further economic integration, but only if accompanied by flanking social measures (Bieler, 2006). Ultimately, this position has done little to halt neoliberal restructuring and austerity, reflected in the four freedoms of the Internal Market, the convergence criteria of Economic and Monetary Union (EMU) from the late 1980s through to the early 1990s and eastward enlargement in the 2000s (Bieler, 2012), or more recently with the introduction of the new economic governance structure, as discussed in Chapter 9. Partly, this is the result of a change in structural power linked to the manner in which production and finance have become transnationalised across the sociospatial landscape of European political economy. While the annual average of inward FDI flows into the EU between 1989 and 1994 was $76,634 million USD (UNCTAD, 2001: 291), inward FDI in 2007 as a pre-crisis peak year was $842,311 million (UNCTAD, 2009: 247). The corresponding figures for outward FDI are $105,194 million as annual average between 1989 and 1994 (UNCTAD, 2001: 296), and $1,192,141 million in 2007 (UNCTAD, 2009: 247). As for the EU financial system, 'the European Union has moved decisively in the direction of a more transnationalised, marketised, and desegmented financial system based on a single legislative framework' (Underhill, 1997: 118). This increase in capital's structural power has put European labour on the defensive. Moreover, the institutional set-up has disadvantaged trade unions. The strategic selectivity (Jessop, 1990: 260, 268) of the EU form of state is heavily skewed towards the interests of transnational capital and the way it enjoys privileged access to the key Commission Directorates responsible for Competition, Internal Market, and Economics and Finances in contrast to the side-lining of trade unions, social movements and NGOs (Bieler, 2006: 179–82). This is compounded by the way the new economic governance structure has nationalised social conflict, while the main drivers for austerity are implemented at the European level (Erne, 2015). Nevertheless, as in the case of Syriza in Greece, it was also the programmatism of trade unions that contributed to labour's inability to stop and redirect neoliberal restructuring. As Asbjørn Wahl points out, many of the large, established European trade unions have succumbed to a social partnership ideology. They assume that 'the social progress of the welfare state was not the result of the preceding struggles but of class cooperation and tripartite negotiations in themselves' (Wahl, 2011: 35). This stance overlooks that it was also the collective militancy of labour movements that assisted in curbing the power of capital with labour's power having been built up in successful moments of class struggle, which underpinned the gains of the welfare state in Europe after 1945. Tripartite negotiations, i.e. the willingness of employers and state managers to take demands by the labour movements seriously, were themselves the result of trade unions' structural power in society. By continuing to rely on participating in European and national institutions, while the underlying power structure had changed as a result of the transnationalisation of production and finance, trade unions were less and less able to mobilise their members, never mind establish wider connections across the social factory. In sum, a combination of a change in structural power towards capital alongside particularly skewed institutional arrangements and misguided strategies resulted in a situation in which organised labour has become largely sidelined within the political economy of Europe.

The ESF process mentioned earlier seemed to provide an alternative to mainstream trade unions' participation in formal bipartite and tripartite social institutions. It provided regular meeting points of established European trade unions but also more radical, rank-and-file trade unions as well as social movements and NGOs to exchange their critical positions on neoliberalisation as well as organise various events of contestation at the meetings and beyond (Bieler and Morton, 2004b, 2007). Nevertheless, while enthusiastically welcomed at the first ESF in Firenze/ Italy in November 2002, over time this process lost traction as participants became disenchanted, arguing that the forum process had not resulted in joint actions challenging neoliberalism. It was thought that the forums had failed to develop a significant impact on policymaking.

At the fifth ESF in Malmö in September 2008, the Social Conference in Europe was initiated, with its first meeting taking place in March 2011. Unlike the ESF events, membership was not open. Instead, similarly minded organisations had been carefully selected with the overall objective in mind to move towards joint action. Nevertheless, similar to the AlterSummit launched in November 2012, it did not meet expectations and petered out. The Firenze 10+10 meeting in November 2012, another attempt to revise opposition to neoliberalism by the European left, did not fare better. 'Whereas the first ESF in 2002, which had more than 60,000 participants, has widely been considered a success, the Firenze 10+10 meeting, which was attended by fewer than 1,000 people, lacked resonance in the media and attracted little attention from the wider public' (Wigger and Horn, 2014: 252). The sixth and final instalment of the ESF had taken place in Istanbul/Turkey in 2010, marking the end of the social forum process in Europe. In sum, the European left had been fragmented and weak even before the financial crisis and the subsequent Eurozone crisis struck in 2007/2008, partly due to a shift in structural power towards capital and partly due to the misguided strategies of programmatism by trade unions.

Importantly, resistance to neoliberalism must not be regarded as automatically progressive. The vacuum on the left provided space which the extreme right has been successful at exploiting. 'When people are marginalised and underprivileged, if respect and dignity is refused to them, if their social status is threatened, nationalism is one way to compensate for that, in particular, in the absence of an emancipatory alternative' (Wahl, 2017: 159). Across Europe, nationalist, xenophobic parties have been on the rise since 2007 with the near victory by the extreme right-wing candidate in the Austrian presidential elections in 2016 and the strong performance of the Front National candidate Marine Le Pen in the French presidential elections in May 2017 as some of the key moments, not to mention the election of Donald Trump as U.S. president in November 2016. The British referendum on EU membership in June 2016 is an interesting case here in relation to struggles against austerity. When analysing the social base of support for Brexit, different authors identify different groups. A significant minority of left-wing people voted for Brexit because they regarded it as an opportunity to embolden anti-neoliberal policies (Kagarlitsky, 2017). Others point to a substantial social group that has lost out during the large processes of restructuring in the United Kingdom since the mid-1980s (Mckenzie, 2017), while others refer to those who, economically well off, have experienced declining living standards as a result of ongoing austerity (Antonucci et al., 2017). As Bob Jessop concludes, 'the dominance of neoliberalism indicates that the choice posed in the referendum was misleading: the real choice should have been in or out of neoliberalism rather than in or out of the European Union' (Jessop, 2017: 137). In its concrete manifestation, Brexit was a nationalist response to austerity, often linked to xenophobic, anti-migration rhetoric. 'The populist and racist right has been able to exploit this development most effectively, paradigmatically UKIP, which has fused together Euroscepticism and anti-migrant racism into a powerful anti-elitist discourse' (Callinicos, 2017: 11).

If we simply look at the electoral terrain across Europe, the outlook from a left perspective is indeed bleak, notwithstanding at the time of writing the bounce back of Jeremy Corbyn as leader of the Labour Party in the June 2017 general election. The majority of governments currently in power are clearly of a centre-right to right disposition. If unrest against increasing inequality and social deprivation erupts, it is often of an extreme-right, nationalist dimension. From a left, progressive perspective, resistance against ongoing neoliberal restructuring and austerity seems fruitless. This stance is taken up by some observers who have argued that 'the paradox of a monetary union that endures despite its contradictions, social costs and conflicts can be seen as an ordoliberal iron cage' (Ryner, 2015: 276), an iron cage that cannot easily be escaped (Ryner and Cafruny, 2017: 219–27). Nevertheless, we must be careful not to restrict our analysis to the electoral terrain and the quest for state power. Resistance always takes place across the whole social factory, as discussed in Chapter 6. In the next section, we therefore indicate how a focus on more ruptural forms of mobilisation may reveal an array of different progressive moments of resistance and alternatives to neoliberal capitalism across the social factory in Europe. The imposition of austerity is neither smooth nor completely assured but constantly contested.

Ruptural Struggles and the Social Factory

In a leading contribution to understanding neoliberalisation, Nikolai Huke, Mònica Clua-Losada and David Bailey have developed what they describe as a disruption-oriented approach to resistances which overcomes a negative assessment of the state of the left by pointing out that 'social struggle has not ceased to exist but ... has instead shifted in form towards mass mobilisations and collective, autonomous, self-organisation' (Huke, Clua-Losada and Bailey, 2015: 745). There is a danger, these authors argue, that a critical political economy focus solely on the electoral terrain obscures ongoing contestation of neoliberal restructuring. Rather, a disruption-oriented approach can reveal that neoliberalisation is anything but stable and assured in and beyond Europe. It 'should instead be viewed as a fragile, troubled and hard-fought development' (Bailey et al., 2017: 214). In order to analyse the ongoing disruption of neoliberalism, we therefore need to move beyond a focus only on the struggle for state power and also widen the optic to encompass different territories in resistance and radical ruptures (Zibechi, 2012). The Arab Uprisings in 2011 are a case in point of such forms of class struggle with this wave of radical ruptures involving: 1) mass riots capable of widespread diffusion, while targeting specific spaces and territories; 2) the transformation of that territory into occupation; and 3) attempts to extend from central spaces to surrounding areas by means of demonstrations, neighbourhood assemblies, solidarity strikes and blockades with the constituents involving women, graduates, the surplus population, youth and organised workers (Endnotes, 2013: 32–3). Rather than assuming a pre-constituted set of identities in the movement of squares, 'the virtue of the occupations was to create a space between an impossible class struggle and a tepid populism, where protesters could momentarily unify, in spite of their divisions' (Endnotes, 2013: 48). Moreover, from this emphasis on radical ruptures, 'one might say that the riot and its repression became a sort of proxy way in which class relations were regulated, in the absence of the "normal" mode of regulation exercised by wage bargaining' (Endnotes, 2015: 297). From Tahrir Square in Cairo, to Syntagma Square in Athens, to Puerta del Sol in Madrid, these urban-based social movements grounded in grassroots democracy and practices of civil disobedience in occupying prominent public squares have been a crucial experience for the formation of collective power of bodies in public space (Harvey, 2012). For example, in Spain El Movimiento 15-M, or the *indignados* movement, 'acted as a breeding ground for subsequent movements to emerge, including the movement against the privatisation of hospitals and health centres in Madrid (*marea blanca*), protests in the education sector (*marea verde* or sos Educació), and unconventional forms of radical strike action from below' (Bailey et al., 2016: 15).

This disruption-oriented approach dovetails well with the radical ruptural emphasis placed on cycles of struggle earlier in our argument. As indicated in Chapter 6, neoliberal restructuring and austerity in the wake of the GFC has had a gendered impact on societies. 'The ensuing cuts in public sector services in the heartlands of the crisis disproportionately affected women' (Hozić and True, 2016: 8). As revealed by Ian Bruff and Stefanie Wöhl, authoritarian modes of governance, as part of restructuring in the Eurozone, are underpinned by highly masculinised norms of competitiveness. These norms 'have provided for a tight coupling of increasingly authoritarian state practices and an enhanced affirmation of the "benefits" of competitiveness for society as a whole. Moreover ... this strategy to displace the effects of the crisis from the "public" to the "private" has intensified the crisis of social reproduction experienced by households across Europe' (Bruff and Wöhl, 2016: 97). Unsurprisingly, many of the currently ongoing moments of contestation are precisely taking place in the sphere of social reproduction and here in particular housing, healthcare services, education and the welfare state more generally. When the housing bubble burst in Spain in 2008 due to the global financial market crisis, the socio-spatial political economy of Spain went into crisis. In 2012, in order to secure the country's financial sector, the Spanish government had 'to borrow from the European Financial Stability Facility (EFSF) of the so-called "troika", and in turn was required to sign a Memorandum of Understanding which brought with it draconian austerity measures' (Bailey et al., 2017: 132). As a result, the healthcare sector in Madrid was earmarked for privatisation. 'After the plans became public, employees enclosed themselves in the hospitals (*encierros*) and organised assemblies with a massive participation of the workforce. This represented the birth of the *marea blanca*. Regular assemblies took place in every one of the affected hospitals that quickly expanded to include users of health services' (Bailey et al., 2017: 135). In short, constituents across the social factory – in this case militant workers and public healthcare users – came together to protect healthcare as a public good and ultimately succeeded in halting privatisation. Education was similarly attacked as a result of austerity with severe cuts to the Spanish education budget. In response, trade unions organising in the sector – together with pupils and their parents – mobilised widely to contribute to a situation in which support for public education remains high. These social movements 'drew on the repertoire of action and political climate created by 15-M. The movements were also often subsumed under the label, *marea verde*, a name derived from green shirts, with the demand for public schools for everyone, which became a symbol of the protest' (Bailey et al., 2017: 169; see also Béroud 2014: 52–3). Another notable example of ruptures in/against neoliberalism can be identified in the housing sector, in which many people have been faced with eviction since the onset of the global financial crisis, as they were no longer able to keep up mortgage payments. The Platform for People Affected by Mortgages (Plataforma de Afectados por la Hipoteca) (PAH) has been successful not only in stopping physical evictions through civil disobedience but also in managing to turn individual hardship into a collective, political issue. 'The PAH has been struggling to use collective organising as a means of overcoming isolation and forming a collective identity, that is, to transform a problem that is widely perceived as being a private one, into a collective, political problem. This way, individuals who had previously been overwhelmed with strong feelings of failure, guilt, loneliness and uncertainty can become agents of political transformation' (Bailey et al., 2017: 210). In Spain, this struggle around housing adopted a particular gendered dimension in that it was often women who became empowered as a result of struggle and were leading resistance. 'The PAH has become a space of political socialisation and struggle for working-class women, and also a space for developing social bonds and finding emotional support' (Bailey et al., 2017: 211).

In Greece too, contestation of austerity is ongoing despite the climb down of the Syriza government in the summer of 2015. As a result of cuts, the healthcare sector in Greece has been decimated, with many unemployed Greeks no longer being covered by health insurance and thus, unable to access healthcare. In response, across the country 'healthcare clinics' have emerged which cater for these people's healthcare needs for free. The clinics are run by volunteers and depend on donations of money, equipment and facilities. While successful in covering people's needs, they also have a political objective. 'Emphasising solidarity as the dominant principle of action repoliticises austerity and restructuring, and how it is having a generalised impact on the socio-economic functioning of Greece and its people' (Jordan, 2017: 253). These clinics are embedded within wider networks of social solidarity. For example, one such healthcare clinic has been set up on the premises of Vio.me, a large metallurgy factory in the north of Greece, which has been run under workers' control with twenty-five members since February 2013. 'The "factory-clinic" formation co-constitutes a multiplicity of socio-spatial relations, such as workers' struggle to take control over their work, the struggle against austerity and unemployment or the struggle for free health care that can enact new modes of resistance in the future' (Daskalaki and Kokkinidis, 2017: 1315). The factory-clinic, in other words, is a coming together of resistance across the whole social factory against exploitation in the form of job cuts as well as cuts to the public healthcare service, while at the same time fostering new ways of solidarity and economy organising.

Nevertheless, as indicated in Chapter 9, it is not only in the crisis countries of the Eurozone that austerity has been imposed. Cuts to public budgets have been implemented across the EU, including, for example, in the United Kingdom, where Conservative-led governments have passed one austerity budget after another since 2010. And yet, here too, we can identify ongoing ruptures, new movements challenging austerity. Education came under attack in austerity Britain with an increase in tuition fees in higher education of up to £9,000 per year. Nonetheless, this has also become an area of disruption. 'The student movement in the UK represented one of the most vibrant and ongoing instances of popular opposition to the austerity measures associated with the post-2008 period' (Bailey et al., 2017: 166). When it comes to the housing crisis, especially in London, students have again been highly active. In 2015 and 2016, students at University College London engaged in large-scale rent strikes in protest over increasingly unaffordable student accommodation. 'The final outcome saw the Cut the Rent group announce a victory, as UCL agreed to make available £350,000 for the academic year 2016–17 to fund accommodation bursaries for those students in most need of financial support, and £500,000 for the following year, as well as agreeing to freeze rent for 2016–17' (Bailey et al., 2017: 201–2). One of the most vicious areas of austerity in the United Kingdom has been around cuts to welfare services. A new, highly aggressive 'narrative stressed the need of coercion through tougher benefit sanctions. Consequently, the change of discourse around unemployment, the stricter rules, the intimidation of claimants by the job centres, the rise of sanctions and compulsory work placements caused hardship and poverty as well as mental and physical illnesses' (Weghmann, 2017: 179–80). Nevertheless, even social groups, perceived by many as some of the weakest members in society, have been able to organise collectively and fight back against state repression with considerable success. As Vera Weghmann (2017: 199) reveals, for example, 'in Dundee, which has become known colloquially as "sanctions city" due to its disproportioned high number of sanctions in Scotland, the advocacy practices of the Scottish Unemployed Workers Network led to a 40 per cent reduction in sanctions.' Unsurprisingly, in the United Kingdom too the gendered nature of austerity is visible. For example, as noted by Daniela Tepe-Belfrage and Johnna Montgomerie (2016: 83), 'it is women and children who are being vilified and services to poor families that are being cut; the sharp end of the neoliberal stick is not wielded uniformly.' They outline how especially women with children were identified as a problem for public finances and, therefore, were subjected to 'reform' measures such as the Troubled Families Programme.

The examples of ruptural instances of resistance discussed so far include struggles in the sphere of reproduction as part of the social factory around housing, education, healthcare services and welfare benefits. Nevertheless, workplaces too have increasingly become sites of rupture and experiments in alternative ways of organising production and living. George Kokkinidis has analysed a number of worker-run cooperatives including, for example, Pagkaki, a workers' collective coffee shop, Syn.all.ois, a cooperative for alternative and solidarity trade, and Unfollow, a collectively run magazine. Importantly, different forms of organising production are perceived as political projects of transformation. 'Autonomy is not a mere organisational tool but a way of doing politics, of bringing the future into the present, which is simultaneously a collective act of refusal and creation: refusing a set of values and practices embedded in capitalist relations while experimenting with anti-capitalist practices' (Kokkinidis, 2015b: 848). Crucial to this different way of organising commerce is the emphasis on workplace democracy – not forms of representative democracy as this often excludes the voice of others – but, rather, forms of participatory democracy within horizontal, non-hierarchical structures (Kokkinidis, 2012). In sum, organisationally, these cooperatives are based on direct democratic remuneration schemes. 'Their established egalitarian remuneration schemes are indicative of their perception of work as a collective effort, fostering a collective spirit necessary for practicing horizontality' (Kokkinidis, 2015a: 430). When it comes to decision-making, the emphasis is on consensus reached in general assemblies. This is not a way to avoid difficult discussions. Rather, consensus 'is a means of creating a space where diverse opinions flourish rather than being suppressed, reinforced by practices of horizontality' (Kokkinidis, 2015b: 866).

As a reflection of their political ambitions, many of these cooperatives are also involved in political activities, including the organisation of seminars on issues such as fair trade or sustainable farming, the participation in strikes or the publication of political leaflets. These sorts of cooperatives have increasingly become involved in establishing a social factory network of solidarity economy, not only across Greece with links to other worker-run factories in Europe and Argentina but elsewhere too. Whether it is the Caravan for Struggle and Solidarity, run by the recuperated Vio.me factory, which travels around Greece promoting the factory's cause, or the establishment of a solidarity fund in order to provide support for other cooperatives and struggles, or the Members' Mobility Scheme, which allows members of solidarity initiatives to experience operations in other workers' cooperatives, there is clearly an attempt to link up various autonomous alternatives within the social factory of ruptural struggle (Daskalaki and Kokkinidis, 2017: 1316–18). In sum, the expression of these cooperatives is, first, rooted in the way they are collectively set up and run and, second, based in their participation in wider political activities. 'As grassroots initiatives with clear economic and political objectives, they are part of the wider anti-neoliberal movement in Greece' (Kokkinidis, 2015a: 430). Whether the extremes of 'horizontalism' (or changing the world through 'anti-power'; see Holloway, 2002 or Day, 2005) and strict 'verticalism' (or capturing state power as a vehicle of political transformation; see Robinson, 2007b: 154 or Petras, 2008: 477) can be blended is an argument that goes beyond the constraints of the present discussion. Yet our position is that it would be misleading to characterise the former stress as a 'no-power' approach to social change just as much as it would be remiss to underestimate the tangible forms of autonomy based on collective action and organisation-building that has as its target struggles within and against the state (see, respectively, Petras and Veltmeyer, 2007, and Holloway, 2002). Instead, such struggles attest to the point that social movement activism with a focus on autonomous politics can nonetheless form broad alliances emphasising the importance of influencing state policymaking, as our turn to struggles against water privatisation and for public water in Europe now demonstrates.

Accumulation by extra-economic means has also ventured into previously decommodified areas and public services have been a primary target in this respect. The privatisation of public assets has created a global infrastructure market, considered 'a profitable source of private investment with a range of competing investment funds providing good returns relative to other types of investment' (Whitfield, 2010: 91). Water services are no exception in this respect. 'A disturbing trend in the water sector is accelerating worldwide. The new "water barons" – the Wall Street banks and elitist multibillionaires – are buying up water all over the world at an unprecedented pace' (Yang, 2012). And yet, from the Cochabamba water wars in 2000, to the United Nations' declaration of water as a human right in 2010, from the re-municipalisation of water in Grenoble in 2000, to the successful European Citizens' Initiative (ECI) on 'Water is a Human Right' in 2012 and 2013, the struggle against water privatisation has gained momentum and is a clear rupture of resistance against further neoliberal restructuring. A number of key aspects can be identified when thinking about the reasons of impact: 1) the unique quality of water; 2) the long history of water struggles across multiple geographical scales; and 3) the broad alliances across the social factory of trade unions, social movements and environmental NGOs underpinning the struggles. First, water is widely recognised in terms of its intrinsic symbolic power as a fundamental source of life, as a human right and as part of the global commons. This discourse resonated, for example, with the Catholic Social Doctrine during the campaign for the Italian water referenda in 2011 and facilitated the mobilisation of Catholic groups that highlighted the moral, symbolic and cultural aspects of water (Bieler, 2015a: 39–40). Second, from the successful campaign against the privatisation of water in the Bolivian city of Cochabamba to the UN declaration of water as a human right in 2010 at the global level, back to the ruptural resistance of local struggles in Italy from the late 1990s onwards and up to the national level of Italian water referenda in 2011 leading to the ECI on water across the EU in 2012 to 2013, water struggles have gained increasing traction across multiple scales of resistance, with activists engaged in concrete actions of solidarity across borders. While witnessing the hearing of the ECI in the European Parliament through a video link, activists from the Thessaloniki citizens' movement against water privatisation decided to hold their own independent referendum about the privatisation of water services in their city on 18 May 2014. The European Federation of Public Service Unions (EPSU) and the Italian water movement, as well as others from the European water movement, all sent monitors in support (Bieler, 2017: 313). Finally, both the campaigns in the Italian referenda and the ECI at the European level were based on broad social factory alliances. Environmental groups, including, for example, the Italian Legambiente and the German Grüne Liga, all equally participated because, it was argued, when water becomes privatised and the sector is dominated by the profit motive, the protection of ecologies is usually regarded as secondary. In general, trade unions have also been concerned about the privatisation of water and the potential implications for salaries and working conditions (Jakob and Sanchez, 2015: 76). In turn, social movements have organised consumers worried about the potentially higher prices as well as mobilising other social groups that have been equally concerned about being cut off in case of an inability to pay. Thus, the struggle for water as a human right and against privatisation is precisely a struggle taking place in the wider social factory against exploitation in production, the sphere of social reproduction and the appropriation of nature in an attempt to sustain access to water for everyone.

Looked at more closely, struggles for public water indicate the combination of autonomous and vertical politics. One of the signal contributions of the Italian water movement has been to emphasise the possibilities of potable water as a 'global' commons and thus something that stands outside of both state and privately run services. The commons are understood as 'elements that we maintain or reproduce together, according to rules established by the community: an area to be rescued from the decision-making of the post-democratic elite and which needs to be self-governed through forms of participatory democracy' (Fattori, 2011). Thus, the focus on the commons is combined with an emphasis on a different, more participatory form of democracy, a form of democracy which 'guarantees citizens' direct participation in local government and the administration of the commons, which goes beyond the mere participation in local public institutions' (Carrozza and Fantini,

2013: 77). In other words, it is the internal combination of a new struggle for democracy and a new understanding of how to organise economies that also brings with it this ruptural transformative dimension. As Madelaine Moore clarifies, water struggles as 'spaces of protest are concurrently sites of production and re-production, sharpening these contradictions and forcing the movements and activists to begin to unpack capitalism as a whole – highlighting their potential in any larger anti-capitalist strategy' (Moore, 2017: 31). Struggles across the social factory, in other words, include the potential for an anti-capitalist, transformative dynamic to gain hold.

Discussing solutions around the notion of the commons has also been part of struggles against water privatisation in Greece. The citizens of the group K136 against water privatisation in Thessaloniki viewed the crisis 'as an opportunity to intensify the search for democratic alternatives' (Steinfort, 2014). Working on how to mobilise different ways of running the city's water services, it adopted this notion of a new struggle for democracy. 'The model is based on direct democracy, meaning that decisions are taken at open assemblies and are based on the principles of self-management and one person, one vote' (Steinfort, 2014). Similar experiments are carried out elsewhere. In Paris and Grenoble, for example, 'civil society representatives sit on the Board of Directors together with local government representatives, and have equal voting rights [moreover,] citizen observatories have been established to open spaces for citizens to engage in strategic decisions on investment, technology options and tariff setting' (Lobina, Kishimoto and Petitjean, 2014: 5). In the Spanish city of Zaragoza, trade unions signed an agreement with other civil society organisations, political parties and the municipality for public water management in order to secure the human right to water (EPSU, 2014). While there is no blueprint on how these new struggles for democracy should be designed, experiments of the type in Grenoble, Paris or Zaragoza, in which trade unions, municipalities, public water managers and social movements from across the social factory come together, can help to explore new anti-capitalist ways of organising water and sanitation for all.

Conclusion: Dialectics of Uneven and Combined Development

Touching on some of these contours and in closing this book we want to finish by arguing that struggles against accumulation by extra-economic means are at the centre of the internal unity of Global Capitalism, Global War, Global Crisis. By considering such struggles, in our case through a focus on the social factory and the rise of China, the Eurozone crisis and then wider gendered, ecological and class ruptures within neoliberalisation, we have endeavoured to address how elements of productive and unpaid reproductive labour beyond the place of work play a clear role in the constitution and contestation of the movement of value within contemporary capitalism. Concurrent with David Harvey (2005: 202) we are still aghast that, 'when many progressives were increasingly persuaded that class was a meaningless or at least long defunct category, ... progressives of all stripes seem to have caved in to neoliberal thinking since it is one of the primary functions of neoliberalism that class is a fictional category.' Pithy claims that a focus on class is tantamount to believing in a 'great refusal' are belied by the multitude and diversity of class struggles existing today, the outcome of which, of course, is contingent on the cohering of structured agency within the uneven and combined developmental crises of local and global capitalism. Philip McMichael captures these relations of force well when summarising the contemporary epoch.

The series of crises ... are not uniformly coordinated so much as expressing the uneven and combined development of global political economy. The political distance between the Latin rebellions (over economic sovereignty) and the Arab uprising (over popular sovereignty) is as striking as is their combined revolt against neoliberalism's impact (however distinct to their region). (McMichael, 2012: 259)

Throughout this book we have asserted the hallmark of historical materialism in pointing to the internally combined relation of Global Capitalism, Global War, Global Crisis, which implies dialectics. This chapter has revealed through its focus on combative ruptures of class struggle how 'the development of such (anti-)political "prefigurative" forms of struggle is as necessary, and as internally related, to building a socialist society as was state formation to the bourgeois order' (Sayer, 1985: 251). Our argument makes an original intervention by advancing a necessarily historical materialist approach to the philosophy of internal relations that is capable of delivering a radically open-ended dialectics. This book finishes, then, by emphasising the relations of interiority between Global Capitalism, Global War, Global Crisis shaped through the uneven and combined development of class struggle.

Bibliography

Adler, Emmanuel (1997) 'Seizing the Middle Ground: Constructivism in World Politics', *European Journal of International Relations* 3(3): 319–63.

Adler, Emmanuel and Peter M. Haas (1992) 'Epistemic Communities, World Order, and the Creation of a Reflective Research Program', *International Organization*, 46(1): 367–90.

Agnew, John (2011) 'Capitalism, Territory and "Marxist Geopolitics"', *Geopolitics*, 16(1): 230–3.

Alker, Hayward R. (1996) *Rediscoveries and Reformulations: Humanistic Methodologies for International Studies*. Cambridge: Cambridge University Press.

Alker, Hayward R. and Thomas Biersteker (1984) 'The Dialectics of World Order: Notes for a Future Archaeologist of International Savoir Faire', *International Studies Quarterly*, 28(2): 121–42.

Allinson, Jamie and Alex Anievas (2010) 'The Uneven and Combined Development of the Meiji Restoration: A Passive Revolutionary Road to Capitalist Modernity', *Capital & Class*, 34(3): 469–90.

Althusser, Louis (1968/2005) *For Marx*, trans. Ben Brewster. London: Verso.

Althusser, Louis (2003) *The Humanist Controversy and Other Writings*, ed. François Matheron, trans. G. M. Goshgarian. London: Verso.

Althusser, Louis, Étienne Balibar, Roger Establet, Jacques Rancière and Pierre Macherey (1965/2015) *Reading Capital: The Complete Edition*, trans. Ben Brewster and David Fernbach. London: Verso.

Amin, Samir (1976) *Unequal Development: An Essay on the Social Formations of Peripheral Capitalism*, trans. Brian Pearce. New York: Monthly Review Press.

Amin, Samir (2013a) *The Implosion of Contemporary Capitalism*. New York: Monthly Review Press.

Amin, Samir (2013b) 'China 2013', *Monthly Review*, 64(10): 14–33.

Amoore, Louise (2004) 'Risk, Reward and Discipline at Work', *Economy and Society*, 33(2): 174–96.

Amoore, Louise (2006) '"There Is No Great Refusal": The Ambivalent Politics of Resistance', in Marieke de Goede (ed.) *International Political Economy and Poststructuralist Politics*. London: Palgrave, pp. 255–73.

Anderson, Kevin (2010) *Marx at the Margins: On Nationalism, Ethnicity and Non-Western Societies*. Chicago: University of Chicago Press.

Anderson, Perry (1974a) *Passages from Antiquity to Feudalism*. London: Verso.

Anderson, Perry (1974b) *Lineages of the Absolutist State*. London: Verso.

Anderson, Perry (1983) *In the Tracks of Historical Materialism*. London: Verso.

Anderson, Perry (1992) *English Questions*. London: Verso.

Anderson, Perry (2013) 'American Foreign Policy and Its Thinkers', *New Left Review* (II), Special Issue, 83: 5–167.

Anderson, Perry (2017) *American Foreign Policy and Its Thinkers*. London: Verso.

Anievas, Alexander (2008) 'Theories of a Global State: A Critique', *Historical Materialism*, 16(2): 190–205.

Anievas, Alexander (2014) *Capital, the State and War: Class Conflict and Geopolitics in the Thirty Years' Crisis, 1914–1945*. Ann Arbor: University of Michigan Press.

Anievas, Alexander and Kamran Matin (eds.) (2016) *Historical Sociology and World History: Uneven and Combined Development over the Longue Durée*. London: Rowman & Littlefield International.

Anievas, Alexander and Kerem Nişancıoğlu (2015) *How the West Came to Rule: The Geopolitical Origins of Capitalism*. London: Pluto Press.

Antentas, Josep Maria (2016) 'Podemos and the Spanish Political Crisis', *Labor History*. Online first: DOI: 10.1080/0023656X.2017.1255544.

Antonucci, Lorenzo, Laszlo Horvath, Yordan Kutiyski and André Krouwel (2017) 'The Malaise of the Squeezed Middle: Challenging the Narrative of the "Left Behind" Brexiter', *Competition & Change*. Online first: DOI: 10.1177/1024529417704135.

Archer, Margaret (1982) 'Morphogenesis versus Structuration: On Combining Structure and Action', *British Journal of Sociology*, 33(4): 455–83.

Archer, Margaret (1990) 'Human Agency and Social Structure: A Critique of Giddens', in Jon Clark, Celia Modgil and Sohan Modgil (eds.) *Anthony Giddens: Consensus and Controversy*. London: Falmer Press, pp. 73–84.

Archer, Margaret (1995) *Realist Social Theory: The Morphogenetic Approach*. Cambridge: Cambridge University Press.

Aronowitz, Stanley (1981) 'A Metatheoretical Critique of Immanuel Wallerstein's *The Modern World-System*', *Theory and Society*, 10(4): 503–20.

Arrighi, Giovanni (1994) *The Long Twentieth Century: Money, Power and the Origins of Our Time*. London: Verso.

Arrighi, Giovanni (2007) *Adam Smith in Beijing: Lineages of the Twenty-First Century*. London: Verso.

Ashley, Richard K. (1983) 'Three Modes of Economism', *International Studies Quarterly*, 27(4): 463–96.

Ashley, Richard K. (1984) 'The Poverty of Neorealism', *International Organization*, 38(2): 225–86.

Ashley, Richard K. (1989) 'Living on Border Lines: Man, Poststructuralism and War', in James Der Derian and Michael Shapiro (eds.) *International/Intertextual Relations: Postmodern Readings of World Politics*. Toronto: Lexington Books, pp. 259–321.

Ashley, Richard K. (1996) 'The Achievements of Poststructuralism', in Steve Smith, Ken Booth and Marysia Zalweski (eds.) *International Theory: Positivism and Beyond*. Cambridge: Cambridge University Press, pp. 240–53.

Ashley, Richard K. and R. B. J. Walker (1990) 'Speaking the Language of Exile: Dissident Thought in International Studies', *International Studies Quarterly*, 34(3): 259–68.

Ashman, Sam (2006) 'Symposium: On David Harvey's "The New Imperialism"', *Historical Materialism*, 14(4): 3–166.

Ashman, Sam (2010) 'Capitalism, Uneven and Combined Development, and the Transhistoric', in Alexander Anievas (ed.) *Marxism and World Politics: Contesting Global Capitalism*. London: Routledge, pp. 189–202.

Association of American Universities (2006) 'National Defense Education and Innovation Initiative: Meeting America's Economic and Security Challenges in the 21st Century', www.aau.edu/reports/NDEII.pdf; accessed 9 April 2009.

Bailey, David J., Mònica Clua-Losada, Nikolai Huke and Olatz Ribera-Almandoz (2017) *Beyond Defeat and Austerity: Disrupting (the Critical Political Economy of) Neoliberal Europe*. London: Routledge.

Bailey, David J., Mònica Clua-Losada, Nikolai Huke, Olatz Ribera-Almandoz and Kelly Rogers (2016) 'Challenging the Age of Austerity: Disruptive Agency after the Global Economic Crisis', *Comparative European Politics*. Online first: DOI: 10.1057/s41295-016-0072-8.

Bakker, Isabella and Stephen Gill (eds.) (2003) *Power, Production and Social Reproduction: Human In/security in the Global Political Economy*. London: Palgrave.

Banaji, Jairus (2010) *Theory as History: Essays on Modes of Production and Exploitation*. Leiden: Brill.

Barker, Colin (2013) 'Class Struggle and Social Movements', in Colin Barker, Laurence Cox, John Krinsky and Alf Gunvald Nilsen (eds.) *Marxism and Social Movements*. Leiden and Boston: Brill, pp. 41–61.

Bauer, Michael W. and Stefan Becker (2014) 'The Unexpected Winner of the Crisis: The European Commission's Strengthened Role in Economic Governance', *Journal of European Integration*, 36(3): 213–29.

Bechtel (2004) 'USAID Awards Bechtel National Iraq Infrastructure II Contract' (6 January), www.bechtel.com/2004-01-06.html; accessed 27 December 2008.

Bellofiore, Riccardo and Joseph Halevi (2011) '"Could Be Raining" – The European Crisis after the Great Recession', *International Journal of Political Economy*, 39(4): 5–30.

Béroud, Sophie (2014) 'Une mobilisation syndicale traversée par le souffle des Indignés ? La "marée verte" dans le secteur de l'éducation à Madrid', *Savoir/agir*, 27: 49–54.

Bhambra, Gurminder (2007) *Rethinking Modernity: Postcolonialism and the Sociological Imagination*. London: Palgrave.

Bhaskar, Roy (1975) *A Realist Theory of Science*, second edition. London: Verso.

Bhaskar, Roy (1993) *Dialectic: The Pulse of Freedom*. London: Verso.

Bieler, Andreas (2000) *Globalisation and EU Enlargement: Austrian and Swedish Social Forces in the Struggle over Membership*. London: Routledge.

Bieler, Andreas (2006) *The Struggle for a Social Europe: Trade Unions and EMU in Times of Global Restructuring*. Manchester: Manchester University Press.

Bieler, Andreas (2011) 'Labour, New Social Movements and the Resistance to Neoliberal Restructuring in Europe', *New Political Economy*, 16(2): 163–83.

Bieler, Andreas (2012) 'Globalisation and European Integration: The Internal and External Dimensions of Neoliberal Restructuring', in Petros Nousios,

Henk Overbeek and Andreas Tsolakis (eds.) *Globalisation and European Integration: Critical Approaches to Regional Order and International Relations.* London: Routledge, pp. 196–216.

Bieler, Andreas (2013) 'The EU, Global Europe and Processes of Uneven and Combined Development: The Problem of Transnational Labour Solidarity', *Review of International Studies*, 39(1): 161–83.

Bieler, Andreas (2014) 'Transnational Labour Solidarity in (the) Crisis', *Global Labour Journal*, 5(2): 114–33.

Bieler, Andreas (2015a) '"Sic Vos Non Vobis" (For You, But Not Yours): The Struggle for Public Water in Italy', *Monthly Review*, 67(5): 35–50.

Bieler, Andreas (2015b) 'Social Europe and the Eurozone Crisis: The Importance of the Balance of Class Power in Society', in Amandine Crespy and Georg Menz (eds.) *Social Policy and the Euro Crisis.* London: Palgrave, pp. 24–44.

Bieler, Andreas (2017) 'Fighting for Public Water: The First Successful European Citizens' Initiative "Water and Sanitation Are a Human Right"', *Interface: A Journal for and about Social Movements*, 9(1): 300–26; available online: www.interfacejournal.net/wordpress/wp-content/uploads/2017/07/Int erface-9-1-Bieler.pdf; accessed 8 July 2017.

Bieler, Andreas, Werner Bonefeld, Peter Burnham and Adam David Morton (2006) *Global Restructuring, State, Capital and Labour: Contesting Neo-Gramscian Perspectives.* London: Palgrave.

Bieler, Andreas, Sümercan Bozkurt, Max Crook, Peter Cruttenden, Ertan Erol, Adam David Morton, Cemal Burak Tansel and Elif Uzgören (2016) 'The Enduring Relevance of Rosa Luxemburg's *The Accumulation of Capital*', *Journal of International Relations and Development*, 19(3): 420–47.

Bieler, Andreas, Ian Bruff and Adam David Morton (2010) 'Acorns and Fruit: From Totalisation to Periodisation in the Critique of Capitalism', *Capital & Class*, 34(1): 25–37.

Bieler, Andreas and Roland Erne (2014) 'Transnational Solidarity? The European Working Class in the Eurozone Crisis', in Leo Panitch and Greg Albo (eds.) *The Socialist Register: Transforming Classes.* London: Merlin Press, pp. 157–77.

Bieler, Andreas and Jamie Jordan (2015) 'Austerity and Resistance: The Politics of Labour in the Eurozone Crisis', in Vishwas Satgar (ed.) *Capitalism's Crises: Class Struggles in South Africa and the World.* Johannesburg: Wits University Press, pp. 97–122.

Bieler, Andreas and Chun-Yi Lee (2017) 'Exploitation and Resistance: A Comparative Analysis of the Chinese Cheap Labour Electronics and High-Value Added IT Sectors', *Globalizations*, 14(2): 202–15.

Bieler, Andreas and Ingemar Lindberg (eds.) (2010) *Global Restructuring, Labour and the Challenges for Transnational Solidarity.* London: Routledge.

Bieler, Andreas, Ingemar Lindberg and Werner Sauerborn (2010) 'After Thirty Years of Deadlock: Labour's Possible Strategies in the New Global Order', *Globalizations*, 7(1–2): 247–60.

Bieler, Andreas and Adam David Morton (2003) 'Globalisation, the State and Class Struggle: A "Critical Economy" Engagement with Open Marxism', *British Journal of Politics and International Relations*, 5(4): 467–99.

Bieler, Andreas and Adam David Morton (2004a) 'A Critical Theory Route to Hegemony, World Order and Historical Change: Neo-Gramscian Perspectives in International Relations', *Capital & Class*, 82: 85–113.

Bieler, Andreas and Adam David Morton (2004b) '"Another Europe Is Possible"? Labour and Social Movements at the European Social Forum', *Globalizations*, 1(2): 303–25.

Bieler, Andreas and Adam David Morton (2007) 'Canalising Resistance: The Historical Continuities and Contrasts of "Anti-capitalist" Movements at the European Social Forum', in Andrew Gamble, Steve Ludlam, Andrew Taylor and Stephen Wood (eds.) *Labour, the State, Social Movements and the Challenge of Neoliberal Globalisation*. Manchester: Manchester University Press, pp. 204–22.

Bieler, Andreas and Adam David Morton (2008) 'The Deficits of Discourse in IPE: Turning Base Metal into Gold?', *International Studies Quarterly*, 52(1): 103–28.

Bieler, Andreas and Adam David Morton (2014) 'Uneven and Combined Development and Unequal Exchange: The Second Wind of Neoliberal "Free Trade"?', *Globalizations*, 11(1): 35–45.

Bieling, Hans-Jürgen (2011) 'European Statehood', in Alexander Gallas, Lars Bretthauer, John Kannankulam and Ingo Stützle (eds.) *Reading Poulantzas*. London: Merlin Press, pp. 201–15.

Black, Jeremy (2011) 'Towards a Marxist Geopolitics', *Geopolitics*, 16(1): 234–5.

Blaut, James M. (1993) *The Colonizer's Model of the World: Geographical Diffusionism and Eurocentric History*. New York: The Guilford Press.

Blaut, James M. (1999) 'Marxism and Eurocentric Diffusionism', in Ronald H. Chilcote (ed.) *The Political Economy of Imperialism: Critical Appraisals*. Dordrecht: Kluwer, pp. 127–40.

Block, Fred (2001) 'Using Social Theory to Leap over Historical Contingencies: A Comment on Robinson', *Theory and Society*, 30(2): 215–21.

Block, Fred and Margaret Somers (2014) *The Power of Market Fundamentalism: Karl Polanyi's Critique*. Oxford: Oxford University Press.

Blyth, Mark (2002) *Great Transformations: Economic Ideas and Institutional Change in the Twentieth Century*. Cambridge: Cambridge University Press.

Blyth, Mark (2007) 'Powering, Puzzling, or Persuading? The Mechanisms of Building Institutional Orders', *International Studies Quarterly*, 51(4): 761–77.

Blyth, Mark (2013) *Austerity: The History of a Dangerous Idea*. Oxford: Oxford University Press.

Bohle, Dorothee and Béla Greskovits (2012) *Capitalist Diversity in Europe's Periphery*. Ithaca, NY: Cornell University Press.

Bond, Patrick, Ashwin Desai and Trevor Ngwane (2013) 'Uneven and Combined Marxism within South Africa's Urban Social Movements', in Colin Barker, Laurence Cox, John Krinsky and Alf Gunvald Nilsen (eds.) *Marxism and Social Movements*. Leiden: Brill, pp. 233–55.

Bonefeld, Werner (1992) 'Social Constitution and the Form of the Capitalist State', in Werner Bonefeld, Richard Gunn and Kosmas Psychopedis (eds.) *Open Marxism, Vol. 1: Dialectics and History*. London: Pluto Press, pp. 93–132.

Bonefeld, Werner (2008) 'Global Capital, National State, and the International', *Critique: Journal of Socialist Theory*, 36(1): 63–72.

Bonefeld, Werner, Alice Brown and Peter Burnham (1995) *A Major Crisis? The Politics of Economic Policy in Britain in the 1990s*. Aldershot: Ashgate Publishing.

Bonner, Christine and David Spooner (2011) 'Organising in the Informal Economy: A Challenge for Trade Unions', *International Politics and Society*, 2: 87–105.

Brancaccio, Emiliano (2012) 'Current Account Imbalances, the Eurozone Crisis, and a Proposal for a "European Wage Standard"', *International Journal of Political Economy*, 41(1): 47–65.

Brenner, Neil (1997) 'State Territorial Restructuring and the Production of Spatial Scale: Urban and Regional Planning in the Federal Republic of Germany, 1960–1990', *Political Geography*, 16(4): 273–306.

Brenner, Robert (1977) 'The Origins of Capitalist Development: A Critique of Neo-Smithian Marxism', *New Left Review* (I), 104: 25–92.

Brenner, Robert (1985a) 'Agrarian Class Structure and Economic Development in Pre-industrial Europe', in T. H. Aston and C. H. E. Philpin (eds.) *The Brenner Debate: Agrarian Class Structure and Economic Development in Pre-industrial Europe*. Cambridge: Cambridge University Press, pp. 10–63.

Brenner, Robert (1985b) 'The Agrarian Roots of European Capitalism', in T. H. Aston and C. H. E. Philpin (eds.) *The Brenner Debate: Agrarian Class Structure and Economic Development in Pre-industrial Europe*. Cambridge: Cambridge University Press, pp. 213–327.

Brenner, Robert (1986) 'The Social Basis of Economic Development', in John Roemer (ed.) *Analytical Marxism*. Cambridge: Cambridge University Press, pp. 23–53.

Brenner, Robert (2001) 'The Low Countries in the Transition to Capitalism', *Journal of Agrarian Change*, 1(2): 169–241.

Brenner, Robert and Christopher Isett (2002) 'England's Divergence from China's Yangzi Delta: Property Relations, Microeconomics and Patterns of Development', *The Journal of Asian Studies*, 61(2): 609–62.

Breslin, Shaun (2009) *China and the Global Political Economy*. London: Palgrave.

Breslin, Shaun (2011a) 'The "China Model" and the Global Crisis: From Friedrich List to a Chinese Mode of Governance?', *International Affairs*, 87(6): 1323–43.

Breslin, Shaun (2011b) 'China and the Crisis: Global Power, Domestic Caution and Local Initiative', *Contemporary Politics*, 17(2): 185–200.

Breslin, Shaun (2014) 'Financial Transitions in the PRC: Banking on the State?', *Third World Quarterly*, 35(6): 996–1013.

Brincat, Shannon (2010) 'Towards a Social-Relational Dialectic for World Politics', *European Journal of International Relations*, 17(4): 679–703.

Brincat, Shannon (2014) 'Introduction: Dialectics and World Politics', *Globalizations*, 11(5): 581–6.

Bromley, Simon (1994) *Rethinking Middle East Politics: State Formation and Development*. Cambridge: Polity Press.

Bromley, Simon (2005) 'The United States and the Control of World Oil', *Government and Opposition*, 40(2): 226–55.

Bromley, Simon (2006) 'Blood for Oil?', *New Political Economy*, 11(3): 419–34.

Bruff, Ian (2009) 'The Totalisation of Human Social Practice: Open Marxists and Capitalist Social Relations', *British Journal of Politics and International Relations*, 11(2): 332–51.

Bruff, Ian (2011) 'What about the Elephant in the Room? Varieties of Capitalism, Varieties in Capitalism', *New Political Economy*, 16(4): 481–500.

Bruff, Ian (2012) 'The Relevance of Nicos Poulantzas for Contemporary Debates on "the International"', *International Politics*, 49(2): 177–94.

Bruff, Ian (2014) 'The Rise of Authoritarian Neoliberalism', *Rethinking Marxism*, 26(1): 113–29.

Bruff, Ian and Stefanie Wöhl (2016) 'Constitutionalising Austerity, Disciplining the Household: Masculine Norms of Competitiveness and the Crisis of Social Reproduction in the Eurozone', in Aida A. Hozić and Jacqui True (eds.) *Scandalous Economics: Gender and the Politics of Financial Crises*. Oxford: Oxford University Press, pp. 92–108.

de Brunhoff, Suzanne (1978) *The State, Capital and Economic Policy*, trans. Mike Sonenscher. London: Pluto Press.

Bryant, Gareth (2018) *Carbon Markets in a Climate-Changing Capitalism: Appropriating, Commodifying and Capitalising Nature*. Cambridge: Cambridge University Press.

Bryant, Gareth, Siddhartha Dabhi and Steffen Böhm (2015) '"Fixing" the Climate Crisis: Capital, States and Carbon Offsetting in India', *Environment and Planning A*, 47(10): 2047–63.

Brzezinski, Zbigniew (2003/4) 'Hegemonic Quicksand', *The National Interest*, 74: 5–16.

Buci-Glucksmann, Christine (1980) *Gramsci and the State*, trans. David Fernbach.London: Lawrence and Wishart.

Bukharin, Nikolai (1917) *Imperialism and World Economy*, intro. V. I. Lenin. New York: Monthly Review Press.

Bulmer, Simon (2014) 'Germany and the Eurozone Crisis: Between Hegemony and Domestic Politics', *West European Politics*, 37(6): 1244–63.

Burawoy, Michael (1989) 'Two Methods in Search of Social Science: Skocpol versus Trotsky', *Theory and Society*, 18(6): 759–805.

Burawoy, Michael (2003) 'For a Sociological Marxism: The Complementary Convergence of Antonio Gramsci and Karl Polanyi', *Politics & Society*, 31(2): 193–261.

Burnham, Peter (1990) *The Political Economy of Postwar Reconstruction*. London: Macmillan.

Burnham, Peter (1994) 'Open Marxism and Vulgar International Political Economy', *Review of International Political Economy*, 1(2): 221–31.

Burnham, Peter (1995) 'State and Market in International Political Economy: Towards a Marxian Alternative', *Studies in Marxism*, 2: 135–59.

Burnham Peter (1998) 'The Communist Manifesto as International Relations Theory', in Mark Cowling (ed.) *The Communist Manifesto: New Interpretations*. Edinburgh: Edinburgh University Press, pp. 190–201.

Burnham, Peter (2000) 'Globalisation, Depoliticisation and "Modern" Economic Management', in Werner Bonefeld and Kosmas Psychopedis (eds.) *The Politics of Change: Globalisation, Ideology and Critique*. London: Palgrave, pp. 9–30.

Burnham, Peter (2003) *Remaking the Postwar World Economy: Robot and British Policy in the 1950s*. London: Palgrave.

Burron, Neil (2012) *The New Democracy Wars: The Politics of North American Democracy Promotion in the Americas*. Farnham: Ashgate Publishing.

Busch, Klaus, Christoph Hermann, Karl Hinrichs and Thorsten Schulten (2013) 'Euro Crisis, Austerity Policy and the European Social Model', *International Policy Analysis*, Friedrich Ebert Stiftung, http://library.fes.de/pdf-files/id/ipa/09656.pdf; accessed 1 June 2013.

Buttigieg, Joseph A. (1995) 'Gramsci on Civil Society', *Boundary 2*, 22(3): 1–32.

Cafruny, Alan and Timothy Lehmann (2012) 'The U.S. and Iraq', *New Left Review* (II), 73: 5–16.

Cahill, Damien (2014) *The End of Laissez-Faire? On the Durability of Embedded Neoliberalism*. Cheltenham: Edward Elgar.

Callinicos, Alex (1989) 'Bourgeois Revolutions and Historical Materialism', *International Socialism*, Second Series, No. 43: 113–71.

Callinicos, Alex (2003a) *An Anti-capitalist Manifesto*. Cambridge: Polity Press.

Callinicos, Alex (2003b) *The New Mandarins of American Power: The Bush Administration's Plans for the World*. Cambridge: Polity Press.

Callinicos, Alex (2005) 'Imperialism and Global Political Economy', *International Socialism*, 108 (Second Series): www.isj.org.uk/?id=140.

Callinicos, Alex (2009) *Imperialism and Global Political Economy*. Cambridge: Polity Press.

Callinicos, Alex (2010a) 'Does Capitalism Need the State-System?', in Alexander Anievas (ed.) *Marxism and World Politics: Contesting Global Capitalism*. London: Routledge, pp. 13–26.

Callinicos, Alex (2010b) 'The Limits of Passive Revolution', *Capital & Class*, 34(3): 491–507.

Callinicos, Alex (2011) 'The Crisis of Our Time', *International Socialism*, No. 132; available at http://isj.org.uk/the-crisis-of-our-time/; accessed 7 June 2016.

Callinicos, Alex (2014) *Deciphering Capital: Marx's Capital and Its Destiny*. London: Bookmarks.

Callinicos, Alex (2017) 'Britain and Europe on the Geopolitical Roller-Coaster', *Competition & Change*. Online first: DOI: 10.1177/1024529417700428.

Callinicos, Alex and Justin Rosenberg (2008) 'Uneven and Combined Development: The Social-Relational Substratum of "the International"? An Exchange of Letters', *Cambridge Review of International Affairs*, 21(1): 77–112.

Camfield, David (2002) 'Beyond Adding on Gender and Class: Revisiting Feminism and Marxism', *Studies in Political Economy*, 68: 37–54.

Camfield, David (2016) 'Theoretical Foundations of an Anti-racist Queer Feminist Historical Materialism', *Critical Sociology*, 42(2): 289–306.

Cammack, Paul (2007) 'Forget the Transnational State'. Papers in the Politics of Global Competitiveness, No. 3, Institute for Global Studies, Manchester Metropolitan University, e-space Open Access Repository; www.e-space.mmu.ac.uk.

Campbell, David (1996) 'Political Prosaics, Transversal Politics and the Anarchical World', in Michael J. Shapiro and Hayward R. Alker (eds.) *Challenging Boundaries: Global Flows, Territorial Identities*. Minneapolis: University of Minnesota Press, pp. 7–31.

Campbell, David (1999) 'The Deterritorialisation of Responsibility: Levinas, Derrida and Ethics after the End of Philosophy', in David Campbell and Michael J. Shapiro (eds.) *Moral Spaces: Rethinking Ethics and World Politics*. Minneapolis: University of Minnesota Press, pp. 29–56.

Campbell, David (2001) 'International Engagements: The Politics of North American International Relations Theory', *Political Theory*, 29(3): 432–48.

Cao, Xuebing and Quan Meng (2017) 'Dockworkers' Resistance and Union Reform within China's Globalised Seaport Industry', *Globalizations*, 14(2): 272–84.

Carlsnaes, Walter (1992) 'The Agency–Structure Problem in Foreign Policy Analysis', *International Studies Quarterly*, 36(3): 245–70.

Carrozza, C. and E. Fantini. 2013. 'Acqua paradigma dei beni comuni: tra epica e pratica', in C. Carrozza and E. Fantini (eds.) *Si scrive acqua . . . Attori, pratiche e discorsi nel movimento italiano per l'acqua bene commune*. Torino: Accademia University Press, pp. 75–99.

Cerny, Philip G. (2010) *Rethinking World Politics: A Theory of Transnational Neopluralism*. Oxford: Oxford University Press.

Chakrabarty, Dipesh (2007) *Provincializing Europe: Postcolonial Thought and Historical Difference*, new edition. Princeton, NJ: Princeton University Press.

Chan, Chris King-chi and Elaine Sio-ieng Hui (2017) 'Bringing Class Struggles Back: A Marxian Analysis of the State and Class Relations in China', *Globalizations*, 14(2): 232–44.

Chan, Jenny, Ngai Pun and Mark Selden (2013) 'The Politics of Global Production: Apple, Foxconn and China's New Working Class', *New Technology, Work and Employment*, 28(2): 100–15.

Chan, Jenny and Mark Selden (2014) 'China's Rural Migrant Workers, the State, and Labour Politics', *Critical Asian Studies*, 46(4): 599–620.

Chan, Jenny and Mark Selden (2017) 'The Labour Politics of China's Rural Migrant Workers', *Globalizations*, 14(2): 259–71.

Chandrasekarn, Rajiv (2006) *Imperial Life in the Emerald City: Inside Baghdad's Green Zone*. London: Bloomsbury.

Charnock, Greig and Guido Starosta (eds.) (2016) *The New International Division of Labour: Global Transformation and Uneven Development*. London: Palgrave.

Chase-Dunn, Christopher (1989) *Global Formations: Structures of the World-Economy*. Oxford: Blackwell Publishers.

Chibber, Vivek (2013) *Postcolonial Theory and the Specter of Capital*. London: Verso.

Chilcote, Ronald H. (2010) *The Portuguese Revolution: State and Class in the Transition to Democracy*. Lanham, MD: Rowman & Littlefield.

China Labour Bulletin (February 2014), Searching for the Union, the Workers Movement in China 2011–13, www.clb.org.hk/en/sites/default/files/File/resear ch_reports/searching%20for%20the%20union%201.pdf; accessed 6 July 2014.

Chodor, Tom (2015) *Neoliberal Hegemony and the Pink Tide in Latin America: Breaking Up with TINA?*. London: Palgrave.

Chomsky, Noam (2003) *Hegemony or Survival*. London: Penguin Books.

Chomsky, Noam (2007) *Failed States: The Abuse of Power and the Assault on Democracy*. London: Penguin Books.

Ciccariello-Maher, George (2017) *Decolonizing Dialectics*. Durham, NC: Duke University Press.

Clauwaert, Stefan and Isabelle Schomann (2012) 'The Crisis and National Labour Law Reforms: A Mapping Exercise', ETUI – Working Paper 2012.04, available at: www.etui.org/Publications2/Working-Papers/The-crisis-and-national-labour-law-reforms-a-mapping-exercise.

Cleaver, Harry (1979/2000) *Reading Capital Politically*, second edition. Leeds: Anti/Theses.

Coates, David (2000) *Models of Capitalism: Growth and Stagnation in the Modern Era*. Cambridge: Polity Press.

Colás, Alejandro and Gonzalo Pozo (2011) 'The Value of Territory: Towards a Marxist Geopolitics', *Geopolitics*, 16(1): 211–20.

Cooper, Luke (2013) 'Can Contingency Be "Internalised" into the Bounds of Theory? Critical Realism, the Philosophy of Internal Relations and the Solution of "Uneven and Combined Development"', *Cambridge Review of International Affairs*, 26(3): 573–97.

Coronil, Fernando (1992) 'Can Postcoloniality Be Decolonised? Imperial Banality and Postcolonial Power', *Public Culture*, 5(1): 90–115.

Corrigan, Philip, Harvie Ramsey and Derek Sayer (1980) 'The State as a Relation of Production', in Philip Corrigan (ed.) *Capitalism, State Formation and Marxist Theory*. London: Quartet Books, pp. 1–25.

Cox, Laurence and Alf Gunvald Nilsen (2014) *We Make Our Own History: Marxism and Social Movements in the Twilight of Neoliberalism*. London: Pluto Press.

Cox, Robert W. (1981) 'Social Forces, States and World Orders: Beyond International Relations Theory', *Millennium: Journal of International Studies*, 10(2): 126–55.

Cox, Robert W. (1983) 'Gramsci, Hegemony and International Relations: An Essay in Method', *Millennium: Journal of International Studies*, 12(2): 162–75.

Cox, Robert W. (1985/1996) 'Realism, Positivism, Historicism', in Robert W. Cox with Timothy J. Sinclair, *Approaches to World Order*. Cambridge: Cambridge University Press, pp. 49–59.

Cox, Robert W. (1987) *Production, Power and World Order: Social Forces in the Making of History*. New York: Columbia University Press.

Cox, Robert W. (1989) 'Production, the State and Change in World Order', in Ernst-Otto Czempiel and James N. Rosenau (eds.) *Global Changes and Theoretical Challenges: Approaches to World Politics for the 1990s*. Lexington, MA: Lexington Books, pp. 37–50.

Cox, Robert W. (1992/1996) 'Towards a Posthegemonic Conceptualisation of World Order: Reflections on the Relevancy of Ibn Khaldun', in Robert W. Cox with Timothy J. Sinclair, *Approaches to World Order*. Cambridge: Cambridge University Press, pp. 144–73.

Cox, Robert W. (1995) 'Critical Political Economy', in Björn Hettne (ed.) *International Political Economy: Understanding Global Disorder*. London: Zed Books, pp. 31–46.

Crespy, Amandine (2017) *Welfare Markets in Europe. The Democratic Challenge of European Integration*. London: Palgrave.

Dalla Costa, Mariarosa (2008) 'Capitalism and Reproduction', in Werner Bonefeld (ed.) *Subverting the Present, Imagining the Future: Class Struggle, Commons*. Brooklyn, NY: Autonomedia, 87–98.

Daskalaki, Maria and George Kokkinidis (2017) 'Organising Solidarity Initiatives: A Socio-spatial Conceptualization of Resistance', *Organization Studies*, 38(9): 1303–25.

Davidson, Neil (2006) 'China: Unevenness, Combination, Revolution?', in Hugo Radice and Bill Dunn (eds.) *100 Years of Permanent Revolution: Results and Prospects*. London: Pluto Press, pp. 211–29.

Davidson, Neil (2010) 'From Deflected Permanent Revolution to the Law of Uneven and Combined Development', *International Socialism*, No. 128; available at www.isj.org.uk/?id=686; accessed 30 March 2014.

Davies, Matt and Magnus Ryner (eds.) (2006) *Poverty and the Production of World Politics: Unprotected Workers in the Global Political Economy*. London: Palgrave.

Day, Richard J. F. (2005) *Gramsci Is Dead: Anarchist Currents in the Newest Social Movements*. London: Pluto Press.

De Ville, Ferdi and Jan Orbie (2014) 'The European Commission's Neoliberal Trade Discourse since the Crisis: Legitimising Continuity through Subtle Discursive Change', *British Journal of Politics and International Relations*, 16(1): 149–67.

Degryse, Christophe (2012) 'The New European Economic Governance'. ETUI Working Paper 2012.14, available at: www.etui.org/Publications2/Working -Papers/The-new-European-economic-governance.

Deng, Ping (2013) 'Chinese Outward Direct Investment Research: Theoretical Integration and Recommendations', *Management and Organization Review*, 9(3): 513–39.

Dessler, David (1989) 'What's at Stake in the Agent–Structure Debate?', *International Organization* 43(3): 441–73.

Dirlik, Arif (1994) 'The Postcolonial Aura: Third World Criticism in the Age of Global Capitalism', *Critical Inquiry* 20(2): 328–56.

Dönmez, Pınar and Alex Sutton (2016) 'Revisiting the Debate on Open Marxist Perspectives', *British Journal of Politics and International Relations*, 18(3): 688–705.

Doty, Roxanne Lynn (1997) 'Aporia: A Critical Exploration of the Agent–Structure Problematique in International Relations Theory', *European Journal of International Relations* 3(3): 365–92.

Drainville, André (1994) 'International Political Economy in the Age of Open Marxism', *Review of International Political Economy*, 1(1): 105–32.

Drainville, André (1995) 'Of Social Spaces, Citizenship and the Nature of Power in the World Economy', *Review of International Political Economy*, 20(1): 51–79.

Edgerton, D. (1991) 'Liberal Militarism and the British State', *New Left Review* (I), 185: 138–69.

Edkins, Jenny (1999) *Poststructuralism & International Relations: Bringing the Political Back In*. Boulder, CO: Lynne Rienner.

Edkins, Jenny and Véronique Pin-Fat (1999) 'The Subject of the Political', in Jenny Edkins, Nalini Persram and Véronique Pin-Fat (eds.) *Sovereignty and Subjectivity*. Boulder, CO: Lynne Rienner, pp. 1–18.

Edkins, Jenny and Véronique Pin-Fat (2005) 'Through the Wire: Relations of Power and Relations of Violence', *Millennium: Journal of International Studies*, 34(1): 1–24.

Edkins, Jenny, Véronique Pin-Fat and Michael J. Shapiro (eds.) (2004) *Sovereign Lives: Power in Global Politics*. London: Routledge.

Edkins, Jenny and Maja Zehfuss (2005) 'Generalising the International', *Review of International Studies*, 31(3): 451–72.

Endnotes (2008) *Preliminary Materials for a Balance Sheet of the Twentieth Century* (October). London: Endnotes.

Endnotes (2010) *Misery and the Value Form* (April). London: Endnotes.

Endnotes (2013) *Gender, Race, Class and Other Misfortunes* (September). London: Endnotes.

Endnotes (2015) *Unity in Separation* (October). London: Endnotes.

Engels, Friedrich (1883/1987) *Dialectics of Nature*, in Karl Marx and Friedrich Engels, *Collected Works*, Vol. 25. London: Lawrence and Wishart.

Engels, Friedrich (1884/1990) 'On the Decline of Feudalism and the Emergence of National States', in Karl Marx and Friedrich Engels, *Collected Works*, Vol. 26. London: Lawrence and Wishart, pp. 556–65.

Epstein, Charlotte (2013) 'Constructivism or the Eternal Return of Universals in International Relations: Why Returning to Language Is Vital to Prolonging the Owl's Flight', *European Journal of International Relations*, 19(3): 499–519.

Epstein, Charlotte (2015) 'Minding the Brain: IR as a Science?', *Millennium: Journal of International Studies*, 43(2): 743–8.

EPSU (2014) 'Mass Mobilisation Stops Privatisation in Alcazar de San Juan' (Spain) (21 February 2014); www.epsu.org/a/10216; accessed 14 December 2014.

EPSU (2015) 'EU Social Partners Reach Landmark Agreement on Rights for Central Government Employees' (21 December 2015); available at www.epsu.org/sites/default/files/article/files/PR_2015_12_21_landmark_agreement_EU_social_part ners_Central_Government_Administrations.pdf; accessed 23 December 2016.

Erne, Roland (2012) 'European Industrial Relations after the Crisis: A Postscript', in Stijn Smismans (ed.) *The European Union and Industrial Relations – New Procedures, New Context*. Manchester: Manchester University Press, pp. 225–35.

Erne, Roland (2015) 'A Supranational Regime That Nationalises Social Conflict: Explaining European Trade Unions' Difficulties in Politicizing European Economic Governance', *Labor History*, 56(3): 345–68.

EuroMemo Group (2013) 'The Deepening Crisis in the European Union: The Need for a Fundamental Change', in *European Economists for an Alternative Economic Policy in Europe*. www2.euromemorandum.eu/uploads/eu romemorandum_2013.pdf; accessed 26 June 2013.

European Commission (2013a) 'MIP Scoreboard'. http://ec.europa.eu/econo my_finance/economic_governance/macroeconomic_imbalance_procedure/mi p_scoreboard/; accessed 22 November 2013.

European Commission (2013b) 'The Economic Adjustment Programme for Portugal – Seventh Review – Winter 2012/2013', European Economy, Occasional Papers 153, June 2013.

European Commission (2016a) 'Vice-President Dombrovskis and the Commissioner Thyssen Sign Joint Statement 'New Start for Social Dialogue' (27 June 2016); available at http://ec.europa.eu/social/main.jsp?langId=en&ca tId=329&newsId=2562&furtherNews=yes; accessed 23 December 2016.

European Commission (2016b) 'Recommendation for a Council Recommendation on the Economic Policy of the Euro Area' (16 November 2016); available at htt ps://ec.europa.eu/info/sites/info/files/2017-european-semester-recommendation-euro-area_en_0.pdf; accessed 23 December 2016.

European Council (2013) 'Fiscal Compact Enters into Force on 1 January 2013'. www.european-council.europa.eu/home-page/highlights/fiscal-compact-enter s-into-force-on-1-january-2013?lang=en; accessed 23 April 2013.

Evans, Peter (1997) 'The Eclipse of the State? Reflections on Stateness in an Era of Globalisation', *World Politics*, 50(1): 62–87.

Fattori, Tommaso (2011) 'Fluid Democracy: The Italian Water Revolution', *transform! Europe*, www.transform-network.net/en/publications/yearbook/arti cle//fluid-democracy-the-italian-water-revolution/; accessed 1 March 2014.

Federici, Silvia (2004) *Caliban and the Witch: Women, the Body and Primitive Accumulation*. Brooklyn, NY: Autonomedia.

Federici, Silvia (2006) 'Prostitution and Globalisation: Notes on a Feminist Debate', in Matt Davies and Magnus Ryner (eds.) *Poverty and the Production of World Politics: Unprotected Workers in the Global Political Economy*. London: Palgrave, pp. 112–36.

Federici, Silvia (2012) *Revolution at Point Zero: Housework, Reproduction and Feminist Struggle*. Oakland, CA: PM Press.

Femia, Joseph V. (1981) *Gramsci's Political Thought: Hegemony, Consciousness and the Revolutionary Process*. Oxford: Clarendon Press.

Femia, Joseph V. (1998) *The Machiavellian Legacy: Essays in Italian Political Thought*. London: Macmillan Press.

Ferdinand, Peter (2016) 'Westward Ho – The China Dream and "One Belt, One Road": Chinese Foreign Policy under Xi Jinping', *International Affairs*, 92(4): 941–57.

Ferguson, Susan (2016) 'Intersectionality and Social-Reproduction Feminisms: Toward an Integrative Ontology', *Historical Materialism*, 24(2): 38–60.

Fine, Ben and Alfredo Saad-Filho (2004) *Marx's Capital*, fourth edition. London: Pluto Press.

Finnemore, Martha and Kathryn Sikkink (1998), 'International Norm Dynamics and Political Change', *International Organization*, 52(4): 887–917.

Fioramonti, Lorenzo (2013) *Gross Domestic Problem: The Politics behind the World's Most Powerful Number*. London: Zed Books.

Fitzsimons, Alejandro Luis and Guido Starosta (2017), 'Global Capital, Uneven Development and National Difference: Critical Reflections on the Specificity of

Accumulation in Latin America', *Capital & Class*, (2017). Online first: DOI: 10.1177/030981681762126.

Flassbeck, Heiner and Costas Lapavitsas (2013) 'The Systemic Crisis of the Euro – True Causes and Effective Therapies', *Studien – Rosa Luxemburg Stiftung*: 1–45.

Fletcher, Bill and Fernando Gapasin (2008) *Solidarity Divided: The Crisis in Organised Labor and a New Path toward Social Justice*. Berkeley: University of California Press.

Flibbert, Andrew (2006) 'The Road to Baghdad: Ideas and Intellectuals in Explanations of the Iraq War', *Security Studies*, 15(2): 310–52.

Foucault, Michel (1972) *The Archaeology of Knowledge*, translated by A. M. Sheridan Smith. New York: Pantheon Books.

Foucault, Michel (1977) *Language, Counter-memory, Practice: Selected Essays and Interviews*. Cornell, NY: Cornell University Press.

Foucault, Michel (1980) *Power/Knowledge: Selected Interviews and Other Writings, 1972–1977*. London: Harvester-Wheatsheaf.

Foucault, Michel (1999) 'Who Are You, Professor Foucault?', interview with P. Caruso [1967], in Michel Foucault, *Religion and Culture*, ed. J. R. Carrette. London: Routledge, pp. 87–100.

Foucault, Michel (2000) 'The Subject and Power', in *Power: Essential Works of Foucault, 1954–1984*, Vol. 3, ed. James D. Faubion, trans. Robert Hurley and others. New York: The New Press, pp. 326–48.

Foucault, Michel (2003) *Society Must Be Defended*, trans. David Macey. London: Penguin.

Fraser, Nancy (2014) 'Behind Marx's Hidden Abode: For an Expanded Conception of Capitalism', *New Left Review* (II), 86: 55–72.

Freeman, Richard (2010) 'What Really Ails Europe (and America): The Doubling of the Global Workforce', *The Globalist;* available at www.theglobalist.com/what-really-ails-europe-and-america-the-doubling-of-the-global-workforce/; accessed 16 December 2014.

Friedman, Eli (2014) *Insurgency Trap: Labor Politics in Postsocialist China*. Ithaca, NY: Cornell University Press.

Gallagher, John and Ronald Robinson (1953) 'The Imperialism of Free Trade', *The Economic History Review*, Second Series, 6(1): 1–15.

Gallagher, Mary E. (2014) 'China's Workers Movement and the End of the Rapid-Growth Era', *Daedalus: The Journal of the American Academy of Arts and Sciences*, 143(2): 81–95.

Gallin, Dan (2001) 'Propositions on Trade Unions and Informal Employment in Times of Globalisation', in Peter Waterman and Jane Wills (eds.) *Place, Space and the New Labour Internationalisms*. Oxford: Blackwell, pp. 227–45.

Gallin, Dan (2012) 'Informal Economy Workers and the International Trade Union Movement: An Overview'. Paper presented at the Critical Labour Studies 8th Symposium, University of Salford/UK (18–19 February 2012).

Gemici, Kurtuluş (2007) 'Karl Polanyi and the Antinomies of Embeddedness', *Socio-Economic Review*, 6(1): 5–33.

Gereffi, Garry, John Humphrey and Timothy Sturgeon (2005) 'The Governance of Global Value Chains', *Review of International Political Economy*, 12(1): 78–104.

German, Randall (ed.) (2016) *Susan Strange and the Future of Global Political Economy: Power, Control and Transformation*. London: Routledge.

Gibson-Graham, J. K. (1996/2006) *The End of Capitalism (As We Knew It): A Feminist Critique of Political Economy*, new edition. Minneapolis: University of Minnesota Press.

Gibson-Graham, J. K. (2014) 'Rethinking the Economy with Thick Description and Weak Theory', *Current Anthropology*, 55(S9): S147–53.

Gibson-Graham, J. K., Jenny Cameron and Stephen Healey (2013) *Take Back the Economy: An Ethical Guide for Transforming Our Communities*. Minneapolis: University of Minnesota Press.

Gibson-Graham, J. K., Stephen Resnick and Richard Wolff (2001) 'Towards a Poststructuralist Political Economy', in J. K. Gibson-Graham, Stephen Resnick and Richard Wolff (eds.) *Re/Presenting Class: Essays in Postmodern Marxism*. Durham, NC: Duke University Press, pp. 1–22.

Giddens, Anthony (1984) *The Constitution of Society: Outline of the Theory of Structuration*. Cambridge: Polity Press.

Gill, Stephen (1991) 'Reflections on Global Order and Sociohistorical Time', *Alternatives*, 16(3): 275–314.

Gill, Stephen (1992) 'The Emerging World Order and European Change: The Political Economy of European Union', in Ralph Miliband and Leo Panitch (eds.) *The Socialist Register: New World Order?* London: Merlin Press, pp. 157–96.

Gill, Stephen and David Law (1988) *The Global Political Economy: Perspectives, Problems and Policies*. London: Harvester-Wheatsheaf.

Gilpin, Robert (1987) *The Political Economy of International Relations*. Princeton, NJ: Princeton University Press.

Giroux, Henry A. (2007) *The University in Chains: Confronting the Military-Industrial-Academic Complex*. Boulder, CO: Paradigm Publishers.

Glassman, Jim (2003) 'Rethinking Overdetermination, Structural Power and Social Change: A Critique of Gibson-Graham, Resnick and Wolff', *Antipode*, 35(4): 678–98.

Glassman, Jim (2006) 'Primitive Accumulation, Accumulation by Dispossession, Accumulation by "Extra-Economic" Means', *Progress in Human Geography*, 30(5): 608–25.

Godelier, Maurice (1986) *The Mental and the Material: Thought Economy and Society*, trans. Martin Thom. London: Verso.

de Goede, Marieke (2001) 'Discourses of Scientific Finance and the Failure of Long-Term Capital Management', *New Political Economy*, 6(2): 149–70.

de Goede, Marieke (2003) 'Beyond Economism in International Political Economy', *Review of International Studies*, 29(1): 79–97.

de Goede, Marieke (2004) 'Repoliticising Financial Risk', *Economy and Society*, 33(2): 197–217.

de Goede, Marieke (2005) *Virtue, Fortune, and Faith: A Genealogy of Finance*. Minneapolis: University of Minnesota Press.

de Goede, Marieke (2006) 'Introduction: International Political Economy and the Promises of Poststructuralism', in Marieke de Goede (ed.) *International Political Economy and Poststructuralist Politics*. London: Palgrave, pp. 1–20.

Goldfrank, Walter (1975) 'World System, State Structure and the Onset of the Mexican Revolution', *Politics and Society*, 5(4): 417–39.

Goldstein, Judith and Robert O. Keohane (1993) 'Ideas and Foreign Policy: An Analytical Framework', in Judith Goldstein and Robert O. Keohane (eds.) *Ideas and Foreign Policy: Beliefs, Institutions, and Political Change*. Ithaca, NY: Cornell University Press, pp. 3–30.

Gow, Michael (2017) 'The Core Socialist Values of the Chinese Dream: Towards a Chinese Integral State', *Critical Asian Studies*, 49(1): 92–116.

de Graaff, Naná and Bastiaan van Apeldoorn (2011) 'Varieties of U.S. post–Cold War Imperialism: Anatomy of a Failed Hegemonic Project and the Future of U.S. Geopolitics', *Critical Sociology*, 37(4): 403–27.

Gramsci, Antonio (1971) *Selections from the Prison Notebooks*, ed. and trans. Quintin Hoare and Geoffrey-Nowell Smith. London: Lawrence and Wishart.

Gramsci, Antonio (1977) *Selections from Political Writings, 1910–1920*, ed. Quintin Hoare, trans. John Matthews. London: Lawrence and Wishart.

Gramsci, Antonio (1978) *Selections from Political Writings, 1921–1926*, ed. and trans. Quintin Hoare. London: Lawrence and Wishart.

Gramsci, Antonio (1985) *Selections from Cultural Writings*, ed. David Forgacs and Geoffrey Nowell-Smith, trans. William Boelhower. London: Lawrence and Wishart.

Gramsci, Antonio (1992) *Prison Notebooks*, Vol. 1, ed. and intro. Joseph A. Buttigieg, trans. Joseph A. Buttigieg and Antonio Callari. New York: Columbia University Press.

Gramsci, Antonio (1994a) *Pre-prison Writings*, ed. Richard Bellamy, trans. Virginia Cox. Cambridge: Cambridge University Press.

Gramsci, Antonio (1994b) *Letters from Prison*, Vol. 2, ed. Frank Rosengarten, trans. Raymond Rosenthal. New York: Columbia University Press.

Gramsci, Antonio (1995) *Further Selections from the Prison Notebooks*, ed. and trans. D. Boothman. London: Lawrence and Wishart.

Gramsci, Antonio (1996) *Prison Notebooks*, Vol. 2, ed. and trans. Joseph A. Buttigieg. New York: Columbia University Press.

Gramsci, Antonio (2007) *Prison Notebooks*, Vol. 3, ed. and trans. Joseph A. Buttigieg. New York: Columbia University Press.

Gray, Kevin (2010) 'Labour and the State in China's Passive Revolution', *Capital & Class*, 34(3): 449–67.

Gray, Kevin (2015) *Labour and Development in East Asia: Social Forces and Passive Revolution*. London: Routledge.

Greenwood, Ian and Jo McBride (2009) 'Conclusion', in Jo McBride and Ian Greenwood (eds.) *Community Unionism: A Comparative Analysis of Concepts and Contexts*. London: Palgrave, pp. 210–20.

Guzzini, Stefano (2011) 'Marxist Geopolitics: Still a Missed Rendezvous?', *Geopolitics*, 16(1): 226–9.

Haas, Peter M. (1992) 'Introduction: Epistemic Communities and International Policy Coordination', *International Organization*, 46(1): 1–35.

Hall, Peter A. (2012) 'The Economics and Politics of the Euro Crisis', *German Politics*, 21(4): 355–71.

Hall, Peter A. (2014) 'Varieties of Capitalism and the Euro Crisis', *West European Politics*, 37(6): 1223–43.

Hall, Peter A. and David Soskice (2001) 'An Introduction to Varieties of Capitalism', in Peter A. Hall and David Soskice (eds.) *Varieties of Capitalism*. Oxford: Oxford University Press, pp. 1–68.

Hall, Stuart (1986) 'The Problem of Ideology: Marxism without Guarantees', *Journal of Communication Inquiry*, 10(2): 28–44.

Hall, Stuart (1996) 'On Postmodernism and Articulation' [an interview ed. Lawrence Grossberg], in D. Morley and K.-H. Chen (eds.) *Stuart Hall: Critical Dialogues in Cultural Studies*. London: Routledge, pp. 131–50.

Hall, Stuart (1997) 'Culture and Power', Interview with Peter Osbourne and Lynne Segal [London, June 1997], *Radical Philosophy*, 86: 24–41.

Halperin, Sandra (2011) 'The Political Economy of Anglo-American War: The Case of Iraq', *International Politics*, 48(2/3): 207–28.

Hameiri, Shahar and Lee Jones (2015) *Governing Borderless Threats: Non-traditional Security and the Politics of State Transformation*. Cambridge: Cambridge University Press.

Hameiri, Shahar and Lee Jones (2016) 'Rising Powers and State Transformation: The Case of China', *European Journal of International Relations*, 22(1): 72–98.

Hancké, Bob (2013) *Unions, Central Banks, and EMU: Labour Market Institutions and Monetary Integration in Europe*. Oxford: Oxford University Press.

Hardy, Jane (2017) 'China's Place in the Global Divisions of Labour: An Uneven and Combined Development Perspective', *Globalizations*, 14(2): 189–201.

Hardy, Jane and Adrian Budd (2012) 'China's Capitalism and the Crisis', *International Socialism*, No. 133; available at www.isj.org.uk/?id=777; accessed 27 June 2014.

Harootunian, Harry (2015) *Marx after Marx: History and Time in the Expansion of Capitalism*. New York: Columbia University Press.

Harris, Jerry (2005) 'The Military-Industrial Complex in Transnational Class Theory', in Richard P. Appelbaum and William I. Robinson (eds.) *Critical Globalization Studies*. London: Routledge, pp. 141–54.

Harris, Jerry (2006) *The Dialectics of Globalization: Economic and Political Conflict in a Transnational World*. Newcastle-upon-Tyne: Cambridge Scholars Publishing.

Harris, Jerry (2008) 'U.S. Imperialism after Iraq', *Race & Class*, 50(1): 37–58.

Harris, Jerry (2012) 'Outward Bound: Transnational Capitalism in China', *Race & Class*, 54(1): 13–52.

Harrod, Jeffrey (1987) *Power, Production and the Unprotected Worker*. New York: Columbia University Press.

Hart-Landsberg, Martin (2013) *Capitalist Globalization: Consequences, Resistance, and Alternatives*. New York: Monthly Review Press.

Hart-Landsberg, Martin (2015) 'From the Claw to the Lion: A Critical Look at Capitalist Globalization', *Critical Asian Studies*, 47(1): 1–23.

Hart-Landsberg, Martin (2016) 'The Pitfalls and Possibilities of Socialist Transformation: The Case of Greece', *Class, Race and Corporate Power*, 4(1): 1–24.

Harvey, David (1975/2001) 'The Geography of Capitalist Accumulation: A Reconstruction of the Marxian Theory', in David Harvey, *Spaces of Capital: Towards a Critical Geography*. Edinburgh: Edinburgh University Press, pp. 237–66.

Harvey, David (1982/2006) *The Limits to Capital*, new edition. London: Verso.

Harvey, David (1985) 'The Geopolitics of Capitalism', in D. Gregory and J. Urry (eds.) *Social Relations and Spatial Structures*. London: Macmillan, pp. 128–63.

Harvey, David (1989) *The Condition of Postmodernity*. Oxford: Basil Blackwell Ltd.

Harvey David (1996) *Justice, Nature and the Geography of Difference*. Oxford: Blackwell Publishing.

Harvey, David (2000) 'The Insurgent Architect at Work', in David Harvey, *Spaces of Hope*. Edinburgh: Edinburgh University Press, pp. 233–56.

Harvey, David (2003a) *Paris, Capital of Modernity*. London: Routledge.

Harvey, David (2003b) *The New Imperialism*. Oxford: Oxford University Press.

Harvey, David (2005) *A Brief History of Neoliberalism*. Oxford: Oxford University Press.

Harvey, David (2006a) 'Neoliberalism and the Restoration of Class Power', in David Harvey (ed.) *Spaces of Global Capitalism: Towards a Theory of Uneven Geographical Development*. London: Verso, pp. 7–68.

Harvey, David (2006b) *Spaces of Global Capitalism: Towards a Theory of Uneven Geographical Development*. London: Verso.

Harvey, David (2012) *Rebel Cities: From Right to the City to the Urban Revolution*. London: Verso.

Harvey, David (2016) 'Abstract from the Concrete', Lecture delivered to the Harvard University Graduate School of Design, Cambridge, MA. (28 March). Harvard University: Graduate School of Design Sternberg Press.

Hay, Colin (1995) 'Structure and Agency', in David Marsh and Gerry Stoker (eds.) *Theory and Methods in Political Science*. Basingstoke: Macmillan Press, pp. 189–206.

Hein, Eckhard and Matthias Mundt (2013) 'Financialisation, the Financial and Economic Crisis, and the Requirements and Potentials for Wage-led Recovery', in Marc Lavoie and Engelbert Stockhammer (eds.) *Wage-Led Growth: An Equitable Strategy for Economic Recovery*. London: Basingstoke, pp. 153–86.

Heine, Christian and Benno Teschke (1996) 'Sleeping Beauty and the Dialectical Awakening: On the Potential of Dialectic for International Relations', *Millennium: Journal of International Studies*, 26(2): 455–70.

Heino, Brett (2018) *Regulation Theory and Australian Capitalism: Rethinking Social Justice and Labour Law*. London: Rowman & Littlefield International.

Heinrich, Michael (2012) *An Introduction to the Three Volumes of Karl Marx's Capital*. New York: Monthly Review Press.

Held, David, Anthony McGrew, David Goldblatt and Jonathan Perraton (1999) *Global Transformations: Politics, Economics and Culture*. Cambridge: Polity Press.

Herod, Andrew (2006) 'Trotsky's Omission: Labour's Role in Combined and Uneven Development', in Hugo Radice and Bill Dunn (eds.) *100 Years of Permanent Revolution: Results and Prospects*. London: Pluto Press, pp. 152–65.

Herring, Eric and Glen Rangwala (2006) *Iraq in Fragments: The Occupation and Its Legacy*. London: Hurst and Company.

Hesketh, Chris (2016) 'The Survival of Noncapitalism', *Environment and Planning D*, 34(5): 877–94.

Hesketh, Chris (2017a) *Spaces of Capital/Spaces of Resistance: Mexico and the Global Political Economy*. Athens: University of Georgia Press.

Hesketh, Chris (2017b) 'Passive Revolution: A Universal Concept with Geographical Seats', *Review of International Studies*, 43(3): 389–408.

Hesketh, Chris and Adam David Morton (2014) 'Spaces of Uneven Development and Class Struggle in Bolivia: Transformation or Trasformismo?', *Antipode*, 46(1): 149–69.

Higginbottom, Andrew (2011) 'Gold Mining in South Africa Reconsidered: New Mode of Exploitation, Theories of Imperialism and Capital', *Économies et Sociétés*, 45(2): 261–88.

Hilary, John (2014) *The Transatlantic Trade and Investment Partnership: A Charter for Deregulation, an Attack on Jobs, and End to Democracy*. Brussels: Rosa Luxemburg Stiftung, available at http://rosalux.gr/sites/default/files/publica tions/ttip_web.pdf; accessed 11 February 2015.

Hirsch, Joachim and John Kannankulam (2011) 'The Space of Capital: The Political Form of Capitalism and the Internationalisation of the State', *Antipode*, 43(1): 12–37.

Hirst, Paul and Grahame Thompson (1999) *Globalisation in Question: The International Economy and the Possibilities of Governance*, second edition. Cambridge: Polity Press.

Hobsbawm, Eric (1962) *The Age of Revolution, 1789–1848*. London: Weidenfeld & Nicolson.

Hobsbawm, Eric (1965) 'The Crisis of the Seventeenth Century', in Trevor Aston (ed.) *Crisis in Europe, 1560–1660: Essays from Past & Present*. London: Routledge, pp. 5–58.

Hobsbawm, Eric (1975) *The Age of Capital, 1848–1875*. London: Weidenfeld & Nicolson.

Hobson, John M. (1997) *Wealth of States: A Comparative Sociology of International Economic and Political Change*. Cambridge: Cambridge University Press.

Hobson, John M. (2004) *The Eastern Origins of Western Civilisation*. Cambridge: Cambridge University Press.

Hobson, John M. (2011) 'What's at Stake in the Neo-Trotskyist Debate? Towards a Non-Eurocentric Historical Sociology of Uneven and Combined Development', *Millennium: Journal of International Studies*, 40(1): 147–66.

Holgate, Jane (2015) 'Community Organising in the UK: A "New" Approach for Trade Unions?', *Economic and Industrial Democracy*, 36(3): 431–55.

Hollis, Martin and Steve Smith (1990) *Explaining and Understanding International Relations*. Oxford: Clarendon Press.

Holloway, John (1994) 'Global Capital and the National State', *Capital & Class*, 52: 23–49.

Holloway, John (2002) *Change the World without Taking Power: The Meaning of Revolution Today*. London: Pluto Press.

Holloway, John and Sol Picciotto (1977) 'Capital, Crisis and the State', *Capital & Class*, 2: 76–101.

Holmstrom, Nancy (ed.) *The Socialist Feminist Project: A Contemporary Reader in Theory and Politics*. New York: Monthly Review Press.

Hossein-Zadeh, Ismael (2006) *The Political Economy of U.S. Militarism*. London: Palgrave.

Hozić, A. Aida and Jacqui True (2016) 'Making Feminist Sense of the Global Financial Crisis', in Aida A. Hozić and Jacqui True (eds.) *Scandalous Economics: Gender and the Politics of Financial Crises*. Oxford: Oxford University Press, pp. 3–20.

Hsu, Sarah (2015) 'China's Efforts to Boost Consumption: Are They Enough?', *The Diplomat*, 3 May; available at http://thediplomat.com/2015/05/chinas -efforts-to-boost-consumption-are-they-enough/; accessed 4 December 2015.

Hui, Elaine Sio-ieng (2014) 'Hegemonic Transformation: The State, Laws, and Labour Relations in Post-Socialist China', PhD thesis, Faculty of Social Sciences, University of Kassel.

Hui, Elaine Sio-ieng (2016a) 'Putting the Chinese State in Its Place: A March from Passive Revolution to Hegemony', *Journal of Contemporary Asia*, 47(1): 66–92.

Hui, Elaine Sio-ieng (2016b) 'The Labour Law System, Capitalist Hegemony and Class Politics in China', *The China Quarterly*, 226 (June): 431–55.

Huke, Nikolai, Mònica Clua-Losada and David J. Bailey (2015) 'Disrupting the European Crisis: A Critical Political Economy of Contestation, Subversion and Escape', *New Political Economy*, 20(5): 725–51.

Humphrys, Elizabeth and Damien Cahill (2016) 'How Labour Made Neoliberalism', *Critical Sociology*. Online first: https://doi.org/10.1177/089692 0516655859.

Ikenberry, G. John (2008) 'The Rise of China and the Future of the West', *Foreign Affairs*, 87(1): 23–37.

Inman, Phillip (2016) 'Irish Economy Surges 26% as Revised Figures Take in Foreign Investment', *The Guardian* (12 July 2016); available at www .theguardian.com/business/2016/jul/12/irish-economic-growth-revised-figures -foreign-investment-aircraft; accessed 22 December 2016.

Iraq Inquiry (2016) *Report of the Iraq Inquiry*. 12 Vols. London: HMO.

Ives, Peter (2004a) *Gramsci's Politics of Language: Engaging the Bakhtin Circle and the Frankfurt School*. Toronto: University of Toronto Press.

Ives, Peter (2004b) *Language and Hegemony in Gramsci*. London: Pluto Press.

Ives, Peter and Nicola Short (2013) 'On Gramsci and the International: A Textual Analysis', *Review of International Studies*, 39(3): 621–42.

Jacobsen, John K. (2003) 'Duelling Constructivisms: A Post-mortem on the Ideas Debate in Mainstream IR/IPE', *Review of International Studies*, 29(1): 39–60.

Jakob, Christine and Pablo Sanchez (2015) 'Remunicipalisation and workers: Building New alliances', in Satoko Kishimoto, Emanuele Lobina and Olivier Petitjean (eds.) *Our Public Water Future: The Global Experience with Remunicipalisation*. Transnational Institute; available online at: www .municipalservicesproject.org/sites/municipalservicesproject.org/files/publica tions/Kishimoto-Lobina-Petitjean_Our-Public-Water-Future-Global-Experie nce-Remunicipalisation_April2015_FINAL.pdf; accessed 7 July 2015.

Jauch, Herbert (2011) 'Chinese Investments in Africa: Twenty-First Century Colonialism?', *New Labor Forum*, 20(2): 49–55.

Jessop, Bob (1990) *State Theory: Putting the Capitalist State in Its Place*. Cambridge: Polity Press.

Jessop, Bob (2011) 'Poulantzas' *State, Power, Socialism* as a Modern Classic', in Alexander Gallas, Lars Bretthauer, John Kannankulam and Ingo Stützle (eds.) *Reading Poulantzas*. London: Merlin Press, pp. 42–55.

Jessop, Bob (2017) 'The Organic Crisis of the British State: Putting Brexit in Its Place', *Globalizations*, 14(1): 133–41.

Johnston, Alison and Aidan Regan (2016) 'European Monetary Integration and the Incompatibility of National Varieties of Capitalism', *Journal of Common Market Studies*, 54(2): 318–36.

Jordan, Jamie (2016) 'The Uneven and Combined Development of the Eurozone Debt Crisis in Greece and Portugal'. Paper presented at the 2016 SPERI conference 'Political Economy in an Age of Great Uncertainty', University of Sheffield (4–6 July).

Jordan, Jamie (2017) 'Global Restructuring and Resistance in an Age of Austerity: A Critical Political Economy Approach to the Eurozone Crisis in Greece and Portugal', PhD thesis, School of Politics and International Relations, University of Nottingham.

Joseph, Jonathan (2007) 'Critical Realism and Causal Analysis in IR', *Millennium: Journal of International Studies*, 35(2): 345–59.

Joseph, Jonathan and Colin Wight (eds.) (2002) *Scientific Realism and International Relations*. London: Palgrave.

Kagarlitsky, Boris (2017) 'Brexit and the Future of the Left', *Globalizations*, 14(1): 110–17.

Katz, Claudio J. (1993/1999) 'Karl Marx on the Transition from Feudalism to Capitalism', in Bob Jessop and Russell Wheatley (eds.) *Karl Marx's Social and Political Thought: Critical Assessments II*, Vol. 6. London: Routledge, pp. 59–82.

Katzenstein, Peter J., Robert O. Keohane and Stephen D. Krasner (1998) 'International Organization and the Study of World Politics', *International Organization*, 52(4): 645–85.

Kautsky, Karl (1914/1970) 'Ultra-imperialism', *New Left Review* (I), 59: 41–6.

Kelpie, Colm (2013) 'Italy, Spain Criticised among Countries at Risk of Breaking EU Budget Rules', www.independent.ie/business/irish/italy-spain-criticised -among-countries-at-risk-of-breaking-eu-budget-rules-29758927.html; accessed 16 November 2013.

Kettell, Steven (2004) *The Political Economy of Exchange Rate Policy-Making: From the Gold Standard to the Euro*. London: Palgrave.

Kiely, Ray (2007) *The New Political Economy of Development: Globalization, Imperialism, Hegemony*. London: Palgrave.

Kiely, Ray (2010) *Rethinking Imperialism*. London: Palgrave.

Kiely, Ray (2012) 'Spatial Hierarchy and/or Contemporary Geopolitics: What Can and Can't Uneven and Combined Development Explain?', *Cambridge Review of International Affairs*, 25(2): 231–48.

Kiely, Ray (2015) *The BRICs, U.S. 'Decline' and Global Transformations*. London: Palgrave.

Klare, Michael T. (2004) *Blood and Oil: The Dangers and Consequences of America's Growing Petroleum Dependency*. London: Penguin Books.

Klein, Naomi (2007) *The Shock Doctrine: The Rise of Disaster Capitalism*. London: Penguin.

Knafo, Samuel (2010) 'Critical Approaches and the Legacy of the Agent/Structure Debate in International Relations', *Cambridge Review of International Affairs*, 23(3): 493–516.

Knafo, Samuel (2014) *The Making of Modern Finance: Liberal Governance and the Gold Standard*. London: Routledge.

Kokkinidis, George (2012) 'In Search of Workplace Democracy', *International Journal of Sociology and Social Policy*, 32(3): 233–56.

Kokkinidis, George (2015a) 'Post-capitalist Imaginaries: The Case of Workers' Collectives in Greece', *Journal of Management Inquiry*, 24(4): 429–32.

Kokkinidis, George (2015b) 'Spaces of Possibilities: Workers' Self-Management in Greece', *Organization*, 22(6): 847–71.

Kouvelakis, Stathis (2016) 'Syriza's Rise and Fall', *New Left Review* (II), 97: 45–70.

Kratochwil, Friedrich (1988) 'Regimes, Interpretation and the "Science" of Politics: A Reappraisal', *Millennium: Journal of International Studies*, 17(2): 263–84.

Kratochwil, Friedrich (1989) *Rules, Norms and Decisions: On the Conditions of Practical and Legal Reasoning in International Relations and Domestic Affairs*. Cambridge: Cambridge University Press.

Kratochwil, Friedrich and John G. Ruggie (1986) 'International Organization: A State of the Art on an Art of the State', *International Organization*, 40(4): 753–75.

Krippner, Greta (2001) 'The Elusive Market: Embeddedness and the Paradigm of Economic Sociology', *Theory and Society*, 30(6): 775–810.

Kristol, William and Robert Kagan (1996) 'Toward a Neo-Reaganite Foreign Policy', *Foreign Affairs*, 75(4): 18–32.

Kurki, Milja (2008) *Causation in International Relations: Reclaiming Causal Analysis*. Cambridge: Cambridge University Press.

Lacher, Hannes (2006) *Beyond Globalization: Capitalism, Territoriality and the International Relations of Modernity*. London: Routledge.

Laffey, Mark (2004) 'The Red Herring of Economism', *Review of International Studies*, 30(3): 459–68.

Laffey, Mark and Jutta Weldes (1997) 'Beyond Belief: Ideas and Symbolic Technologies in the Study of International Relations', *European Journal of International Relations*, 3(2): 193–237.

Lamas, Andrew T., Todd Wolfson, and Peter N. Funke (eds.) (2017) *The Great Refusal: Herbert Marcuse and Contemporary Social Movements*. Philadelphia, PA: Temple University Press.

Lambert, Rob and Edward Webster (2017) 'The China Price: The All-China Federation of Trade Unions and the Repressed Question of International Labour Standards', *Globalizations*, 14(2): 313–26.

Langley, Paul (2004a) 'In the Eye of the "Perfect Storm": The Final Salary Pensions Crisis and Financialisation of Anglo-American Capitalism', *New Political Economy*, 9(4): 539–58.

Langley, Paul (2004b) '(Re)politicising Global Financial Governance: What's "New" about the "New International Financial Architecture"?', *Global Networks*, 4(1): 69–87.

Lapavitsas, Costas, A. Kaltenbrunner, G. Labrinidis, D. Lindo, J. Meadway, J. Michell, J. P. Painceira, E. Pires, J. Powell, A. Stenfors, N. Teles and L. Vatikiotis (2012) *Crisis in the Eurozone*. London: Verso.

Lapavitsas, Costas (2013) *Profiting without Producing: How Finance Exploits Us All*. London: Verso.

Laskos, Christos and Euclid Tsakalotos (2013) *Crucible of Resistance: Greece, the Eurozone and the World Economic Crisis*. London: Pluto Press.

Lavoie, Marc and Engelbert Stockhammer (2013) 'Introduction', in Marc Lavoie and Engelbert Stockhammer (eds.) *Wage-Led Growth: An Equitable Strategy for Economic Recovery*. London: Palgrave, pp. 1–12.

Lebowitz, Michael (1992/2003) *Beyond* Capital: *Marx's Political Economy of the Working Class*, second edition. London: Palgrave.

Ledwith, Sue (2006) 'The Future as Female? Gender, Diversity and Global Labour Solidarity', in Craig Phelan (ed.) *The Future of Organised Labour: Global Perspectives*. Oxford: Peter Lang, pp. 91–134.

Lee, Ching Kwan and Yonghong Zhang (2013) 'The Power of Instability: Unraveling the Microfoundations of Bargained Authoritarianism in China', *American Journal of Sociology*, 118(6): 1475–508.

Lee, Seung-Ook, Joel Wainwright and Jim Glassman (2017) 'Geopolitical Economy and the Production of Territory: The Case of U.S.–China Geopolitical–Economic Competition in Asia', *Environment and Planning A*. Online first: DOI: 10.1177/0308518X17701727.

Lefebvre, Henri (1974/1991) *The Production of Space*, trans. Donald Nicholson-Smith. Oxford: Blackwell Publishing.

Lefebvre, Henri (1975/2009) 'The State in the Modern World', in Henri Lefebvre, *State, Space, World: Selected Essays*, ed. Neil Brenner and Stuart Elden, trans. Gerald Moore. Minneapolis: University of Minnesota Press.

Lehndorff, Steffen (2015) 'Acting in Different Worlds: Challenges to Transnational Trade Union Cooperation in the Eurozone Crisis', *Transfer: European Review of Labour and Research*, 21(2): 157–70.

Lenin, V. I. (1916/1964) *Imperialism, the Highest Stage of Capitalism: A Popular Outline*, in *Collected Works*, Vol. 22, by V. I. Lenin. London: Lawrence and Wishart.

Leverett, Flynt and Wu Bingbing (2016) 'The New Silk Road and China's Evolving Grand Strategy', *The China Journal*, 77: 110–32.

Lim, Kean Fan (2017) 'Variegated Neoliberalism as a Function and Outcome of Neo-authoritarianism in China', in Burak Tansel (ed.) *States of Discipline: Authoritarian Neoliberalism and the Contested Reproduction of Capitalist Order*. London: Rowman & Littlefield International, pp. 255–73.

Lobina, Emanuele, Satoko Kishimoto and Olivier Petitjean (2014) *Here to Stay: Water Remunicipalisation as a Global Trend.* Greenwich: PSIRU. Available at www .psiru.org/sites/default/files/2014–11-W-HeretoStay.pdf; accessed 14 December 2014.

Lundborg, Tom and Nick Vaughan-Williams (2015) 'New Materialisms, Discourse Analysis and International Relations: A Radical Intertextual Analysis', *Review of International Studies*, 41(1): 3–25.

Lüthje, Boy and Florian Butollo (2017) 'Why the Foxconn Model Does Not Die: Production Networks and Labour Relations in the IT Industry in South China', *Globalizations*, 14(2): 216–31.

Luxemburg, R. (1913/2003) *The Accumulation of Capital*, trans. Agnes Schwarzschild. London: Routledge.

Malm, Andreas (2016) *Fossil Capital: The Rise of Steam Power and the Roots of Global Warming.* London: Verso.

Mandel, Ernest (1975) *Late Capitalism*, trans. Ben Fowkes. London: New Left Books.

Mandel, Ernest (1976/1990) 'Introduction', in Karl Marx, *Capital*, Volume 1, trans. Ben Fowkes. London: Penguin.

Mann, Michael (1986) *The Sources of Social Power*, Volume I: *A History of Power from the Beginning to AD 1760.* Cambridge: Cambridge University Press.

Margesson, Rhoda and Curt Tarnoff (2003) 'Iraq: Recent Developments in Humanitarian and Reconstruction Assistance (1 April 2003)', http://fpc.state .gov/documents/organization/19705.pdf; accessed 14 April 2009.

Marsden, Richard (1999) *The Nature of Capital: Marx after Foucault.* London: Routledge.

Marx, Karl (1843/1975) 'On the Jewish Question', in Karl Marx and Friedrich Engels, *Collected Works*, Vol. 3. London: Lawrence and Wishart.

Marx, Karl (1847/2010) *The Poverty of Philosophy*, in Karl Marx and Friedrich Engels, *Collected Works*, Vol. 6. London: Lawrence and Wishart.

Marx, Karl (1850/1978) *The Class Struggles in France, 1848–1850*, in Karl Marx and Friedrich Engels, *Collected Works*, Vol. 10. London: Lawrence and Wishart.

Marx, Karl (1852/1984) *The Eighteenth Brumaire of Louis Bonaparte.* London: Lawrence and Wishart.

Marx, Karl (1859/1987) *A Contribution to the Critique of Political Economy*, in Karl Marx and Friedrich Engels, *Collected Works*, Vol. 29. London: Lawrence and Wishart.

Marx, Karl (1857–8/1973) *Grundrisse: Foundations of the Critique of Political Economy*, trans. Martin Nicolaus. London: Penguin Books.

Marx, Karl (1867/1990) *Capital*, Vol. 1, intro. Ernest Mandel, trans. Ben Fowkes. London: Penguin.

Mark, Karl (1894/1991) *Capital*, Vol. 3, intro. Ernest Mandel, trans. Ben Fowkes.London: Penguin.

Marx, Karl and Friedrich Engels (1848/1998) 'Manifesto of the Communist Party', in Mark Cowling (ed.) *The Communist Manifesto: New Interpretations*. Edinburgh: Edinburgh University Press, pp. 14–37.

Matin, Kamran (2013) *Recasting Iranian Modernity: International Relations and Social Change*. London: Routledge.

Mayer, Arno J. (1981/2010) *The Persistence of the Old Regime: Europe to the Great War*. London: Verso.

Mckenzie, Lisa (2017) '"It's Not Ideal": Reconsidering "Anger" and "Apathy" in the Brexit Vote among an Invisible Working Class', *Competition & Change*. Online first: DOI: 10.1177/1024529417704134.

McMichael, Philip (1990) 'Incorporating Comparison within a World-Historical Perspective: An Alternative Comparative Method', *American Sociological Review*, 55(3): 385–97.

McMichael, Philip (2001) 'Revisiting the Question of the Transnational State: A Comment on William Robinson's "Social Theory and Globalisation"', *Theory and Society*, 30(2): 201–10.

McMichael, Philip (2012) *Development and Social Change*, fifth edition. London: Sage Publications.

McNally, David (2015) 'The Dialectics of Unity and Difference in the Constitution of Wage-Labour: On Internal Relations and Working-Class Formation', *Capital & Class*, 39(1): 131–46.

Meardi, Guglielmo (2013) *Social Failures of EU Enlargement: A Case of Workers Voting with Their Feet*. London: Routledge.

Mearsheimer, John (2006) 'China's Unpeaceful Rise', *Current History*, 105: 160–2.

Mies, Maria (1986/2014) *Patriarchy and Accumulation on a World Scale: Women in the International Division of Labour*. London: Zed Books.

Mills Wright, C. (1959) *The Sociological Imagination*. Oxford: Oxford University Press.

Mohanty, Chandra T. (2002) 'Women Workers and Capitalist Scripts: Ideologies of Domination, Common Interests, and the Politics of Solidarity', in Nancy Holmstrom (ed.) *The Socialist Feminist Project: A Contemporary Reader in Theory and Politics*. New York: Monthly Review Press, pp. 160–80.

Mohanty, Chandra T. (2003) *Feminism without Borders: Decolonizing Theory, Practicing Solidarity*. Durham, NC: Duke University Press.

Moore, Jr., Barrington (1958) *Political Power and Social Theory: Seven Studies*. New York: Harper & Row Publishers.

Moore, Jr., Barrington (1967/1993) *Social Origins of Dictatorship and Democracy: Lord and Peasant in the Making of the Modern World*, foreword by Edward Friedman and James C. Scott. Boston, MA: Beacon Press.

Moore, Jason W. (2015) *Capitalism in the Web of Life: Ecology and the Accumulation of Capital*. London: Verso.

Moore, Madelaine (2017) 'Common Ground: Applying Social Reproduction Feminism to the Study of Contemporary Social Movements'. Paper presented at the European Sociological Association conference '(Un)Making Europe: Capitalism, Solidarities, Subjectivities'; Athens/Greece (29 August–1 September).

Morgenthau, Hans J. (1946) *Scientific Man vs. Power Politics*. Chicago: University of Chicago Press.

Morgenthau, Hans J. (1966) *Politics among Nations: The Struggle for Power and Peace*, Third edition. New York: Alfred A. Knopf.

Morton, Adam David (2002) '"La Resurrección del Maíz": Globalisation, Resistance and the Zapatistas', *Millennium: Journal of International Studies*, 31(1): 27–54.

Morton, Adam David (2005) 'The Age of Absolutism: Capitalism, the Modern States-System and International Relations', *Review of International Studies*, 31(3): 495–517.

Morton, Adam David (2006) 'The Grimly Comic Riddle of Hegemony in IPE: Where Is Class Struggle?', *Politics*, 26(1): 62–72.

Morton, Adam David (2007a) *Unravelling Gramsci: Hegemony and Passive Revolution in the Global Political Economy*. London: Pluto Press.

Morton, Adam David (2007b) 'Waiting for Gramsci: State Formation, Passive Revolution and the International', *Millennium: Journal of International Studies*, 35(3): 597–621.

Morton, Adam David (2007c) 'Disputing the Geopolitics of the States System and Global Capitalism', *Cambridge Review of International Affairs*, 20(4): 599–617.

Morton, Adam David (2010a) 'The Continuum of Passive Revolution', *Capital & Class*, 34(3): 315–42.

Morton, Adam David (2010b) 'The Geopolitics of Passive Revolution', in Alexander Anievas (ed.) *Marxism and World Politics: Contesting Global Capitalism*. London: Routledge, pp. 215–30.

Morton, Adam David (2011/2013) *Revolution and State in Modern Mexico: The Political Economy of Uneven Development*, updated edition. Lanham, MD: Rowman & Littlefield.

Morton, Adam David (2013) 'The Limits of Sociological Marxism?', *Historical Materialism*, 21(1): 129–58.

Morton, Adam David (2015) 'The Warp of the World: Geographies of Space and Time in the Border Trilogy by Cormac McCarthy', *Environment and Planning D*, 33(5): 831–49.

Morton, Adam David (2017a) *Revolución y Estado en el México moderno: La economía política del desarrollo desigual*. México, D.F.: Siglo XXI.

Morton, Adam David (2017b) 'The Architecture of Passive Revolution: Society, State and Space in Modern Mexico', *Journal of Latin American Studies*, 50(1): 117–52.

Morton, Adam David (2017c) 'Spatial Political Economy', *Journal of Australian Political Economy*, 79 (Winter): 21–38.

Munck, Ronaldo (2013) *Rethinking Latin America: Development, Hegemony and Social Transformation*. London: Palgrave.

Murray, Andrew and Lindsey German (2005) *Stop the War: The Story of Britain's Biggest Mass Movement*. London: Bookmarks.

National Intelligence Council (2004) 'Mapping the Global Future: Report of the National Intelligence Council's 2020 Project', www.foia.cia.gov/2020/2020 .pdf; accessed 4 January 2009.

National Security Council (2002) 'The National Security Strategy of the United States of America', www.whitehouse.gov/nsc/nss/2002/nss.pdf; accessed 4 January 2009.

Ness, Immanuel (2015) *Southern Insurgency: The Coming of the Global Working Class*. London: Pluto Press.

Neufeld, Mark A. (1995) *The Restructuring of International Relations Theory*. Cambridge: Cambridge University Press.

Nilsen, Alf Gunvald (2009) '"The Authors and the Actors of Their Own Drama": Towards a Marxist Theory of Social Movements', *Capital & Class*, 99: 109–39.

Nilsen, Alf Gunvald (2010) *Dispossession and Resistance in India: The River and the Rage*. London: Routledge.

Nilsen, Alf Gunvald and Laurence Cox (2013) 'What Would a Marxist Theory of Social Movements Look Like?', in Colin Barker, Laurence Cox, John Krinsky and Alf Gunvald Nilsen (eds.) *Marxism and Social Movements*. Leiden: Brill, pp. 63–81.

Nişancıoğlu, Kerem (2013) 'The Ottoman Origins of Capitalism: Uneven and Combined Development and Eurocentrism', *Review of International Studies*, 40(2): 325–47.

Nitzan, Jonathan and Shimshon Bichler (2002) *The Global Political Economy of Israel*. London: Pluto Press.

Nitzan, Jonathan and Shimshon Bichler (2004) 'Dominant Capital and the New Wars', *Journal of World-Systems Research*, 10(2): 255–327.

Nowak, Jörg (2015) 'Mass Strikes in Brazil, South Africa and India after 2008', in Andreas Bieler et al., (eds.) *Labour and Transnational Action in Times of Crisis*. London: Rowman & Littlefield International, pp. 53–68.

Nowak, Jörg (2016) 'The Spatial Patterns of Mass Strikes: A Labour Geography Approach', *Geoforum*, 75: 270–3.

Nye, Joseph S. (2010) 'American and Chinese Power after the Financial Crisis', *The Washington Quarterly*, 33(4): 143–53.

Ó Tuathail, Gearóid and John Agnew (1992) 'Geopolitics and Discourse: Practical Geopolitical Reasoning in American Foreign Policy', *Political Geography*, 11(2): 190–204.

Ó Tuathail, Gearóid, Simon Dalby and Paul Routledge (1998) *The Geopolitics Reader*. London: Routledge.

Ó'Beacháin, Donnacha, Vera Sheridan and Sabina Stan (2012) (eds.) *Life in Post-communist Eastern Europe after EU Membership: Happy Ever After?* London: Routledge.

Oberndorfer, Lukas (2015) 'From New Constitutionalism to Authoritarian Constitutionalism: New Economic Governance and the State of European Democracy', in Johannes Jäger and Elisabeth Springler (eds.) *Asymmetric Crisis in Europe and Possible Futures: Critical Political Economy and post-Keynesian Perspectives*. London: Routledge, pp. 186–207.

OECD Employment Outlook (2016) 'OECD Employment Outlook 2016', www .oecd-ilibrary.org/employment/oecd-employment-outlook_19991266; accessed 7 September 2016.

OECD/WTO. (2014) 'Trade in Value-Added (TIVA) Indicators', www.oecd.org/i ndustry/ind/measuringtradeinvalue-addedanoecd-wtojointinitiative.htm; accessed 21 March 2014.

Ohmae, Kenichi (1990). *The Borderless World: Power and Strategy in the Interlinked Economy*. London: Harper Collins.

Ohmae, Kenichi (1995) *The End of the Nation State: The Rise of Regional Economies*. London: Harper Collins.

Ollman, Bertell (1976) *Alienation: Marx's Conception of Man in Capitalist Society*, second edition. Cambridge: Cambridge University Press.

Ollman, Bertell (2003) *Dance of the Dialectic: Steps in Marx's Method*. Chicago: University of Illinois Press.

Ollman, Bertell (2014) 'Dialectics and World Politics', *Globalizations*, 11(5): 573–9.

Ollman, Bertell (2015) 'Marxism and the Philosophy of Internal Relations; or, How to Replace the Mysterious "Paradox" with "Contradictions" That Can Be Studied and Resolved', *Capital & Class*, 39(1): 7–23.

Overbeek, Henk and Bastiaan van Apeldoorn (eds.) (2012) *Neoliberalism in Crisis*. London: Palgrave.

Palan, Ronan (2000) 'A World of Their Making: An Evaluation of the Constructivist Critique in International Relations', *Review of International Studies*, 26(4): 575–98.

Paley, Dawn (2014) *Drug War Capitalism*. Oakland, CA: AK Press.

Panitch, Leo (1994) 'Globalisation and the State', in Ralph Miliband and Leo Panitch (eds.) *The Socialist Register: Between Globalism and Nationalism*. London: Merlin Press, pp. 60–93.

Panitch, Leo (2000) 'The New Imperial State', *New Left Review* (II), 2: 5–20.

Panitch, Leo and Sam Gindin (2003) 'Global Capitalism and American Empire', in Leo Panitch and Colin Leys (eds.) *The Socialist Register: The New Imperial Challenge*. London: Merlin Press, pp. 1–42.

Panitch, Leo and Sam Gindin (2005a) 'Finance and American Empire', in Leo Panitch and Colin Leys (eds.) *The Socialist Register: The Empire Reloaded*. London: Merlin Press, pp. 46–81.

Panitch, Leo and Sam Gindin (2005b) 'Superintending Global Capital', *New Left Review* (II), 35: 101–23.

Panitch, Leo and Sam Gindin (2012) *The Making of Global Capitalism: The Political Economy of American Empire*. London: Verso.

Panitch, Leo and Sam Gindin (2014) 'The Integration of China into Global Capitalism', *International Critical Thought*, 3(2): 146–58.

Pareto, Vilfredo (1902) *Les systèmes socialistes*. Paris: V. Giard & E. Brière.

Patomäki, Heikki (2012) *The Great Eurozone Disaster: From Crisis to Global New Deal*. London: Zed Books.

Paul, Darel E. (2007) 'The Siren Song of Geopolitics: Towards a Gramscian Account of the Iraq War', *Millennium: Journal of International Studies*, 36(1): 51–76.

Peck, Jamie (2010) *Constructions of Neoliberal Reason*. Oxford: Oxford University Press.

Peck, Jamie and Jun Zhang (2013) 'A Variety of Capitalism ... with Chinese Characteristics?', *Journal of Economic Geography*, 13(3): 357–96.

Però, Davide (2014) 'Class Politics and Migrants: Collective Action among New Migrant Workers in Britain', *Sociology*, 48(6): 1156–72.

Persram, Nalini (1999) 'Coda: Sovereignty, Subjectivity, Strategy', in Jenny Edkins, Nalini Persram and Véronique Pin-Fat (eds.) *Sovereignty and Subjectivity*. Boulder, CO: Lynne Rienner, pp. 163–75.

Petras, James (2008) 'Social Movements and Alliance-Building in Latin America', *Journal of Peasant Studies*, 35(3): 476–528.

Petras, James (2015) 'u.s.–China Relations: the Pentagon versus High Tech', *Latin American Perspectives*: Political Report #1081; available at http://laperspec tives.blogspot.co.uk/2015/10/political-report-1081-us-china.html; accessed 3 March 2016.

Petras, James and Henry Veltmeyer (2007) 'The "Development State" in Latin America: Whose Development, Whose State?', *Journal of Peasant Studies*, 34(3): 371–407.

Phillips, Nicola (2005) 'State Debates in International Political Economy', in Nicola Phillips (ed.) *Globalizing International Political Economy*. London: Palgrave.

van der Pijl, Kees (1984) *The Making of an Atlantic Ruling Class*. London: Verso.

van der Pijl, Kees (1998) *Transnational Classes and International Relations*. London: Routledge.

van der Pijl, Kees (2011), 'Arab Revolts and Nation-State Crisis', *New Left Review* (II), 70: 27–49.

van der Pijl, Kees (2015) 'The Uneven and Combined Development of International Historical Sociology', in Radhika Desai (ed.) *Theoretical Engagements in Geopolitical Economy*. Bingley: Emerald Group Publishing, Ltd., pp. 45–83.

Pine, Álvaro and Ildeberta Abreu (2012) 'Portugal: Rebalancing the Economy and Returning to Growth through Job Creation and Better Capital Allocation'. *OECD Economics Department Working Papers*, No. 994, OECD Publishing, http://dx.doi.org/10.1787/5k918xjjzs9q-en; accessed on 27 June 2013.

Polanyi, Karl (1944/1957) *The Great Transformation: The Political and Economic Origins of Our Time*. Boston, MA: Beacon Press.

Polanyi, Karl (1953/1959) 'Anthropology and Economic Theory', in Morton H. Fried (ed.) *Readings in Anthropology*, Volume II: *Readings in Cultural Anthropology*. New York: Thomas Y. Cromwell, pp. 161–84.

Politi, Daniel and André Verlöy (2003) 'Advisors of Influence: Nine Members of the Defense Policy Board Have Ties to Defense Contractors' (28 March), www .publicintegrity.org/2003/03/28/3157/advisors-influence-nine-members-defen se-policy-board-have-ties-defense-contractors; accessed 11 January 2018.

Poulantzas, Nicos (1976) *The Crisis of the Dictatorships: Portugal, Greece, Spain*, trans. David Fernbach. London: Verso.

Poulantzas, Nicos (1969) 'The Problem of the Capitalist State', *New Left Review* (I), 58: 67–78.

Poulantzas, Nicos (1973) *Political Power and Social Classes*, trans. T. O'Hagan. London: New Left Books.

Poulantzas, Nicos (1974/2008) 'Internationalisation of Capitalist Relations and the Nation-State', in James Martin (ed.) *The Poulantzas Reader: Marxism, Law, and the State*. London: Verso, pp. 220–57.

Poulantzas, Nicos (1975) *Classes in Contemporary Capitalism*, trans. D. Fernbach. London: New Left Books.

Poulantzas, Nicos (1978) *State, Power, Socialism*, trans. Patrick Camiller. London: Verso.

Pozo-Martin, Gonzalo (2006) 'A Tougher Gordian Knot: Globalisation, Imperialism and the Problem of the State', *Cambridge Review of International Affairs*, 19(2): 223–42.

Pradella, Lucia (2014) 'New Developmentalism and the Origins of Methodological Nationalism', *Competition & Change*, 18(2): 180–93.

Price, Richard and Christian Reus-Smit (1998) 'Dangerous Liaisons? Critical International Theory and Constructivism', *European Journal of International Relations*, 4(3): 259–94.

Pringle, Tim (2013) 'Reflections on Labour in China: From a Moment to a Movement', *The South Atlantic Quarterly*, 112(1): 191–202.

Pringle, Tim (2015) 'Labour under Threat: The Rise and (Possible) Fall of "Collective Bargaining" in South China', *International Union Rights*, 22(4): 3–5.

Pringle, Tim (2017) 'A Class against Capital: Class and Collective Bargaining in Guangdong', *Globalizations*, 14(2): 245–58.

Project for the New American Century (1997a) 'About PNAC', www.newamericancentury.org/aboutpnac.htm; accessed 14 April 2009.

Project for the New American Century (1997b) 'Statement of Principles', www.newamericancentury.org/statementofprinciples.htm; accessed 14 April 2009.

Qi, Hao (2014) 'The Labor Share Question in China', *Monthly Review*, 65(8): 23–35.

Quaglia, Lucia (2011) 'The "Old" and "New" Political Economy of Hedge Fund Regulation in the European Union', *West European Politics*, 34(4): 665–82.

Radcliffe, Sarah A. (2007) 'Geographies of Modernity in Latin America: Uneven and Contested Development' in Nicola Miller and Stephen Hart (eds.) *When Was Latin America Modern?* London: Palgrave, pp. 21–48.

Radice, Hugo (2014) 'Enforcing Austerity in Europe: The Structural Deficit as a Policy Target', *Journal of Contemporary European Studies*, 22(3): 318–28.

Radice, Hugo (2015) 'After the Crisis: Global Capitalism and the Critique of Political Economy', *Spectrum: Journal of Global Studies*, 7(1): 32–40.

Resnick, Stephen A. and Richard D. Wolff (1987) *Knowledge and Class: A Marxian Critique of Political Economy*. Chicago: University of Chicago Press.

Resnick, Stephen A. and Richard D. Wolff (2006) *New Departures in Marxian Theory*. London: Routledge.

Retort (2005) *Afflicted Powers: Capital and Spectacle in a New Age of War*. London: Verso.

Rioux, Sébastien (2013) 'The Fiction of Economic Coercion: Political Marxism and the Separation of Theory and History', *Historical Materialism*, 21(4): 92–128.

Rioux, Sébastien (2015) 'Mind the (Theoretical) Gap: On the Poverty of International Relations Theorising of Uneven and Combined Development', *Global Society*, 29(4): 481–509.

Roberts, Philip (2015) 'Passive Revolution in Brazil: Struggles over Hegemony, Religion and Development', *Third World Quarterly*, 36(9): 1663–81.

Robinson, William I. (1996) *Promoting Polyarchy: Globalization, U.S. Intervention and Hegemony*. Cambridge: Cambridge University Press.

Robinson, William I. (2001a) 'Social Theory and Globalisation: The Rise of a Transnational State', *Theory and Society*, 30(2): 157–200.

Robinson, William I. (2001b) 'Transnational Processes, Development Studies and Changing Social Hierarchies in the World System: A Central American Case Study', *Third World Quarterly*, 22(4): 529–63.

Robinson, William I. (2003) *Transnational Conflicts: Central America, Social Change and Globalisation*. London: Verso.

Robinson, William I. (2004) *A Theory of Global Capitalism: Production, Class, and State in a Transnational World*. Baltimore, MD: John Hopkins University Press.

Robinson, William I. (2007a) 'The Pitfalls of Realist Analysis of Global Capitalism: A Critique of Ellen Meiksins Wood's *Empire of Capital*', *Historical Materialism*, 15(3): 71–93.

Robinson, William I. (2007b) 'Transformative Possibilities in Latin America', in Leo Panitch and Colin Leys (eds.) *The Socialist Register: Global Flashpoints – Reactions to Imperialism and Neoliberalism*. London: Merlin Press, pp. 141–59.

Robinson, William I. (2008) *Latin America and Global Capitalism: A Critical Globalisation Perspective*. Baltimore, MD: Johns Hopkins University Press.

Robinson, William I. (2012) '"The Great Recession" of 2008 and the Continuing Crisis: A Global Capitalism Perspective', *International Review of Modern Sociology*, 38(2): 169–98.

Robinson, William I. (2011) 'Globalisation and the Sociology of Immanuel Wallerstein: A Critical Appraisal', *International Sociology*, 26(6): 723–45.

Robinson, William I. (2014) *Global Capitalism and the Crisis of Humanity*. Cambridge: Cambridge University Press.

Robinson, William I. (2015) 'The Transnational State and the BRICS: A Global Capitalism Perspective', *Third World Quarterly*, 36(1): 1–21.

Robinson, William I. and Jerry Harris (2000) 'Towards a Global Ruling Class? Globalisation and the Transnational Capitalist Class', *Science & Society*, 64(1): 11–54.

Rodrigues, João and José Reis (2012) 'The Asymmetries of European Integration and the Crisis of Capitalism in Portugal', *Competition & Change*, 16(3): 188–205.

Rogers, Chris (2009) 'From Social Contract to Social Contrick: The Depoliticisation of Economic Policy-Making under Harold Wilson, 1974–75', *British Journal of Politics and International Relations*, 11(4): 634–51.

Rogers, Chris (2013) '"Hang on a Minute, I've Got a Great Idea": From the Third Way to Mutual Advantage in the Political Economy of the British Labour Party', *British Journal of Politics and International Relations*, 15(1): 53–69.

Romagnolo, David J. (1975) 'The So-Called "Law" of Uneven and Combined Development', *Latin American Perspectives*, 1(2): 7–31.

Rosenberg, Justin (1994) *The Empire of Civil Society: A Critique of the Realist Theory of International Relations*. London: Verso.

Rosenberg, Justin (2000) *The Follies of Globalisation Theory*. London: Verso.

Rosenberg, Justin (2006) 'Why Is There No International Historical Sociology?', *European Journal of International Relations*, 12(3): 307–40.

Rosenberg, Justin (2013a) 'Kenneth Waltz and Leon Trotsky: Anarchy in the Mirror of Uneven and Combined Development', *International Politics*, 50(2): 183–230.

Rosenberg, Justin (2013b) 'The "Philosophical Premises" of Uneven and Combined Development, *Review of International Studies*, 39(3): 569–97.

Roth, Felix, Daniel Gros and Felicitas Nowak-Lehmann D. (2014) 'Crisis and Citizens' Trust in the European Central Bank – Panel Data Evidence for the Euro Area, 1999–2012', *Journal of European Integration*, 36(3): 303–20.

Ruccio, David F. (2009) 'Rethinking Gramsci: Class, Globalisation and Historical Bloc', in Joseph Francese (ed.) *Perspectives on Gramsci: Politics, Culture and Social Theory*. London: Routledge, pp. 145–62.

Ruccio, David F. (2011) *Development and Globalization: A Marxian Class Analysis*. London: Routledge.

Ruggie, John G. (1982) 'International Regimes, Transactions and Change: Embedded Liberalism in the Postwar Economic Order', *International Organization*, 36(2): 379–415.

Ruggie, John G. (1983) 'Continuity and Transformation in the World Polity: Toward a Neorealist Synthesis', *World Politics*, 35(2): 261–85.

Ruggie, John G. (1993) 'Territoriality and Beyond: Problematising Modernity in International Relations', *International Organization*, 47(1): 139–74.

Ruggie, John G. (1998) *Constructing the World Polity: Essays on International Institutionalisation*. London: Routledge.

Rupert, Mark (1995) *Producing Hegemony: The Politics of Mass Production and American Global Power*. Cambridge: Cambridge University Press.

Rupert, Mark (2000) *Ideologies of Globalization: Contending Visions of a New World Order*. London: Routledge.

Ryan, Matthew (2017) '"Authoritarian Neoliberalism": Crisis, the State and the Challenge of Periodisation', MPhil thesis, Department of Political Economy, The University of Sydney.

Ryner, Magnus (2015) 'Europe's Ordoliberal Iron Cage: Critical Political Economy, the Euro Area Crisis and Its Management', *Journal of European Public Policy*, 22(2): 275–94.

Ryner, Magnus and Alan Cafruny (2016) *The European Union and Global Capitalism: Origins, Development, Crisis*. London: Palgrave.

Saad-Filho, Alfredo (2014) 'The "Rise of the South": Global Convergence at Last?', *New Political Economy*, 19(4): 578–600.

Sacchetto, Devi (2007) 'Isolani dell'arcipelago. Delocalizzatori e forza lavoro in Romania', in Feruccio Gambino and Devi Sacchetto (eds.) *Un arcipelago produttivo. Migranti e imprenditori tra Italia e Romania*. Roma: Carocci, pp. 133–70.

Sacom (2012) 'Open Letter to the Guangdong Government'; available at http://sacom.hk/archives/953; accessed 11 January 2018.

Sahoo, Sarbeswara (2012) 'Organizing Informal Women Workers for Green Livelihoods: The Self Employed Women's Association in Gujarat', in

Sarah Mosoetsa and Michelle Williams (eds.) *Labour in the Global South: Challenges and Alternatives for Workers.* Geneva: International Labor Organization, pp. 181–99.

Salleh, Ariel (2003) 'Ecofeminism as Sociology', *Capitalism, Nature, Socialism,* 14(1): 61–74.

Salleh, Ariel (1997/2017) *Ecofeminism as Politics: Nature, Marx and the Postmodern,* second edition. London: Zed Books.

Sassoon, Anne S. (1987) *Gramsci's Politics,* second edition. Minneapolis: University of Minnesota Press.

Saull, Richard (2012) 'Rethinking Hegemony: Uneven Development, Historical Blocs, and the World Economic Crisis', *International Studies Quarterly,* 56(2): 323–38.

Sayer, Derek (1985) 'The Critique of Politics and Political Economy: Capitalism, Communism and the State in Marx's Writings of the mid-1840s', *Sociological Review,* 33(2): 221–53.

Sayer, Derek (1987) *The Violence of Abstraction: The Analytic Foundations of Historical Materialism.* London: Basil Blackwell.

Sayer, Derek and Philip Corrigan (1983) 'Late Marx: Continuity, Contradiction and Learning', in Theodor Shanin (ed.) *Late Marx and the Russian Road: Marx and 'the Peripheries of Capitalism'.* New York: Monthly Review Press, pp. 77–93.

Schimmelfennig, Frank (2014) 'European Integration in the Euro Crisis: The Limits of Postfunctionalism', *Journal of European Integration,* 36(3): 321–37.

Schmalz, Stefan and Matthias Ebenau (2012) 'After Neoliberalism? Brazil, India, and China in the Global Economic Crisis', *Globalizations,* 9(4): 487–501.

Schmalz, Stefan, Brandon Sommer and Hui Xu (2017) 'The Yue Yuen Strike: Industrial Transformation and Labour Unrest in the Pearl River Delta', *Globalizations,* 14(2): 285–97.

Sennett, Richard (1977/2002) *The Fall of Public Man.* London: Penguin.

Shanin, Theodor (1983) 'Late Marx: Gods and Craftsmen', in Theodor Shanin (ed.) *Late Marx and the Russian Road: Marx and 'the Peripheries of Capitalism'.* New York: Monthly Review Press, pp. 3–39.

Shields, Stuart (2012) *The International Political Economy of Transition: Neoliberal Hegemony and Eastern Central Europe's Transformation.* London: Routledge.

Siles-Brügge, Gabriel (2014) 'Explaining the Resilience of Free Trade: The Smoot-Hawley Myth and the Crisis', *Review of International Political Economy,* 21(3): 535–74.

Silver, Beverly J. (2003) *Forces of Labor: Workers' Movements and Globalisation since 1870.* Cambridge: Cambridge University Press.

Simonazzi, Annamaria, Andreas Ginzburg and Gianluigi Nocella (2013) 'Economic Relations between Germany and Southern Europe', *Cambridge Journal of Economics,* 37(3): 653–75.

Sklair, Leslie (2001) *The Transnational Capitalist Class.* Oxford: Wiley.

Skocpol, Theda (1977) 'Wallerstein's World Capitalist System: A Theoretical and Historical Critique', *American Journal of Sociology,* 82(5): 1075–90.

Skocpol, Theda (1979) *States and Social Revolutions: A Comparative Analysis of France and Russia.* Cambridge: Cambridge University Press.

Smith, John (2012) 'The GDP Illusion: Value Added versus Value Capture', *Monthly Review*, 64(3): 86–102.

Smith, John (2016) *Imperialism in the Twenty-First Century: Globalization, Super-Exploitation and Capitalism's Final Crisis*. New York: Monthly Review Press.

Smith, Neil (1984/2008) *Uneven Development: Nature, Capital and the Production of Space*, third edition. Athens: University of Georgia Press.

Smith, Neil (2000) 'What Happened to Class?', *Environment and Planning A*, 32(6): 1011–32.

Smith, Neil (2004) 'The Geography of Uneven Development', in Bill Dunn and Hugo Radice (eds.) *100 Years of Permanent Revolution: Results and Prospects*. London: Pluto Press, pp. 180–95.

Smith, Steve (1995) 'The Self-Images of a Discipline: A Genealogy of International Relations Theory', in Ken Booth and Steve Smith (eds.) *International Relations Theory Today*. Cambridge: Polity Press, pp. 1–37.

Smith, Steve (1996) 'Positivism and Beyond', in Steve Smith, Ken Booth and Marysia Zalewski (eds.) *International Theory: Positivism and Beyond*. Cambridge: Cambridge University Press, pp. 11–44.

Soederberg, Susanne (2014) *Debtfare States and the Poverty Industry: Money, Discipline and the Surplus Population*. London: Routledge.

Sotirakopoulos, Nikos and George Sotiropoulos (2013) '"Direct Democracy Now!": The Greek *Indignados* and the Present Cycle of Struggles', *Current Sociology*, 61(4): 443–56.

Sotiris, Panagiotis (2017) 'The Authoritarian and Disciplinary Mechanism of Reduced Sovereignty in the EU: The Case of Greece', in Cemal Burak Tansel (ed.) *States of Discipline: Authoritarian Neoliberalism and the Contested Reproduction of Capitalist Order*. London: Rowman & Littlefield International, pp. 171–87.

Spivak, Gayatri (1987/2006) *In Other Worlds: Essays in Cultural Politics*. London: Routledge.

Stan, Sabina and Roland Erne (2014) 'Explaining Romanian Labor Migration: From Development Gaps to Development Trajectories', *Labor History*, 55(1): 21–46.

Standing, Guy (2011) *The Precariat: The New Dangerous Class*. London: Bloomsbury Academic.

Steinfort, Lavinia (2014) 'Thessaloniki, Greece: Struggling against Water Privatisation in Times of Crisis', *Water Justice* (3 June), Amsterdam: Transnational Institute. Available at www.tni.org/article/thessaloniki-greece-struggling-against-water-privatisation-times-crisis; accessed 11 January 2015.

Stephen, Matthew D. (2014) 'Rising Powers, Global Capitalism and Liberal Global Governance: A Historical Materialist Account of the BRICs Challenge', *European Journal of International Relations*, 20(4): 912–38.

Stockhammer, Engelbert (2011) 'Peripheral Europe's Debt and German Wages. The Role of Wage Policy in the Euro Area', *Research on Money and Finance, Discussion Paper*, 29; available at www.boeckler.de/pdf/v_2011_10_27_stock hammer.pdf; accessed 7 June 2016.

Strange, Susan (1988) *States and Markets*, second edition. London: Pinter Publishers.

Strange, Susan (1996) *The Retreat of the State: The Diffusion of Power in the World Economy*. Cambridge: Cambridge University Press.

Ste. Croix, G. E. M. de (1981) *The Class Struggle in the Ancient Greek World from the Archaic Age to the Arab Conquests*. London: Duckworth.

Stewart, Paul et al., (2009) 'Introduction', in Jo McBride and Ian Greenwood (eds.) *Community Unionism: A Comparative Analysis of Concepts and Contexts*. London: Palgrave, pp. 13–20.

Stockhammer, Engelbert (2013) 'Why Have Wage Shares Fallen? An Analysis of the Determinants of Functional Income Distribution', in Marc Lavoie and Engelbert Stockhammer (eds.) *Wage-Led Growth: An Equitable Strategy for Economic Recovery*. London: Palgrave, pp. 40–70.

Stockhammer, Engelbert (2016) 'Neoliberal Growth Models, Monetary Union and the Euro Crisis: A Post-Keynesian Perspective', *New Political Economy*, 21(4): 365–79.

Stockhammer, Engelbert and Karsten Köhler (2015) 'Linking a Post-Keynesian Approach to Critical Political Economy: Debt-Driven Growth, Export-Driven Growth and the Crisis in Europe', in Johannes Jäger and Elisabeth Springler (eds.) *Asymmetric Crisis in Europe and Possible Futures: Critical Political Economy and Post-Keynesian Perspectives*. London: Routledge, pp. 34–49.

Stokes, Doug (2005) 'The Heart of Empire? Theorising U.S. Empire in an Era of Transnational Capitalism', *Third World Quarterly*, 26(2): 217–36.

Stokes, Doug and Sam Raphael (2010) *Global Energy Security and American Hegemony*. Baltimore, MD: Johns Hopkins University Press.

Struna, Jason (ed.) (2015) *Global Capitalism and Transnational Class Formation*. London: Routledge.

Sturn, Simon and Till van Treeck (2013) 'The Role of Income Inequality as a Cause of the Great Recession and Global Imbalances', in Marc Lavoie and Engelbert Stockhammer (eds.) *Wage-Led Growth: An Equitable Strategy for Economic Recovery*. London: Palgrave, pp. 125–52.

Suganami, Hidemi (1999) 'Agents, Structures, Narratives', *European Journal of International Relations* 5(3): 365–86.

Sum, Ngai-Ling (2017) 'The Makings of Subaltern Subjects: Embodiment, Contradictory Consciousness, and Re-hegemonisation of the Diaosi in China', *Globalizations*, 14(2): 298–312.

Sum, Ngai-Ling and Bob Jessop (2013) *Towards a Cultural Political Economy: Putting Culture in Its Place in Political Economy*. Cheltenham: Edward Elgar.

Sutton, Alex (2015) *The Political Economy of Imperial Relations: Britain, the Sterling Area and Malaya, 1945–1960*. London: Palgrave.

Tansel, Cemal Burak (2015a) 'State Formation and Social Change in Modern Turkey', PhD thesis, University of Nottingham.

Tansel, Cemal Burak (2015b) 'Deafening Silence? Marxism, International Historical Sociology and the Spectre of Eurocentrism', *European Journal of International Relations*, 21(1): 76–100.

Tansel, Cemal Burak (2016) 'Geopolitics, Social Forces and the International: Revisiting the "Eastern Question"', *Review of International Studies*, 42(3): 492–512.

Tansel, Cemal Burak (ed.) (2017a) *States of Discipline: Authoritarian Neoliberalism and the Contested Reproduction of Capitalist Order*. London: Rowman & Littlefield International.

Tansel, Cemal Burak (2017b) 'Authoritarian Neoliberalism: Towards a New Research Agenda', in Cemal Burak Tansel (ed.) *States of Discipline: Authoritarian Neoliberalism and the Contested Reproduction of Capitalist Order*. London: Rowman & Littlefield International, pp. 1–28.

Tattersall, Amanda (2009) 'Using Their Sword of Justice: The NSW Teachers Federation and Its Campaigns for Public Education between 2001 and 2004', in Jo McBride and Ian Greenwood (eds.) *Community Unionism: A Comparative Analysis of Concepts and Contexts*. London: Palgrave, pp. 161–86.

Taylor, Cliff (2016) 'Ireland's GDP Figures: Why 26% Economic Growth Is a Problem', *The Irish Times* (15 July 2016); available at www.irishtimes .com/business/economy/ireland-s-gdp-figures-why-26-economic-growth-is-a-problem-1.2722170; accessed 22 December 2016.

Taylor, Ian (2017) *Global Governance and Transnationalizing Capitalist Hegemony: The Myth of the 'Emerging Powers'*. London: Routledge.

Tepe-Belfrage, Daniela and Johnna Montgomerie (2016) 'Broken Britain: Post-crisis Austerity and the Trouble with the Troubled Families Programme', in Aida A. Hozić and Jacqui True (eds.) *Scandalous Economics: Gender and the Politics of Financial Crises*. Oxford: Oxford University Press, pp. 79–91.

Teschke, Benno (1998) 'Geopolitical Relations in the European Middle Ages: History and Theory', *International Organization*, 52(2): 325–58.

Teschke, Benno (2003) *The Myth of 1648: Class, Geopolitics and the Making of Modern International Relations*. London: Verso.

Teschke, Benno and Can Cemgil (2014) 'The Dialectic of the Concrete: Reconsidering Dialectic for IR and Foreign Policy Analysis', *Globalizations*, 11(5): 605–25.

Teschke, Benno and Hannes Lacher (2007) 'The Changing "Logics" of Capitalist Competition', *Cambridge Review of International Affairs*, 20(4): 565–80.

Therborn, Göran (2017) *Cities of Power: The Urban, the National, the Popular, the Global*. London: Verso.

Thomas, Peter D. (2009) *The Gramscian Moment: Philosophy, Hegemony and Marxism*. Leiden: Brill.

Thomas, Peter D. (2013) 'Hegemony, Passive Revolution and the Modern Prince', *Thesis Eleven*, 117(1): 20–39.

Thompson, E. P. (1968) *The Making of the English Working Class*. London: Penguin.

Thompson, E. P. (1975) *Whigs and Hunters: The Origin of the Black Act*. London: Penguin.

Thompson, E. P. (1978) 'Eighteenth-Century English Society: Class Struggle without Class?', *Social History*, 3(2): 133–65.

Tosun, Jale, Anne Wetzel and Galina Zapryanova (2014) 'The EU in Crisis: Advancing the Debate', *Journal of European Integration*, 36(3): 195–211.

Trading Economics (2013a) 'Germany Balance of Trade'. www .tradingeconomics.com/germany/balance-of-trade; accessed 10 May 2013.

Trading Economics (2013b) 'Greece Exports'. www.tradingeconomics.com/gre ece/exports; accessed 30 August 2013.

Trotsky, Leon (1906/2007) 'Results and Prospects', in L. Trotsky, *The Permanent Revolution and Results and Prospects*, intro. M. Löwy. London: Socialist Resistance, pp. 24–100.

Trotsky, Leon (1928/1970) *The Third International after Lenin*. New York: Pathfinder Press.

Trotsky, Leon (1929/2007) 'The Permanent Revolution', in L. Trotsky, *The Permanent Revolution and Results and Prospects*, intro. M. Löwy. London: Socialist Resistance, pp. 111–256.

Trotsky, Leon (1936/1980) *The History of the Russian Revolution*, 3 volumes. New York: Pathfinder Press.

True, Jacqui (2016) 'The Global Financial Crisis's Silver Bullet: Women Leaders and "Leaning In"', in Aida Hozić and Jacqui True (eds.) *Scandalous Economics: Gender and the Politics of Financial Crisis*. Oxford: Oxford University Press, pp. 41–56.

Tsai, Frederick (2008) 'The False Binary Choice between Multilateralism and Unilateralism', *SAIS Review of International Affairs*, 28(2): 45–8.

Tsolakis, Andreas (2010) 'Opening Up Open Marxist Theories of the State: A Historical Materialist Critique', *British Journal of Politics and International Relations*, 12(3): 387–407.

UNCTAD (2001) *World Investment Report 2001: Promoting Linkages*. New York: United Nations.

UNCTAD (2008) *World Investment Report 2008: Transnational Corporations and the Infrastructure Challenge*. Geneva/New York: United Nations. Available at http://unctad.org/en/Docs/wir2008_en.pdf; accessed 18 December 2014.

UNCTAD (2009) *World Investment Report 2009: Transnational Corporations, Agricultural Production and Development*. New York: United Nations.

UNCTAD (2013) *Global Value Chains: Investment and Trade for Development. World Investment Report 2013*. New York/Geneva: United Nations. Available at http://u nctad.org/en/PublicationsLibrary/wir2013_en.pdf; accessed 18 December 2014.

UNCTAD (2014) *Bilateral FDI Statistics 2014*. Geneva: UNCTAD; available at http://unctad.org/en/Pages/DIAE/FDI%20Statistics/FDI-Statistics-Bilateral .aspx; accessed 10 June 2014.

UNCTAD (2017) *Investment and the Digital Economy. World Investment Report 2017*. New York/Geneva: United Nations. Available at http://unctad.org/en/ PublicationsLibrary/wir2017_en.pdf; accessed 27 June 2017.

Underhill, Geoffrey R. D. (1997) 'The Making of the European Financial Area: Global Market Integration and the EU Single Market for Financial Services', in Geoffrey R. D. Underhill (ed.) *The New World Order in International Finance*. London: Palgrave, pp. 101–23.

USAID (2007) 'Acquisition and Assistance Activities', www.usaid.gov/iraq/activ ities.html; accessed 29 October 2008.

Vacca, Giuseppe (1982) 'Intellectuals and the Marxist Theory of the State', in Anne Showstack Sassoon (ed.) *Approaches to Gramsci*. London: Writers and Readers, pp. 37–69.

Van Apeldoorn, Bastiaan (2002) *Transnational Capitalism and the Struggle over European Integration*. London: Routledge.

Van Apeldoorn, Bastiaan and Naná de Graaff (2014) 'Corporate Elite Networks and U.S. Post–Cold War Grand Strategy from Clinton to Obama', *European Journal of International Relations*, 20(1): 29–55.

Van Apeldoorn, Bastiaan and Naná de Graaff (2016) *American Grand Strategy and Corporate Elite Networks: The Open Door since the End of the Cold War*. London: Routledge.

Vanaik, Achin (2014) 'Capitalist Globalisation and the Problem of Stability: Enter the New Quintet and other Emerging Powers', in Kevin Gray and Craig N. Murphy (eds.) *Rising Powers and the Future of Global Governance*. London: Routledge, pp. 12–31.

Vogel, Lise (1983/2013) *Marxism and the Oppression of Women: Toward a United Theory*, intro. Susan Ferguson and David McNally. Leiden: Brill.

Wahl, Asbjørn (2011) *The Rise and Fall of the Welfare State*. London: Pluto Press.

Wahl, Peter (2017) 'Between Eurotopia and Nationalism: A Third Way for the Future of the EU', *Globalizations*, 14(1): 157–63.

Wallerstein, Immanuel (1974a) *The Modern World-System I: Capitalist Agriculture and the Origins of the European World-Economy in the Sixteenth Century*. London: Academic Press.

Wallerstein, Immanuel (1974b) 'The Rise and Future Demise of the World Capitalist System: Concepts for Comparative Analysis', *Comparative Studies in Society and History*, 16(4): 387–415.

Wallerstein, Immanuel (1979) *The Capitalist World-Economy*. Cambridge: Cambridge University Press.

Wallerstein, Immanuel (1990) 'Patterns and Perspectives of the Capitalist World Economy', in P. R. Viotti and M. V. Kauppi (eds.) *International Relations Theory Today: Realism, Pluralism, Globalism*. New York: Macmillan, pp. 501–12.

Wallerstein, Immanuel (1992) 'The West, Capitalism and the Modern World-System', *Review: A Journal of the Fernand Braudel Center*, 15(4): 561–619.

Wallerstein, Immanuel (2004) *World-Systems Analysis: An Introduction*. Durham, NC: Duke University Press.

Waltz, Kenneth N. (1979) *Theory of International Politics*. Reading, MA: Addison-Wesley.

Waltz, Kenneth N. (1990) 'Realist Thought and Neorealist Theory', *Journal of International Affairs*, 44(1): 21–37.

Waltz, Kenneth N. (2000) 'Globalisation and American Power', *The National Interest*, 59: 46–56.

Webber, Jeffrey R. (2016) 'Evo Morales and the Political Economy of Passive Revolution in Bolivia, 2006–15', *Third World Quarterly*, 37(10): 1855–76.

Webster, Edward (2015) 'Labour after Globalisation: Old and New Sources of Power', in Andreas Bieler et al., (eds.) *Labour and Transnational Action in Times of Crisis*. London: Rowman & Littlefield International, pp. 115–27.

Webster, Edward, Rob Lambert and Andries Beziudenhout (2008) *Grounding Globalization: Labour in the Age of Insecurity*. Oxford. Wiley-Blackwell.

Weghmann, Vera (2017) 'Employability and the Rise of Unpaid Work: Organising in the No-Wage Economy', PhD thesis, School of Politics and International Relations, University of Nottingham.

Wei, Lim Tai (2016) 'Introduction', in Lim Tai Wei, Henry Chan Hing Lee, Katherine Tseng Hui-Yi and Lim Wen Xin (eds.) *China's One Belt, One Road Initiative*. London: Imperial College Press, pp. 3–18.

Weiss, Linda (1998) *The Myth of the Powerless State: Governing the Economy in a Global Era*. Cambridge: Polity Press.

Wendt, Alexander (1987) 'The Agent–Structure Problem in International Relations', *International Organization*, 41(3): 335–70.

Wendt, Alexander (1992b) 'Anarchy Is What States Make of It: The Social Construction of Power Politics', *International Organization*, 46(2): 393–425.

Wendt, Alexander (1994) 'Collective Identity Formation and the International State', *American Political Science Review*, 88(2): 384–96.

Wendt, Alexander (1999) *Social Theory of International Politics*. Cambridge: Cambridge University Press.

Wendt, Alexander (2003) 'Why a World State Is Inevitable', *European Journal of International Relations*, 9(4): 491–542.

Whitfield, Dexter (2010) *Global Auction of Public Assets: Public Sector Alternatives to the Infrastructure Market & Public Private Partnerships*. Nottingham: Spokesman.

Widmaier, Wesley W., Mark Blyth and Leonard Seabrooke (2007) 'Exogenous Shocks or Endogenous Constructions? The Meanings of Wars and Crises', *International Studies Quarterly*, 51(4): 747–59.

Wight, Colin (1996) 'Incommensurability and Cross-Paradigm Communication in International Relations Theory: "What's the Frequency Kenneth?"', *Millennium: Journal of International Studies*, 25(2): 291–319.

Wight, Colin (1999) 'They Shoot Dead Horses Don't They? Locating Agency in the Agent–Structure Problematique', *European Journal of International Relations*, 5(1): 109–42.

Wight, Colin (2004) 'State Agency: Social Action without Human Activity?', *Review of International Studies*, 30(2): 269–80.

Wight, Colin (2006) *Agents, Structures and International Relations: Politics as Ontology*. Cambridge: Cambridge University Press.

Wight, Colin (2007) 'A Manifesto for Scientific Realism in IR: Assuming the Can-Opener Won't Work!', *Millennium: Journal of International Studies*, 35(2): 379–98.

Wigger, Angela and Laura Horn (2014) 'Uneven Development and Political Resistance against EU Austerity Politics', in Lucia Pradella and Thomas Marois (eds.) *Polarizing Development: Alternatives to Neoliberalism and the Crisis*. London: Pluto Press, pp. 248–59.

Wilson, Edmund (1940/1972) *To the Finland Station: A Study in the Writing and Acting of History*. New York: New York Review of Books.

Wissel, Jens (2011) 'The Transnationalisation of the Bourgeoisie and the New Networks of Power', in A. Gallas, L. Bretthauer, J. Kannankulam and I. Stützle (eds.) *Reading Poulantzas*. London: Merlin Press, pp. 216–30.

Wolf, Eric R. (1982/1997) *Europe and the People without History*, with a new preface. Berkeley: University of California Press.

Wolff, Richard (2013) *Democracy at Work: A Cure for Capitalism*. Chicago: Haymarket Books.

Wood, Ellen Meiksins (1986) *The Retreat from Class: A New 'True' Socialism*. London: Verso.

Wood, Ellen Meiksins (1991) *The Pristine Culture of Capitalism: An Historical Essay on Old Regimes and Modern States*. London: Verso.

Wood, Ellen Meiksins (1995) *Democracy against Capitalism: Renewing Historical Materialism*. Cambridge: Cambridge University Press.

Wood, Ellen Meiksins (1997) 'Modernity, Postmodernity or Capitalism?', *Review of International Political Economy*, 4(3): 539–60.

Wood, Ellen Meiksins (1999) 'Unhappy Families: Global Capitalism in a World of Nation-States', *Monthly Review*, 51(3): 1–12.

Wood, Ellen Meiksins (2002a) *The Origin of Capitalism: A Longer View*. London: Verso.

Wood, Ellen Meiksins (2002b) 'The Question of Market Dependence', *Journal of Agrarian Change*, 2(1): 50–87.

Wood, Ellen Meiksins (2002c) 'Global Capital, National States', in Mark Rupert and Hazel Smith (eds.) *Historical Materialism and Globalisation*. London: Routledge, pp. 17–39.

Wood, Ellen Meiksins (2002d) 'Capitalism and Human Emancipation: Race, Gender, and Democracy', in Nancy Holmstrom (ed.) *The Socialist Feminist Project: A Contemporary Reader in Theory and Politics*. New York: Monthly Review Press, pp. 277–92.

Wood, Ellen Meiksins (2003) *Empire of Capital*. London: Verso.

Wood, Ellen Meiksins (2007) 'A Reply to My Critics', *Historical Materialism*, 15(3): 143–70.

Woods, Ngaire (1995) 'Economic Ideas and International Relations: Beyond Rational Neglect', *International Studies Quarterly*, 39(2): 161–80.

Woodward, Bob (2004) *Plan of Attack*. New York: Pocket Books.

Yang, Jo-Shing (2012) 'The New "Water Barons": Wall Street Mega-Banks are Buying up the World's Water'. www.marketoracle.co.uk/article38167.html; accessed 28 October 2014.

Yee, Albert S. (1996) 'The Causal Effects of Ideas on Policies', *International Organization*, 50(1): 69–108.

Zhang, Ziru (2012) 'Guangdong NGOs Face Grand-Scale Regulation: The Government Is Using a Two-handed Policy, Suppression and Incorporation' (in Chinese), www.szwlg.org/news/lgnew/2012/0608/911.html; accessed 6 July 2014.

Zibechi, Raúl (2012) *Territories in Resistance: A Cartography of Latin American Social Movements*, trans. Ramor Ryan. Oakland, CA: AK Press.

Index